I0802970

THIS

GREAT

NATIONAL

OBJECT

Surmounting the Niagara Escarpment, c. 1928. The First Welland Canal (built 1824–29) followed the small channel at the lower left, while the Second Welland (1840–45) with its large weir pond, is at the right. The Third Welland (1872–81) runs across the top of this picture, with construction of the twentieth-century canal underway. (St Catharines Centennial Library)

THIS GREAT NATIONAL OBJECT

Building the Nineteenth-Century Welland Canals

Roberta M. Styran and Robert R. Taylor

McGill-Queen's University Press
Montreal & Kingston · London · Ithaca

© McGill-Queen's University Press 2012
ISBN 978-0-7735-3893-1

Legal deposit second quarter 2012
Bibliothèque nationale du Québec

Printed in Canada on acid-free paper that is 100% ancient forest free (100% post-consumer recycled), processed chlorine free

McGill-Queen's University Press acknowledges the support of the Canada Council for the Arts for our publishing program. We also acknowledge the financial support of the Government of Canada through the Canada Book Fund for our publishing activities.

Library and Archives Canada Cataloguing in Publication

Styran, Roberta M. (Roberta McAfee), 1927–
This great national object : building the nineteenth-century Welland canals / Roberta M. Styran and Robert R. Taylor.

Includes bibliographical references and index.
ISBN 978-0-7735-3893-1

1. Welland Canal (Ont.) – History.
I. Taylor, Robert R., 1939– II. Title.

HE401.W4S794 2012 386'.470971338 C2011-904886-8

Set in 9.5/12.5 Baskerville 10 Pro with Aviano Slab
Book design & typesetting by Garet Markvoort, zijn digital

CONTENTS

LIST OF ILLUSTRATIONS

INTRODUCTION

Almost a century and a half ago, engineer and historian William Kingsford wrote of the Welland Canal: "The history of this important work is so marvellous and so little known, to some extent even so misrepresented, that a consecutive narrative is indispensable, correctly to understand the vicissitudes through which it has passed. So far as the writer knows, no connected account of it exists."[1] How little has changed since 1865! As canal historian Robert F. Legget observed in 1987: "The Welland Canal is still but little known to most Canadians, [despite the fact that] the Welland today is one of the very few great ship canals of the world."[2] The present work is an attempt to address this knowledge gap by recounting the astonishing saga of construction and reconstruction of Niagara's waterway.

Our two illustrated histories of the Welland Canals have already been published by The Boston Mills Press, our book of "then and now" photographs of the Canal corridor issued by Vanwell Press, and our documentary history of the Welland printed by the University of Toronto Press for The Champlain Society. Could there be more to say on the subject? True, John N. Jackson has written several books relating to the Welland, and a number of shorter works exist.[3] However, even the Introduction to The Champlain Society volume is a mere hundred pages, and neither the Vanwell nor The Boston Mills Press books contain lengthy text. We believe, therefore, that Canadians – and readers abroad – will welcome more insight into Niagara's remarkable canal.

The Welland was only one of several canals built in the Canadas during the "canal fever" of the early nineteenth century. The Rideau Canal, for example, which connected Montreal and Kingston (via what became known as Ottawa), was constructed between 1826 and 1832, and the Lachine, designed to avoid the St Lawrence rapids near Montreal, was finished in 1825. This book recounts the story of three-quarters of a century of what is arguably Canada's most important man-made waterway. As early as 1856, a St Catharines journalist described the Welland as "the great swivel link in the big arterial chain of that mighty and vast inter-oceanic water communication, now stretching from the Atlantic to the head waters of Lake Superior."[4] Despite changes in trading volumes and patterns, it remains just that today. Hence it seems vital for Canada's heritage that we present in some detail the history of how this canal was built ... and rebuilt.

The saga of the construction of the nineteenth-century Welland Canals is long and complex, involving thousands of men (and animals) from 1824 to the 1880s, and documenting the progress from simple picks and shovels to steam-powered earth-moving machines. It is a tale of changing ship-building and construction technology and of increasingly sophisticated building materials from timber to stone to concrete. Among its protagonists are wind and rain, ice and blazing summer heat, floods and landslides, jolts to the existing social order, and shocking accident and violent death. It is set in the context of dramatic political and economic change in the Niagara peninsula and on the national and international stage. Moreover, its immutable technological and geological challenges had to be met by fallible human beings. And so the story of the canals' construction grants us many glimpses into the characters and personalities of the men who built the waterway – the unskilled labourers, the talented artisans, the self-trained or formally educated engineers, the harassed or inventive contractors, and ultimately the conscientious – and not so conscientious – bureaucrats.

In other words, the Welland Canals' construction is more than a simple account of digging an increasingly large ditch to enable increasingly large ships to bypass the physical obstacle of Niagara Falls. It is many stories, interweaving hope and despair, triumph and defeat, humour and violence, generosity and selfishness ... a reflection of the whole human comedy.

Half a dozen studies could be written on the history of the Welland Canals – on their financing, on their political ramifications, and so on. For our part we have asked: "How did human brains, muscle, and ingenuity conspire to overcome natural obstacles and create an artificial river linking the Great Lakes and the St Lawrence?" We bring responses from the perspective of engineers, contractors, entrepreneurs, labourers, and by-standers "on the ground," and we hope our work will stimulate others to delve still further into the multiple aspects of this rich and fascinating subject.

We begin with a brief sketch of the political, social, and economic background to the canal-building era, and follow with a discussion of the various routes contemplated for these canals. A chapter on the engineers responsible for planning and overseeing the work, and the many contractors charged with implementing the plans leads into a description of the actual construction and working conditions. We continue by looking at the major features of each canal – the locks, the aqueducts, and the bridges. Finally, we consider the passions and problems of the men involved, the "cast of thousands" that included William Hamilton Merritt, his supporters and detractors, and the "navvies" who provided the labour. We do not know the names of the great majority of the workers who did the grubbing and digging, who wielded the picks and shovels, or manned the excavators and draglines – but it seems important to acknowledge that without them the Welland Canals could not have been built.

Construction of the First Welland Canal began in November 1824, on a north-south axis that would ultimately connect lakes Ontario and Erie. A project of private enterprise, specifically William Hamilton Merritt's Welland Canal Company, it was formally opened in November 1829. This canal was supplied by a "Feeder" canal that brought water from the Grand River, and it gave access to Lake Erie via Chippawa Creek (or the Welland River) and the Niagara River (figs. Int.1, Int.2). The northern terminus was at the mouth of Twelve Mile Creek. Here, where a dam created a harbour and a lock connected the canal to Lake Ontario, the town of Port Dalhousie developed. In 1833 a direct cut to Lake Erie was opened to Gravelly Bay (later Port Colborne).

The forty locks of the first canal, known as "Mr. Merritt's Ditch," were built of wood, and large enough to receive vessels up to 100 feet (30.5 m) long, bearing 185 tons.[5] A wooden aqueduct carried the canal over Chippawa Creek. Because sailing ships could not travel the Welland by themselves, they were pulled by teams of horses and/or mules along a towpath that ran mainly along the east side of the canal. Designing this towpath was itself a minor engineering achievement; many creeks and reservoirs drained into the canal, necessitating wooden bridges for the towhorses as well as occasional diversions to the west side, as in St Catharines.

Few traces of these locks exist today, although Lock 24 was excavated, studied, and reburied in 1987. The remains of Lock 1 are buried in Port Dalhousie, as are those of Lock 6 in Centennial Park in St Catharines. Much of the Feeder channel is still extant, but remnants of the main waterway, predicted in 1818 to be a "grand and most useful work,"[6] are now hard to find and remain a subject of conjecture. The most tangible and easily located remnant (aside from the Feeder) is a recently discovered narrow ditch, parallel to part of the Feeder, of the "Western Section" leading from the Forks of Chippawa Creek

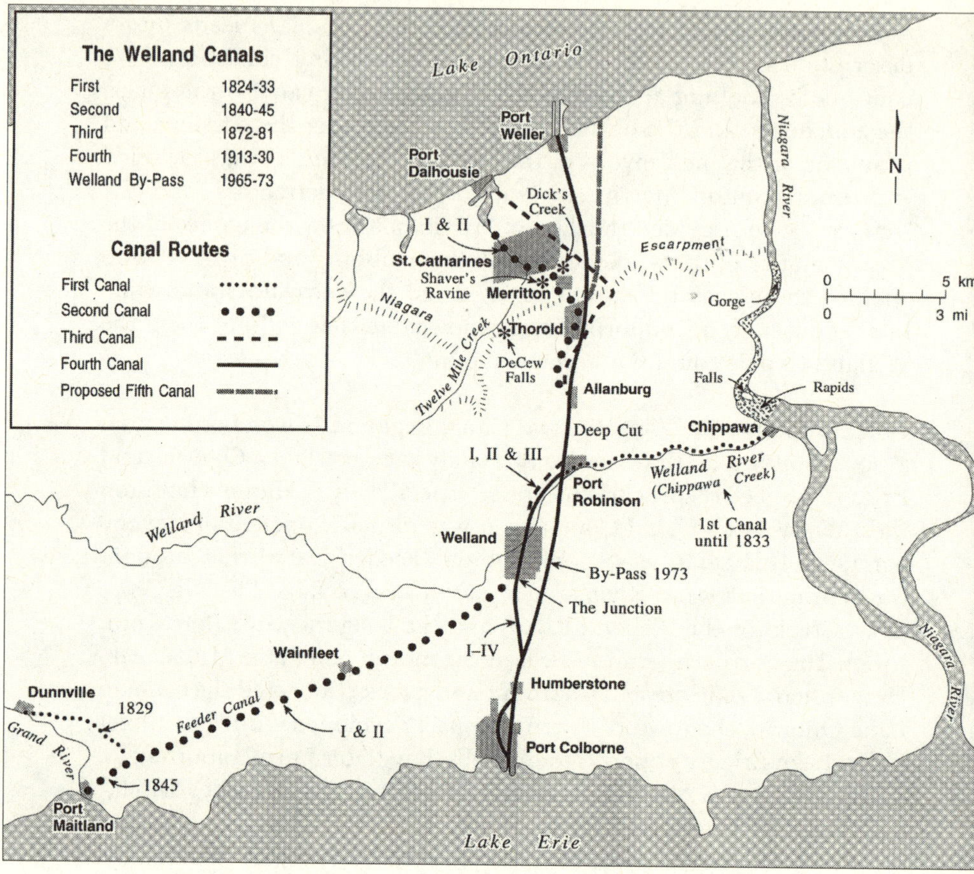

Int.1 (*above*) The Welland Canals (Loris Gasparotto, Department of Geography, Brock University)

Int.2 (*opposite*) The First Welland Canal (1829–45) (Loris Gasparotto, Department of Geography, Brock University)

to Broad Creek, constructed in 1828 but never incorporated into the navigation (fig. 2.3).

The efficiency of the First Welland Canal as a channel for shipping was almost immediately a subject of controversy – and the debate continues – but the waterway's success must be measured in more than just annual tonnage figures. Its construction involved materials produced by Niagara artisans and food grown by local farmers, providing an economic infusion that must have invigorated the building trades and the production of consumer goods, as well as employing

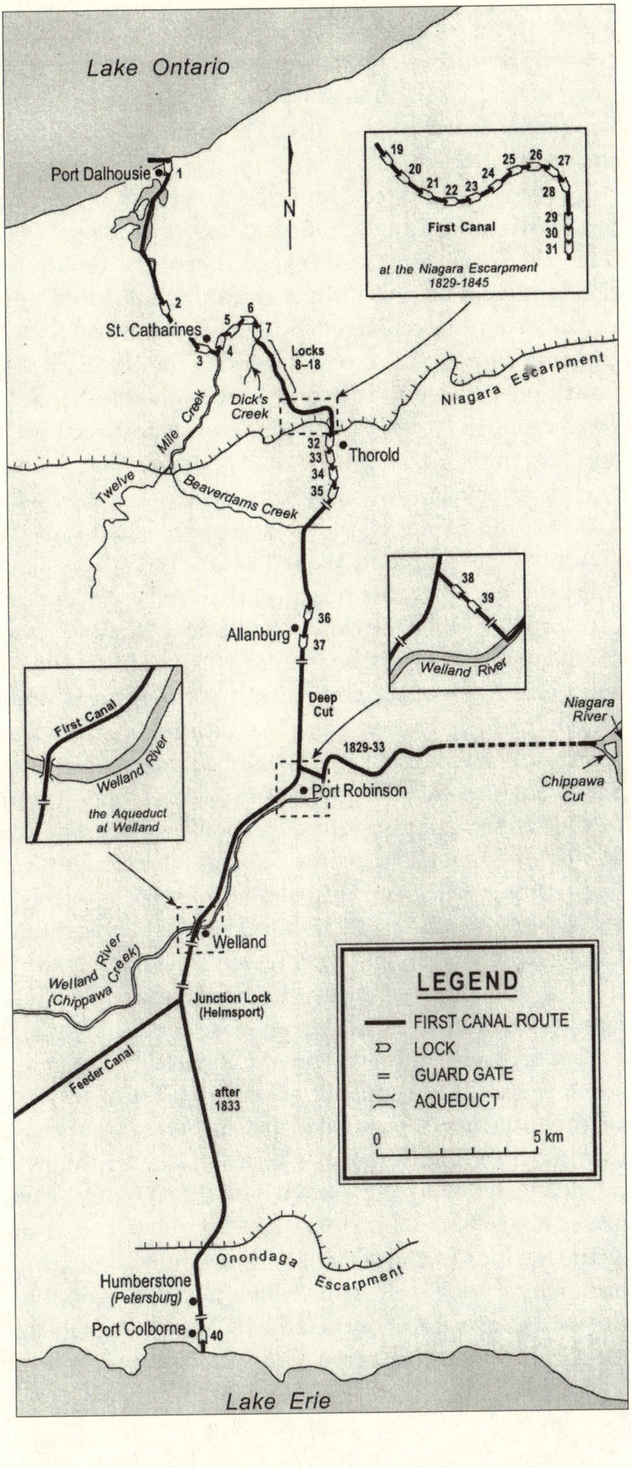

Lake Ontario
Port Dalhousie
N
St. Catharines
Locks 8–18
Dick's Creek
Twelve Mile Creek
Beaverdams Creek
Niagara Escarpment
Thorold
First Canal
at the Niagara Escarpment 1829-1845
Allanburg
Deep Cut
Welland River
1829-33
Niagara River
Chippawa Cut
Port Robinson
First Canal
Welland River
the Aqueduct at Welland
Welland
Welland River (Chippawa Creek)
Junction Lock (Helmsport)
Feeder Canal
after 1833
LEGEND
FIRST CANAL ROUTE
LOCK
GUARD GATE
AQUEDUCT
0
5 km
Onondaga Escarpment
Humberstone (Petersburg)
Port Colborne
Lake Erie

hundreds of local men. Furthermore, the First and Second Welland canals provided water power for mills, directly stimulating local industry.[7] The Welland also linked the British settlements on Lake Ontario with those on the north shore of Lake Erie, thus strengthening the unity of Upper Canada.[8]

"A canal of this size," reported surveyors James and Samuel Clowes to the Welland Canal Company board in 1824, "will pass all the produce that may be necessary for a century to come."[9] How seriously they underestimated! Fully operational for only about a decade, faulty in construction, damaged by winter draining, and challenged by increasing ship size and trade volume, the waterway soon had to be rebuilt and enlarged. This reconstruction, the Second Welland Canal, was begun in late 1840 and was completed via Port Maitland in 1845 and to Port Colborne in 1850 (fig. Int.3). Navigation began in 1848, and the new canal was officially declared open by Governor General Lord Elgin in 1850. In the next decade, it had to be further deepened.

Actually, the Second Welland Canal had been formally initiated in August 1838, when the board of the Welland Canal Company had approved rebuilding the canal from Lock 7 to Lock 35 and then, in January 1839, asked for estimates for this work. In June 1841 royal assent was given to place the company under the exclusive control of the government of the United Canadas, although the company continued to exist until December 1843. Minor changes were undertaken between St Catharines and Port Dalhousie, with a bigger harbour being completed by the opening of navigation in 1848. The route was virtually identical to that of the First Canal, but its twenty-seven locks were now of cut stone. Most of these chambers were 150 feet (45.7 m) long and 26.5 feet (8.1 m) wide.[10] The aqueduct, too, was rebuilt in stone. Ships 140 feet (42.7 m) long carrying 750 tons could now be lifted from 9.5 to 14.25 feet (2.9–4.3 m) up the Escarpment. The reconstructed canal was also served by a towpath, whose route now ran sometimes on the west side, sometimes on the east side of the channel. The growth of communities and industries along the banks of the Welland, as well as the continued presence of other watercourses, necessitated this shifting back and forth. Where the old and the new canals ran side by side, moreover, the towpath of the First Canal supplemented the newer one.[11]

The Second Welland Canal – "a wonderful developement [sic] of experimental art,"[12] said two contemporaries – doubled the capacity of the waterway's locks and channel. Many of its locks, some with their identifying numbers carved into the walls, still stand, notably at the

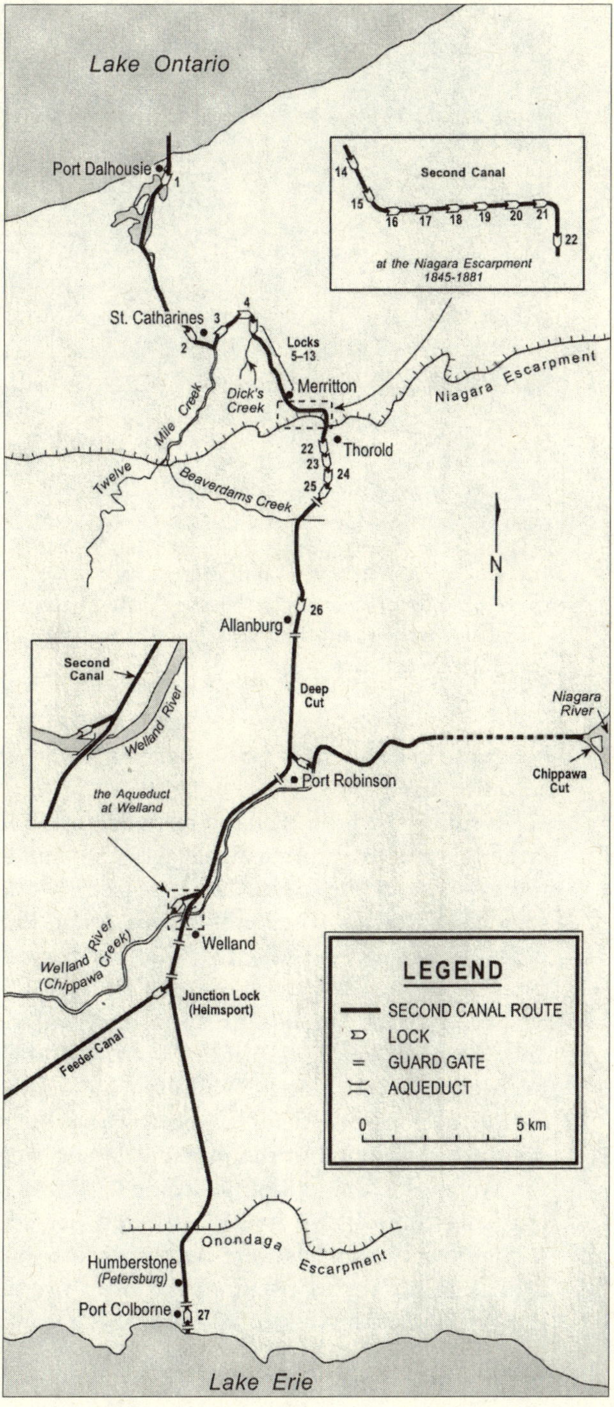

Int.3 The Second Welland Canal (1845–81) (Loris Gasparotto, Department of Geography, Brock University)

Int.4 Lock 18, Second Canal, Merritton, c. 1980, with its number elegantly carved by stonemasons into the wing wall. Such inscriptions helped captains orient themselves and their vessels in the waterway. These stone walls still stand. (Photo: R.R.T.)

Niagara Escarpment in St Catharines, where the channel also can be seen (fig. Int.4).

No sooner had the Welland been enlarged, however, than it was enlarged again! Beginning in 1853, the embankments were raised and the capacity of the locks was increased by adding another course of stones to the walls. Then in 1857 the Annual Report of the Department of Public Works envisioned yet another enlargement of the locks.[13] In 1871 Department of Public Works Chief Engineer John Page noted that more than "one hundred and forty millions of bushels" of grain and "immense quantities of lumber and timber" had been handled at five different lake ports. The following year Page indicated that the "wholy [sic] unprecedented" speed with which the Great Lakes economy had developed in the previous twenty years required rebuilding the Welland. Competition for trade had grown, with New York State reducing the tolls on its canals by 50 per cent. Larger, iron-hulled, steam-powered vessels were becoming predominant, with the result, said Page, that over twenty Lake Erie "propellers" were too big for the Welland.[14] The inadequate size of the waterway, however, had not prevented the traffic on it from increasing.

Canadian national ambitions came into play at the same time. After 1871, Ottawa sought to create a uniform system of inland water transportation, eliminating trans-shipments on the Welland and St Lawrence canals, to allow big lake freighters to pass directly from Lake Superior through to Montreal. The "National Policy" of Prime Minister John A. Macdonald (1815–1891) urged the enlargement of the St Lawrence canals and the Welland to a uniform scale with a depth of 12 feet (3.6 m) and locks 270 feet (81 m) by 45 feet (13.5 m).

The Welland, therefore, was again rebuilt, beginning in 1871 (fig. Int.5). The world depression slowed the work, but the Third Welland Canal was completed in 1881 to a depth of 12 feet (3.65 m), with twenty-six stone locks. Lifts could now receive ships of approximately 255 feet (77.7 m) in length bearing 3,000 tons. Another, larger stone aqueduct was built to take the canal over Chippawa Creek. Despite the proliferation of steam-powered vessels, a towpath was again provided, now on both sides of the canal, to accommodate the large number of sailing vessels still in service.

From Port Dalhousie to the Escarpment, this third waterway followed a new route, bypassing St Catharines. The older line was deepened and widened from the Escarpment to Port Colborne. In July 1881 water was let into the canal directly from Lake Erie, replacing the Grand River and the Feeder Canal from Dunnville as sources of water. Opened in April 1882 (except for the unfinished aqueduct), the Third Welland Canal was finally completed in 1887 to a depth of 14 feet (4.2 m). In fact, by the mid-1880s the water transport goals of Macdonald's National Policy had been achieved, and by 1895, when the Sault Ste Marie Canal was opened, the whole system had been deepened to 14 feet (4.3 m). The Canadian route ran uninterrupted from the Atlantic to Lake Superior (fig. Int.1).

The Welland's builders hoped that "the Enlargement" (as it was called) would double the capacity of the Old Canal (as it became known at the time), but the Third Canal too was soon obsolete! Nevertheless, this channel operated for longer than its two predecessors – over forty years – until it was superseded by the Fourth Canal, the Welland Ship Canal, so named to differentiate it from the Erie *Barge* Canal. Begun in 1913, this waterway was formally opened in 1932. As our chronicle suggests, the Welland has never really been "finished." In fact, authorities discussed yet another reconstruction in the 1960s.[15]

As historians, we too have occasionally felt that our work on the history of the Welland canals would never be finished. After a quarter-century of research, however, we believe that we have a remarkable

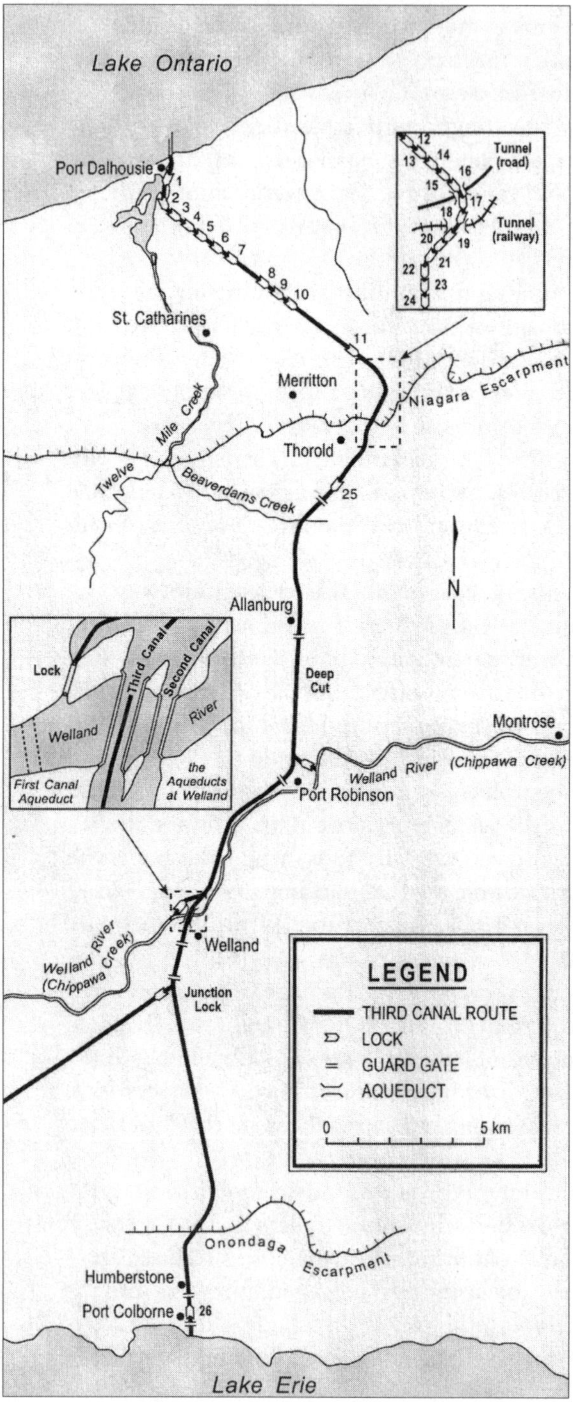

Int.5 The Third Welland Canal (1881–1930) (Loris Gasparotto, Department of Geography, Brock University)

tale to recount. As for our years of labour in archives, libraries, and on abandoned canal sites, the experience has often been exhilarating, sometimes exasperating. Most students of history will understand the exhilaration, but the exasperation may need explaining.

For example, our readers will note the frustrating dearth of technical information and graphic illustrations for the period of the First Canal's construction (1824–33). Several factors explain this paucity. Not only had the camera not yet been invented, but the soldier-artists, such as those of the Royal Engineers, who built and sketched (for their masters in London) the building of the Rideau Canal, had no part in the construction of the First Welland. It was built by the private Welland Canal Company, whose directors could easily ride up and down the line in person to inspect the work's progress. The occasionally cavalier business practices of the company meant that diagrams and drawings, vital to later historians, were misplaced or simply not filed. Early written records are scanty, too, with the result that many questions cannot be answered. Contractors presumably kept "time books" in which every labourer's name was recorded, along with the work he did, but these also have long vanished. Matters improved after the government of the United Canadas took control of the canal after 1841 and as the professionalization of engineering evolved, resulting in the augmentation of our knowledge through detailed reports and drawings. However, labourers' names and related personal details emerge only after disasters or disputes. We do not know of *any* contractors' records of men employed, while the Departments of Public Works and Railways and Canals kept records only of their own employees.[16]

"The past is messy," one researcher remarked to us. As noted, virtually no contemporary drawings or paintings of the First Canal exist. Nor are there many images of the Second Canal until the 1860s, from which era a few photographs survive. For us, the unreliability of existing maps and plans has been a particularly frustrating problem. Early cartographers made mistakes. For example, the Welland Canal Company conducted a "Survey of Lands" in connection with their purchase of land necessary for the First Canal's construction. However, on the "Diagram of J[ohn]. Martindales land in Grantham," a contemporary has considerately written: "In this diagram, the Tow-path is drawn on the wrong Side – it should be on the East Side" (fig. Int.6).[17] In this case, fortunately, the cartographer warned the user, but such anomalies – unflagged – exist on most early maps. Researchers beware!

In other cases, maps do not tell the whole story. We are indebted to Professor Alun Hughes of Brock University for indicating the anomaly

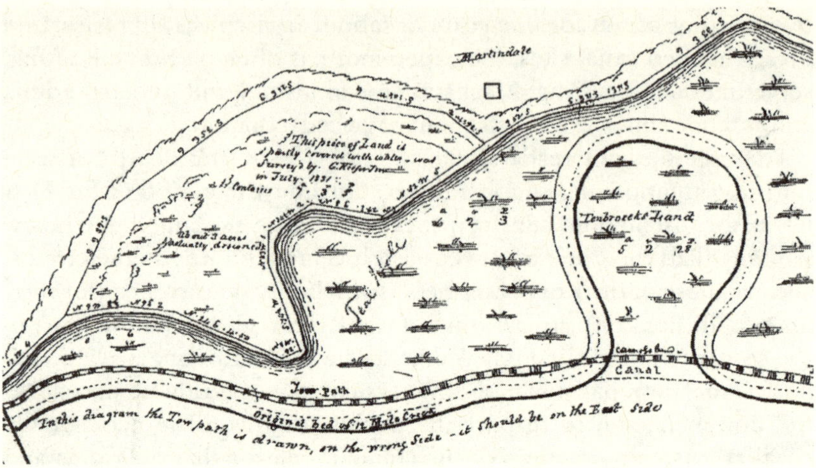

Int.6 "Drowned Land" on the First Canal on Twelve Mile Creek, south of Port Dalhousie, c. 1831: "This piece of Land is partly covered with water … About 3 acres actually drowned." The cartographer notes an error in the map – a warning to historians and students! (James A. Gibson Library, Brock University, Special Collections: Survey of Lands "1826" [1834], 21)

of the First Canal's curve at Allanburg, which appears on only one map (Captain Alexander's) and never in the Welland Canal Company's records (chapter 2). Maps must be carefully studied – but even then, they are not necessarily accurate.

Confusion of terminology is another stumbling block for the historian or student of the First Canal. For example, when is a lock not a lock – that is, not two sets of gates, forming a water-filled enclosure, resembling a bathtub – but simply one gate (a two-leaf structure holding back water in a channel)? The "Guard lock" shown on the map "Survey of Land, belonging to John Hellems"[18] is quite clearly one set of gates, not a lock. An unwary scholar reading the document and trying to count genuine locks could be led astray. A variation on this problem is found in Ogden Creighton's 1830 book, which provides a map showing "regulating locks" at Stromness and Port Robinson. The term "regulating" might suggest that each of the aforementioned structures was a single set of gates (two leaves) used to control the flow of water, but in fact, Creighton is referring to a genuine lock whose main function was to control water flow.[19] Occasionally, however, early nineteenth-century cartographers were more precise. For example, a "Guard gate" shown at Port Robinson uses the same symbol as the aforementioned feature and is obviously merely two leaves. Here the object is accurately described as a safety measure on an important stretch of the waterway. On the other hand, engineers H.H. Killaly (as he was known) and Nicol Hugh Baird used the terms "Guard Lock" for the same site in Port Robinson on the map of their 1837 survey.[20]

An observant student of Welland Canal construction might also be confused at first by that map drawn by Killaly and Baird in 1837, which shows the symbol for lock gates at Port Colborne with the mitre pointing north (that is, against the flow of water).[21] Should not the mitre point south, against the pressure of Lake Erie? The answer to this perfectly reasonable question is that, at this time, the flow of water from the Feeder divided at the junction with the canal – some flowed north, while some flowed south to the lake. Killaly and Baird were correct.

Another puzzle for the neophyte researcher is the numbering of First Canal locks. In most of the secondary material – and in much of the primary documentation – "Lock One" is at Port Dalhousie, with the rest numbered consecutively southward. However, in the reports and letters of contemporary engineers and contractors, "Lock One" is at the top of the Niagara Escarpment, where construction began.[22]

Then there is the question of how many locks were built on the First Canal. Confusion arises partly over the aforementioned naming of guard gates as "locks." The result is that different sources give different totals; some say thirty-nine, while others say forty. Historians must decide how they are going to count! Ignoring guard gates, we have declared there to be forty locks on the First Canal.

In our time, appreciation is often expressed for the advances in communication offered by the computer and the Internet. Similarly, the engineers building the Third and especially the Fourth Canals were helped in the transfer of vital information and decisions by the invention of the telephone. Unfortunately for the historian, however, certain links in the cause-and-effect chain became impossible to trace, because decisions taken seem to have been communicated verbally by long-distance phone. No paper trail exists.[23]

Needless to say, few of these obstacles were apparent to us when we started our research in the libraries of the Niagara Peninsula, where we found the most available artifacts, maps, and documents – often photocopied from originals stored elsewhere – on the history of the Welland Canals. The Archives of Ontario in Toronto also provided useful material. At that point, however, vital information was lacking, and so Dr Styran went off to the National Archives of Canada (now Library and Archives Canada) in Ottawa, and asked if they held any documentary material relating to the history of the Welland. An archivist replied that, unfortunately, there was not very much on hand.

True, there is not a lot that deals specifically with "the Welland Canal." But departmental records abound for the period after the government takeover in 1841. Dr Styran began to use the finding aids, and lo! – hundreds of "volumes" of documents (often in large boxes) came to light, along with innumerable letters, memoranda, and reports from the Departments of Public Works and Railways and Canals! A tiny fraction of these are included in our volume of documents for The Champlain Society.[24]

Despite these frustrations, our research has been stimulating and enjoyable. For that reason alone, we hope that future scholars will continue the work we have begun. As the directors of the Welland Canal Company said in June 1833, "much is yet to be done."[25]

ACKNOWLEDGMENTS

Acknowledging the scores of individuals who have assisted us in our research would take several more pages. However, special thanks are owed to Donald G. Anger, John Burtniak, Dennis Gannon, Alun Hughes, William L. Lewis, Jane McLeod, Stephen Otto, Robert Passfield, Carmela Patrias, Arden Phair, Lynne Prunskus, Robert John Taylor, Keith Tinkler, Wesley B. Turner, Edie Williams, and Sheila Wilson. As well, we are indebted to the staffs of the James A. Gibson Library (Brock University), the St Catharines Centennial Library (Special Collections), the St Catharines Museum, the St Lawrence Seaway Management Corporation (Niagara Region, St Catharines), the Welland Historical Museum, the Port Colborne Historical and Marine Museum, the Archives of Ontario (Toronto), the Metropolitan Toronto Reference Library, and Library and Archives Canada (Ottawa). Without the advice and assistance of the staff of McGill-Queen's University Press, this volume would not have been possible. We are especially grateful to our editor, Jane McWhinney.

Every effort has been made to trace the ownership of all copyright material reprinted in the text. Any errors in this book remain our responsibility and, if discovered, will be corrected in subsequent editions.

THIS

GREAT

NATIONAL

OBJECT

CHAPTER ONE

This Great National Object

To you, to whom is fairly attributed the successful working out of this great national object, it must be a source of very deep gratification to find it once occupying that place in Public attention and Estimation to which its vast importance fully justifies it.

This 1842 tribute to William Hamilton Merritt, the first of many, was long in coming but richly deserved.[1] The saga of the Welland Canals' construction may be said to have begun with Merritt as a twenty-year-old. On a summer night in 1812 a lonely rider patrolled the west bank of the Niagara River, which swirled below him. Young Lieutenant Merritt of the Second Lincoln Militia, in charge of forty soldiers, was well acquainted with the area between the village of Chippawa and Fort Erie in Upper Canada. On this night he and his companions were on the alert. His young eyes constantly ranged the opposite bank, where American troops were about to execute their plans to invade the British colony. As he rode, ever-watchful, his brain was as active as his eyes. A thought flitted through his mind, an idea which, while pushed aside by the demands of war, would later evolve into the concept of a man-made river to connect two of the Great Lakes, Erie and Ontario, to circumvent the spectacular, but inconvenient, Niagara Falls.[2]

Merritt was captured in 1814, and spent nearly eight months as a prisoner of the Americans. Shortly after his release in July 1815, he married Catharine, daughter of Dr Jedediah Prendergast of Mayville, New York. They had met when her father was living for a few years in St Catharines, situated on Twelve Mile Creek in the Niagara Peninsula, where Merritt's parents resided. The correspondence between Merritt and his wife is a rich source of material for this account. The couple remained together until her death in January 1862.

By the time the young Merritts were settled in their own home "on the Twelve," Hamilton (as he preferred to be known) was well aware that canals were exercising the minds of many Upper Canadians. Even before the War of 1812, suggestions had been made to improve the portage road along the Niagara River and possibly to construct some kind of canal.[3] But it was Robert Gourlay, a Scots immigrant and activist,[4] who concentrated such thinking by sending out a questionnaire in 1817–18 to the townships of Upper Canada, asking (among other questions) if "water conveyance" could be "obtained, extended, or improved, by means of canals, locks, &c. &c."[5]

Merritt, who by now owned several enterprises on Twelve Mile Creek, including a general store, saw- and gristmills, and a distillery, as well as a cooper's shop, smithy, potashery, and salt well, was stimulated to action. He may have been thinking only of a hydraulic raceway to power his mills,[6] but he may not have forgotten his original inspiration by the Niagara River. Certainly, he was aware of the great "canal fever" rampant in Britain and the United States. In England and Wales, for example, the extent of the canal network had more than doubled between 1760 and 1800,[7] as capitalists, encouraged by the profits from early canals, flocked to invest. Canals were also being constructed on the Continent in the late eighteenth century and, while North America was slow to get started, by 1792 thirty waterway companies had been incorporated in the United States, although only a hundred miles of canal had been built by 1816.[8] As we have seen, by the late 1820s the Lachine and Rideau canals were in operation in the Canadas. Many of the canal companies, on both sides of the Atlantic, were privately financed by stockholders, but others had government backing.

By the time Merritt chaired a meeting of Grantham Township settlers, including fellow-merchants William Chisholm, Charles Ingersoll (Merritt's business partner), and Paul Shipman (who owned a tavern on "the Twelve") – a meeting called to formulate a response to Gourlay – he and his colleagues were all familiar with waterway developments in Canada and abroad as well as across the Niagara River. "A water communication within a mile and half of the village of St. Catharine's," they wrote to Gourlay, "is capable of being extended and improved, by means of a canal of three miles distant, which will bring the Chippawa creek [Welland River] into the Twelve Mile Creek."[9] Similar responses were submitted by all but two other townships in the Niagara Peninsula. As Merritt's son put it, "a mania for canalling seemed to possess the people."[10] But it was the Grantham Township dream that would come to fruition.

What may have begun as merely a ditch to provide a steady supply of water to Merritt's mills became a canal to carry barges (later, ships) between lakes Erie and Ontario. This waterway – "Mr. Merritt's ditch" – evolved into the linchpin of today's St Lawrence Seaway. The Rideau Canal was built (1826–32) by the British government (specifically the Royal Engineers) under Colonel John By. The Erie was constructed (1817–25) by the government of New York State, inspired by Governor DeWitt Clinton (1769–1828).[11] In contrast, both the concept and the inception of the Welland were due largely to the efforts of one man — not yet a well-connected politician nor a strategically placed bureaucrat, nor a much-travelled soldier, but a struggling miller in a sleepy pioneer village.

In the early years of the nineteenth century, although Merritt was only on the threshold of a distinguished career, without his vision, energy, determination, calculation, and political acumen, the Welland Canal might never have come into existence. Called by some the "Father of Canadian Transportation," he was a commanding figure in British North America in the first half of the nineteenth century. Even his greatest critic, William Lyon Mackenzie (1795–1861),[12] dubbed him "the prime mover of the whole machine."[13] Some of his contemporaries complained that he was never knighted by Queen Victoria.[14] Upper Canada's Chief Justice John Beverley Robinson (1791–1863) did not exaggerate when he praised Merritt's "unremitting and extraordinary exertions"[15] in spearheading construction of the First Welland Canal. Merritt was obviously no unsung hero in his own time. In 1842 a contemporary wrote: "If our neighbors wish to see proofs of Canadian enterprise, let them travel along the line of the canal, from Dunnville to Port Dalhousie, and I am confident they will not hesitate to affirm, that William Hamilton Merrit [sic] is the Clinton of Canada."[16]

The Visionary

Who was this man, whose personal motto was "I undertake and I persevere"?[17] William Hamilton Merritt (1793–1862) (fig. 1.1) was born on 3 July 1793 in Bedford, New York, the son of Thomas Merritt and Mary Hamilton. The family became "late" Loyalists and moved to what became St Catharines, Upper Canada, in 1796. His formal education was not extensive, nor could it be, given the pioneer conditions in the British colony at the turn of the eighteenth century. However, it was varied, both in subject matter and location. After some primary tutoring at home, he attended Richard Cockerell's school in Ancaster, which later moved to Niagara. From the Reverend John Burns he received a traditional classical education. With his uncle Nehemiah in Halifax, he spent a short apprenticeship, learning the rudiments of

1.1 Portrait Gallery 1. *Clockwise from top left*: William Hamilton Merritt (1793–1862) (H.R. Page, *Illustrated Historical Atlas*, 2); George Keefer Senior (1773–1858) (LAC: PA-134907); George Ramsay, 9th Earl of Dalhousie (1770–1838) (Metropolitan Toronto Library: T–31639); John Barentse Yates (1784–1836) (Village Hall, Chittenango, New York)

business, as well as surveying. Before he was sixteen he had visited Montreal, Quebec City, Trois-Rivières, Halifax, Saint John, New York City, and Bermuda. Once settled back in St Catharines after his war service, he became a farmer, miller, and distiller and dabbled in various speculations such as lumber and land.

An Anglican church-goer, he was conservative in his politics; yet he had qualities that made him one of the most dynamic "movers and shakers" of the time. James Johnson has remarked that the American-born Merritt possessed many of the same characteristics as the Scots who were prominent in Upper Canada at the time: "bustling and successful out of proportion to their numbers."[18] His "heart and feelings [were] ardently British," wrote two of his early biographers, "while his manner and style of thought were eminently American ... On questions of progress," they continued, "he knew no rest."[19] Indeed, Merritt wholeheartedly subscribed to the nineteenth-century notion that material advancement was equivalent to the moral development of Western civilization.

As a politician, Merritt achieved much of what he wanted, at least concerning the Welland Canal, but, being too single-minded or, as his contemporaries said, "too independent" to submit to party discipline, he was not a "leader of men."[20] He had little patience with unimaginative or penny-pinching members of the Legislative Assembly who did not share his enthusiasm for "progress." "They are fearful of some imaginary evil," he complained in his journal, "and do not dwell on the great Public Good."[21] They had to be prodded and encouraged: "As a matter of course, it is absolutely necessary I should remain at the elbow of the Members untill the business [the First Welland] is compleated as *they do not understand and scarcely have an idea of it*" [Merritt's emphasis].[22]

Self-Interest and Vision

Merritt's initial vision was undeniably partly motivated by self-interest. The supply of water from Twelve Mile Creek to his mills was unreliable – limited in the summer months, causing a backlog of grain and timber in his and other businesses, and tending to flood in the spring. This imbalance was a natural result of pioneer clearance of the land; as forest cover was removed, less water was held in the soil and runoff increased. Hence streams would be swollen and dangerous in the spring, but much reduced in flow after a hot summer. So, perhaps recalling his inspiration as a young soldier, Merritt said, "I ...

conceived the Idea of obtaining a further supply from the Chippewa [Creek]."[23]

Other factors impelled the mature Merritt to consider the canal enterprise. As a result of a monetary crisis in England, prices for agricultural produce such as grain dipped in the 1820s. The Corn Laws (revised only in 1827 and 1828) inhibited the export of colonial wheat to the British market. Merritt's own financial embarrassment also played a role in his conception of a Niagara canal. Unable to pay his debts to Montreal creditors, he seems to have looked about for a new way to ensure a steady income.[24]

Hence, on 28 September 1818, Merritt, his friend George Keefer Sr (1778–1858) (fig. 1.1),[25] and several other millers and merchants of the area, carried out a survey for a possible canal route. Using a water level, the only instrument available to them, they ran a line from the eastern branch of Twelve Mile Creek, near what is now Allanburg, due south to the Chippawa, a distance of 2 miles (3.2 km), including a rise of land later known as the Summit Ridge. Unfortunately, their amateur conclusions were inaccurate – the height to be negotiated was double their estimate! But so encouraged were they that their plans for a Niagara canal became a veritable crusade.

As we have noted, Merritt's concept of a man-made channel evolved over time. When construction began on the Erie Canal in 1817, Merritt's vision of a feeder channel from the Welland River (Chippawa Creek) evolved into the bolder idea of a canal that could take small boats between Lake Erie and Lake Ontario. At first, a canal for barges, like the Erie, seemed appropriate. However, by 1825, in a letter to his father-in-law, Dr Prendergast, he wrote of a waterway large enough for sailing ships: "By making a sloop navigation large enough to admit any vessel on Lake Erie, we will at once draw all the Transit from Lake Erie to New York through our Canal, as a vessel can sail from any point to Oswego at once."[26] Merritt saw "his" canal as part of a trade route to rival the American Erie Canal, which opened in the year of this letter. He also projected a connection between the Welland River and the Grand River. As he had earlier written to his father-in-law on 1 January 1824, this channel "opens the whole Western Country to us at once."[27] In fact, Merritt saw further afield as well. As early as 21 July 1824 he had expressed his vision of a British water route to connect the hinterland of North America with the Atlantic, a view he reiterated in his address at the sod-turning on 30 November 1824.

Merritt and his colleagues found support both in and beyond the Niagara Peninsula. The impressive falls of Niagara were increasingly seen as a handicap to traffic, and the legislatures of both Upper and

Lower Canada, as well as naval and army officials in England, were interested in bypassing the cataract. Lower Canadian businessmen supported the project, as evidenced by an 1818 report in the Montreal *Gazette*, the voice of English-speaking Quebec merchants. It was, they declared, "highly gratifying" to learn of Merritt's plan. In March 1824 Quebec businessmen passed a resolution at a meeting, noting that "the said [Welland] Canal when in operation would tend to draw forth the Commercial and Agricultural resources of the extensive interior of the Upper Province, and become the means of preserving to the Canadas a valuable trade, which without such a Channel of Communication would be lost to these Provinces and pass to the United States."[28]

In Upper Canada, committees and commissions were named, and reports made. The legislatures of both Upper and Lower Canada voted money for surveys, and surveyors were hired to see what routes might be suitable. Despite this widespread interest and activity, however, Merritt himself was the catalyst for action taken "on the ground." By 9 March 1823 he wrote to his wife, "The waters of Chip Cr. will be down the 12 in 2 years from this time as certain as fate."[29] This particular optimistic prophecy, based as it was on the 1818 survey, was not to be fulfilled. Nevertheless, Merritt worked assiduously during the coming years in order to realize his dream. Public meetings, letters to newspapers, and frequent trips to recruit support among members of the Family Compact, were among his efforts.

Not unexpectedly, everyone had an opinion about his scheme, and opposition arose both at the local level and in the Upper Canadian legislature. "Have been very much harased [sic] both in body and mind," he wrote in March 1823; "have met with obstacles and opposition on every hand."[30] Despite this perceived harassment, the publicity efforts of Merritt and his friends succeeded. On 19 January 1824 royal assent was given to an Act incorporating the Welland Canal Company, consisting of Merritt, his father Thomas (1759–1842), local businessmen George Keefer, George Adams (1774–1844), William Chisholm, and others. Merritt became the superintendent of construction and related business (general agent), and the company's first office was in Merritt's own home overlooking Twelve Mile Creek. The directors, encouraged by the formation of the company, undertook further surveys and, by mid-November 1824, sufficient money was in hand to award the initial contracts.[31] The first sod was turned on 30 November at what is now Allanburg in a ceremony at which Merritt was the chief speaker.

Having succeeded in convincing the members of the Legislature, as well as the powerful clique that made up the Family Compact, of the wisdom of his canal scheme, Merritt went about widening his influence. In Montreal, New York, and London, his passion impelled others, who had initially taken little interest in Upper Canadian developments, to support him. Yet he was more than just a huckster. Because he had come to understand both the methods of modern finance and the way to raise funds for an undertaking that he could not afford with his own resources, he was, writes S.J.R. Noel, "a prototypical broker of genius," suggesting that the cunning Merritt was able to persuade the sympathetic members of the Family Compact as well as his American supporters "to go just a little too far to turn back."[32]

Although an uncomfortable politician, "naturally and constitutionally a grave and monotonous speaker,"[33] Merritt's letters and papers reveal him to be a dedicated family man, at least within the parameters of Victorian patriarchal society. For example, in 1823, when away from home, he wrote to his wife, Catharine, "I am quite lonesome, write me our Family matters."[34] In 1825, in a letter from their home when she was visiting her relatives in New York State, he wrote wistfully: "Your letter met me at home I was delighted with your description of the little shaver I am very desirous to see you & them, we have never yet had so long a separation ... I have felt the loss of your society and the prattle of those little innocents."[35]

Canal Crusader

From such letters and from his wife's descriptions, Merritt's delight in the building of the First Welland becomes almost palpable. Accompanying her husband on a wintry tour of the construction site, Catharine Merritt recalled: "H. stoped the sleigh oposite Hartsell [a local farmer] for us to listen to the chopers the axes made a compleat clatter and H. appeared more delighted with it than at hearing a band of music."[36] His enthusiasm for the project rebounded despite the "obstacles and opposition" recorded in his journal even before the first sod was turned.[37] "You know how it is if business call," wrote Catharine to her mother, "if he is able to crawl he will go."[38] Another of Merritt's characteristics – his optimism – must have been contagious for some colleagues. In November 1825, for example, he predicted that the entire canal would be finished "within a year." At the same time, in another letter, he again incorrectly predicted, "May 1827 at farthest."[39] Moreover, as we have seen, he never stopped speculating about and enlarging on his concept of a Niagara waterway.

If Merritt's optimism and vision were impressive, so, too, was his command of English. Abundant examples of his turn of phrase exist, such as his remark in an 1828 article addressed to an American audience: "Lake Erie will be connected with the Ocean by canals ... which will render this extensive lake coast a sea coast."[40]

Despite his undeniable loyalty to his adopted country, Merritt was clearly no altruist. The First Welland was initiated more than partially for his own benefit, especially because its line ran past his mills. In 1824 he wrote to his father-in-law, "I consider that I will be richly paid in the enhanced value of my property." Later, struggling to defend "his" route for the canal against proponents of the alternate route to Niagara-on-the-Lake, which would have bypassed his property, he admitted some duplicity to Dr Prendergast: "I am satisfied ... that there is a cheaper route than ours – which shall be nameless at present."[41]

There is no question that Merritt profited from the canal. John MacTaggart, Clerk of Works on the Rideau, knew this when he described the smaller size of the locks south of St Catharines: "There must be some private interests of individuals at work in this erroneous alteration."[42] That Merritt campaigned for a route that would benefit his properties is also obvious. Nevertheless, in 1831 he felt compelled to defend himself from the charge of speculation: "I have refrained from purchasing any situation on the line of the Canal since its commencement to avoid all ground for suspicion of having speculated for my private advantage."[43] This remark suggests that Merritt was sensitive to the ethical issues raised by his intimate connection with the Niagara economy and the new canal. Like several of his protestations, however, his defence does not ring quite true in hindsight. By 1831 he was a lessee of water rights in St Catharines and, by 1834, had acquired potentially valuable property in Port Colborne close to the new harbour.

It would be wrong, on the other hand, to accuse Merritt of greed. One could argue that a more personally ambitious and financially astute businessman would have amassed much more personal wealth than he did.[44] His dealings with contractors exhibit a desire to do them justice – and hint at an almost nonchalant attitude to distinctions between personal and company bookkeeping. To the 1836 Select Committee investigating charges of fiscal mismanagement laid by William Lyon Mackenzie, the contractor Love Newlove defended Merritt's probity. He recalled that once, when he was arguing with the company secretary about the amount owed to him, "Mr. Merritt came in, and said if there is a penny due to Newlove let him have it ... He always paid me whenever and wherever I met with him and wanted it, if he had not the money of the Company he paid me with his own."[45]

If Merritt was the instigator of the canal project, he was much more as well. While the board of the Welland Canal Company as a whole was responsible for raising the funds necessary to construct the First Welland, Merritt also played a key role in fundraising. At the same time as supervising the work itself, he was urging governments and prominent merchants to support the endeavour, both by letter and through personal visits. Merritt's efforts to spearhead his grand project may have taken a toll on his psyche,[46] but he nevertheless took pleasure in them. After he had been authorized by the board of the Welland Canal Company to travel to New York and "any other place, where he may think proper"[47] to sell stock, for instance, Merritt crowed to his wife from Bridgewater, New York: "It has ever been a greater gratification to be the harbinger of good news to those so deeply interested in my welfare than to realize it myself – I have now the satisfaction to say that I have succeeded far beyond my most sanguine expectations – Have got the necessary Amt of Stock subscribed by the most respectable and influential men in the Money Market in New York."[48]

Creative Brokerage

In promoting "his" canal, Merrit was an accomplished, persuasive salesman, using what has been called "creative brokerage."[49] On these junkets and in these person-to-person meetings between the visionary and optimistic Merritt and prospective stockholders, the force of his personality must have played a great role. That the rich and powerful agreed to support Merritt's project cannot be ascribed solely to their political or financial calculations. But despite what validity there may have been in Mackenzie's later charges of financial sloppiness on the part of Merritt and other directors, we cannot agree with his charge that Merritt was trying "to decoy wealthy foreigners into the concern as stockholders."[50] More insightful is the view of M.J. Patton that, while Merritt was indeed far-seeing, "sometimes he saw too far into the realms of the remotely possible as to make him forget the limitations of the actual."[51]

Part of Merritt's talent as a broker lay in knowing how to bring men, money, and ideas together, and how to present his project in the most favourable language. To Major George Hillier, secretary to Sir Peregrine Maitland (1777–1854), then lieutenant-governor (1818–28), he described the advantages of draining the area of Cranberry Marsh, through which the canal would pass, as follows: "A grant of these lands would enable them [the Canal Company] by draining it to contribute to the health of the District and the Health of that part of the country and by giving an effectual impulse to the Company it would be an additional inducement of Capital to come forward and assist in the internal improvement of the country."[52]

Public health, economic growth, and "progress," as the nineteenth century envisaged it, are all present in this remark. In his speech at the sod-turning, Merritt expanded on the link to the Grand River,[53] noting: "The banks of the River Welland and the Grand River abound with an almost inexhaustible supply of pine timber, now useless, which will be floated down to our establishments, converted into lumber, and transported to the entrance to the American canal at Tonawanda ... There are likewise important quarries of the purest white gypsum, or plaster, on the banks of the Grand River, which will soon become a profitable article of commerce ... By entering the mouth of the Grand River one month earlier every Spring, we will draw all the early transit from the American shore, even should they join their own canal again at Tonawanda."

He could also skillfully stress the nostalgic, the economically practical, and the military in his appeals for support. For example, he wrote to a former comrade-in-arms, Sir John Harvey, then commander of the British army at Quebec, explaining the military importance of the proposed waterway. He recalled their common experience in the War of 1812 and stressed the ongoing commercial competition between British North America and the United States. "I can bring every part of this route forcibly to your recollection. It commences ten miles up the Chippewa [Welland] River; passes De Cew's (the house we retreated to after we were beaten from Fort George) and terminates at the Twelve Mile Creek, the place where our boats generally landed during the War."[54]

As a measure of the esteem he was accorded in some quarters, when Merritt was sent to Quebec in 1827 as a broker for the company, he took with him despatches from Lieutenant-Governor Maitland to Lord Dalhousie (1770–1838, governor-in-chief of the Canadas, 1819–28) (fig. 1.1).[55] The latter spoke of the canal before the Quebec Legislature, which was inspired to pass a bill granting £25,000 to the company.

Early in 1828 Merritt was again on his travels. He went first to New York, where he encouraged J.B. Yates (1784–1836) (fig. 1.1), a prominent New York financier and early supporter of his plans, to subscribe a further amount. Failing to acquire sufficient guarantees there, he sailed for England to try his luck. In Britain the advantages of easier interlake communication were apparent to both commercial and military interests. In March, when he found that the London *Times* editor repeatedly postponed their appointment, Merritt declared that he could describe the canal project in five minutes. When the editor looked at his watch and allowed him to proceed, Merritt pulled a map out of his pocket, and said, "Here is Lake Erie, here are the Falls of Niagara, this is Lake Ontario, the St. Lawrence and the Atlantic, and here is the route of the great Welland Canal."[56] While this anecdote may be apocryphal, it effectively portrays Merritt's adaptability and insight – and determination.

As much as he was an ambassador for the canal project, Merritt was a "hands-on" entrepreneur who took a lively interest in the details of its progress. His journal entry for July 1825, for example, shows his attention to every aspect of the early construction:

> [July] 8. Wrote 3 letters to Hovey & Beach & Co. to Ridgeway, Rochester & Montesuma — wrote Chapman likewise — went up to give the Engineer instructions, very hard went up to [deep] cut, paid Platter & Kennedy — Men quite discouraged. 22 quit work on Dobbins job. Encouraged them to go on, but find many men have left the line — all pleased to hear Hovey has taken the contract.
>
> Wrote Sylvester Hatheway & Mr. Lemon Lockport — Niagara County John TenBroecks farm 150 acres will sell for $4500 ...
>
> 12th — Went to Decous, Miss Hicks — Swaisy, Hopkins, Wilson &c to get relinquishments of land — all want to think of it until next week — No work done on Canal today. Orange celebration. Clows put in bottom line & commenced the Beaver Dam route — sent James Clowes yesterday to level from the Welland & Grand River to Marsh ...
>
> 14th called on Hiram Swaizy, George Marlatt, Widow Smith & Thos Nihan to sign off their lands — to which but one agreed until taken into consideration
>
> 15th Spent the whole of this day in the Office drawing off reports, proceedings of the Meeting & attending to Fenelon [re contract for harbour]
>
> 16th Rode to deep cut and find the men much dissatisfied — the men on Simpson's job getting on badly with the Ditch ...
>
> Hovey arrived & Fenlon went over to Black Rock with a letter from me to Smith & Chapman
>
> It will be necessary to let out the Canal from Harbor to near the Mountain go where it may for the purpose of conveying Stone to Harbor, it will cost but a very small sum of money and be adding much to its popularity having so much finished in so short a period ...
>
> 18th attended the Arbitrators and left it with Mr. Keefer to settle — Assigned operations with Mr. Hovey for the prompt prosecution of the work

get Mr. Roberts to examine the whole rout as soon as possible and leave it to his decision.[57]

Merritt was always intimately associated with the work "on the ground," travelling up and down the line on horseback, inspecting jobs, and making notes. In an 1827 memorandum to the board he noted: "I have to attend to the whole line keep a detail of the proceedings on each Job — a copy of all accounts, decide on all plans & Specifications of Engineers encourage & alternately censure each Contractor, urge them on as well as the Engineer, particularly that part which requires most labor, look out for Contractors find out which different Jobs cost to compare the value of excavation & have my whole mind and attention placed on the Work, to answer & attend to the various applications, settle disputes, spend as much time in talking as working."[58]

This catalogue may sound like discontented complaining, but one doubts that Merritt would have had it any other way! Of course, his ability to handle all these responsibilities might be questioned. The investigation of 1836 suggested, credibly, that he and others on the company's board of directors often took on more than their experience or ability could manage. Nevertheless, Merritt's contemporaries recognized his pivotal and practical role in the canal project. When he broke his leg in a stagecoach accident, in September 1828, after his trip to England, and had returned to St Catharines, the company secretary wrote: "We feel the loss of his active service and already find his presence has given the spur to the work."[59] His direct engagement continued as the company's focus turned toward further stages of the project.

Merritt's Continuing Role

As early as 1825 Merritt had envisaged what would become the Second Canal, referring (once again in a letter to his father-in-law) to the project underway as "the small Canal" and predicting that the public would demand a larger one in the future.[60] In that same year he called a meeting at Niagara to institute a survey of the St Lawrence River. In 1832 a pamphlet on the need for improving the Canadian canal system was published in St Catharines by "A Projector" – Merritt himself.[61]

He was undaunted by Mackenzie's muck-raking in 1835–36 (see below), and continued to champion a long-term vision of the Welland Canal. In a detailed memorandum of 1837, he urged the Canal Company to take over the Grand River Navigation Company, expanding (in effect) the Welland's maritime connections.[62] Two years later, impatient with Canadian and British politicians, he castigated them for their neglect of Canada's canal network, condemning "the negligence, ignorance, supineness and powerless situation of two divided Legislatures, as well as ... the want of attention to our best interests, on the part of the Home Government."[63] That he maintained his vision of what would eventually become the St Lawrence Seaway is evident in his support for a canal at "The Soo." In 1850 he wrote: "Another link of this great chain, is the connexion of Lakes Huron and Superior ... It requires but one lock, and a short canal, on the Sault Ste. Marie."[64]

When the Welland Canal passed into the hands of the Board of Works in the early 1840s, Merritt may well have felt sidelined. But his concern for the project remained intense. On 22 July 1844, for example, he accepted a temporary appointment with the Board of Works, for the "superintendence of the Public Works, on and above the Niagara Peninsula.[65] Two days later he entered a long memorandum in his journal, in which he detailed necessary improvements to the canal (already undergoing reconstruction), including widening some locks, improving waste weirs and embankments, and strengthening the Grand River dam. The document reads more like the technical musings of a trained engineer than the strategy of a businessman.[66] Then, in 1845, he wrote to Samuel Power, superintending engineer of the Welland: "There are one or two subjects to which your early attention should be directed."[67]

Although he was not an engineer, Merritt's commitment and efforts continued to be appreciated by laymen and engineers alike. For example, engineer Hamilton Killaly, first chairman of the Board of Works, wrote to him in 1842: "I feel persuaded that your general Agency and energy, and the intimate acquaintance you have acquired with such matters, could be made extremely useful in forwarding the various preliminary arrangements necessary for the full and final opening of the St. Lawrence navigation throughout."[68]

During the period of construction of the Second Canal, Merritt served as a member of the House of Assembly of both Upper Canada (for Haldimand County, 1832–41) and the Province of Canada (for Lincoln County, 1841–60). In April 1850 he was named Chief Commissioner of Public Works, thus assuming a more formal public role in Upper Canadian life. Unhappily, his schemes to further reform the department and his more far-reaching suggestions to improve Canada's canals were not well received by his political masters. His plans, wrote historian J.E. Hodgetts, were "rudely disowned by every one of his colleagues."[69] The real problem was essentially that he was neither a bureaucrat nor a politician. He resigned in February 1851 because, said two contemporaries, "the restraints of office were ... in the last degree irksome to him."[70] The chief commissioner, they said, "was neither a party man nor a politician ... His popularity sprang from his independence, his purity of character, and from the practical nature of his aims."[71] That popularity was further acknowledged when he was elected to represent Niagara in the Legislative Council in 1860.

Merritt died on 5 July 1862, not inappropriately aboard a steamship in the Cornwall Canal, returning from Montreal. He had been to the east coast on a rare holiday and was working on a study of inland navigation – in short, doing what he loved. It is not too much to imagine, however, that Merritt had been at his happiest and most fulfilled in the 1820s, riding up and down the line of "his" canal, inspecting unfinished locks, conferring with engineers and contractors over plans, deeply excited by what he knew to be (in MacTaggart's words) "one of the most wonderful of the hydraulic contrivances of man."[72]

This brief portrait of William Hamilton Merritt shows clearly that the development of the Welland Canals was intimately linked to political, military, social, economic, and technological interests, both domestic and foreign. The War of 1812 was still very much in the collective memory of Upper Canadians when the site of the First Welland was under discussion. One requirement, therefore, was the need to locate the canal a sufficient distance from the international boundary to provide security in the event of another American invasion. The rebuilding of the canal in stone was affected by the recession of 1837, the Rebellions of 1837–38, and the bureaucratic reorganization occasioned by the union of Upper and Lower Canada in 1841. Construction of the Third Canal was delayed by the impending Confederation of 1867, and then was incorporated into the political aspirations of Prime Minister John A. Macdonald and his National Policy. The project was further influenced by the economic depression that afflicted the Western world in the 1870s and 1880s. The building of the Welland Canals, therefore, cannot be fully understood without an appreciation of factors beyond the energy and commitment of its prime mover and the technical challenges of directing water and ships through an ever-larger ditch.

THE POLITICIANS

From the time French missionaries and explorers first confronted Niagara Falls, it was clear that this spectacular natural wonder was also a barrier to transportation by water. As early as the 1700s, French officials had considered a canal to circumvent the cataract and to secure their growing empire. Concluding that the enterprise would be too expensive, however, the naval commissioner of New France, Francis Clairambault D'Aigremont, in 1710 declared his scepticism about "any sort of connection from Lake Ontario to Lake Erie which would have us avoid the portage."[73] While the French made no attempt to build such a canal, they retained control of Fort Niagara, on the east side of the Niagara River (at its mouth) until the British took it over in 1759. By 1764 the British had control of both banks of the river – including the portage route on the east side long used by the French. When the British lost the Thirteen Colonies in the American Revolutionary War, the Treaty of Paris (1783) made the Niagara River the boundary between British territory and the new republic. As trade and commerce grew in the course of the subsequent peace, both the Americans and the British maintained portage routes around the Falls, but neither built a canal.

The British Constitutional Act of 1791 created the largely anglophone Upper Canada (later Canada West, then the Province of Ontario) and the mainly francophone Lower Canada (later Canada East and then the Province of Quebec). Newark (later Niagara, now Niagara-on-the-Lake) on the British side of the Niagara River mouth became the capital of Upper Canada, with a government consisting of an appointed lieutenant-governor, legislative and executive councils, and an elected legislative assembly. As the nineteenth century dawned, this authority, later based in York (Toronto from 1834), began to regard a link between lakes Ontario and Erie as important not only to the local region but also as part of a larger waterway. In 1818, therefore, they sent commissioners to confer with their counterparts in Lower Canada on the matter of British North American canals. The resulting report of 30 October 1818 indicated that, while Lower Canada was prepared to commence surveys of the St Lawrence and Ottawa rivers, Upper Canada did not have financial resources to contribute. Nevertheless, in November 1818, the Upper Canada Assembly voted a sum, not to exceed £2,000, toward the cost of such a survey. The matter was studied further and in 1821 a Select Committee on Internal Resources recommended both the improvement of the St Lawrence and the construction of a canal between lakes Erie and Ontario. On the latter subject the committee reported: "That it is perfectly practicable to connect the lakes Erie and Ontario with Montreal by canals of sufficient depth to enable vessels of burthen to sail without unloading direct to that port cannot be doubted."[74] One of Merritt's relatives identified a major impediment, however, writing in 1823: "Upper Canada is too poor to undertake such an expensive business."[75] Indeed, even by early nineteenth-century standards, the colony was far from prosperous. Its rich natural resources remained still largely untapped and its population, mainly agricultural, was still small. Entrepreneurs had not had time to become rich and influential – or daring.

The Perceived Value of a Niagara Canal

The economic weakness of Upper Canada did not, however, preclude optimism about the future, an attitude based in part on activities in New York State. The committee encouraged the colonial government to emulate "the successful enterprise of our jealous neighbours" who had started to build the Erie Canal in 1817.[76] Moreover, any waterway through British territory would have strategic as well as economic value. No one had forgotten the American invasions of 1812–14, when significant battles had been fought in the militarily crucial Niagara Peninsula (at Beaver Dams and Stoney Creek in 1813), and the burning of Newark by American forces in late 1813. The memory of this conflict would also affect the choice of the site of a trans-peninsula canal. Reporting in 1825, a committee studying the improvement of navigation in British North America noted that "such a work [a Niagara canal] would undoubtedly facilitate military operations in defence of the Province."[77]

Ultimately, the interest that influential individuals in Upper Canada and elsewhere took in the Welland Canal project was crucial to its success. "Many gentlemen of character and high respectability,"[78] boasted the Welland Canal Company directors, later supported the enterprise. In truth, Merritt was careful to encourage the colonial gentry to take up positions on the company's board of directors and to let their participation be known.[79] In 1825 he toured colonial centres to raise money for his canal, selling stock subscriptions in York, Kingston, Montreal, and Quebec. More important in the long run, in York, he convinced John Henry Dunn (1792–1854), receiver general, and John Beverley Robinson, attorney-general, both members of the "Family Compact," to support his endeavour. In Kingston, he interested Commodore Robert Barrie (1774–1841) of the Royal Navy, as well. Robinson, in particular, described by a biographer as the "bone and sinew of the Compact,"[80] was deeply interested in developing water communication on the Great Lakes, and was therefore happy to promote the building of the Welland Canal.

In May 1825 Merritt sent a map of the planned canal to Lieutenant-Governor Maitland, who had a twenty-room summer house on the Niagara Escarpment near St David's, a fact that may have made him somewhat more aware than others in the political elite of the nature of Niagara's geography. Perhaps in his summer retreat here, he had social contacts with local leaders and businessmen. In any event, Port Robinson (originally Port Beverley) was named for the attorney-general; Port Dalhousie was named in tribute to the encouragement of the Earl of Dalhousie; Port Maitland for Sir Peregrine Maitland; and Dunnville in honour of John Dunn, the receiver general.

Whatever their political views, the Family Compact leaders were broad-visioned enough to see the worth of Merritt's project. At least one later lieutenant-governor agreed: "In no one of the United States," wrote Sir Francis Bond Head (1793–1875) proudly, "has a public work equal to the Welland Canal been carried through by a country so young and so thinly inhabited."[81] Moreover, without the assistance of the lieutenant-governor and the legislative council in piloting bills for the company's financing through the Assembly, the continuation of the canal scheme could not have been secure.

On the way to Montreal in 1825, Merritt impressed several prominent businessmen, including the MacDonalds, Gananoque millowners. In Montreal he called a meeting of businessmen, some of whom subscribed. In Quebec City an old acquaintance, James Irwin, offered support and, after a meeting of the Board of Trade, £1,000 of stock in the company was purchased. Equally important, Governor General Dalhousie agreed to raise the subject with the British government. Leaving no stone unturned, Merritt also had a pamphlet printed in French.

Contacts in New York State were equally vital to the success of the project. On 30 March 1825 Merritt met with Governor Clinton, who had instigated the building of the Erie Canal. Merritt's father-in-law, Dr Prendergast, a state senator, introduced him to New York businessmen, some of whom took up considerable stock in the company – lending crucial support to the endeavour. Far from crippling the development by exploitation or restrictions, American interests galvanized the project. For example, New York stockholders (who purchased substantial amounts of stock) persuaded the Welland Canal Company directors to enlarge the waterway's dimensions from barge to ship canal size, thus laying the foundation for the channel's later – however qualified – commercial success.[82] Altogether, Merritt and his colleagues raised about £100,000 from private investors outside the Canadas – that is, in the United States and Britain. However, at this time return on private investment in canals proved everywhere to be low. Canal-building projects in Upper Canada, as in the States, required government involvement. In York this fact was not at first obvious, but in 1825 the Upper Canada government amended the company's charter and increased the amount of authorized capital.

The Welland Canal Company and the Colonial Elite

With such support the way was cleared for the Legislature to pass an act on 19 January 1824 incorporating the Welland Canal Company and setting out the general lines on which it was to operate. The company's original directors were mainly local men, with the exception of the president, John Henry Dunn, who declined to serve in the newly incorporated company and was succeeded by Merritt's friend and fellow millowner, George Keefer. However, from 1825 forward the list of directors included the names of several powerful Upper Canadians not resident in Niagara. For example, Dunn later did assume the role of president and served until 1832; Henry John Boulton (1790–1870), solicitor general, served as vice-president until 1827 and remained on the board until June 1832. William Allan (1771–1853), president of the Bank of Upper Canada (1822–35), was also a director from 1825 to 1832. It is scarcely surprising that, given this strong political support from 1824 until 1837, both the Upper Canadian and the British governments made loans and grants to the company.

If today it seems irregular – if not actually illegal – for individual members of a government to hold stock in a private company that is financially supported by the same government, it was not unusual at this time. The Burlington Bay Canal, to give one example, was financed in a similar way.[83] Whether we speak of "York," the "Family Compact," or "the Upper Canadian government," important members of the colonial administration had a great investment in the Welland. Common political and economic sense, therefore, dictated that men such as Dunn and Robinson, as well as Boulton, Allan, and Colonel Joseph Wells – some of "the powers that be" – should remain interested in its fate. On more than one occasion, they saved the Welland from abandonment.

On the other hand, while the desperate straits in which the Welland Canal Company often found itself were frequently caused by its own inefficiency, the colonial government was at other times as much a hindrance as a help. For example, in 1830 York demanded that the canal be opened for commerce before it would offer any more financial help. "Hasty make-shift credit arrangements"[84] were therefore entered into with contractors, who agreed to receive partial payment for work done, in proportion to the company's available funds. Thus, normal methods of contracting were abandoned and the door was left open to contractors who, themselves desperate for payment, did shoddy work. At other times the company resorted to questionable measures to add to their revenue, such as selling water-power rights along the canal, in particular to John B. Yates, whose Hydraulic Company was established in 1830, a measure that was of little assistance to the directors in the subsequent inquiry.

For its part, York did not invest blindly. In 1830 Robert Randal, MPP, was appointed as commissioner to inspect the canal and report on the wisdom of the government's granting a further loan to the company. He visited the Deep Cut, where he found that recent landslides would not impede navigation, but that the Grand River Dam had settled as much as 16 inches (40.6 cm) since completion. He found some of the locks already in disrepair and thought that the Port Dalhousie harbour should be deepened and the entrance lock there widened. While his assessment was on the whole positive, he nevertheless warned: "A considerable outlay will yet be required to complete the Welland Canal."[85]

The First Welland Canal, although built on a route safe from American invasion and useful to the British army and navy, was by no means an efficient waterway. By the mid-1830s its deteriorating wooden locks required rebuilding in stone on a larger scale. But this justifiable and technically feasible undertaking was delayed, as the Welland Canal Company became trapped in the crossfire between the Family Compact and a vigorous political reform movement. The radical William Lyon Mackenzie had targeted the company as early as 1830, when he moved in the House of Assembly that a Select Committee be appointed to study the management of the Welland, before the government made it another grant. In his efforts to discredit the colonial political elite, Mackenzie found the canal a useful weapon. In 1831 he moved in the House that the company's directors produce a statement of their business and its practices, but the Legislature refused to support his motion. Mackenzie persisted and, as a government-appointed member of the company's board of directors in 1835, claimed to have found matters that disturbed him. In December of 1835 Mackenzie published *The Welland Canal: A Weekly Journal*, which publicly documented his concern about the canal's financing, construction, and operation. In January 1836, on a motion put forward by Merritt himself, the government felt compelled to establish a Select Committee to investigate

Mackenzie's thirty allegations,[86] which included "defalcation of the funds of the Company."[87]

While Mackenzie was clearly gunning for the Family Compact, he may have had a point. The Welland Canal was indeed a private institution that had swallowed up a great deal of public money – about a million dollars in loans and grants (see below). And so, whatever Mackenzie's motives, such an inquiry was probably justifiable. No responsible person in authority in Toronto could ignore his claim that, on studying the account books, he had discovered "many errors, additions and crossings out." Neglect of basic business practices, he declared, had led to "an endless round of taking, resigning, modifying, amending, altering and making of contracts ... nothing is fixed."[88] The company directors had been improperly elected, he said; investors were tricked into buying stock; hydraulic leases and canal contracts were given to personal friends of the directors; and large sums of money were unaccounted for. As for Merritt, Mackenzie further claimed, he had allegedly charged to the company luxuries such as theatre tickets and cigars.[89] The gist of Mackenzie's accusations was that the account books were improperly kept – and deliberately so – in order to defraud the public and the stockholders.

Mackenzie's language was intemperate and his charges politically motivated, but the company's procedures were admittedly unorthodox, even by the standards of early nineteenth-century colonial finances. Moreover, he was quite correct in recognizing in Merritt the canny and occasionally disingenuous businessman. On the other hand, Mackenzie associated Merritt's healthy self-interest and the directors' slapdash habits with private moral corruption and abuse of public money. In this latter judgment, he was mistaken. The investigating committee ultimately declared the allegations of fraud unfounded: "[They] cannot say that any intentional fraud against the public or canal proprietors, has been brought home to any individual officer of the Company, or that the misconduct complained of in this respect is calculated to benefit the individuals connected with the management of the canal."[90]

Merritt must have been relieved by this judgment, and also by the committee's conclusion that the reason the affairs of the company had been conducted "in a very loose and unsatisfactory manner" was that the canal builders were "frequently much cramped for means to carry on the necessary repairs required to keep the canal open." Merritt and his colleagues were judged not-guilty of "any intentional abuse of the powers vested in them."[91] According to his son's biography, Merritt wrote to his wife: "The farce has ended. And after being tried by our enemies, we have been acquitted with credit. Even my political opponents expressed their astonishment ... But it is no gratification to me personally."[92]

The Political Value of a Completed Welland

By the early 1830s provincial authorities could not ignore the evidence that the Welland Canal was not going to become a source of income for the province or for its private investors. In fact, the company could not meet its interest payments and continually had to seek public help for operation and repairs. Eventually, expenditure on the Welland and other public works projects would nearly bankrupt Upper Canada. Already in 1834 a Committee of the House of Assembly had recommended consideration of government purchase. By 1841, as we shall see, about a quarter of the province's entire public debt had been incurred by the Welland Canal,[93] and the idea of the government taking over the company had much wider currency.

At the end of 1835, however, the company was still staggering along. Repairs to the waterway were desperately needed, the company was deeply in debt, traffic (hence toll revenue) had not yet met expectations, and destructive rumours about the canal were circulating in New York newspapers. The board was forced to issue its own promissory notes to workers and contractors, notes that, although of dubious legality, were accepted as legal tender. And by this time, York's confidence in the Welland project had been virtually eroded: the company had made constant calls on public resources, and its statements and reports had been vague and contradictory. The waterway was "ever on the verge of completion," wrote early canal historian William Kingsford, "and never finished."[94]

The year 1836 was marked not only by Mackenzie's damaging inquiry but also by the closure of the waterway for over three months of the navigation season (93 out of 184 days). Decay of the locks continued and, alarmingly, the Americans were talking about building their own Niagara canal and were making surveys to that effect. In November 1836 the company asked for yet another loan from the government.

In short, the project was obviously foundering in many problems, not least of which was the company's great debt – which the toll revenues could not pay off. The expense of repairing the deteriorating locks would probably be greater than the company's income. The original intention of the directors had been not merely to recoup the costs of operation, but to make a profit for its shareholders, assuming that the tolls charged on goods in transit would be sufficient for both purposes. As it transpired, sales of stock, even with the considerable participation of New York investors, did not meet expectations; nor did the tolls. Loans from individuals and the government of Upper Canada and, later, England, had proved necessary. Despite considerable aid from the Legislature of Upper Canada, the situation was sufficiently critical by late 1836 that the directors, having received approval from the stockholders, petitioned both legislatures to take over the privately held stock in the company.

In view of these dire conditions, the Family Compact took on a more "pro-active" role. In an Act of 4 March 1837, the government converted its loans to the company (£102,000) into stock and subscribed a further £250,000 in public stock. This Act, while keeping the company alive, also reduced the number of directors on the board to five, so that the three government-appointed members had a majority. The last meeting of the old Welland Canal Company board was held on 3 April 1837, and a new board, with the government-appointed members, met just two weeks later, on 18 April. Private control of the Welland Canal effectively ended, although actual ownership did not pass into government hands until January 1842.

The 1837 Act also provided that the Welland Canal Company directors should hire "two scientific and practical engineers," and two British civil engineers, Killaly and Nicol Baird (fig. 3.1), were engaged to report on the state of the Welland and to survey for an enlargement. They did so in 1837–38,[95] recommending that the locks be rebuilt in stone, the channel deepened, and a new route excavated north of the escarpment (fig. 1.2). Unfortunately, their survey coincided with the economic slowdown of 1837 and the Rebellions of 1837–38. By 1838 matters were desperate: the anticipated buy-out of the private stockholders by the government had been delayed and every avenue was being explored to ease the financial situation. For a while, the very survival of the Welland was in doubt. The directors, under the presidency of J.S. Macaulay (1791–1855), opined that, given the great expense involved in repairing the canal, "it may well be questioned whether it will be more wise to let the Canal go to decay, using it only as a source of water power for driving ... machinery."[96] Shortly after this, it was suggested in the House of Assembly that, "in the present state of the Province and its finances, it is inexpedient to pass any positive Act in relation to the Welland Canal."[97] The pessimistic Macaulay was under no illusion: "I have a clear conception of the *ruinous expenditure* to be incurred [in reconstruction]" [his emphasis].[98] He was not mistaken for, in 1840 alone, £15,000 was spent on canal maintenance, out of a

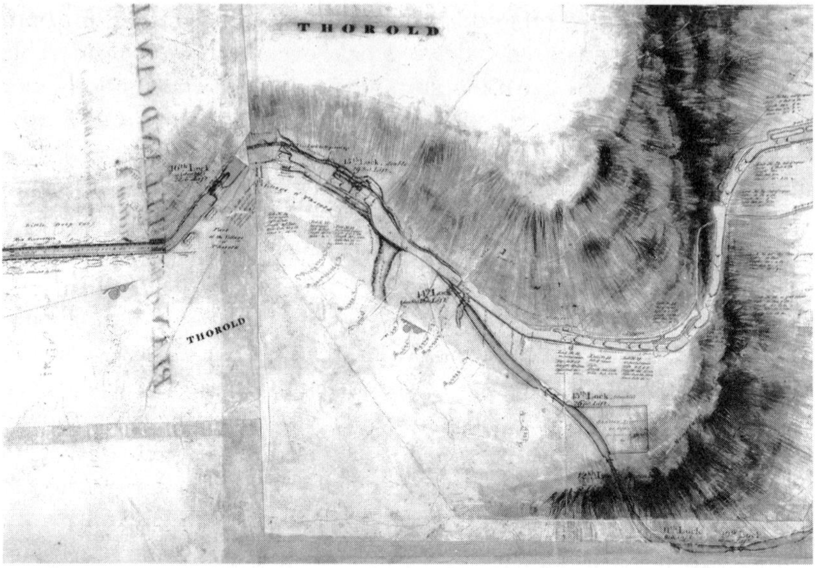

1.2 A section of Baird and Killaly's survey of the First Canal, 1838, showing the curved "path of least resistance" approach to the Niagara Escarpment and the route of their suggested improvement. The fine print on the original map often notes that a lock is "out of repair." (LAC: NMC-11848)

total public works budget of £36,000. Nevertheless, despite the fact that the Welland was already the most expensive public works project in Upper Canada, the government of the United Canadas (the new Province of Canada) allocated £450,000 to rebuild the Welland Canal locks in stone.[99] In the meantime, by 1842 the province of Canada West had acquired 42.9 per cent of the company's stock.

Despite the pessimism of 1838, the political authorities had remained committed to improving the Welland. In 1839 the new governor general, Lord Durham (1792–1840),[100] asked Lieutenant-Colonel George Phillpotts (d. 1853) of the Royal Engineers to report on the condition of all Canadian canals. Unimpressed by the state of the Welland, Phillpotts agreed with Killaly and Baird that the canal's capacity would have to be enlarged, especially given changing ship technology. The most significant aspect of his report was his suggestion for crossing the Escarpment. Like his two predecessors, he envisaged a more direct approach along a "loop" via Ten Mile Creek, with three sets of flight locks, a great reservoir atop the bluff, and larger locks to accommodate steamers (fig. 1.3).[101]

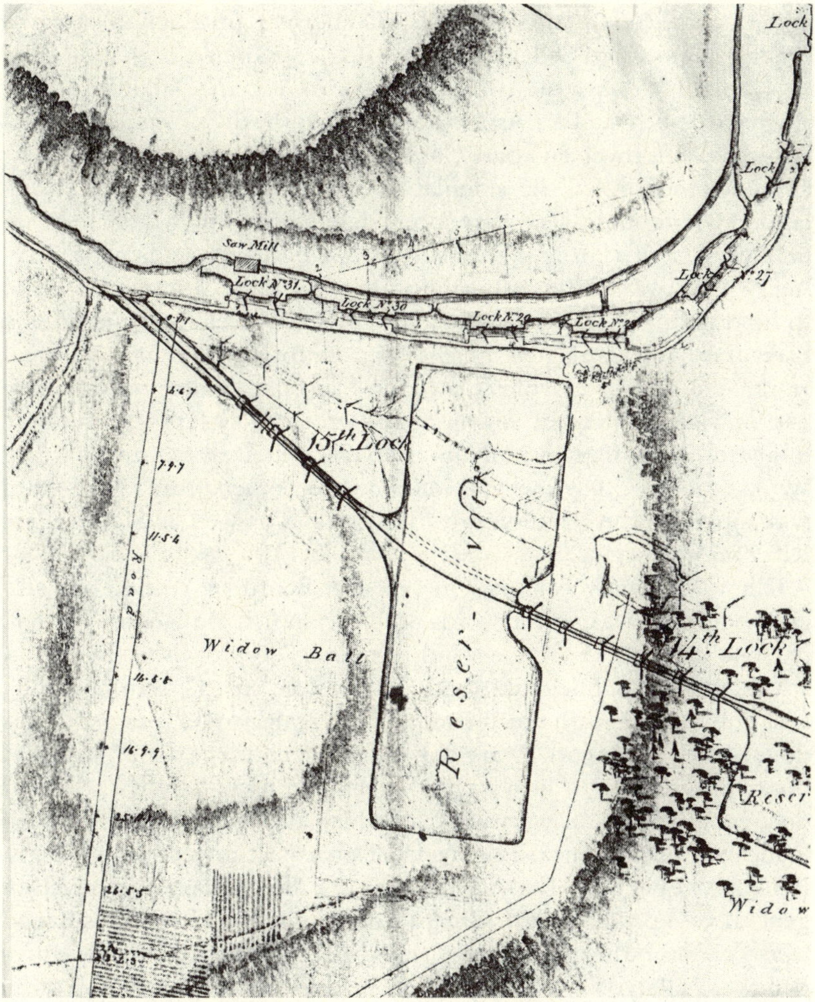

1.3 Part of George Phillpotts's map in his 1842 report. His suggestion for rebuilding was similar to Baird and Killaly's, but with massive reservoirs. The presence of a saw mill at Lock 31 documents the beginning of the town of Thorold to the south. (SCM: 979.56.2)

Lord Durham's term as governor general and his historic report did not affect the location of a new waterway, but his advice to London on the constitution of the Canadas did influence the Welland Canal's future. His recommendation for a "United Province of Canada" was implemented in the Act of Union of 1840, which linked the former Upper and Lower Canadas as the Province of Canada (Canada West and Canada East). After Sir John Colborne's brief tenure as governor general, Lord Sydenham (1799–1841), appointed to that office in 1839, sought to have the two Canadas work together smoothly. Merritt regarded Sydenham as the ideal man to lead "a commercial and industrial improvement party,"[102] and was heartened when the new appointee continued the colonial government's interest in the Welland. Merritt must also have been delighted with Sydenham's announcement that an imperial loan of £1.5 million (the Canada Loan Act of 1842) would be forthcoming to reduce the colony's debt and to fund public works. Sydenham was critical of what he believed had been the haphazard government support for the Welland, a "great work," but one upon which £400,000 had been "most improvidently and unwisely expended, owing to the wretched system ... heretofore followed."[103] In 1841 Sydenham established a five-member Board of Works (under Killaly), which would oversee expenditure of the grant and supervise the rebuilding of the Welland as well as St Lawrence River improvements.

Killaly, not only commissioner of the Board of Works, but also chief engineer, was, in the words of historian J.E. Hodgetts, "a strong personality, with an engineer's 'direct action' approach to the task of advancing the public works with all possible speed" and "spending vast public funds with the abandon of the zealot anxious to get things done whatever the cost."[104] He did, indeed, "get things done" – and the board "plunged into heavy engagements with contractors, which at once committed it on every work for which an appropriation had been made, without any regard to the wholesome checks imposed by Legislative enactment."[105] The Act creating the board gave the governor general veto power over the board's decisions, but Sir Charles Bagot, who took over after Sydenham's unexpected death, exerted little control over Killaly.

By 1845 allegations of excessive expenditure on public works led to the appointment of a Royal Commission to investigate the board's management. Killaly's dual role as commissioner and chief engineer had contributed to a centralization of power that made it virtually beyond the reach of any political control. The commission's investigation recommended a number of changes designed to increase accountability, which were enacted in June 1846. The five-man board was replaced by a chief commissioner and an assistant commissioner (both political appointees), the position of chief engineer was to be responsible to the political head, and the board became known as the Department of Public Works. Killaly was ousted from his position, but remained with the department. He had over-stepped his authority while chairman and put a great strain on the province's coffers.[106]

It was clear that, from then on, the construction and maintenance of the Welland would be a true public work and, as such, would continue to be influenced as much by political as by technological factors.[107] The days of uncontrolled expenditure were over. In keeping with the new mood, in the fall of 1846 Samuel Keefer (1811–90, fourth son of George Keefer, Sr) (fig. 3.1), who had replaced Samuel Power as the Welland's engineer,[108] was told to suspend "all works unconnected with the main trunk of the Canal."[109] Keefer protested, citing the "injury of the navigation and consequent reduction of tolls – damage or destruction of works from being left in an unfinished state – compensation to contractors for delay – increased cost of work remaining to be done – injury to the Credit of the Province." He preferred to await the decision of the chief commissioner of Public Works, W.B. Robinson (1797–1873), who, in Keefer's words, understood "the extreme impropriety of suspending the works." Robinson had, however, enjoined Keefer "to keep down expenses as much as possible."[110]

Work did continue, but in June 1848 Keefer received another order to discontinue all work that was not absolutely necessary. Accordingly, he ordered the suspension of works at Port Colborne, the Broad Creek lock, and the aqueduct, and stopped the dredging at Port Dalhousie and the Deep Cut. In addition, the method of paying contractors was changed from cash to debentures payable at varying times (usually in five years)[111] and, whenever possible, contracting out of work was abandoned in favour of the use of day labour. The retrenchment also affected personnel, including the engineers. John Page, assistant engineer on the First Division of the Welland (and later chief engineer of the Department of Public Works, and that of Railways and Canals) was among those let go for lack of funds to pay his salary.

In November 1848 Killaly, now engineer on the Welland, made a tour of inspection on the construction site and reported extensively to the Department, stressing that he awaited instruction from the commissioners "with great anxiety."[112] While the Welland's financial situation had improved with the 1841 grant for the Board of Works, by late December 1848 the Department was advising thinner paper for letters and reports and avoiding the use of the expensive and unreliable telegraph. A month later Killaly informed the board that he was sending with one of the contractors "sundry documents to save postage."[113]

Why the retrenchment and the apparently nit-picking parsimony? Generally speaking, the late 1840s was a time of economic stress in both the United States and Britain, and Canada West was no exception. The problem originated in part in British commercial policy. Until the mid-1840s Canadian exporters enjoyed preference in the Imperial market, but the notion of free trade took hold in Britain, and the long-standing Corn Laws and Navigation Acts (which protected Canadian exports to the mother country) were abolished in 1846, with the result that Canada's trade with Britain declined dramatically. Wheat prices plummeted and the wheels of many grist and flour mills ground to a halt. Grain, of course, was a staple cargo of the Welland. In 1846, moreover, the American government developed a rival system whereby goods from Canada West could be transported to the Atlantic through the States in bond over American canals or railways.

In addition, 1848 was a tumultuous year in Europe, with revolts breaking out in France, the Germanies, the Italian Peninsula, and elsewhere. England saw the last gasp of Chartism, and, in the United Canadas, a political "revolution" occurred as representative government was finally achieved. Robert Baldwin (1804–1858) and Louis-Hippolyte Lafontaine (1807–1864), supported by an election majority, constituted a Reform ministry in March 1848, a milestone in the development of Canadian democracy but a cause of Tory outrage. In Montreal, English-speaking conservatives rioted, setting the parliament buildings there on fire. Lord Elgin (1811–1863), the new governor general (1847–54), did not seek to interfere with the new government, but believed himself in danger of being physically assaulted if he appeared in public. Lafontaine's house, moreover, was vandalized.

The belt-tightening continued into 1849, with Thomas Begly (secretary of the Department of Public Works, 1841–58) urging Killaly to use "the strictest economy upon all matters."[114] Meanwhile, Killaly had to endure protests from unpaid contractors, such as the "clamerous [sic] complaints"[115] of a James Cotton, who was working on the harbours. Of course, unpaid contractors meant unpaid labourers, and the result was strife among the navvies. (See chapters 9 and 10.) As a new cholera epidemic threatened in the summer of 1849, these political and economic stresses combined with recurrent labour unrest to nearly stop work on the Second Canal. Matters were slow to improve, even though the government had by July 1849 found some of the funds Killaly needed. Despite these vicissitudes, the Second Welland was completed all the way to Port Colborne in 1850, and was later deepened. As of the 1860s, however, accompanying developments on the political stage, pressure for further enlargement was renewed.

Confederation and the Canal

By the latter part of the nineteenth century, Niagara and its canal builders were entering an era of well-founded optimism and confidence. While the American Civil War (1861–65) provoked concern for the safety of the Welland Canal, its conclusion – and Canadian Confederation in 1867 – seemed to offer greater opportunities for Canadian economic prosperity, opportunities more than partly based on a canal network. The railway boom, culminating in the construction of the Canadian Pacific Railway (1880–85), while it might have been an impediment, did not prevent the second reconstruction of the Welland (1871–81).

In fact, the advent of Confederation set some observers to worrying about the piecemeal development of Canada's canal system. In 1865 William Kingsford, in documenting Canadian canals, complained that the recent Quebec Conference had not extensively discussed the need for waterway expansion. He noted that the emerging state had no overall policy regarding transportation.[116] The meetings and negotiations over Confederation may have actually deflected attention from moves to reconstruct the Welland. In addition, the need to obtain water from Lake Erie rather than from the Grand River had exercised the minds of the Welland's engineers for many years. When, in May 1867, the Welland's then superintendent, Samuel Woodruff (1819–1904), wanted to begin lowering the summit level to admit water from the lake, he was advised by the Department of Public Works that it was not "desirable to enter upon any large contracts until after the formation of the Confederate Govt."[117]

However, pressure for enlargement of the Welland was growing not only in Niagara but also throughout the Great Lakes–St Lawrence system. From at least 1869 the *Daily Times* of St Catharines waved the banner, urging local people to "Agitate, Agitate,"[118] and criticizing Niagara MPs (members of the newly formed Parliament of Canada) Lauchlin McCallum (1823–1903) and Thomas Rodman Merritt (1824–1906), as well as Senator James Benson (1807–1885), for not pushing the project vigorously enough in Ottawa.[119] The Liberal *Times* was suspicious of local Conservative MP John Charles Rykert (1831–1913) for obvious partisan reasons. The prospect of the Georgian Bay Canal – promoted by "a few ... Toronto schemers"[120] – also alarmed the *Times*. After a well-attended public meeting in St Catharines on 15 March 1870, a deputation was sent to meet the Minister of Public Works, Hector-Louis Langevin (1826–1906), in Ottawa to argue the Welland's case.

Perhaps by coincidence, on 31 March 1870, the government announced that funding was available to start the enlargement. When matters were not expedited to its satisfaction, the *Times* continued to lambaste Public Works throughout 1871. "A batch of two surveyors and half a dozen theodolites have been appearing and disappearing in the neighbourhood of St. Catharines and Dunnville," wrote the editor in August 1871, but he despaired of the work commencing soon.[121] And so it went, with the *Times* chronicling local interest in an enlargement throughout the year, until reconstruction actually began.

As with the reconstruction of the 1840s, the increasing size and power of Great Lakes ships was the primary catalyst to rebuilding the Welland in the 1870s. But this second reconstruction – the Third Canal – occurred under federal control with a more formal, bureaucratic approach. Increasingly, the Welland was recognized as the vital link in a national waterways system. In November 1870 Macdonald appointed a Royal Commission, whose report concluded that a policy of "Canal enlargement and extension" was "one which will best stimulate the commercial development of the whole Dominion."[122] Considerable detail was added. The Canadian waterway system must be extended and enlarged in order to capture a greater part of the growing inland commerce of North America. All the canals on the St Lawrence–Great Lakes network must be of a uniform size and depth, allowing large ships to pass freely from the western end of Lake Superior to Montreal. As to the Welland itself, it should be enlarged and improved. A new and more direct route should be opened up between Thorold and Port Dalhousie because reaches between locks on the Escarpment were too short and too narrow to support an enlarged canal. On the present "mountain route," if bigger locks were built, they would have to be placed so close together that not even a vessel's length would lie between them – tantamount to combined locks, which would slow down the movement of ships. The locks, banks, and weirs on the Second Canal (which should be retained) must be raised to give 12 feet of water; the harbours at Port Colborne and Port Dalhousie should be deepened to 15 feet of water; the main line between Thorold and Port Colborne should be widened to 110 feet at bottom and deepened to 13 feet; a second lock should be built at Port Colborne to allow more water into the canal; and the floor of the aqueduct should be sunk 2 feet and perhaps another aqueduct be built beside it to maintain the greater supply of water needed to feed larger locks.

The federal government had instigated studies "on the ground" as well. In August 1870, Chief Engineer John Page (1815–1890) (fig. 3.1) was authorized to have surveys made and to report on the practicability of enlarging the canal. Engineer Thomas Monro (sometimes Munro) (1831–1903) (fig. 3.1)[123] was put in charge of surveys, which began in October and continued for several months. Then, as we have seen, in 1870 the Royal Commission was struck to study Canada's canal system and the possibility of deepening the Welland as well as the St Lawrence route.

While it had seemed that financial constraints would delay the project, work on the Third Canal was able to start in December 1871. The depression that began in the early 1870s caused "a general stagnation of business in all parts of the country," said the Welland's superintendent, Ebenezer Bodwell (b. 1826) in 1875.[124] The slump retarded reconstruction, as did the fact that burgeoning interest in railways provided a competitor for public funds. Indecision about the future of Canada's canals was deepened by a failure to appreciate the potential growth of the wheat trade.[125] These economic difficulties affected contractors in specific ways. For example, in 1873 the Department of Public Works allowed contractors to import necessary equipment or goods free of duties and to send necessary items such as coal through the canal toll-free. The depression of the mid-seventies led to the rescinding of the latter privilege: now, said Public Works, "Contractors are on same footing as the general public."[126]

That the Welland Canal was now a matter of national concern is evident not only from the appointment of the Royal Commission but also from the editorial campaigns of the 1870s beyond Niagara. The Welland was perceived to be vital to the economy of the new Dominion of Canada and so should be deepened as soon as possible. In 1875, for example, the Toronto *Mail* condemned the Liberal government of Alexander Mackenzie (1822–1892) for its "dilatory conduct," especially for not making the new waterway 14 feet deep.[127] In 1880 the Toronto *Globe* detected mismanagement and favouritism as the source of delays in completing the canal.[128] The topic of Niagara's canal now appeared regularly in House of Commons debates and in the deliberations of Commons committees, with local Members of Parliament such as Rykert, James Norris (1820–1891), and others defending their constituents' interests in Ottawa.

Some of the political issues that could swirl – or be made to swirl – around the awarding of contracts on the Welland are exemplified by the Larkin Affair of 1875. The contract for Section One at Port Dalhousie had been awarded to Denison, Belden & Co., of Syracuse, New York. But when American authorities accused them of wrong-doing with regard to contracts in New York State, the Department took the contract from them and awarded it to Captain Patrick Larkin, a Canadian contractor and a Conservative. Although Larkin's tender had been the next lowest, the St Catharines *Daily Times* smelled patronage and repeatedly said so throughout August and September of 1875. Larkin was "absolutely necessary to the success of the Party in power in the District," said a letter to the editor – unlike the Americans, Larkin was a contractor who could vote. "Surely if Canadian contractors take advantage of cheap American labour, the country ought to take advantage of cheap American contractors."[129] Today, the issue seems to have been trumped up by the *Times* editors, who ended their diatribes with the sarcastic comment, "Now, fetch on the champagne, Captain."[130] Such political sniping nonetheless illustrates the importance of the Welland to the nation's leaders.

By the late 1870s, the construction of the Third Welland had become part of a far-reaching plan. In the 1878 election campaign, the policy of Macdonald's Liberal-Conservative party was to stimulate the new state's economy, to settle the prairies (the Dominion Lands Act, designed to develop their potential for wheat export), and to build a transcontinental railroad. This National Policy also included tariff protection for Canadian manufacturers and reduced customs duties on raw materials entering the country. As well, wanting to encourage east-west trade within the country, Macdonald provided aid to the Canadian Pacific Railway in the form of subsidies, mineral rights, and land to support its construction – and especially the difficult line through Crow's Nest Pass. An improved canal system was part of this overall plan, with its role of assisting in the transport of Canadian manufactured products to farmers on the prairies, while carrying their wheat to wider markets. To this end, a new Department of Railways and Canals was created in 1879, relieving the Department of Public Works of those responsibilities. All this – Macdonald hoped – should broaden the base of the Canadian economy and maintain confidence in development of the new country.

Despite various delays, controversies, and contractors' failures, by September 1881 the Third Canal was opened to a depth of twelve feet (3.65 m).[131] It was, said a reporter for the New York *Tribune* in 1883, "a magnificently structured work and excites surprise that the Americans should have permitted the Canadians to anticipate them."[132] But the Americans had not been idle; in the 1870s, a movement to build a ship canal on the American side of the Niagara River developed. While supporters managed to have a bill to effect its construction introduced into the House of Representatives in January 1884, nothing was achieved.

The glow of satisfaction at a job well done did not last. Pessimism about the future of the Welland and other waterways was again evident in 1893, when Thomas C. Keefer (another son of George, a founding director of the Welland Canal Company) expressed his concern that "our canals, instead of becoming as expected, a source of revenue, have become a charge upon the public purse."[133] Nevertheless, and regardless of the financial hurdles to be overcome, a third reconstruction – the Welland Ship Canal – would begin in 1913. That story, however, belongs to another epoch in the Welland's evolution, one in which Canadian political leaders continued to invest much money and thought.[134]

The Military

At all stages of the nineteenth-century Welland Canals, support from the political elite was augmented by the approbation of military leaders. Both the British army and the navy needed a secure through route from the inland colony to the Atlantic. The British army would finance construction of the St Lawrence canals in the late eighteenth and early nineteenth centuries, and the Rideau Canal to connect the Ottawa and Rideau rivers with the St Lawrence at Kingston, from 1826 to 1834. Once the First Welland was under construction, Colonel John By (1779–1836), in charge of building the Rideau, frequently insisted to British authorities that the locks of the Niagara canal, like those of the Rideau "and all the Canals at present projected" in the colony, should be large enough to pass the new steam-powered warships.[135] In 1825 the Duke of Wellington organized a commission of Royal Engineers under the chairmanship of Major General Sir James Carmichael Smyth (1779–1838) to investigate British North American defence needs. Like Colonel By, Carmichael Smyth was concerned that an interior route should be available for transporting gunboats at least into Lake Erie. In his report, he described the Welland as a useful addition to Britain's defences in North America, but deplored the fact that the 1824 Act incorporating the Welland Canal Company had not specified dimensions.[136] As it turned out, although Merritt's canal would be smaller than Carmichael Smyth wanted, colonial military leaders remained interested in the waterway.

Military considerations played a role also in the selection of the route for the Welland (fig. Int.1). A line running from Queenston through St Davids and up to Chippawa, more or less on the portage route, made both economic and commercial sense. But British soldiers, as well as local supporters and Upper Canadian politicians, afraid of renewed American aggression, believed that this line was much too close to the easily crossed Niagara River. The result was that a route based on Twelve Mile Creek farther inland was approved.[137] The voice of the Royal Navy was also heard: Commodore Barrie objected to the Welland Canal Company's original plan to dam the Grand River at its mouth. "If I am to build gun boats on the Grand River," he wrote to Lieutenant-Governor Maitland in 1824, "I should like to construct them on a plan which will admit of their being passed into either Lake by this canal."[138] The proposed dam at the river's mouth would have no lock, and would therefore impede passage of gunboats from the Grand or the Feeder to Lake Erie. (Entrance to the canal from the southern lake was planned for the junction of Chippawa Creek and the Niagara River.) For this reason, the company was compelled to move the site of the dam five miles (8 km) upstream to what is now Dunnville (chapter 2). British soldiers and sailors agreed, however, on the strategic value of Merritt's canal.

By mid-nineteenth century, the defence of Canada and the security of its water transportation routes were still of concern to both the colonial and the British governments. Knowing this, Killaly and Baird had noted in their 1838 report that their recommendations for a new route would "allow of the concentration of our armaments upon either Lake, as circumstances might require."[139] In his report of 1842, George Phillpotts of the Royal Engineers had also stressed the military usefulness of the Welland "in the event of any misunderstanding with the United States."[140] In 1841, when Killaly was chair of the new Board of Works, he explained to the governor general that an enlarged Welland would provide: "the advantage which would be obtained in time of War, from having the power of concentrating our Naval forces upon either Lake as might be required ... The large Lock which is proposed at each end, would allow (in case of danger) of the Steamers being brought up many miles inland."[141]

However, the Second Canal, completed in 1845, still left much to be desired from a military standpoint – or so wrote the then governor general, Lord Cathcart (1783–1859), to the colonial secretary, Lord Stanley (1799–1869), in 1845, observing that "to render it better adapted for Military purposes" would involve "enormous expense." Since fears of invasion persisted, a line "more retired from the Frontier" would have to be built.[142]

The question of making the canal part of the colony's defences was also on Samuel Keefer's mind in 1846. He suggested that the projected houses for locktenders could be made defensible and that, "If the Ordnance Department could be prevailed upon to contribute a ... sum of £3000 or £4000, Block Houses might be built in some of the most commanding positions which would answer both purposes as upon the Rideau and other Military Canals."[143] Apparently the Ordnance Department was not willing, for no blockhouses were built.

When tensions arose fifteen years later during the American Civil War (1861–65), the plan to build blockhouses along the canal was revived.[144] In 1883 the canal authorities may have heard of an American admiral's appeal to Washington to place a "heavy ironclad" on Lake

Erie near Buffalo to destroy the Port Colborne terminus of the Welland in case of war with Britain.[145] At any rate, although it was believed necessary to station troops along the waterway in both World Wars, the Welland was never fortified; nor were twentieth-century rebuilding plans ever influenced much by defence considerations.

THE MEN ON THE GROUND

Just as the building and operation of the First Welland highlights the political, military, and economic context of Upper Canada, the history of its construction also reflects the dramatic social history of the British colony. In the 1780s a major influx of Amercians had brought thousands of United Empire Loyalists, mainly Anglo-Saxons, to settle on the north shores of the St Lawrence, Lake Ontario, and Lake Erie. The Niagara Peninsula, a natural link to New York State, was one of the first areas populated by these relatively well-educated and politically sophisticated farmers and discharged military personnel. This peaceful invasion of Americans brought settlers of intelligence, education, and broad horizons to Upper Canadian life. Merritt's own family were by no means impoverished or unlettered, and remained up-to-date on contemporary matters, maintaining links with professional friends and relatives in the United States. Among other things, they were interested in canals as transportation and communication networks as features of a modern society.[146]

A Changing Population and a Changing Workplace

Between 1825 and 1842 the population of Upper Canada tripled.[147] The newcomers to Niagara were mainly English, Irish, and Scottish, coming this time directly from Britain. The virtual army of labourers who built the First Welland were largely men of Irish descent from New York State, who came seeking work when the Erie Canal was completed in 1825. Poverty-stricken and often unskilled, these miserable navvies added a disconcerting element to the social fabric of Upper Canada and their difficulties in becoming integrated would be the cause of alarming disturbances in the 1840s.

Although only slightly less than a decade passed between the completion of the cut to Lake Erie in 1833 and the start of the reconstruction in stone in 1840 for the Second Canal, relations between construction labourers (still largely Irish) and their employers changed dramatically in that period. The situation on the Welland reflected a pattern prevalent throughout eastern Canada and the United States.[148] Contractors

– like employers everywhere in the industrializing world – were now taking a new attitude to their employees. The old master-apprentice relationship, which implied a certain responsibility on the part of the master/employer for the well-being of his labourers (journeymen or apprentices), was in decline. Relations between employer and employee were becoming more impersonal and detached. The worker was now "free" – a positive achievement by liberal-capitalist standards – yet for many workers on the Second Welland Canal construction site, as elsewhere, this meant "free" to starve.

When reconstruction work on the Erie Canal ceased in 1842, the situation on the Welland was further complicated. Workers and their families crossed the Niagara River by the thousands. Their arrival coincided with the arrival of many immigrants from Britain, also seeking work. As a result, labour became cheap and unemployment was rampant. Moreover, as we shall see, religious and social tensions among the navvies themselves contributed to the misery of life in the shanty towns along the Welland. Perhaps inevitably, canal labourers became more aggressive in demanding better conditions. By the late 1830s workers elsewhere were already resorting to strikes to realize their ends, and in the 1840s strikes by the navvies created a state of latent civil war along the banks of the Welland (chapters 9 and 10).

Matters were exacerbated by underfunding. Despite the additional monies made available after the union of Upper and Lower Canada, such funding was not always evident "on the ground." In 1843 Killaly, as chairman of the Board of Works, had already been obliged to nag his superiors to free up money to pay contractors quickly: "The utmost energy should be exerted in driving on the works," he urged. In 1844 he encouraged Superintendent Samuel Power to "assist some of the contractors by advances ... to encourage the speedy completion of the works."[149] In October 1845 Thomas Begly, secretary of the Board of Works, admitted to Power that, "there being no funds [available]," certain contractors would not be paid on time. A month later, Power had to remind Begly: "For many months past no funds have been received by Mr. Prescott [paymaster in the Welland Canal office] for the payment of the wages due to the locktenders, laborers, and various other persons employed on this work."[150] The workers' situation continued to deteriorate, and in February 1846, "the Paymaster not having received any funds and the banks having refused to lend any," Power was reduced to issuing certificates "as the only means of providing the money required for the payments of the laborers' wages."[151] This state of affairs forced the board to request that the governor general authorize an advance in order to operate and maintain the canal.

An Evolving Society

Other social developments in the 1840s and 1850s had an impact on the Welland's construction as well. The increase in population in Canada West[152] was most noticeable in towns and cities, and this population was becoming more mobile, as the first railroads were built. The Niagara Peninsula lost much of its "frontier" aspect and became settled and stable – more "Victorian" in attitudes and mores. Moreover, by the 1840s the Welland, as part of a St Lawrence–Lake Ontario waterway, had captured the imagination of the general public in the British colony. In their 1865 biographies of leading Canadians, William Notman and Jennings Taylor wrote that the Second Welland "represent[ed] progress,"[153] and that technological developments amounted to prosperity, stability, and moral advancement. Events on the Welland would challenge that confidence.

On the building sites of the Third Welland Canal, some social problems were identical to those of forty years earlier: abuse of liquor, a problem from the start, remained an issue, and ethnic conflict continued. On the other hand, the outlines of a modern industrial society were taking shape in that period, and new approaches to the difficulties of the men constructing the waterway reflected that development. Modern labour relations, increasingly widespread literacy, greater professional sophistication, and Canada's multicultural society were in formation.

Take, for example, the rise of trade unions. They had made little progress in Canada West (Ontario) before the 1870s, but in 1872 the federal government passed the Trade Union Act, which lifted from nascent unions the threat of indictment for "conspiracy in restraint of trade." The depression of the 1870s slowed union growth, however, and many collectives actually ceased to exist in this difficult time. We have found no evidence of extensive trade union organization among Third Canal labourers. However, the itinerant lives of many of these men, and Ontario's improved transportation, postal, and educational systems, probably account for the greater assertiveness that we notice among the navvies in the 1880s. They had heard (or even read) about the Knights of Labour crusade, and no doubt some of them had had their "consciousness raised." We do know that the American Knights of Labor organized assemblies in Ontario in 1880, and that by 1885 the Trades and Labour Congress of Canada was formed. This group put pressure on the provincial government to bring about passage of the Factories' Act of 1884 (an attempt to regulate working conditions) and the Workman's Compensation Act of 1886. In 1889 a Royal Commission on the Relations of Labour and Capital became the federal government's pioneering effort at understanding the realities of modern capitalist working conditions, and in 1900 the federal Department of Labour was created.

THE BUSINESSMEN

In addition to providing a livelihood for thousands of workers, the building of the first three Welland Canals was an anticipated godsend to capitalists near and far. When the Seven Years War ended in 1763 and political control of Canada passed into British hands, the colonial economy (although primitive by later standards) promised profit and prosperity to businessmen, especially shippers. A thriving lumber industry was in the offing in Upper Canada as its forests began to be cleared. Loyalist settlers taking up the land needed basic supplies such as salt, and would soon seek markets for their new grain crops. By the late eighteenth century the importance of Lake Ontario as part of a British North American trade nexus was already apparent. In 1795 at least three merchant ships of approximately sixty to a hundred imperial tons were sailing its waters; in that year alone, they made eleven voyages. By 1816 over sixty schooners were engaged in freight and passenger traffic, and that year saw the first steam-powered vessel on the lake.[154] Lake Erie, on the other hand, remained almost a foreign sea to Upper Canadian businessmen, forwarders, and travellers. The obstacle was Niagara Falls.

The Niagara Portage

In the early years of the nineteenth century the age-old portages around the Falls were still much used for trade. After the American Revolutionary War, British soldiers and traders expanded the route on the river's west side, and by 1799 large wagons carried rum and other supplies up the Escarpment and furs downward. Teams of oxen provided the power and as many as fifty wagons passed daily between Queenston and Chippawa.[155] Flat-bottomed batteaux were used to transport goods from Chippawa to Fort Erie, where schooners loaded the cargoes for destination ports on Lake Erie and the Upper Lakes.

Thus the nascent colonial economy was kept alive but, to Upper Canadian businessmen, the trans-shipment at the portage began to seem more and more inefficient. One complaint was that the "Upper Settlers" (on the northern shore of Lake Erie) could not bring timber down to Lake Ontario.[156] From late in the eighteenth century, therefore, an increasing number of proposals were put forward to improve access between the lakes for the transport of military personnel and supplies, civilian travellers, and especially merchants and traders and their commodities. One of the most striking was the plan of merchants Robert Hamilton (1753–1809) and Thomas Clark of Queenston, and George Forsyth (1755–1806) of Newark, who in 1799 presented to the Assembly of Upper Canada "A Bill to Improve and Amend the Communication between the Lakes Erie and Ontario by Land and Water." Their plan involved both an improvement of the road between Queenston and Fort Erie and "a canal or artificial channel, with the necessary locks for raising the water to a sufficient height for the easy passage of boats at or near the rapids of Fort Erie."[157] The merchants planned to maintain the waterway themselves, profiting by the tolls charged. Their bill, however, met opposition from nearby townships, and the Assembly was not impressed by the prospect of a private monopoly of such a vital transportation link – so the matter was dropped in 1800.

Throwing Off Lethargy

Meanwhile, however, the colonial elite faced the growing indebtedness of Upper Canada: how could the colony be made more solvent? They were not unaware of the difficulties of businessmen and merchants, given the low wheat prices of the time and the difficulty of penetrating the protected British market. Furthermore, the American economy and its expanding canal network might prove an even greater threat to the Upper Canadian economy. Not only did Americans need a strategically secure route from the Great Lakes to the Atlantic but they wanted to bind the new states of the mid- and northwest to the rest of the Union. By the end of the second decade of the nineteenth century, it was conceivable that, having failed to conquer British North America in 1812–14 by military means, they might achieve the same goal by economic and technological strategies. Illinois, Indiana, and Ohio had burgeoning agricultural industries seeking an ocean outlet under American control. The Erie Canal, begun in 1817 to connect Lake Erie and New York City via the Hudson River, was complete by 1825. Although only a barge canal, the Erie would clearly threaten the economy of the young British colony, a fact recognized by ambitious businessmen and politicians alike. In 1818 promoters of a Niagara canal in Upper Canada warned the Legislative Assembly: "The grand object of the American people appears to be opening a navigation with Lake Erie, which design our canal, if effected soon, would counteract and take down the whole of the produce from the Western country."[158]

Possibly goaded by such a warning, the government established the aforementioned 1818 Commission to confer with their counterparts in the Lower Province on the matter.

As for the Americans, they were well aware of the purpose of the Erie. In 1819, a New York State native told James Strachan, a British observer: "As to Canada, and especially Montreal, this undertaking [the Erie] is extremely detrimental." Strachan, however, thought that a Canadian Niagara canal might be "more easily effected than ... commonly supposed"; thirty-four locks would be needed, and perhaps an incline railway.[159] When Merritt's waterway was completed, on the other hand, a committee of the New York State legislature recognized the threat to America: "The lethargy under which the people of Canada have slumbered for the last century has been thrown off." The American commissioners saw this development as an "evil," because the Welland offered shippers access to Lake Ontario from the Upper Lakes "with facility and for a trifling expense." Cleveland, they lamented, "will be within sixty hours ride of Montreal."[160] In 1839 the American Benjamin Wright (1770–1842),[161] described as "an old experienced engineer," went even further: "None of the intended and already established routes can compete, in cheapness of transportation, with that via the Welland Canal and St. Lawrence River."[162]

Merritt himself may have been the author of an article in the Niagara *Gleaner* in November 1823 summarizing the ideal Upper Canadian response to the threat of the Erie: "It becomes our duty and should be our sole aim to endeavour to draw the whole trade from the Western District and keep it within ourselves, by means of Canal and other improvements, we have remained too long in a dormant state, but we should rejoice to perceive that a few spirited individuals have at length taken the welfare of the District into consideration by exerting themselves in order to faciliate the opening of a Canal from the Grand River to the Chippawa Creek, and from thence across to the Beaver Dams, where it will intersect the Twelve Mile Creek, and continue on to Lake Ontario."[163]

If the Erie Canal destroyed Montreal's commercial empire on the lower Great Lakes, Britain's hold on a sizable part of North America would be at risk. A vigorous Canadian riposte was essential, and the First Welland Canal, which opened for business in late 1829, with a direct line to Lake Erie in 1833, was Upper Canada's response to this economic and possibly political threat.

The Welland Canal Company directors must have been disappointed that, even in the early 1830s, despite a respectable number of vessel passages, their canal did not attract as much American commerce as had been anticipated. Traffic on Lake Ontario increased after the canal opened, but trade between the lakes did not grow substantially. On the other hand, it appears that, thanks to high grain prices in Britain, by the end of 1841 over two million bushels of wheat and flour had been sent through the Welland and St Lawrence and across the Atlantic, generating income from tolls. Similar fees levied on the lumber trade were also lucrative. Indeed, according to this analysis, income from all tolls for the 1841 season was nearly twice as high as that in 1839.[164] For this reason, as Christopher Andreae has recently suggested, the First Welland Canal "was immediately popular and its capacity was soon overwhelmed."[165]

The Welland had one major advantage over the Erie; it was free of ice earlier in the navigation season than the mouth of the American canal at Buffalo. The 10 April opening of the Canadian route in 1847, as Samuel Keefer reminded Alvin Bronson, an American merchant, would "still be an early opening compared with Buffalo." Reflecting a widely held aspiration, Keefer observed ten days later: "Business people say that this will have the effect of giving us a larger share of the trade than usual, this season."[166]

Despite its decaying locks, the First Welland had become a fixture in the minds of businessmen, and commercial interests from Montreal to the American Great Lakes ports were now frequently concerned with its efficiency. Therefore, although at one point the benefit of the expense of keeping the canal viable had been questioned, no serious plan to abandon it ever materialized. Rather, the pressure was for enlargement and, as we have seen, Merritt used his reputation and his political contacts to good advantage to ensure financial support for the first enlargement of the canal in the 1840s. Still, the new colonial government faced an interesting political dilemma. Contemporary experts urged the improvement of both the Welland and the St Lawrence system. As Hodgetts noted: "Either the government must write off the vast capital outlay on the canals as a dead loss, or else it must continue spending money on improvements."[167] They chose to continue improvement, but probably undertook too ambitious a program of construction: not only was the Welland to be rebuilt but the Lachine, Cornwall, and Beauharnois canals were to be completed. Given that there was now plenty of labour, railway construction was advancing and potential competition from trains had to be considered. Nevertheless, the canal program continued – at a total reconstruction cost by 1867 of more than $7.5 million.[168]

An Adjunct to the Erie Canal

Despite some rosy views, several historians now believe that the First Canal was not commercially successful.[169] Annual freight passing through remained far below what had been estimated – the anticipated cargoes never arrived.[170] Meanwhile, traffic on the Erie Canal continued to expand: in fact, it appears that the First Welland was merely "an adjunct to the Erie Canal,"[171] as most of the ships passing through it were American, sailing between American ports. Forwarders in Toledo, Ohio, for example, would send their merchandise north through the Welland to harbours such as Oswego in New York State, and from there onto the Erie, or in the other direction. Ultimately, the Welland did not help Montreal secure control of Canadian and American western trade, as had been hoped.

It was for this reason (as we have noted) that the Board of Works of the Canadas decided in the 1840s to proceed both with the construction of the enlarged and improved Second Canal and with the improvement of the navigation of the St Lawrence River. These works together provided a more efficient waterway than the Erie: the locks were fewer and larger, and freight rates through Montreal were cheaper than through New York. But the American city offered a better ocean port and, as it turned out, was never supplanted by Montreal. Nevertheless, the Department of Public Works began the further deepening of the Second Welland in 1851 (continued until 1861) and experimented with a temporary reduction of tolls (1860–62). The Welland Railway (which ran parallel to the canal) was inaugurated in 1853 in a further attempt to attract more cargo, since it could operate in the winter, when the canal was closed.

As a water link between western Upper Canada – the new Lake Erie settlements – and the older Lake Ontario communities, the Welland played a role in strengthening economic, social, and political ties among otherwise little-connected British North Americans. (For example, timber produced in some of the mills on Lake Erie's north shore was used in the First Canal's locks.) Moreover, the canal functioned as the germ cell of a Canadian "seaway," linked, of course, with American ports and traders, but functioning as part of the economic spine of a new state. In 1871 a St Catharines journalist declared: "The number of vessels passing through the Welland Canal is immense this year. On Sunday, no less than twenty ships arrived at Port Dalhousie in less than an hour and by the time the Canal opened on Monday morning, they were lined up end-to-end at distance of ¾ of a mile and thick in the harbor. There were so many that it took until Tuesday to clear the ships and lock them through."[172]

Allowing for local pride, this report correctly suggests that, twenty-five years after its opening, the Second Canal was in turn being utilized to capacity. Moreover, as with its predecessor, its features were beginning to decay. The east pier at Port Dalhousie was found to be rotten as a result of timbers being stored on it. Sparks from passing ships had caused fires on the pier, adding to its decrepitude, and the lighthouse was dilapidated and in danger of falling into the lake.

Mortgaging the National Wealth

"Our Canadian neighbours are mortgaging their entire earthly possessions to put their water route in condition to meet the requirements of cheap water transportation," said an American observer in 1882.[173] Canada's leaders did not in truth resort to such desperate measures, but they were aware that Great Lakes trade was growing and that the pioneer colonial economy based on agricultural produce and raw materials was evidently changing to an industrial one in this period. The mercantile classes and their supporters were still lobbying for an aggressive canal-improvement scheme to direct more of the Great Lakes trade to Montreal. Not that the old staple of wheat was declining as a commodity; it was precisely the fact that by 1850s a large amount of the western trade in grain was still going to the Atlantic via New York City which disturbed many observers. Copper and iron, increasingly produced in the hinterland of Lake Superior, were new cargoes which the Welland and the St Lawrence system could profitably carry to the Atlantic.

Many still believed that the cheapest channel was a natural rather than a man-made waterway. Canada had a fine network of lakes and rivers *and* canals. Along the Welland–St Lawrence route, only 69 miles (111 km) of man-made channel and locks lay between Chicago and the sea, compared to the 363 miles (581.1 km) of the Erie Canal.[174] Canadian canals were better constructed and more favourably situated than the Erie, and shipment to Quebec via the St Lawrence was still less costly than shipment to New York City along the Erie.

Why, then, were Canadians not getting a greater share of the trade? Two factors were responsible: the high price of ocean freight from Montreal to Liverpool, and the fact that Canadian seaports were closed by ice for five months of year while New York City was not. This annual cessation of shipping neutralized the superior advantages of the St Lawrence route, and the higher ocean freight rates cancelled the cost advantage of the inland route. Also, while the capacity of the St Lawrence route was nearly twice that of Erie, the use of bigger ships on the Upper Lakes had almost rendered the Second Welland obsolete. By 1860 almost a third of all the vessels in the grain trade were unable to pass through the Second Welland and nearly three-quarters of the propellers (steamships) were too large.[175] The deepening of canals to 10 feet (3 m) in the 1850s had not greatly improved matters, as the locks were still too narrow.

Tolls constituted another dimension of the competition. Throughout the 1850s the Americans had removed tolls on their canals. To compete, the Canadian government was obliged in 1860 to abolish all tolls on the St Lawrence canals and refund 90 per cent of those paid on the Welland if ships went down the Canadian route. While tonnage increased, however, no great expansion in western traffic resulted. When tolls were reimposed in 1863, traffic on the Welland Canal again declined. And so the debate over tolls continued – and continues to this day!

Nevertheless, improvement of the Welland offered some hope for Canadians. Authorities were aware that the Second Welland Canal was the central point in the whole Canadian canal system, and was the source of most of the income from canal tolls.[176] After Confederation in 1867, the federal government felt a greater confidence, motivated by growing Canadian nationalism and pride in being part of the British Empire. Despite the depression of the 1870s, financial resources were more forthcoming than in earlier years. In 1870, even before Macdonald announced his National Policy, the aforementioned Royal Commission was established to study Canada's waterways. Significantly, as part of its mandate, this commission consulted with boards of trade in the American ports of Oswego, Detroit, Toledo, Chicago, and Milwaukee, most of which urged enlargement of the Welland.

Such conditions encouraged the enlargement of the Welland, and work began late in 1871. But even a booming canal system would not have been impervious to economic pressures beyond Canada's borders. A depression slowed construction of the Third Canal, causing the Liberals, when they came to power after November 1873, to practice financial retrenchment. Prime Minister Alexander Mackenzie (1822–1892) alluded to the economic slowdown in March 1877 in the House of Commons; when explaining the delay in awarding contracts, he pointed to the "enormously expensive" nature of the work which had already added to the national debt. His government, therefore, would not put "the whole money" into the work at the present.[177] After the Conservatives returned to power in 1878, the economic situation improved slightly, and canal construction was soon pushed forward again. The deepening of the Welland from 12 to 14 feet (3.65 to 4.3 m) began.

At the same time, and despite the only-qualified success of the Canadian canal system, including the Welland, certain Americans viewed the potential expansion of that system with a jaundiced eye. In the early 1870s, probably cognizant of the Royal Commission report, boards of trade in the American Northwest urged construction of an American canal around Niagara Falls. The New York *Commercial Advertiser* in 1879 urged the conversion of the Erie into a ship canal.[178] In 1882, when the Third Welland Canal was opened, the Buffalo *Telegraph* expressed concern about how much of the grain trade would pass through the rebuilt Welland – and worse: the Canadians were talking again about a Georgian Bay canal, which would be "a thousand miles shorter than the present route via Buffalo to New York."[179] The following year, the New York *Tribune* went as far as to praise the Third Welland, noting: "The facilities for this canal through Canada are much better than through the United States."[180]

Mixed reviews on the part of Americans should not be surprising. Oswego merchants, for example, welcomed any increase of trade that might be channelled through a reconstructed Welland and hence through their town and onto the Oswego Canal, connecting with the Erie – a traditional trade route. Of course, these merchants were in competition with Buffalo businesses, which sought to avoid giving up any commerce to Oswego. In 1880 a resident of that town is reported to have remarked of the Welland, then in reconstruction: "It is God's Providence to Oswego that Buffalo cannot prevent the building of that canal."[181]

There Is No Impediment ...

We have already noted that Merritt's optimism regarding "his" canal began early. In fact, on Monday 21 July 1824, aboard the Montezuma packet, following a visit along the Erie Canal, he wrote confidently in his journal: "There is no impediment whatsoever in our plan ... the course of this canal [the Erie] and all I have conversed with confirm me in this opinion."[182] He could not have foreseen the impact of the many and varied challenges to be faced by the canal builders over the years: the forces of nature, such as adverse weather and landslides; the lack of necessary tools, particularly in the early years; the need to maintain the navigation of the existing canal in later years; the chronic shortage of funds; and what the Welland Canal Company directors referred to in 1825 as "cupidity, envy, jealousy, and distrust."[183] Even before any sod was turned, another major challenge would have to be faced – the choice of a route.

From the early years of the nineteenth century, the usefulness of a waterway across the Niagara Peninsula – a "great national object" – had been apparent to a variety of interests in both Canada and the United States. Politicians, businessmen, the military, the "men on the ground" – all had good and sufficient motives to encourage such a development. The great question, however, was *where* should it cross? The contentious issue of the exact route for the waterway is the subject of the next chapter.

CHAPTER TWO

Choosing the Route

Before ever a tree was felled, a sod turned, or a shovelful of soil removed, the canal planners had to determine a route for the Niagara canal. Given the challenges of swamps, forests, intractable ground, escarpments, east-west watercourses, and storm-battered coastlines, surveyors had difficulty choosing the most suitable line for an artificial channel across the peninsula. In addition, the interests of local landowners, businessmen, and the military had to be considered. While many early nineteenth-century settlers recognized the advantages of connecting lakes Ontario and Erie, no one route was an early favourite. Not surprisingly, the route finally decided on for the First Welland Canal was not the first – or the only – path surveyed or endorsed by parties concerned with a Niagara waterway.

The challenges of geology and geography alone were daunting: the massive Niagara and Onondaga escarpments, whose soil in some places consisted of stiff clay resting on quicksand; the virgin forests that had to be cleared; the numerous small water courses to accommodate; and the variation in level of Lake Erie waters. The climate, too, ranging from extreme heat in summer to deep freeze in winter – not to mention torrential rains and the occasional gales blowing in off the lakes – also merited serious consideration. But the optimism of the day trumped realism.

THE FORCES OF NATURE

Any canal built on a north-south axis across the Niagara Peninsula would have to traverse the Niagara Escarpment, a bluff lying on an east-west line from northern New York State through Niagara to Burlington Bay, where it turns north to the Bruce Peninsula. This is the cliff that creates Niagara Falls, where the waters of the upper Great Lakes, funnelled through the Niagara River, tumble into a turbulent gorge and flow out to Lake Ontario. While "the Falls" are a great natural phenomenon and an alluring tourist attraction, they constituted a major barrier to transportation in an age when water travel was the cheapest and most convenient mode. Local residents were well aware of the paradox posed by the great cataract. In 1875 a Thorold writer wrily observed: "In Niagara Falls we possess one of the sublimest scenes in Nature's great panorama, but as if by the law of compensation Nature intended to make us pay for our luxuries, Niagara [Falls] presents a most formidable obstacle to the navigation of our great water stretches."[1]

Stiff Clay Resting on Quicksand

To circumvent the Falls, a canal across the peninsula had to achieve a total "lift" of 326 feet (100 m). Apart from the height of the Niagara Escarpment itself, it would also have to overcome the gradual rise of land from the shore of Lake Ontario up to that obstacle. If undertaken at this point – from Dick's Creek at St Catharines to "the mountain" – excavation would have to pass only through clay (fig. 2.1). On the escarpment itself, diggers would find a mixture of clay, sand, and limestone. Although this bluff was a challenge, it was not considered insurmountable; in fact, it would provide quarries for stone as well as lime for cement. Nor was the stretch south of Thorold, consisting of clay resting on limestone, thought to present difficulties.

Between Thorold and Chippawa Creek, however, the land was not flat, although it may seem so today. It contains two "summit ridges" – a "Grand Summit" of glacial moraine just north of Port Robinson, consisting of a slight hump of sand and gravel formed by the water level at the margin of the pre-historic ice shelf, and a lesser ridge just south of Thorold.[2] At the Grand Summit, Colonel George Phillpotts reported finding "stiff clay resting on quicksand" – the latter possibly constituting a certain challenge. Along the bank of Chippawa Creek, surveyors and engineers found more "good stiff clay."[3] Further south toward Gravelly Bay, they encountered a flat, low landscape of clay resting on a bed of limestone about 4 feet (1.2 m) below the surface, with marsh in places. Here, the Onondaga Escarpment, a lesser rise than the Niagara, was also not originally considered a problem. The practice of late eighteenth- and early nineteenth-century canal builders, with their limited technical equipment, was to take the easiest – albeit round-about – route, following natural contours where possible. Therefore, the geology of Niagara ostensibly offered few serious obstacles to the builders of the First Canal, and Merritt's confidence that much could be constructed in a short time was at least partly justified.

In order to compensate for the Niagara Escarpment, then, the builders of the First Welland Canal would have to find a gently rising slope associated with the vertical rise, a direct assault on the cliff being

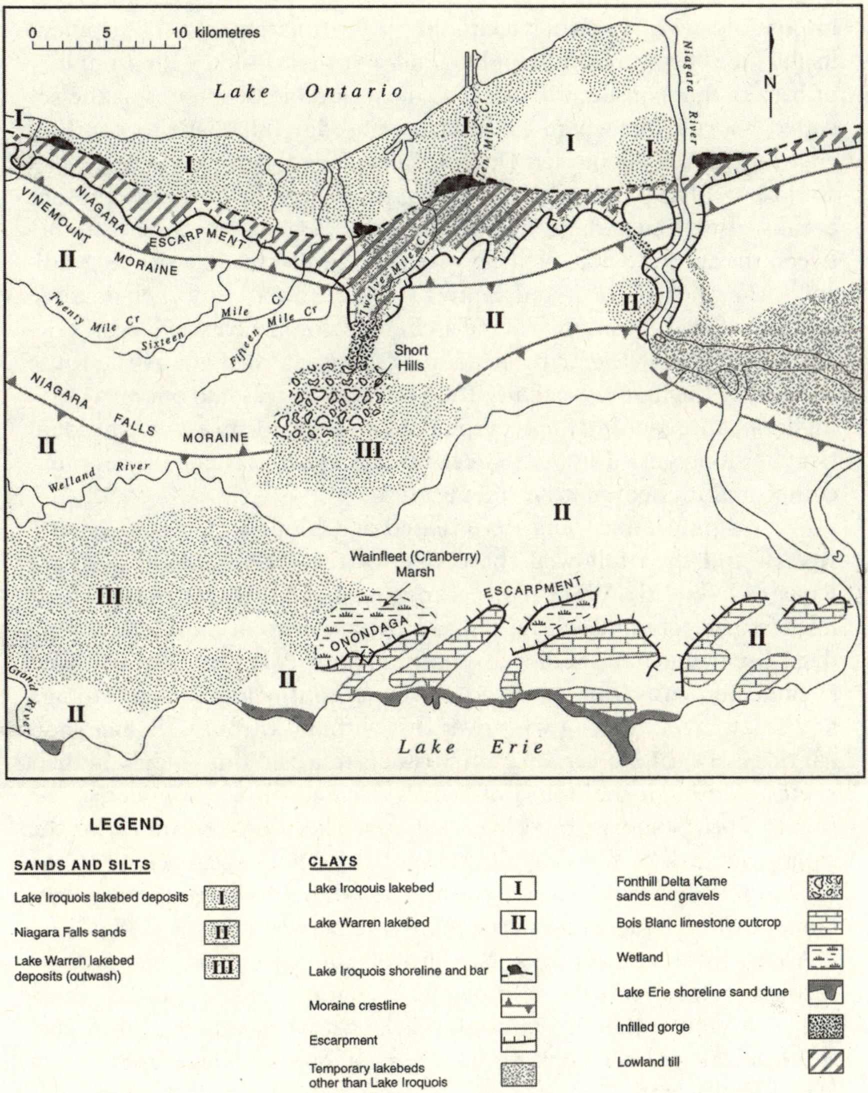

2.1 Geological features of the Niagara Peninsula (Loris Gasparotto, Department of Geography, Brock University)

impossible with available technology. Fortunately, the Escarpment itself – 184 feet (56 m) in height – has a varied profile with a number of breaks that can be utilized. The most notable of these is at the so-called Short Hills, where the escarpment edge falls back to Fonthill, creating the deeply incised DeCew Falls Gorge, a route where a canal could potentially be built into the ridge. East of St Catharines, other breaks also occur where limestone bluffs face to the northeast. Between these headlands, melting glaciers had produced a gentle gradient – the Dick's Creek and Shaver's Ravine area – another possible site for a canal. From the ravine a channel could be excavated up the side of the northeast-facing headland.[4] Ultimately, this was the route chosen for the first two canals. The Third Canal was laid out on a curving loop, approaching the escarpment from the northeast on a gradual rise, but following Ten Mile Creek, another ravine created by a watercourse and incised into the "mountain."

The original First Canal terminated at Chippawa Creek (Welland River), and then followed the course of the creek and the Niagara River to Lake Erie. When a direct route to Lake Erie was later decided upon, surveyors and engineers had to take into account the Onondaga Escarpment, a smaller obstacle north of Port Colborne. At what became known as Ramey's Bend, the canal contractors took advantage of a small creek flowing west over this cliff and through the marshes. All three of the nineteenth-century canals retained this "bend" in their routes. Although the Board of Works decided in 1843[5] to deepen the line to Port Colborne, making Lake Erie the source of water for the canal, the task of blasting the rock of this lesser escarpment – "the rock job" – delayed the accomplishment and necessitated the improvement of the Feeder Canal as the main line between 1845 and 1850.

Apart from the obvious barriers of the two escarpments, cuts through solid rock were rare on the Welland. However, on an abandoned stretch of the Third Canal today, observers can see a "rock cut" south of the present Lock Seven. Here, where the Niagara, St. Catharines & Toronto Railway crossed the canal on a swing bridge, the banks of the waterway are solid stone.[6]

The clay of Niagara could also be an unpredictable challenge, despite first appearances. It could overlay and mask "quicksand," which posed the risk of landslides, especially during the excavation of the prism of the Deep Cut in 1828. The clay could contain large stones or could present a rock-like surface with the hardness of cement (described as "hardpan"), which could be worked only by picks or even blasting. In 1846 and 1848, for example, hardpan delayed construction at Lock Two near St Catharines and at Port Dalhousie harbour.[7]

Alfred Nobel's development of dynamite in 1866 facilitated the work of Third Canal engineers and contractors, as did improvements in steam-powered technology. But, said one journalist in 1880, "the far-famed hardpan" remained a challenge.[8]

Grubbing (Chopping and Clearing)

Above-ground challenges also faced the canal builders of the 1820s. Imagine Niagara without cities, industries, roads, railways, and highways, but covered in trees, specifically, a mature Carolinian forest. Although the United Empire Loyalist settlers of the last decades of the eighteenth century had hewn down many of the original trees for building, fuel, and other justifiable purposes, much of the forest was still standing, potentially useful as timber for canal locks, but also an obstacle on almost any proposed route – as were the stumps left after clearance. Maps of the 1820s show areas such as the "Queen's Bush" on the "brow of mountain," and some specifically note "hard timber, chestnut, black ash."[9] In 1823 the American Hiram Tibbett(s), contracted by Merritt and his friends to survey a canal route, in estimating the task of cutting a "towpath through the woods" at a cost of $100 per mile, emphasized that extensive "grubbing" (clearing of bushes and trees) would be needed.[10] In the early 1830s estimates for the cost of cutting a line to one of the bays on Lake Erie all note the cost of "chopping and clearing."[11] In November 1830 *The Farmer's Journal* picturesquely described the passage of a ship "with her neatly painted hull and towering masts, moving most majestically in her native element, with stumps and trees on either side, between the hills that enclose the valley through which this splendid artificial channel winds its serpentine course."[12] Stands of trees noted as "wood land" appear on surveys well into the 1840s. Phillpotts's 1842 map, based on his survey, shows extensive forests still paralleling the route of the canal.[13] To pioneer engineers, of course, such barriers were not insurmountable, but planning had to factor in the time and cost for their removal.

Water ... Will Have Its Way

Water, although essential to the operation of a canal, can also interfere with construction and inhibit operation. Not enough is a problem, but too much and in the wrong place and at the wrong time can be disastrous, as the Welland Canal Company discovered. While its presence could be sometimes predicted, unexpected water would at times astonish the engineers by rushing from undetected underground streams into a lock pit or a half-excavated channel. As John MacTaggart correctly noted: "Water ... will have its way."[14]

Twelve Mile Creek, Chippawa Creek, and the Grand River proved useful to the canal builders, but other, smaller, watercourses running on an east-west axis turned out to be nuisances. These streams could not simply be blocked because the dammed up water would flood and damage farmers' property. Nor could the water always be directed into the canal because unpredictable freshets could cause the prism to overflow. Consequently, culverts would be needed to divert small streams such as Lyons Creek (between what is now Welland and Port Colborne) or Beaverdams Creek (south of Thorold) underneath the canals.[15]

To save money, time, and effort, builders of nineteenth-century canals used natural watercourses as much as possible. In the case of the Welland, Twelve Mile Creek and Chippawa Creek were the largest streams used, but Dick's Creek and Broad Creek, as well as dry ravines were also exploited. Until 1881 water from the Grand River served to feed the Welland. On the other hand, such watercourses could represent obstacles. Chippawa Creek, for instance, was not initially perceived to be a construction barrier but was to be used as part of the canal connecting to the Niagara River, and as the source of the canal's water supply. When this plan failed, it became necessary to take water from the Grand River through a feeder canal, a project that transformed the Chippawa into a barrier. How to carry the Feeder over it? In chapter 6, we shall see how aqueducts were designed to meet this challenge.

The Welland canals, which would connect the two smaller Great Lakes and ultimately link these "inland seas" with the Atlantic Ocean, had to be protected from those very "seas." The First Canal's lock at Port Colborne was designed to keep the water in the canal at the same level as the waters of Lake Erie, despite their frequent fluctuations. Moreover, because Erie was the most turbulent of the Great Lakes, the engineers of the First Welland felt the need to build two piers out into Gravelly Bay. Two similar breakwaters were constructed at Port Dalhousie, extending at an angle to the northwest from the shoreline (figs. 6.8–6.11). Such breakwaters and piers were essential to protect the canals' harbours from lake gales.

Swampy land north and west of Port Colborne – the Cranberry Marsh or "Tamarac Swamp"[16] – posed a different set of water problems. In fact, a complex of marshes had to be crossed – four in all: the Black Ash Swamp, the Cranberry or Wainfleet Marsh, the Hemlock Marsh, and another bog between the junction of the Feeder and the Onondaga Escarpment. This broad area of wetland, through which the Feeder Canal and the extension to Port Colborne were constructed, presented not only a technical problem of drainage but also a medical hazard, because stagnant water was a potential source of disease. As we have seen, the enterprising Merritt saw a practical solution, pointing out that draining the swamp would improve the health of the surrounding country.[17] The Feeder Canal, linking all three nineteenth-century canals with the Grand River, was built through the most impassable part of this "quagmire," and the area was, in fact, "improved."

Water in the form of freshets or ice was the enemy of many a contractor, but it was also necessary for the functioning of any canal. In the case of the Welland, Lake Erie lies at a higher elevation than Lake Ontario, so what would be more natural than to use the former as a source of supply? As early as 1825 the Welland Canal Company stated: "It was not deemed expedient to trust to the Welland River alone for the supply which will be required, but to render Lake Erie or the Grand River at its mouth at once the summit level and the Feeder of the Canal."[18] However, the impecunious company decided to take its waterway south only as far as Chippawa Creek, not all the way to the Erie shore, and planned to use that stream as the water source through a deep cut. It was only when landslides blocked the Deep Cut that they became obliged to use the Grand River as a source and provide water through a feeder canal. But even when the canal was put through to Gravelly Bay in 1833, Lake Erie was still not tapped. Actually, water entering the canal from the Feeder at "the Junction" flowed out in two directions – north over the aqueduct to connect with Twelve Mile Creek, and south to Port Colborne – feeding Lake Erie itself rather than exploiting it! Nevertheless, Merritt composed a memorandum in 1837 urging that "the Deep Cut must be ... taken down & a supply from Lake Erie obtained."[19]

Others expressed the same concern about the reliability of the Grand River as a source for the larger Second Canal locks. Phillpotts acknowledged that the Grand was "the cheapest" but recommended Lake Erie as being "by far the most commodious and secure when complete."[20] While the Board of Works discussed the possibility in 1843, the first contract appears to have been awarded only in 1846,[21] and the channel between Port Colborne and the junction of the Feeder was emptied and excavated. (The Feeder acted as the main line of the canal during this work.) Unfortunately, the rock of the Onondaga Escarpment and more slides on the Deep Cut brought the project of tapping Lake Erie waters to a halt.

WATER CONVEYANCE ... BY MEANS OF CANALS

When Scottish immigrant Robert Gourlay circulated a questionnaire to the townships of Upper Canada in 1817, to gather data for his *Statistical Account of Upper Canada*, he had not been concerned with such practical matters. Interest in canal building was widespread at the time – it was, after all, the "Age of Canals" worldwide – particularly in the fledging colony where the scarcity and crudity of existing roads helped popularize the idea of building canals. The settlers of the Niagara District townships were not slow to respond to Gourlay's request for information regarding "water conveyance ... by means of canals,"[22] seeing both the need and the potential for improved water communication. They were keen to have easier access to the wider world and its markets, and many suggestions for improving natural waterways and constructing canals ensued. In fact, of the Niagara townships, only Thorold and Pelham did not bring forward suggestions for water routes that might benefit the commerce and transportation of the colony – and especially their own district. But few, if any, of the respondents were aware of the potential difficulties.

As we have seen, William Hamilton Merritt, George Keefer, and others, conducted a survey in 1818 for a route between Lake Ontario and Chippawa Creek. Exactly what motivated them to undertake their survey at this time is not clear. Merritt himself retrospectively stated: "Finding the supply was too limited in the summer months from that source [Twelve Mile Creek], I first conceived the idea of obtaining a further supply from the Chippawa."[23] Gourlay's questionnaire would have reinforced this idea.

The thinking of Merritt and his friends was certainly up-to-date, since from the late eighteenth century on, Europeans, Americans, and Canadians had been fascinated by the potential of canals. By 1850 engineers and entrepreneurs in Britain alone would promote and construct over four thousand miles of canals and improvements to navigable rivers to carry the raw materials and products of the Industrial Revolution. Americans, with only about one hundred miles of canals by 1816, by 1850 could boast over 3,500 miles, including the 363 miles of the Erie.[24] In both Britain and the United States the impetus had come largely from the private sector. In British North America, on the other hand, it was the British military which built early canals along the St Lawrence, the Grenville on the Ottawa, and the Rideau.[25] By 1850 the improved canals on the lower St Lawrence, in conjunction with the crucial link represented by the Welland, provided a waterway from Lake Erie through to the Atlantic.

Despite the widespread enthusiasm for canals, the Niagara project began with no pomp or circumstance. At the sod-turning in November 1824, wrote Thomas C. Keefer later, "there were then present no high official personages, no celebrated engineers, – distinguished commercial or political leaders," only "farmers and country traders, the recent comrades of gallant Brock."[26] Keefer was correct to stress the amateur quality of the endeavour, for none of the enthusiasts of 1818 had been engineers or even surveyors, with the result that their calculations were sometimes flawed. Optimistically, Niagarans sent a petition to the House of Assembly asking for a grant to hire a professional surveyor: "No attention was paid to it," Merritt later snorted in his journal.[27]

Seeking a Natural Navigable Canal

In the 1820s "canal awareness" was marked more by enthusiasm than precision. For example, the residents of the northern Niagara Peninsula, chiefly concerned with finding a "natural navigable canal"[28] to Lake Ontario and a connection to the Atlantic via the St Lawrence, heartily endorsed lines along the main streams running into Lake Ontario; that is, the creeks descriptively named Twelve Mile (which issued into the lake northwest of St Catharines), Fifteen Mile (north of Rockway), Twenty Mile (north of Jordan), and Forty Mile (north of Grimsby).[29] As early as 1817, the inhabitants of the Grimsby area had informed a clerk in the lieutenant-governor's office that they had "for some time" been engaged in considering "the great facility ... with which the waters of the Chippawa & Grand River" could be brought into Forty Mile Creek.[30]

Meanwhile, in 1818 the Commissioners of Internal Navigation had hired James Chewett (1793–1862), a member of the surveyor general's staff, to survey a possible route for a canal linking lakes Ontario and Erie. His report and map of later that year described another trans-peninsula possibility: a lengthy canal extending from Burlington Bay south to the Grand River (fig. 2.2). (It is possible that the government's indifference to Merritt's 1818 petition may be attributed to the existence of this survey.) The military strongly favoured this plan because the canal it recommended would be farther away from the frontier with the United States.[31] However, such a waterway, if built, would have been impractical, requiring a long tunnel and an extensive feeder from the Grand River to the Escarpment.[32] Furthermore, it would have thwarted Merritt's ambitions for his mills. One wonders also how well such a lengthy and round-about route would have served

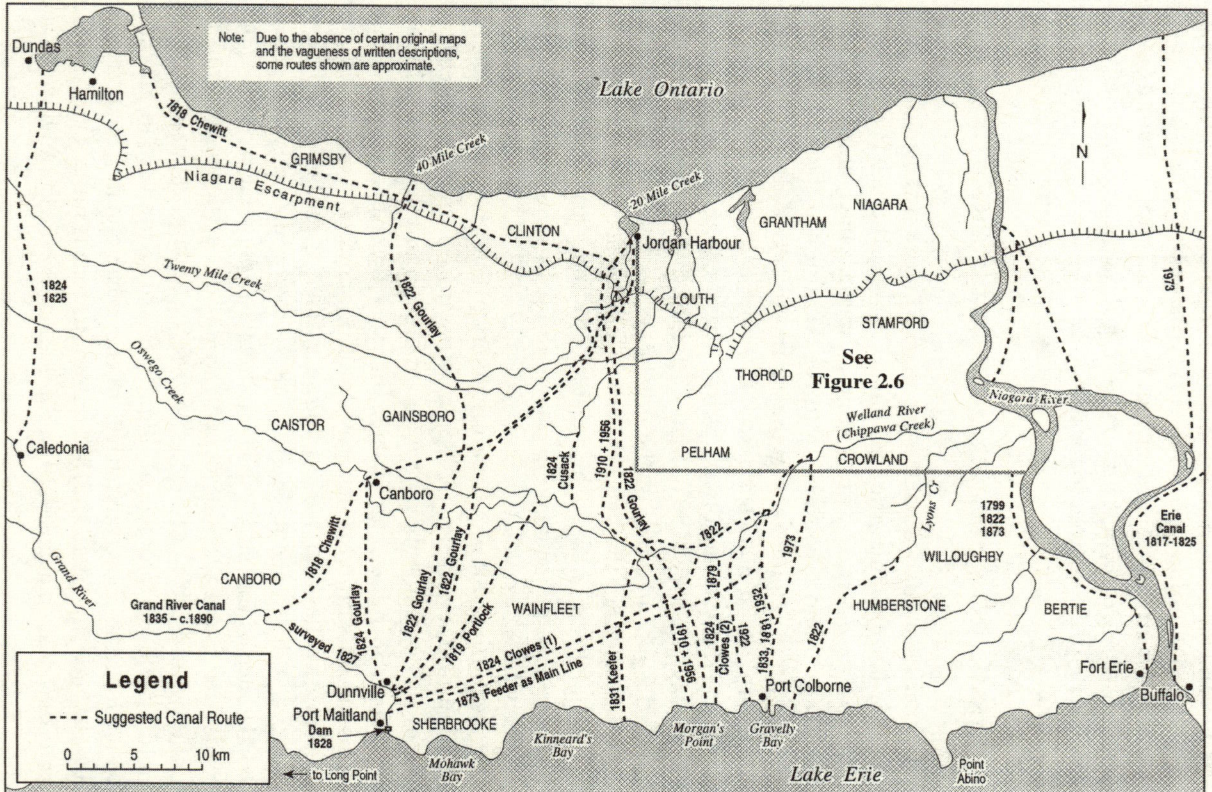

2.2 Suggested canal routes in the Niagara Peninsula. (Loris Gasparotto/ with the permission of The Champlain Society)

in the long run. Nevertheless, the idea persisted even after the ultimate choice of route had been made. As Governor General Lord Cathcart wrote to Lord Stanley in 1845: "If there had been any consideration entertained for the interests of the Mother Country, the present line would not have been adopted, a preferable one existing more retired from the Frontier, by following the course of the Grand River from Lake Erie, as far as Caledonia Bridge or Brantford, and from thence to be carried in the most favorable direction into Burlington Bay with a view to its communication with Lake Ontario."[33] Certainly Merritt and his friends were more concerned with their private business interests than with the defence of the British Empire, although they would not have been unaware of the desirability of having their waterway sufficiently far from the American border to render it relatively secure.

By 1824, then, a number of suggested routes were under consideration. But how realistic were the surveyors and engineers involved in plotting these routes? Surprisingly, their reports make little mention of the problems outlined above. No doubt they were as enthusiastic about the possibilities as were their sponsors, and as reluctant to anticipate trouble. Even the Niagara Escarpment itself appeared to be a minor inconvenience.

THE FRONTIER ROUTE

A glance at any map suggests that a canal simply circumventing the Falls but running parallel to the Niagara River would be "rational." Despite the memory of incursions from the United States in the War of 1812, residents of established commercial centres such as Fort Erie, Chippawa, and Queenston were eager to secure advantageous transport for their goods and people. Consequently, the so-called Frontier Route parallel to the Niagara River had their support. As early as 1799 one portion of this route, a canal to circumvent the Fort Erie rapids, had been suggested,[34] and through the early 1820s local proponents advocated different sections. In 1829 the Upper Canada Legislature did authorize the formation of an incorporated company to build such a canal, but nothing was done.[35] However, the idea remained alive.

No sooner was the First Canal "completed" (with the opening of the line to Port Colborne in 1833) than discussion of rebuilding began. On 3 October 1833 the American engineer Benjamin Wright reported on the work and cost necessary to render the Welland "permanent and complete,"[36] and in November of that year the board began to consider proposals to deepen the main line of the canal, including widening and deepening the Feeder and the Port Colborne route. These projects would involve winter work so that navigation would not be interrupted.[37] The Act of 4 March 1837, which involved government buy-out of the private stock, called for the "permanent completion of the Welland Canal."[38] When in that year the Welland Canal Company hired engineers H.H. Killaly and Nicol Hugh Baird to report on the Welland and to survey routes for an enlargement, they too considered – but rejected – the Niagara River route. Military officials, of course, objected on grounds of its proximity to the United States.[39]

THE MOST DIFFICULT, CIRCUITOUS, AND IMPROPER ROUTE

A number of the creeks running north to Lake Ontario were mentioned as possible routes. When Hiram Tibbett(s) had completed his 1823 survey "between the River Welland, or Chippawa and Lake Ontario," Merritt sent his report to the lieutenant-governor. "The Plan in contemplation," he wrote, "is to petition the Legislature for an Act to Incorporate a Company ... for the purpose of constructing a Canal from Lake Ontario to Chippawa Creek & from thence to the Grand River (to be of the same size as the American Grand Canal)"[40] (fig. 2.2).

The resulting Act of 19 January 1824, which incorporated the Welland Canal Company, unfortunately did not specify a route; hence a flurry of activity ensued as a number of surveyors got to work. Rheddy Cusack (probably Irish) led off with his report of 10 May, for a route from the Welland River via St Johns on Twelve Mile Creek in the Short Hills; on 20 May Samuel and James Clowes (British) proposed a route from the Chippawa to the headwaters of Twelve Mile Creek; another American, Nathan S. Roberts (1776–1852),[41] produced his report on 28 August on both a Twelve Mile Creek route and one to Niagara; on 10 December Francis Hall (a Scot) reported favourably on a route via Twelve Mile Creek.[42]

Twelve Mile Creek seems to have been the most popular choice, but as we have seen, the route via the Niagara River also had strong support in the early years, as evidenced by the fact that in 1825 Hall, in additional reports, proposed both Queenston (February) and the mouth of Twelve Mile Creek (March) as possible northern termini.[43]

Significantly, most of these surveys were undertaken at the instigation of Merritt, either personally or through the Welland Canal Company. Since at that time no reliable maps of Niagara existed, these early surveyors were genuine explorers. Their work, however valuable, was not entirely reliable, at least in part because they lacked effective surveying instruments (chapter 3). As well, local and special interests often dictated who carried out a survey, and where, and of course the difficult terrain presented problems. These early surveys may seem crude or imprecise to modern eyes. The maps that resulted show local landmarks such as "large elm tree" or "cornerstone" – standard types of reference point for many years. Certain habits of the surveyors may also seem questionable, although understandable. Because water was often undrinkable, many men, including surveying teams, drank whisky or ale instead. "Progress on these canal surveys was, therefore, remarkable," writes Don W. Thompson, "and, it might be added, at times exhilarating."[44]

Given all the natural impediments and competing interests, how, then, was the matter ultimately decided? True, the Assembly of Upper Canada settled the issue to an extent by specifying Twelve Mile Creek in a revised Act of 13 April 1825, but it is apparent that, since technical considerations were pretty well evenly divided, the actual route – following Twelve Mile Creek, Dick's Creek, and Shaver's Ravine – owed much to the financial interests of Merritt and his supporters. The legal position was cemented when, on 27 May 1825, a prominent American engineer, James Geddes, hired by the Welland Canal Company, reported on the suitability of the mouth of the Twelve as a harbour.[45]

Even the details of the Twelve Mile Creek line were debated, and the First Canal as completed in 1829 followed only one of several suggestions. Merritt and his colleagues, many of whom were millers, at first intended to have the canal descend the escarpment at John DeCew's mill, near what is still called DeCew Falls. A millowner as canny – if not as aggressive – as Merritt, DeCew (1766–1855) was an early supporter of the Welland Canal and, from May 1824 to April 1825, a director of the Welland Canal Company. In a report of 16 August 1825, Roberts advised against the DeCew route which, he felt, would have necessitated combined locks.[46] This report must have been influential because the decision was made to bypass DeCew's land. Disappointed, DeCew, along with many other disgruntled landowners, withdrew his support and requested a return of the money he had paid for stock.[47] The pioneer miller must have gloated when William Lyon Mackenzie later averred that Merritt had such a great influence on Attorney General Robinson that "the most difficult, circuitous and improper route"[48] had been chosen.[49]

At any rate, by September 1825 Merritt and his friends decided to take the canal over the bluff at what is now Thorold, near a mill belonging to George Keefer, president of the company. Over the next century this route would be challenged by supporters of other possible lines, and there were multiple suggestions for supplementing the main canal with branch waterways.

During construction, specific features of the canal caused problems requiring adjustments to the route. The tunnel originally planned had to be abandoned early on (chapter 4). Late in 1828 landslides in the Deep Cut forced the Canal Company to rely on water from the Grand River instead of Chippawa Creek. This was a major blow, in response to which the company authorized the Feeder to connect the Grand with the Welland at Port Robinson,[50] necessitating the raising of the water level in the Grand above that of Chippawa Creek with the help of a dam at what became Dunnville (chapter 6). The solution to the problem in the Deep Cut also led to another change. As originally constructed, the canal made a tortuous curve to the west and then back eastward at Allanburg. Captain J.E. Alexander's map of c. 1828 is the only contemporary evidence for this bend, and no reference to it occurs in the Canal Company records, although later maps show a boomerang-shaped curve as the "old cut" or "mill race."[51] It is conceivable that the canal builders wanted to take advantage of a watercourse or natural declivity here, but after the changes required in 1828 this curving section became either unnecessary or impractical.

In choosing the route of the Second Canal, less disagreement arose, although alternative suggestions were proposed, especially for the section running north from the Escarpment. Killaly and Baird considered four possible lines, including the Lateral Cut (see below) and the Frontier Route, but Twelve Mile Creek remained their preference. One suggestion was to use the existing course throughout. Another (which they favoured) incorporated a deviation from the existing route between Lock 11 (in the present Merritton) and Thorold on the Escarpment (fig. 1.2). This would have avoided "the dangerous and unfit placing of the locks upon the shelving side of the mountain."[52]

In the event, the former recommendations were endorsed by the Board of Works; that is, using the same natural advantages provided by Dick's Creek and the receding slope of the Escarpment, and retaining Port Dalhousie as the northern terminus.

As had happened with the First Canal, not long after the opening of the Second (1850) the question of further enlargement was again raised. Even by the mid-1850s the possible "considerable widening"[53] of the Welland was being discussed. Furthermore, possible rivals to the Welland were under consideration.[54] As ships became ever-bigger and trade increased, pressure to enlarge the Welland intensified, and in September 1870 engineer Thomas Monro was ordered to commence surveying possible routes. The work of Monro and his crew resulted in a lengthy report in 1872,[55] recommending that the new canal should generally follow the same route from the Escarpment to Lake Erie, but that Twelve Mile Creek should be abandoned in favour of a more direct line from Thorold to Port Dalhousie (which was still to be the northern terminus). St Catharines was not too happy about losing the canal from its centre, but the die was soon cast, and when the Third Canal was finally completed in 1881, "The Twelve" completely ceased to be a major artery – although the line continued in operation for local traffic until the early twentieth century.

The Western Section

As early as 1823 Merritt had envisaged a connection from Chippawa Creek to the Grand River,[56] the utility of which he stressed in his speech at the sod-turning ceremony the following year. Here, again, a number of possible routes were surveyed. Francis Hall, in his report of 7 August 1824, recommended a cut starting at "Misener's Creek, on the first fork of the Chippawa" for two miles, thence to Broad Creek, "about 2 miles above the junction to the Grand River with Lake Erie."[57] A few days later James Clowes reported to the president and directors of the Welland Canal Company on three possible routes, one of which appears to have been similar to Hall's, but specified cutting through Cranberry Marsh to Broad Creek.[58] Then, in September 1825, the Welland Canal Company directors agreed that "Mr. [George] Rykert be employed to survey & lay out the Canal from Grand River to Welland."[59] The Annual Report for that year described progress to date on the "*three great sections*," the third of which was "a cut of about 12 miles from the Welland [River] to the Grand River, through a flat swampy tract of country, called the Canboro' or Wainfleet marsh."[60]

Matters did not end there, however. On 1 September 1827 Alfred Barrett reported on three other possible routes. Feeling that the Clowes/Rykert line required too much "deep cutting," he suggested a line from the Welland River via "Beser's and Kelley's creeks, crossing the north west arm of the Wainfleet Marsh to Broad Creek, near its entrance into the Grand River." This, he pointed out, would not drain the marsh, adding, "not one mile of it will pass through the Company's land." As an alternative, he had the Clowes/Rykert line re-surveyed: from "the forks of the Welland River it passes up the valley of Mill's Creek, terminating at Broad Creek at the same point with the above." He noted that several routes were examined "with reference to a feeder from the Grand River ... raising the level 8 feet, placing two additional locks, constructing a dam across the Grand River, 17 miles above the junction of the canal with the same, 8 feet high, and placing a lock thereon." While the Clowes/Rykert line would be the most expensive, it would "be the most advantageous one for the Board to adopt." He continued: "No time should be lost in placing it under contract, in order to take advantage of the winter's operation; otherwise another entire season will be lost There will be no difficulty in draining it, but the work can only proceed from the two ends."[61]

According to Merritt's son, exactly one week after Barrett submitted his report, notice was given for nine miles of excavation "from the forks of the Welland to Broad Creek – to be finished by 1 Oct. 1828."[62] On 4 October a contract was awarded to Horatio Nelson Monson & James Simpson, and on 10 October the *Farmers' Journal* carried an advertisement for "1000 labourers wanted ... for excavation in Cranberry Marsh near Misener's Mills." A map drawn by Colonel E.W. Durnford, R.E. (included in a report by Sir R.H. Bonnycastle (1791–1847), which suggested a possible canal from Queenston to Thorold and from Port Robinson westward along Chippawa Creek to the Grand River), may be the best approximation we have of that route.[63]

In an 1828 article titled "Account of the Welland Canal, Upper Canada," Merritt traced the route of the entire canal, starting from Lake Erie: "From the mouth of the Grand River on Lake Erie, it continues up that stream by a towing path one hundred and twenty chains, thence up Broad creek seventy chains, thence by a throrough [sic] cut through an extensive marsh ten miles, thence down Mill creek two and a half miles, until it intersects the river Welland, into which it descends by a ship lock of eight feet lift, thence a towing path or track way is constructed ten miles, and thence the canal runs in a northerly direction to Lake Ontario, winding up a ravine about sixty chains with from eight to twelve feet cutting."[64]

In a footnote he adds: "This part of the canal, was placed under contract in October last; a number of men are now employed on the Marsh, which has to be excavated from ten to sixteen feet deep throughout." The article includes a description of an earth-moving "machine" and a "Map of the Niagara Peninsula shewing the Course and a Profile of the Welland Canal Connecting Lakes Erie and Ontario by Ship Navigation," both drawn by George Keefer Jr (fig. 2.3).[65] An Estimate Book of the Welland Canal Company records that the firm of Monson & Simpson worked assiduously from late 1827 through until January 1829, and were paid over $31,000 for work on the "Western Section" and accompanying "Ditch."[66] (The Estimate Book contains no mention of the lock to which Merritt referred.)

2.3 The "Western Section," drawn by George Keefer Jr in 1828, as shown by the hatched line between the Welland and Grand rivers. The original plan involved using a long stretch of the Welland River to connect with the Grand River, via a straight cut through a marshy area. (The American Journal of Science and Arts, vol. 14 (July 1828), n.p.)

The Feeder Canal

While construction of the "Western Section," intended to connect Chippawa Creek (Welland River) with Broad Creek, was undertaken in 1827–28, the landslides in the Deep Cut in November 1828 necessitated a major revision of plans. The Welland Canal Company directors acted with dispatch and called in James Geddes. "The disastrous slips at the Deep Cut," he reported, "present certainty of expense in attempting to remove them, and great uncertainty as to the successful operation of any remedy. These considerations have suggested the expediency of supplying the Canal with Water from the Grand River instead of the Chippawa."[67] At a meeting on 1 January 1829 the company resolved: "the most expedient [plan] is to dam up the Grand River near the mouth – and to proceed in cutting through the marsh for a Feeder to be conducted to the bank of the Welland, at or near Helm's Creek – construct an Aqueduct over the Welland at that point, and dig a Feeder from thence on the north side of the Welland to the

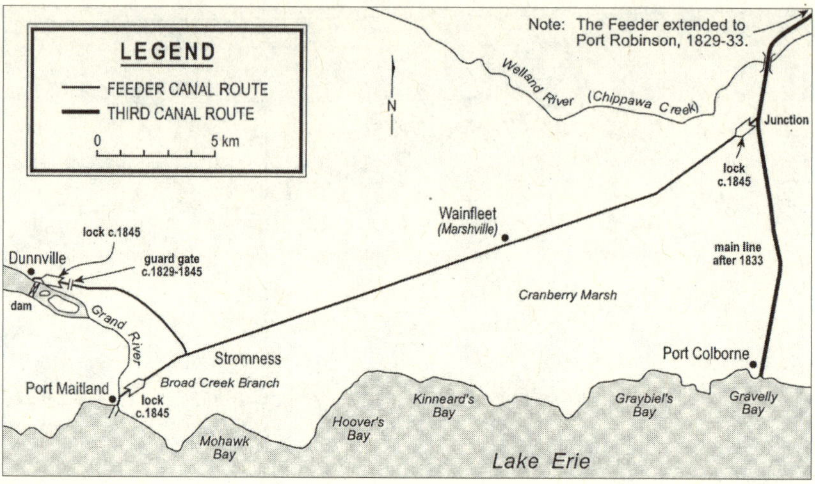

2.4 The Feeder Canal, opened 1829, provided water from the Grand River to the main Canal until 1881. (Loris Gasparatto, Department of Geography, Brock University)

Deep Cut – construct two Locks by which vessels may ascend from the Welland to the Deep Cut upon the proposed level to be procured by means of a Feeder along the Welland."[68]

Contracts were let on 8 February, with Monson sharing a contract for the lockpit, embankment, and puddling. Work proceeded apace, until Commodore Barrie of the Royal Navy objected to locating the dam at the mouth of the Grand, fearing that it would interfere with the naval station there.[69] Once again a rapid change of plan was needed: the southern terminus of the Feeder was moved up the Grand a distance of almost four miles (6 km) to what became Dunnville, and the First Welland Canal could finally open to traffic in late November 1829 (fig. 2.4).

There is no mention in the records of the apparent abandonment of the "Western Branch" and the excavation of what appears to be an entirely new channel for the Feeder. Obviously, the northern portion of the "Western Section" (from the Welland River to the marsh) would have to be replaced by a direct link from the main canal. But although it may seem rather strange that a new cut appears to have been made through the marsh, it was necessary to raise the level of the canal above that of the Welland (thus lowering the level of the Deep Cut). Also, the company may possibly have intended to use the "Western Section" as part of the drainage system.

The Lake Erie Terminus

The southern townships of Upper Canada, especially those bordering Lake Erie (Humberstone, Bertie, and Wainfleet) had also responded to Gourlay's questionnaire. Humberstone, Willoughby, and Crowland envisaged connections with Chippawa Creek and the Niagara River via Lyons Creek (a tributary of the Chippawa), while Canborough and Caistor wanted a connection with Oswego Creek (another tributary of the Chippawa), and Wainfleet suggested a terminus near Morgan's Point on Lake Erie.[70] None of these suggestions was acted upon, however, and it was not until construction of a direct link to Lake Erie (to replace the round-about route via Chippawa Creek and the Niagara River) was considered that the southern route and location of a Lake Erie terminus came to the fore.

One suggestion, on which Clowes had reported in 1824, also noted by Alfred Barrett, was to cut directly from the Welland River south to Lake Erie "at the East end of a Bay formed by Point Industry and Mr. Graybiel's."[71] In 1826 George Keefer Jr produced a survey and map, suggesting three possible lines to the Grand River and Lake Erie. The following year the American journal *The Northern Traveller* published a map (fig. 2.5) showing a route that could follow Twelve Mile Creek to the Niagara Escarpment, and thence along Chippawa Creek, to connect with Lake Erie west of Sugarloaf Mountain.[72]

In fact, only in October 1830, after the first full season of operation, did the need for a more direct line to Lake Erie come under serious discussion. Samuel Keefer began further surveys almost immediately.[73] He reported on four routes, terminating respectively at Kinnaird's, Graybiel's, Hoover's, and Gravelly bays – all lying between the mouth of the Grand and Gravelly Bay (fig. 2.2).[74] Not surprisingly, the best location for a terminus was the subject of much renewed debate. H.J. Boulton (attorney general and a company director) owned property on the Grand River and naturally preferred Kinnaird's Bay.[75] Marshall Lewis, who had built the canal's bridges, reported in 1831 that the mouth of the Grand was "the most natural and best place for a harbour."[76] Commissioner and MPP Robert Randal favoured Graybiel's Bay, partly because the area around Gravelly Bay was "unhealthy."[77] Others noted, on the other hand, that Gravelly Bay had a sandy floor that ships' anchors could grip and that Sugar Loaf Point could protect it from the prevailing winds. This site was also on a line running directly south from the aqueduct, and therefore cheaper to build and offering a shorter route for shippers. In the event, Gravelly Bay, an

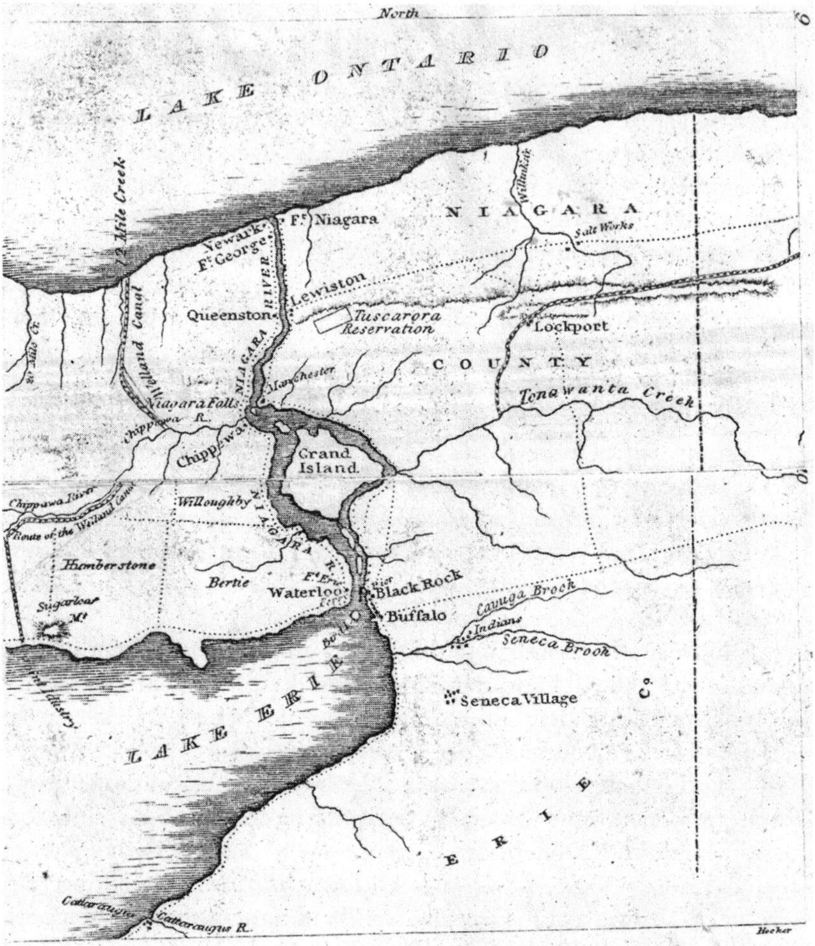

2.5 An American map of the proposed Welland Canal, 1826. Although the First Welland Canal was not completed as shown here, this map expresses fears of an Upper Canadian threat to the Erie Canal. The latter waterway is shown passing through Lockport and connecting via Tonawanda Creek with Black Rock and Lake Erie. (Theodore Dwight, *The Northern Traveller*, 1826, 79 and 99)

"excellent anchorage," was chosen,[78] and the "Lake Erie Extension" was completed in 1833 at what became Port Colborne.

When Killaly and Baird reported on a possible route for the Second Canal in 1838 they made it known what would have been their first choice: "[We] would have preferred, even for a Schooner Navigation, locking down into the Chippewa at the Aqueduct, following the reach of that River as far as the Creek entering it from Marshville Hills, by which we would ascent to the Feeder, pursue it to the head of the Broad Creek, and by it descend into the Grand River – this route would terminate in a Harbor, admitted to be the finest on the Lake for vessels of any class."[79]

Since construction of this line would add £50,000 to the cost, however, even they rejected the idea. George Phillpotts also favoured what would become the Port Maitland area, since it was closer "to the naval establishment on the Grand River," was free of ice earlier than Port Colborne, and was "altogether a much more commodious situation for military purposes."[80]

While these representations were not acted upon in the 1830s, the company's engineer, J.S. Macaulay, in 1840 recommended a second entrance to the Feeder at what became Port Maitland, and since that area was ice-free earlier than Port Colborne, the directors agreed: "at least one month in each year will be gained in the transit of produce between the two lakes."[81] The Board of Works concurred, and by 1845 a cut had been made from Stromness on the Feeder to the mouth of the Grand, with a connecting lock near Port Maitland. In this way, the enlarged canal gained a second Lake Erie terminus. Port Maitland proved of such value that, when plans for the Third Canal were being discussed, Lauchlan McCallum (1823–1903), a Stromness politician and businessman, campaigned to make it the main southern terminus.[82] After Chief Engineer John Page had concluded in 1872 that it was not viable, largely because of the "enormous extent of excavation" required,[83] a group of ship owners petitioned the governor general on Port Maitland's behalf.[84] Despite such pressure, however, the Third Canal terminated at Port Colborne, as would the Fourth Canal in the twentieth century.

THE LATERAL CUT

A number of branch canals were also discussed, including Bonnycastle's 1827 suggestion of a canal linking the Welland to the Short Hills, where the village of St Johns was still a bustling industrial centre.[85] However, the most attractive – as well as most frequently proposed and hotly defended – was the so-called Lateral Cut (or "Side Cut" or "Niagara Cut") from the main Canal to Niagara at the mouth of the Niagara River (fig. 2.2). At that time Niagara was already a prominent mercantile community, far more important than the small settlement on Twelve Mile Creek. Some of the canal's early supporters, being resolutely opposed to the latter route, would have the Niagara Line as the *only* connection between the Escarpment and Lake Ontario. Merchants of Niagara who were involved in the portage trade naturally feared loss of revenue to any route lying to the west. In 1824, encouraged by local support for this route, the Niagara *Gleaner* asserted: "It is become obvious that it [the Canal] will be brought to the River."[86]

A young engineer just entering the profession today might be warned about the amount of "politicking" involved in the job: things were no different in the 1820s, when Francis Hall may have felt himself caught in the crossfire between Niagara supporters of the Lateral Cut and promoters of Twelve Mile Creek. Requested to survey and report in 1824, he preferred the former, noting the "disadvantages" of having a harbour at Port Dalhousie, but he also suggested a canal from Queenston to Chippawa – not exactly what the Lateral Cut enthusiasts wanted![87] To the company directors, he wrote that he wanted a discussion of the matter "in a fair and candid manner," something in which neither group was interested.[88]

The rivalry between the Twelve Mile Creek route and the Niagara Line occasioned acrimonious debate in the newspapers and elsewhere. The views of the Niagara people were "palpably erroneous and idle," said a St Catharines supporter. It was a pity, replied Niagara, that the Twelve Mile Creek folk did not "write with more temperate cool reasoning" – their views were "ridiculous." The Legislative Assembly's support for "cunning" St Catharines was "precipitate," revealing "cruelty and injustice."[89] Back in St Catharines, Niagara's criticism of the company's letting of contracts was dismissed "with a smile of contempt" as "puerile exertions."[90]

The Niagara Line would have the advantage of being five miles shorter than a route from Thorold to Port Dalhousie and, as we have seen, Hall had doubts about the wisdom of a line to the mouth of Twelve Mile Creek.[91] Niagara had a natural harbour and had long been a commercial and administrative centre. A line from the Escarpment to Niagara would be "a far more elegant canal," thought Nathan Roberts.[92] On the other hand, the disadvantages of a Niagara River outlet for any canal – as the only line or as an auxiliary cut – were real: the river had a strong current that carried large floes of ice to the lake in the spring, and across the river loomed the American Fort Niagara. Doing battle against the "Gents from Niagara," Merritt defended his Twelve Mile Creek route on his first appearance in the Upper Canada Assembly. Aware of his limitations as a speaker, he wrote to his wife that "although considerably agitated the first sentence or two," he was "determined not to be embarased [sic]."[93] Geographical factors, however – as well as Merritt's crusade – ultimately determined the choice of the mouth of Twelve Mile Creek, at what became Port Dalhousie, as the northern terminus.

Proponents of the Niagara Line were not easily defeated, although many of them, like those living along the DeCew line, withdrew as shareholders of the company once Twelve Mile Creek was chosen. They received qualified support from George Keefer when, in late 1825, he testified before a Select Committee of the Upper Canada Legislature that a line to Niagara, as an auxiliary canal, might be useful. In January 1827 James Muirhead and other residents of the town of Niagara petitioned the Assembly, indicating that they were "desirous of making a lateral Cut from the River Niagara to intersect with Welland Canal below the Mountain Ridge, of equal dimensions with the Welland Canal."[94] Their request was discussed, but ignored in favour of the existing line.

The Niagara forces were justified in their suspicion that stockholders' and directors' self-interest had also contributed to the choice of Twelve Mile Creek. The editor of the Niagara *Gleaner* suggested that some of that route's supporters were motivated by "cunning and interested views."[95] John MacTaggart, Clerk of Works on the Rideau, was probably unduly skeptical about some aspects of the canal's construction, but he was justified in asking why the only three locks built to accommodate steamships lay on the line between Port Dalhousie and St Catharines. He noted – quite astutely – that "there must be some private interests of individuals at work with this erroneous alteration."[96] Others, such as the contractor Love Newlove, may have been influenced by this view: when questioned by the Select Committee in 1836, he stated: "I would not have gone down Dick's Creek, unless satisfied by the Engineer that it was the best route. I would have gone straight as possible to Port Dalhousie."[97] One of William Lyon Mackenzie's charges in 1836 – his twenty-fifth – was that the canal had been "taken to particular places, to the injury of the company, to serve the purposes of interested individuals."[98]

On the other hand, when Baird and Killaly conducted their survey for the company in the late 1830s, they expressed a preference for Port Dalhousie as a harbour over the Niagara River mouth. With Fort Niagara in mind they pointed out "the national impolicy of adopting for the canal, a termination wholly under the control of the Americans." They noted, as did other engineers and surveyors, the strong current in the river and the lake gales which "create so great a swell and cross sea upon the bar, as to render vessels unmanageable."[99]

The final judgment of the Select Committee investigating Mackenzie's charges in 1836 was non-committal: a shorter route than the Twelve Mile Creek line "might have been judiciously selected, and with less expense to the proprietors, but which would not have been so beneficial to some individuals as the present." Still, they equivocated, believing that they could not "say that the course adopted was with a view of serving the purposes of interested individuals."[100] On the other hand, reminiscing in 1841, Bonnycastle wrote that he had felt the canal "should have been brought to Niagara in the first place."[101]

The idea of a Lake Ontario terminus at Niagara did not die. In 1844 the Board of Works called for estimates for a line to the Niagara River mouth, but in the end decided to stay with the route suggested by Killaly and Baird.[102] Still, interested parties could not let the matter rest. In 1850 Niagara residents petitioned (unsuccessfully) for the Lateral Cut, and in 1854 engineer Walter Shanly recommended to the Mayor of Niagara that the "Cut" should be constructed and be on the same scale as that at Sault Ste Marie.[103] Another petition followed in 1855 and was greeted with the comment that enlargement of the Welland was being considered and that "the expediency of terminating it in Niagara" would receive attention.[104] Unfortunately for Niagarans, discussion concerning Confederation intervened before any decision could be reached. Nevertheless, proponents of the Lateral Cut pushed their case again whenever it looked as if a different route would be considered and possibly chosen. In 1872, for example, an "Ontario and Erie Ship Canal Company" offered to build a branch canal from Thorold to Niagara (fig. 2.6).[105]

The project exercised anonymous letter-writers to the editor of the Toronto *Mail* in early 1873. One of them – "Beaver"– suggested reviving Chippawa as the entrance to a canal connecting to Queenston.[106] Another writer, who called himself "Progress," wrote: "The Niagara River is the proper and natural entrance for the Canal and no improvement will be perfect that does not as a main feature of the work adopt the natural instead of the artificial harbour as the starting point of the undertaking." There followed a series of letters on the subject from "Chip-Away," "Observer," and "An Occasional Correspondent" (the latter two from St Catharines).[107] A petition from the towns of Niagara and Clifton, the township of Stamford and the village of Chippawa begged Hector Langevin, Minister of Public Works, for a survey of the Chippawa-Queenston route. Langevin sent the request to engineers Samuel Keefer, W.J. McAlpine, and Casimir Gzowski, asking their opinion on it, the "Grenville Route" (see below), and the Lateral Cut to Niagara.[108]

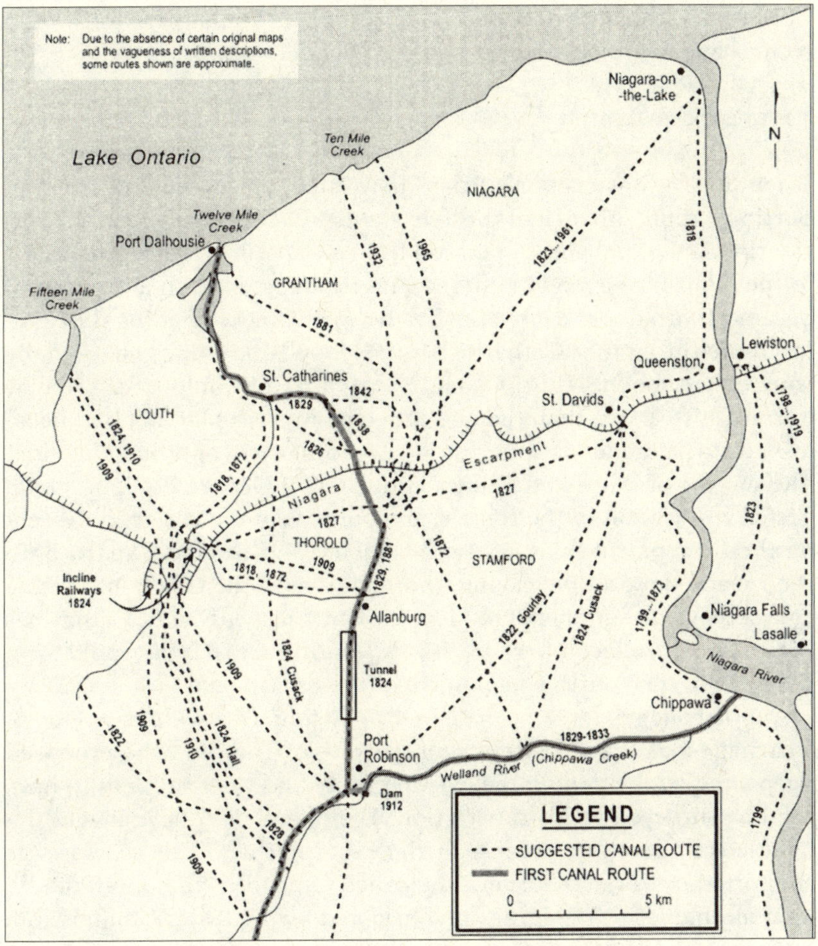

2.6 Suggested canal routes in the Niagara Peninsula (detail). (Loris Gasparotto/with the permission of The Champlain Society)

Chief Engineer Page would hear nothing of these suggestions, noting that the Lateral Cut would not only be four miles (6.4 km) longer, but also would require five flights of "combined locks" at an extra cost of $420,000, and that a harbour at Niagara would be "dangerous to vessels entering the river in thick weather" – the same objections that had been made in the 1830s and 1850s.[109]

One might have thought that Page's rejection in 1872, followed by that of an 1895 Royal Commission on Transportation, which ruled out the possibility of any branch canal being built on the Welland,[110] would have constituted a definitive response. The suggestion would recur – and again be rejected – in the twentieth century.

THE LOOP LINE

Even during construction of the First Canal, voices were raised supporting a route other than the Twelve Mile Creek route – but not necessarily the Lateral Cut. A petition from a Captain Gordon and others to the House of Assembly in 1825 suggested a straight line from what became Thorold to the mouth of Twelve Mile Creek, avoiding the twisting route through St Catharines – the "loop" line which was actually constructed for the Third Canal.[111] Such a route would be shorter by four miles (6.4 km) than the one the company had planned but, needless to say, commercial interests in St Catharines opposed this line! The surveys of Baird and Killaly, and, later, of George Phillpotts, suggested a deviation in the route that would avoid the cramped descent on the Escarpment taken by both the First and Second Canals. Both their maps show a line leaving Thorold at Ten Mile Creek in a gentle curve, then running north to meet the canal just east of St Catharines (figs. 1.2, 1.3). In fact, after 1913, it was Ten Mile Creek that would form the basis of the Fourth Canal north of the Escarpment.

Another suggestion was made in 1872 by John Grenville (1824–1907), a carriage-maker and reeve – later mayor – of Thorold, who proposed deepening and widening the existing route and went so far as to have the line surveyed to his satisfaction. His plan would have involved a double set of combined locks at the Escarpment.[112] This scheme was supported by Thomas Keefer, who called Grenville "an honest, intelligent mechanic."[113] The idea was considered by the Royal Commission, but rejected. In 1886, however, the St Catharines *Journal* wistfully remarked that both Thorold and St Catharines might have been better off, had Grenville's route been chosen.[114]

In the event, a completely new route was taken for the northern stretch of the Third Canal – the "Loop Line" or the "Monro Route," curving to the northeast of Thorold, then running north of St Catharines to Port Dalhousie. "A safe and direct inland navigation"[115] avoided altogether the winding route through Merritton and St Catharines (fig. 2.6). Port Colborne remained the southern harbour. Between Allanburg and Lake Erie, the "New" Canal would be essentially an enlargement of the channel of the Second.

All the controversy and debates concerning the best – or at least the best affordable – route underscore the fact that throughout the nineteenth century the Welland was almost continually in a state of construction and reconstruction. Nor did the deepening of the Third Canal from 12 to 14 feet (3.65 to 4.26 m) in 1886–87 satisfy shipping demands for long. By the 1890s the campaign for an inland deep waterway (what was to become the Seaway) was well underway, including a further enlargement of the Welland–St Lawrence route.[116] The Georgian Bay Ship Canal became an even more serious contender than previously, and other possibilities were on the table as well. It was not until 1912 that the final decision was made, favouring the traditional St Lawrence line including the Welland.

Obviously, the final route of any version of the canal was never a foregone conclusion. Most, if not all, of the suggestions made to Gourlay in 1817–18 were considered at one time or another, and some would re-appear over the years. No doubt historians and canal buffs will continue to debate the pros and cons – and the wisdom, or lack of it – of the choices made. It would be left to the engineers and contractors to implement those choices, and to deal with the consequence, whether for good or ill. The ways in which they fulfilled the plans, and coped with the challenges, make up the subject of the next chapter.

CHAPTER THREE

Surveyors, Engineers, and Contractors

Obviously, no canal could be built without the services of surveyors, engineers, and contractors.[1] While the land surveyors reported on possible routes, and the contractors were essential for managing the actual work, the role of the engineers was pivotal. They were responsible for laying out the lines that had been chosen, checking the soil conditions, dividing the work into sections, overseeing and measuring the contractors' work and authorizing payments for work done, solving the many problems the contractors would encounter, and judging when a contract had been successfully completed. If the work was unsatisfactory, an engineer might be required to arbitrate between the contractor and those who had hired him. In general, the resident engineer was the "boss" on the ground, with responsibilities that reached far beyond the mere technical, which often including handling complaints from not only the workers and contractors but the general public as well. In addition, it was he who had to contend with the decisions of his superiors, the chief engineer, the bureaucrats, and the politicians.

SURVEYORS AND SURVEYING

The early surveyors, especially the American engineer Hiram Tibbett(s) and William Hamilton Merritt himself, made serious errors because of their inexperience, the difficulty of the terrain, and the inadequacy of available equipment. Working often through uncharted lands – virgin forest, marshes, and swamps, uneven contours – and deciding whether to make use of natural watercourses (and in all kinds of weather), their job was not an enviable one. When Merritt and his friends conducted their first survey in 1818, "there being no regular levelling instrument at hand, he borrowed a water level."[2] The survey done by Tibbett(s) in May 1823 was done with a "theodolite" that he brought with him.

Apparently it was customary for an engineer/surveyor to have his own instrument, as Samuel Keefer, the Welland's engineer in 1846, noted that "for the most part the assistants on this Canal have had instruments of their own." This comment accompanied a response to a request from the Department of Public Works for information on instruments held in his office: "1 Good Spirit Level brought from the Beauharnois Canal; 2 bad ones, at present useless, one of them past repair; 2 Theodolites – one good, the other wanting extensive repairs; 4 Levelling Rods, one 50 ft chain and one 66 ft."[3] Surveyors' tools gradually became more sophisticated, however, and more readily available (albeit still from the United States). By 1853 the secretary of the Board of Works could place an order for a number of instruments, including compasses and protractors, confident that they would be provided.[4] Little wonder that originally proposed routes had to be modified as work proceeded.

By the 1870s, with much of the forested land already cleared and equipment improved, surveying routes for the proposed enlargement would be an easier task, and the results more exact in preparing for the engineers' role.

Engineers and Engineering

From the nineteenth century to the present day, both civil engineers and large contractors have been in general a peripatetic breed, following the work from place to place. Indeed, in some cases a canal engineer followed his master, or mentor, as his knowledge was demanded at one canal site or another, and in this way technical knowledge was handed on. We should remember that in the early 1800s the "profession" of engineering was as yet in its infancy; formal training could be acquired only through the military. "Civil engineering" as a separate discipline had just begun to be recognized abroad, and in Britain engineers such as James Brindley (1716–1772), John Rennie (1761–1821), William Jessop (1783–1852), and Thomas Telford (1757–1834) were making names for themselves, especially in canal construction. North Americans naturally looked across the Atlantic for expertise in the late eighteenth and early nineteenth centuries.

Referring to an international "canal network," historian Ronald Shaw recognized the importance of British influence in America, pointing out that the transfer of information on canal building had its origins in personal contacts with some of those British engineers, going back to James Brindley, who had built the Duke of Bridgewater's canal for the transport of coal in northern England, beginning in 1759 and reaching Manchester by 1765. "Brindley's knowledge was shared by William Weston, who came to America to work on the Schuykill and Susquehanna Canal in 1790s [and] shared his leveling instruments with Benjamin Wright ... Weston taught [Loammi] Baldwin and Wright, and Wright taught James Geddes ... Wright and Geddes laid out the greatest portion of the canal line. Canvas White made a trip to England to observe the use of Roman cement and then developed in New York the underwater cement that bound the stone structures for virtually every subsequent American canal ... Nathan Roberts designed the dramatic five-lock flight up the Niagara escarpment at Lockport."[5]

Shaw particularly emphasized the role of the Erie Canal as a virtual "school" for engineers, noting that it was the first to demonstrate on a grand scale that canals could work in North America. Built between 1817 and 1825, it crossed overland 363 miles from the Hudson to Lake Erie, winding its way up the Mohawk Valley and breaking through the Appalachian chain. Popularly known as the "Grand Canal," it became a model for most subsequent canals in America, and its influence on the Welland Canal was significant.

American Influence on the Welland Canal

The American engineers Nathan Roberts, Benjamin Wright, and James Geddes were all consulted by the Welland Canal Company at various times, as we have seen. These three, and many others who worked with them, were involved in construction of most of the early nineteenth-century canals in the United States. In fact, the first professional civil engineers in America were canal engineers. In 1816 probably no more than two engineers or quasi-engineers could be found in each state – "about thirty men altogether."[6] By 1831, however, what would later become Rensselaer Polytechnic Institute in Troy, New York, introduced civil engineering into its curriculum.[7]

It is no coincidence, therefore, that Merritt and the Welland Canal Company directors looked to the Erie Canal for many of their early engineers. While Rheddy Cusack (1824), the Clowes family (1824–26), and Francis Hall (1824, 1835–37) were British, Americans were hired more frequently in the early years: Tibbett(s) in 1823, Roberts in 1824 and 1825 (fig. 3.1),[8] Geddes in 1825 and 1829, and Wright in 1833, were engaged to conduct surveys and report on different routes. Alfred Barrett, as resident engineer from July 1826 to February 1832, Darius Lapham from July 1826 through February 1828, David Thomas from

3.1 Portrait Gallery 2. *Clockwise from top left:* Nicol Hugh Baird (1796–1849) (Mrs A. Foley/James T. Angus); Hamilton Hartley Killaly (1800–1874) (Metropolitan Toronto Library: JRR-788); Samuel Keefer (1811–1890) (LAC: C-21683); Nathan Roberts (1776–1852) (Erie Canal Museum, Syracuse, NY)

3.1 Portrait Gallery 2. *Clockwise from top left:* Oliver Phelps (1779–1851) (SCM: 969.29.1); John Page (1816–1890) (LAC: PA-126256); Thomas C. Keefer (1821–1915) (*Canadian Illustrated News*, 26 September 1863); Thomas Monro (1831–1903) (François Cartier, Canal de Soulanges, 26.)

April 1826 to the end of June 1828, and William Gooding from 1827 to 1830, all made their mark. Their immeasurable influence was in turn passed on to local men, so that the Welland Canal became, in its turn, a "school" of canal engineering of which Samuel and Thomas Coltrin Keefer, Walter Shanly, and John Page (1814–1890) were the most notable "graduates."

Among those early veterans of the Erie Canal was David Thomas (1776–1859), of Quaker background, from Montgomery, Pennsylvania. Having worked on the Erie as an engineer from 1821, when he was paid for a survey for Buffalo harbour, he ended up by 1825 as chief engineer for the section west of Rochester. At the end of that year he was hired by the Welland Canal Company, resigning in June 1827.

Barrett was another Erie veteran. He began work on the Erie in 1818, and was listed as "engineer" in 1821.[9] He was hired by the Welland Canal Company in April 1826 and remained with them until at least February 1832; he then returned to the Erie, but later resigned to come back to the Welland, where he remained through the summer of 1843. He then was sent to oversee the enlargement of the Lachine Canal, and when that was finished in the fall of 1848, he again returned to the Welland. His stay this time was brief – he was let go for financial reasons at the end of 1848, and died the following year in Montreal.

Gooding (1803–1878) also came to Upper Canada in 1826 and apprenticed on the Welland Canal under Barrett. There he remained until the spring of 1829, when he returned to the United States, and later worked on the Wabash and Erie Canal (1835–36), and on the Illinois and Michigan from 1836 to 1871. Lapham, who had worked on the Erie in 1821–25, was hired on the Welland between July 1826 and February 1828.

British Influence

As we have noted, Cusack, Hall, and the Clowes family were employed by the Welland Canal Company in the early years. According to a petition Cusack submitted to Lieutenant-Governor Sir Peregrine Maitland in 1823, he had emigrated from Ireland in 1816, intending to go to Quebec, but had landed instead at Miramichi in New Brunswick. (Miramichi was a common port of call for vessels from Ireland and the west coast of Scotland.) In the absence of roads, he had walked to Quebec, leaving behind all his bedding and most of his clothing. He petitioned for redress, noting that he had "been employed for nine years in canal works, the last five years of which he filled the situation of Assistant Engineer and Land Surveyor; under the Inspector

General of the Honorable Directors General of Inland Navigation."[10] Aside from the fact that he surveyed routes for the Welland Canal in 1824 and 1826, we know nothing else about him.

Among the engineers who brought a British influence to the Welland were the Clowes family (from England), Samuel and his sons John and James. Samuel was paid for work on the Erie Canal in 1821–24, and conducted surveys in 1824 on the Rideau Canal as well as the Welland. James was apparently "one of the pre-canal settlers" in the area of what became known as "Clowes' Quarry" on the Rideau, and was contracted for work during the summer of 1827.[11] James and John also tendered (unsuccessfully) for work on the Welland Canal in 1827.

Hall (1792–1862) was without doubt the best-educated and most influential of the British-trained civil engineers in British North America in the 1820s and '30s. He studied chemistry, mathematics, and philosophy at the University of Edinburgh in 1812, and began his early engineering training with mining engineer Robert Bald of Alloa, Scotland. He then worked under the great civil engineer Thomas Telford, before emigrating to Upper Canada in 1823 and settling in Queenston, where one of his commissions was to design a monument to Sir Isaac Brock. As we have seen, Hall was hired by the Welland Canal Company in 1824, and worked again with them from 1835 through 1837. In the meantime he had been employed as resident engineer on the Shubenacadie Canal in Nova Scotia (1825–32) and, while in the Maritimes, had conducted surveys for a possible canal in New Brunswick. He had also been superintending engineer on the Burlington Bay Canal in 1826, and in 1828 acted as an "expert witness" to a commission investigating construction of the Rideau Canal. After Upper and Lower Canada were united, he continued to work for the Department of Public Works in various capacities until 1851. Hall thus had the distinction of working on canals in all four of the eastern British North American colonies.

While Americans had been the dominant influence in the construction of the First Canal, men of British descent played a crucial role on the Second Canal. By the late 1830s the Welland Canal was already in trouble, as the dilapidated condition of many of the locks was causing frequent delays. When the Act of 1837 recommended that two "scientific and practical engineers" be appointed to survey and report on the condition of the canal, a Scot and an Irishman were hired. Nicol Hugh Baird (fig. 3.1) had learned his trade under his father, Hugh Baird, superintendent of the Forth and Clyde Canal in Scotland. He also worked on reconstruction projects in St Petersburg, Russia,[12] before emigrating to take a position as clerk of works on the Rideau Canal under Col. John By in 1828. In 1837 he, along with Hamilton Hartley Killaly, was hired by the Welland Canal Company. The following year they reported on existing conditions and also on a proposed route and estimates for a "permanent" canal. In 1837 Baird turned down an offer from the Welland Canal Company for a position as permanent engineer. He did, however, return briefly to the Welland in 1843 as a consultant on contracts, and later worked in Montreal.

Baird's colleague, Killaly, an Irishman (fig. 3.1), was possibly the most colourful of the engineers who worked on the Welland Canal, as a contemporary – perhaps exaggerated – description testifies:

> I have seen him at one time promenading a populous city in a dirty, powder-smeared, and blood-stained shooting coat, while his nether man was encased in black dress pantaloons, silk stockings, and highly varnished French leather dancing pumps. At another time, I have met him with one of Gibbs' most recherché dress coats, a ragged waistcoat, and worn-out trousers, all looking as if he had slept in them for weeks, and lain inside of the bed among the feathers. His shirts never had a button on them, which constantly caused his brawny and hairy chest to be exposed to view, while a fringe of ravelled threads from their wrists usually hung dangling over his fat, freckled and dirty hands.
>
> Where he obtained all the old hats he wore puzzled his acquaintances. That he changed hats frequently was evident, for the hat of one day was never the same shape the next. Their general outline was that which might be expected in the hat of an Irishman who had been beaten at a fair — who had encountered a rain-storm as he returned homewards, and who had finally determined to sleep all night in a ditch ... His head was white and his face was purple — a red cabbage in snow ... His temper was as uncertain as the wind toward his subordinates; sometimes familiar as a playfellow, at others as imperious, arbitrary and unreasoning as a Turk.[13]

Killaly unquestionably made his mark on civil engineering, on the Welland Canal and on the Board of Works of the Province of Canada, of which he served as first chairman, 1841–46. Like Baird, he had worked for his father, John, a prominent engineer on Irish canals. Emigrating to Upper Canada in 1835, he found his first permanent engagement as engineer on the Welland in May 1838. The following year Lord Sydenham appointed him chairman of the Board of Works of Lower Canada, and in 1841 chairman of the Board of Works of the

United Province of Canada. He also acted as the board's chief engineer. When he was dismissed as chairman in 1846, he was transferred to the Welland Canal as superintending engineer, remaining in that post until 1851. He then became assistant commissioner of the Department of Public Works. In 1859, following a disagreement with the chief commissioner, he was relieved of this position, but he continued to serve the Department in various capacities for a number of years. In his early years with the Board (later Department) of Public Works, he was instrumental in helping to develop administrative policies that influenced those of other departments in the nascent civil service.[14]

Page, another Scot (1814–1890) (fig. 3.1), was to have an even greater influence on Canadian civil engineering than Killaly. He served his apprenticeship under Robert Stevenson, engineer of the Northern Lighthouse Board in Scotland, and emigrated to the United States in 1838, where he worked on the Erie Canal until 1842. He then came to Upper Canada, where he served a brief stint on the Welland before being transferred for a time to the Williamsburg canals. Between 1844 and 1846 he was an assistant engineer (under Samuel Power) on the Welland "in charge of masonry, bridges & piers."[15] His obituary in the Thorold *Post* on 4 July described him as "an officer of sterling integrity," a characteristic he vividly demonstrated when a contractor attempted to bribe him in 1845, by leaving a parcel on his desk. Power reported the incident to the Department,[16] saying that when Page discovered that the parcel contained bank notes "the amount of which he did not examine," his first impulse was to take the earliest opportunity of inflicting personal chastisement on the man who had, he believed, offered him an insult. "On further reflection & with [Power's] advice" Page decided merely to write a polite but firm note. When Power resigned in 1846, Page was at first unwilling to stay on, but Power convinced him to remain, which he did until he was let go (for financial reasons) in 1848.

Page then served with the Department of Public Works on various canals before being appointed as chief engineer in October 1853. In 1863 he declined the position of deputy minister, preferring to stay on as chief engineer, a role he maintained in the new Ministry of Railways and Canals, formed in 1879. On 2 July 1890 he collapsed and died in his office, having supervised the works on Canada's many canals for thirty-seven years. According to Robert Legget, among his major accomplishments was "the great program of modernizing Canada's canal system [including the Welland] in the 1870s."[17]

The Irish influence extended through Killaly to his protegés the Shanly brothers, Francis (1820–1882) and Walter (1817–1899), and

Thomas Monro. The Shanly brothers were brought to Canada in 1850 by their lawyer father, James. Killaly encouraged them to pursue careers in civil engineering, and both worked on the Welland Canal in the 1840s. Walter was an assistant engineer on the Beauharnois Canal in Quebec by 1843, but was transferred to the Welland in 1846. By August 1848 the brothers were both assistant engineers on the Welland, and both were then let go for financial reasons. They then directed their talents to railway construction in both Canada and the United States. They are perhaps best known for their work on the Hoosac Mountain Tunnel in Massachusetts. Frank had just been appointed chief engineer of the Intercolonial Railway, when he died on a train between Kingston and Brockville. Walter became increasingly well known as a consulting engineer on a variety of major engineering works, and became a colleague and friend of Sir John A. Macdonald.

Monro came to Canada in 1850, worked with Thomas C. Keefer on various railways across Canada for four years, and was then given responsibility for the Grand Trunk Railway construction at Prescott. In 1860 he joined the Department of Public Works, and in 1870, as assistant engineer 1st class, was appointed to head the survey for the proposed Welland Canal Enlargement (Third Canal). Two years later he was placed in charge of the Enlargement, and in 1873 was named resident engineer of the Northern Division. When the superintendent of the Second Canal was suspended, Monro was made acting superintending engineer. He was still in charge of the Northern Division of the Enlargement in 1886, but when the office was shut down in 1889 he was transferred to Ottawa. In early 1891 the Department sent him to England to examine the Manchester Ship Canal, then under construction, for the Department of Railways and Canals. In England he observed the use of solid concrete in construction of the locks, and later that year, when he became superintendent of the work on the Soulanges Canal on the north shore of the St Lawrence, he recommended the extensive use of concrete in the lock structures. In November 1895 the Canadian government appointed him to a commission to meet with a similar commission appointed by the president of the United States to confer on the best line for a deep waterway from the Great Lakes to the Atlantic – what would eventually become the St Lawrence Seaway. That same year he was named president of the Canadian Society for Civil Engineers.

Another influential Irish emigrant, W. George Thompson, first appears in our records when an Order-in-Council dated 25 November 1872 ordered him to report to the Outside Service of the Department of Public Works, to take charge of the enlargement of the Welland

Canal at $250 per month. On 3 December Page, the chief engineer, was instructed to place Thompson "at the upper end" of the work, and then on 31 January 1873 Thompson was appointed resident engineer of the Southern Division. Two years later he was given responsibility for the engineering works at Port Colborne.[18] By late 1889 he was acting as resident government engineer on the construction of the canal at Sault Ste Marie, and on 1 August 1891 he also became superintending engineer on the Welland Canal. He continued in this dual capacity until 1894, when he was relieved of his duties on the "Soo."[19]

Today, we speak of "shuttle diplomacy." Thompson practised "shuttle engineering," travelling back and forth from St Catharines to the Soo, often stopping over in Ottawa en route for consultations with the chief engineer. Little wonder his health broke down! On the evening of 7 January 1892 he was too ill to leave St Catharines for Ottawa, and a week later his doctor reported that he had "grip" and needed "absolute rest and quiet for several days." In fact, he resumed his travels only on 11 April.[20] Then on 30 July 1896 the chief engineer recommended that he be given one month's sick leave with pay, and on 28 September 1896 he was granted "further" leave to 1 October, following an operation in Toronto.[21] On 15 November 1900, he asked to be relieved of his duties, citing a difference of opinion with Chief Engineer Collingwood Schreiber. When in 1903 he asked for superannuation, he was refused, as retirement funding was "not the practice" for officers who had voluntarily resigned.[22] In 1895 and 1897 he served as vice-president of the Society of Civil Engineers, and was president in 1898.

The Welland Canal as Engineering School

In addition to employing the immigrants discussed above, the Welland Canal provided on-the-job training for a number of local men in the days before formal engineering education became available. The earliest of the locals involved with engineering on the Welland was George Rykert (1797–1857) who, like Merritt, had served in the Lincoln Militia in the War of 1812. After working as a school teacher, he qualified as deputy Provincial Land Surveyor in 1821. He conducted a number of surveys throughout the Niagara Peninsula and served as an engineer for the Welland Canal Company from December 1824 to September 1826. In September 1825 Rykert was put in charge of the Western Section, and later worked on surveys on the St Lawrence with Samuel Clowes, and on the Rideau Canal. After 1829 he devoted his energies to local affairs and politics.

No fewer than three sons of George Keefer Sr, the first president of the Welland Canal Company, "cut their teeth" on the Welland: George

(1799–1885, the eldest), Samuel (1811–1890, the fourth), and Thomas Coltrin (1821–1915, the twelfth son). George Keefer Jr was appointed secretary of the Welland Canal Company on 9 June 1824, but he obviously learned surveying as well, since he surveyed three routes for the Western Section in 1826, and produced the map that Merritt used in an 1828 article, as well as the drawing of Phelps's earth-moving "machine" that accompanied that article.[23] He continued to be employed by the company until he was let go in favour of Hall in January 1836. During that time he surveyed a number of properties that had been appropriated by the Welland Canal Company in 1826, and was responsible for laying out the town plan for Port Robinson, and possibly also for Thorold, Marshville, and Dunnville. In some of these activities he was associated with his brother Samuel.[24]

The Second Canal, in particular, served as a practical academy for engineers: the Keefers, Page, and the Shanly brothers are the best known. In 1851 thirty-five men in the Province of Canada referred to themselves as "engineers"; by 1861, 129 did so, and by 1881, 719 used the term.[25] Already in 1842, the Board of Works could reply to one W.B. Gilbert, a civil engineer in Ogdensburg, New York, who had inquired about employment on the Welland, that "the Board can not feel themselves justified, in holding out a prospect of employment to Engineers from a foreign country, while so many competent persons, resident in the province, and who have stronger claims, remain unemployed."[26] In fact, engineers who had cut their teeth on the Welland were soon becoming known in wider circles.

A Canadian Dynasty

While George Keefer Jr began the family's engineering dynasty, and made his mark in the Niagara Peninsula, it was left to two of his brothers to make the name of Keefer prominent far from Niagara. Samuel (fig. 3.1) began his career in 1827, being paid on 10 August (under "Engineers Expenses") £11.13.4 for one sixth of a quarter at £70. He was then granted a raise to £82 per quarter, and was paid £20.10.– on 5 November.[27] He continued to serve as an assistant engineer until 1831. In June 1839 he was sufficiently advanced in his profession to be appointed as the first secretary of the Board of Works of Lower Canada, and became the chief engineer of the Board of Works of the United Canadas in 1841. In July 1846 he was appointed superintending engineer of the Welland Canal, leaving that position only to become chief engineer of the Department of Public Works. In 1853 he left public service for a time, but in May 1859 was appointed deputy commissioner of Public Works, a position he kept until March 1864. In 1870 he became secretary of the Royal Commission on Inland Navigation, and then sat on a Special Committee to consider the route of the Third Canal in 1872. He acted as president of the Canadian Society for Civil Engineers in 1888.[28]

Thomas C. Keefer (fig. 3.1),[29] the youngest of the three engineer-siblings, became Canada's pre-eminent civil engineer. According to George A. Rawlyk, during construction of the First Canal, "many of the canal engineers had lodged in the Keefer home, and had often entertained their hosts by describing in great detail each day's challenging engineering problems. It is not surprising then, that the young Thomas Keefer resolved to become a civil engineer."[30] Unlike his older brothers, however, he began his career in the States as an assistant engineer on the Erie Canal at Stockport, New York, in 1838. He first appears in the Welland Canal records when he was paid at 10/– per day from 24 August to 30 September 1840. On 28 May 1841, as deputy provincial surveyor, he signed a survey of lands sold by the Welland Canal Company to John Vanderburgh, and from then to 1845 he was in charge of the enlargement of the Feeder Canal. From there he was sent to Burlington Bay to take charge of the canal there for a short time. He was soon on the move again, heading for Bytown (later Ottawa). Keefer was also involved in designing water works for several cities, among them Hamilton, Ontario. He did return briefly to the Welland Canal in 1899, to act as a consultant on the harbour improvement at Port Colborne.

In 1888 T.C. Keefer was elected president of the American Society of Civil Engineers, and in 1912 he was appointed London Fellow of the British Institute of Civil Engineers. His honours included being elected as the first president of the Canadian Society for Civil Engineers (later the Engineering Institute of Canada) in 1897.

THE CHAIN OF COMMAND AND THE CHALLENGES

Ideally, while it was the men in "head office" – the politicians and bureaucrats in the political capital – who were ultimately responsible for decisions relating to the construction of the Welland Canals, those decisions were, at least usually and in theory, based on the advice of the engineers. The chief engineer at headquarters, in turn, relied on the on-site engineers who, in most cases, would be more familiar with a given work than "the chief." In fact the system often functioned in reverse: recommendations came from the ground up, with the on-site engineer's advice based not only on observed conditions on site but also on consultation with contractors as to what might, or might not, be practical.

We have already mentioned the inaccurate survey conducted by Merritt and his friends in 1818. Once the Welland Canal Company had been incorporated in 1824, the engineer hired from the Erie worked closely with Merritt, who in turn was in frequent communication with the directors in York. Merritt had already taken the advice of engineers from the Erie Canal, and surveys had been made before the company was officially incorporated. In fact, Merritt's role was unique. He was the direct link between what was happening "on the ground" and the directors in York, and no higher "engineering" authority was available in Upper Canada. Indeed, no formal chain of communication between the directors and the lieutenant-governor and the governor general was in place. (Both of the latter were appointed by the Imperial Government in London, and were ultimately responsible to the Secretary of State for the Colonies.) In a sense this lengthy chain of command was to Merritt's benefit and perhaps gave the early engineers more authority than they might otherwise have had. The major problem was the availability – or lack – of funds.

Fortunately, Merritt had enough knowledge of mathematics and rudimentary surveying not only to work well with the engineers but also to advise them from his knowledge of local conditions. He had access to various encyclopedias, particular that of Abraham Rees, whose *Cyclopædia* devoted considerable space to canal building in England and the United States. It included numerous detailed drawings,[31] and was widely available. With this background, and his unflagging attention to the work, Merritt had all the resources he needed to discuss technical matters directly with engineers and contractors. But once the work began, challenges such as the climate, advances in technology, and – with the government take-over and bureaucratic development – an increase in paperwork, interfered with progress.

Disparagement of the Canadian Climate

The climate was the most obvious of these challenges. "The rigour of a Canadian winter cover[s] the face of the country with snow, and congeal[s] every river, lake and harbour," wrote the British engineer David Stevenson in 1838, marvelling that the ice on Lake Ontario's shore could be nearly two feet thick.[32] In 1850 T.C. Keefer noted, in an understatement: "Much has been advanced in disparagement of the Canadian climate."[33] He, like Stevenson, knew how hot and humid southern Ontario summers are, and how rapidly thunderstorms can flood a construction site. He knew that winters are so severe with frost, ice, and snow that they bring building projects to a standstill – and that spring is not necessarily a relief, for it offers sudden freshets when tonnes of water from seemingly nowhere turn small streams into rivers and fields into swamps.

Climatic problems significantly affected the building of the First Welland. Rain was often a problem, as in 1827, when the directors described the situation on the Deep Cut: "The rains set in last autumn much earlier than usual; and from the stiff and adhesive nature of the clay the work could not be prosecuted with advantage in wet weather, and the contractor thought it most judicious to suspend operations toward the latter end of October – which in the end proved fortunate, as the rain continued during the whole of the following month."[34]

Steam-powered excavators and steam locomotives aided in the building of the Third Canal, but even they were no match for rain and flood. A telegram from Superintendent Bodwell to the Department of Public Works in 1878 says it all: "Incessant rain flood unprecedented. Immense volume of water coming down Twelve Mile Creek. Quantity comes down new canal. Means of escape at Port Dalhousie inadequate. Water nearly beyond control. Still rising."[35] On this occasion, the freshet destroyed the waste weir at Port Dalhousie, and navigation was held up for five days.[36]

Another storm, this time on Lake Erie in 1886, raised the level of the lake more than five feet and forced water through the Port Colborne lock, the gates of which had not yet been closed. The canal, still in the process of being deepened, was flooded up to the head lock at Thorold, and many stretches of the banks were washed out.

Freezing temperatures were another hazard. In December 1829, for example, engineer Barrett reported: "From the severe frosts in the winter the line was not properly laid out until April, although the Engineers were out constantly, nor could the contractors commence before the middle of that month, or the first of May, on many parts of the work."[37]

One of the most graphic descriptions of the effects of inclement winter weather on the work comes from the spring of 1835 in the words of a contractor trying to finish his winter repair work in the Port Robinson area before the canal opened in April:

> All is frost or ice at this time I am now at work weeding the Canal near this place ... which will only be a few day work the winter has been very hard in which time the clay work made but little progress ... the water in Canal and Chapwa [Chippawa] is very high more water comes out of the Swamps than I eversaw before — the ice is not yet of the slopes yet so that it is imposable to do any thing to the bends in the raseway yet but I will attaind

> to them as soon as practable Ostrum was puting down his mitter ceal [mitre sill] on thursday last if not prevented by the high water must be far advanced by this time the acqueduct require sum smal repares before water is let in ... but no water to be seen from Gravelly Bay yet over Jonathan Silverthon goose paster [pasture] is destroyed agane his fences swep away and bridge they are here pestering me.[38]

The contractor's creative spelling and grammar are typical of the era, and his reference to being "pestered" reflects common reactions of local residents to the construction project (chapter 8).

In 1836 the more literate Hall wrote to Merritt with equal vividness: "Only yesterday about ninety feet of the large mill aqueduct at St. Catharines feeder gave way, and other parts of the same structure are likely to follow. The trough or water way has been filled with ice, during the greater part of the winter, and side boards have been placed above the trough, to direct the passage of water to the mills when permitted by the frost to flow. In consequence of leakage at these side boards, the aqueduct has been over loaded with ice; and 90 feet broken down."[39]

Stone could be quarried during the winter months but, even so, severe frost could halt work, as occurred in the winter of 1877, when one contractor lost two to three thousand dollars' worth of stone, "destroyed by frost."[40]

On the other hand, the snows offered "good sleighing" weather, which could be used to bring in supplies over land, as Killaly noted with regard to the delivery of iron parts to Port Colborne's lock gates in January 1849.[41] Ingenious contractors, moreover, could use lake ice to their advantage. As the construction of the Third Canal was underway in 1872, one sent a telegram to the Department of Public Works: "We are anxious to avail ourselves of the sheet of ice now on the Harbor at Port Colborne to get as much of the drilling and blasting done as possible."[42] Depending on the temperature, a covering of ice could make a normally turbulent body of water easier to work on — a common practice at the harbours.

Technological Developments

As much as the climate retarded progress, developments in the shipping industry increased the pressure to keep up with the changing times. A major challenge, which "changed everything," according to a committee of the New York State legislature in 1834, was the advent of steam power.[43] By that time it was evident that the new power source (along with the greater size and draught of ships) would provide both a challenge and an opportunity for engineers and contractors. Steam power became a major catalyst in many aspects of life: construction, industry, and transportation.

By the 1860s, as the expanding economies of the Western world – themselves powered by steam – were producing more raw materials and manufactured goods, iron and steel (now produced more cheaply and efficiently) were applied to ship construction. As these economies (including the nascent modern Canadian economy) expanded their trade, the ships appearing on the Great Lakes were not only bigger but also more numerous.

The first Canadian steam-powered ship had been launched at Montreal in 1809 and others followed, notably the OTTAWA, built at Hawkesbury, Ontario. Driven first by rear- or side-wheels ("pollywogs"), later by propellers (or screws), these ships strained the capacity of the canal's locks and channel, many of the new vessels being simply too large to get through at all. As early as 1825 – before the First Welland was finished – "A Friend to Internal Development" made "Suggestions on the Enlargement of the Welland Canal for Steamboat Navigation," urging a width of 32 feet (9.75 m) for the locks.[44] The interests of the military also made it desirable that locks – whether on the Rideau, Welland or Grenville canals – should be of sufficient size to accommodate steamboats.[45]

At first, the Welland itself provided a stimulus to the development of steam-propelled shipping for, after its opening in 1829, the number of steamboats on Lakes Erie and Ontario increased noticeably. Not until 1843, however, did a steam-powered vessel pass through the entire length of the Welland — the ADVENTURE, built at Niagara, sailing from Quebec to Chicago in September of that year. These larger and faster ships entered and exited the locks literally "under their own steam," not needing to be towed by horses. But, especially when they were fitted with propellers, their greater speed risked damage even to the larger lock gates and walls of the Second Canal. Steam, of course, could be also a great aid to construction and maintenance of the waterway, but it offered a mixed blessing (chapter 4).

Before the depression of the 1870s set in, the size and the numbers of ships grew to the extent that in 1872, a mere decade after the reconstruction then planned, one optimist declared that Great Lakes trade would "demand a double tier of enlarged locks [on the Welland]."[46] Although rebuilt in the 1840s and again in the 1870s and '80s, Niagara's nineteenth-century waterway never completely met the challenge of growing ship size.

Later technological advances affecting the work of the engineers and the operation of the Welland were greeted in turn with varying degrees of enthusiasm – as was the steam engine earlier. The telegraph, first available in Canada West in 1846, was urged on the Department by Samuel Keefer the following year because "there will be many occasions when instantencory [sic] communications to all or part of the line will be of very great advantage."[47] As with most technological developments, early attempts can be unreliable: in 1848 the telegraph was described as "not only expensive, but defective generally."[48] The canal telegraph line was eventually constructed in 1852.

Although the canal had been illuminated with gas since 1853, by 1904 the Minister of Railways and Canals noted "that the shipping interests almost unanimously demanded the electric light."[49] At least some of the contractors were also aware of the advantages of electricity. F.B. McNamee and Co., for example, certainly kept up-to-date on current developments. In 1880 McNamee asked the Department of Railways and Canals to obtain a "machine" from the Montreal Harbor Board so that he could use electric light to finish his contract.[50] This modernization had been strongly opposed in 1882 by then superintendent, William Ellis, who directed a lengthy memo to the Department voicing six strong objections: "The machines are complicated & delicate in construction ... The light is unsteady ...The greatest danger is, the liability to sudden extinguishment ... constant repairs are needed ... At each station wheels, gears, belts &c will have to be kept up and flumes and tail races made & kept in repair ... Electricity is yet but an experiment, and this Canal is too dangerous a place to try it [Ellis's emphasis]."[51]

Either having his own suspicions or heeding Ellis's warning, Chief Engineer Page recommended renewing the contract with the St Catharines and Welland Canal Gas Light Company rather than accepting any of the tenders for electric lighting. And so, as with the Second Canal, gas lighting was installed along the Third – and electricity was not used to light the Welland until the early 1900s. By at least 1915, the canal was illuminated along its entire length by electric lights placed two hundred feet apart.[52]

Other inventions were less spectacular but nonetheless effective. Beginning in 1883 Superintendent Ellis was suggesting that telephone service should be installed along the main line of the Canal, but nothing was done. When Thomas Monro, engineer in charge of construction of the Third Canal's northern section, acted unilaterally and had a telephone installed in his office in April 1886, he was gently reprimanded by the Department.[53] By the fall of that year, however, a private telephone line had been installed between the aqueduct and Thorold, for the purposes of water regulation. Monro's action was typical of the attitude of some engineers who, valuing efficiency and appreciating innovation, grew impatient as the increasing complexities of government bureaucracy tended to cause lengthy delays.

The arrival of dynamite also proved useful for contractors. The deepening of the channel and lock pits meant that, in addition to heavy clay, more of Niagara's limestone would be encountered. Gunpowder had been used to blast away the rock of the Escarpment and elsewhere until Alfred Nobel's invention of dynamite in 1866. At least by November 1875 contractors were using the new blasting compound. Some, however, remained skeptical. The experienced John Brown, for example, preferred gunpowder but also used "Dualine," a form of dynamite that was "so violent in its action that it literally shatters the rock to pieces." He would therefore not employ it if he wanted to use the stone for construction purposes.[54]

Bureaucracy

In responding to increasing demands for professionalism, the builders of the Second Canal had to keep a much closer eye on "paperwork" than previously. The Board of Works wanted its employees to achieve higher standards of accuracy – particularly in drawing up contracts. In 1844, having received copies of contracts from the Welland's secretary, the Board of Works responded, expressing its "extreme displeasure ... at the disgraceful manner in which these documents have been drawn up, as but two, out of the nine contracts sent in are correct."[55] The scolding continued: "No apology whatever will be received for the like inattention in future, as the inaccuracy in completing contracts for the Welland Canal, and the great delay in forwarding them, totally disarranges the system of this Office. If the least trouble were taken in reading over the contracts and completing them all this unpleasant correspondence would be avoided."

At the same time, the board enjoined engineer Power to use "much caution and attention to legal forms" in the drawing up of contracts.[56] Following the reorganization of the Board of Works in 1846, a growth in sophisticated record-keeping and a new concern for efficiency developed. Such methods were time-consuming and led to irritation with the growing bureaucratization of operations "on the ground." In 1849 Killaly, now the Welland's engineer, complained: "Any unnecessary delay in the making of payments creates many embarrassments in the practical management of the works and lays the ground for claims or damages referable to arbitration by the Contractors."[57]

Interrupt the Navigation as Little as Possible

A major new demand was imposed on engineers and contractors when the First Canal required rebuilding: the need to keep the existing Canal in operation during construction of its successor. The authorities were well aware of the problem and, when engineers Baird and Killaly were hired in 1838 to report to the board on possible new routes for the first enlargement, they were instructed to "interrupt the navigation as little as possible."[58] Excavation of a new prism could not take place in too close proximity to the existing canal for fear that the earth between the old channel and the new would give way, flooding the new prism and perhaps also the surrounding countryside. Even where the channel was simply to be enlarged, relatively uncomplicated dredging operations could delay both surface and ship traffic.

The chief imperative on the canal was that navigation, or "the Trade," experience the minimum of delay. Hence, from the 1840s onward, the wording of contracts emphasized the precedence of navigation over construction, with a special clause defining the contractor's responsibility. Typical was an 1842 agreement in which the contractor promised "to make all such arrangements as may seem necessary to the Board of Works or their Engineer to avoid interference with the Navigation."[59] A contract of 1877 with Hunter, Murray and Cleveland was even more explicit: "It is ... to be distinctly understood that if the material [to be excavated] is required to be placed on the east side of the Canal, the arrangements for the disposing of it must be such as not, in any way or shape, to interfere with the free and uninterrupted towage of vessels ... The work throughout must be carried on in such a manner, that the present towing-path shall not be in any way interrupted, or any part of it interfered with during the season of navigation."[60]

Conversely, contractors occasionally found that traffic on the canal could endanger their equipment. In 1887, several contractors complained to the Department of Railways and Canals about the lack of protection for their dredges from vessels passing through the canal.

The Feeder Canal, although less than ideal for major traffic, was used during the 1840s reconstruction as the main line. In April 1880, when the opening of the principal route was delayed, seventy-five propellers and schooners moved through the Feeder to Lake Erie.[61]

While engineers figure prominently in studies of public works, the contractors responsible for the work "on the ground" are often more or less taken for granted. However, without their efforts, construction could not be accomplished. With their sense of the material and financial technicalities of the project, they had to wrestle with myriad details. What follows, therefore, is a description of some of the conditions – legal, professional, and bureaucratic – under which they worked.

CONTRACTORS AND CONTRACTING

As with many aspects of the history of the nineteenth-century Welland Canals, contracting practices changed considerably over time. Not surprisingly, the surviving records concerning tenders and the awarding of contracts are not uniform for the three canals, but they do offer important insights. American influence was strong in the early years, but soon gave way to the exigencies of local conditions. Over time, Canadian-based contractors grew in expertise and the Canadian public began to express concern when non-Canadians were awarded contracts. The evolution of this change is part of our unfolding chronicle.

The Welland's contractors may occasionally have been more subject to human frailty than were the engineers, but on the whole the canal was well served by its many contractors, whether they came from Niagara or farther afield. Some of them could best be described as "colourful characters." A few, alas, must be labelled simply as crooks. The great majority, of course, were ethically upright, skilled, and industrious professionals.

The Contract

Contractors typically made legal agreements to fulfil a certain task for a certain sum, according to specifications laid down by engineers, and usually within an agreed time. They were responsible for hiring, supervising, and paying labour crews, and for supplying the equipment necessary for the excavation and dredging required. Specialization became more common over time, as some contractors developed expertise in dry excavation, dredging, harbour work, and the construction of bridges, locks, or lock gates, while others made themselves responsible for supplying materials: metal parts for bridges and lock gates, lumber, stone or gravel, motors, and – increasingly during the twentieth century – electrical equipment.

Even in the 1820s the terms and practices of the legal contract were well defined. Specifications for a job or jobs were drawn up by the engineer(s), and advertisements placed in newspapers calling for detailed tenders to be submitted by a certain date. At the designated time the tenders were opened and examined, and a choice was made, usually (but not necessarily) for the lowest bid. A contract would then be offered, on condition that the individual or firm could provide sureties to guarantee performance of the work. The sureties were usually two in number, men known to the applicant and the authorities as reputable, and who were willing to put up designated sums (usually in cash or bonds or, sometimes, property), which would be forfeit on failure to fulfill the contract. Contracts also provided for a "drawback" (withholding of a fixed percentage of the estimated value of the work) of usually 10 to 15 per cent. Such a reserve might be drawn upon by the contractor if unusual expenses occurred, but would then be subtracted from a future payment.

The process of tendering for and awarding contracts, on the Welland as elsewhere, was often subject to debate, controversy, even litigation. After the work was underway contractors might find themselves unable to complete the work as specified and be forced to give it up: some went bankrupt, others failed to pay their workers, refused to follow engineer's orders, ran off with equipment, or simply absconded! The number of such "derelictions" tended to decrease over the nineteenth century, as contractors on civil engineering works became more proficient in building canals, railways, highways, municipal water works, and harbour improvements. But it was not unusual for contractors to be chastised for disregarding orders or for committing various derelictions of responsibility.

Contracting on the First Canal: American Predominance

We have already noted three examples of American influence on the First Canal: the choice of a route somewhat removed from the border in case of further military incursion, the considerable funding acquired from New York, and the participation of a number of American engineers. Equally important was Merritt's assurance that, because many of the Erie contractors were out of work, they would "have all their tools on hand and [be] prepared to commence immediately."[62] These men brought with them, not only their tools, but also their method of laying out the sections of work. In his study of American canals, Shaw noted: "Contracts [on the Erie] were let locally, usually for a mile or more to contractors who hired their own labour. More than fifty contractors worked on the first fifty-eight miles."[63] Very few contractors were responsible for more than two sections, and most of the multiple-section contracts were awarded in the 1825 season, when the push was on to complete the work.

Because Merritt had visited the Erie on a number of occasions, and had met with DeWitt Clinton at least once and with various contractors several times, and because the early engineers also came from the Erie, it followed that the work on the Welland would be laid out in a similar fashion – in fairly short sections. The original line, from the Welland River to Lake Ontario, a distance of about 16 miles (9.9 km), was divided into thirty-five sections. While we do not know the precise length of them all, No. 1 was a mere 121 yards (132.3 m); No. 3 was 400 yards (437.4 m, at either end of the tunnel); while the tunnel itself was to be 2 miles (1.24 km) long.

The original line was let out in two instalments: on 20 November 1824 Merritt noted in his journal that twenty proposals had been received "on the line above New Holland [the Allanburg area]," and that on 15 November he "drew out the contracts with Hovey and Kennedy and Co."[64] The following day he wrote in some detail to the Committee of Trade in Quebec: Section 1, consisting of 121 yards from the Welland River to the tunnel mouth was awarded to Horn Kennedy; Section 2, the two-mile tunnel, was taken by Alfred Hovey of Montezuma; Section 3, the 440 yards "at the other end of the tunnel also went to Horn, Kennedy;" and Section 4, "the remainder of open excavation to Lock No. One" was taken by James Simpson.[65] Merritt noted that these men had worked on the Erie, a fact confirmed by the records of payment by the canal commissioners, although in the Welland Canal Company Minutes for 15 November, the firm of Horn, Kennedy is referred to as being based in Queenston (the firm had worked on the Brock monument there) and Simpson as resident in Niagara.[66] In a letter to his wife, Merritt noted that the proposals had been submitted "by at least 50 men who had joined in Companies"[67] – unfortunately, we have no idea who the others may have been! However, we do know that, following the failure of Walter Clendenning of St Catharines to provide adequate security, Theophilus Brundage, who lived in Grantham Township where St Catharines was located, was awarded the contract for timber for the tunnel on 18 December.

By April 1825 the plan for the tunnel had been abandoned, and fifty-five proposals for Sections 1–6 (which included what was to be known as the "Deep Cut") were received on 2 July, submitted by over sixty men divided among twenty-two companies, as well as another five submissions by a single name followed by "& Co." We can identify at least seven of these firms as having worked on the Erie and, while the lowest tender, which was accepted, was from a local group (headed by Erasmus Chapman and including Brundage), they failed to provide the stipulated security of £12,000 and on 7 July the contract was awarded to the American firm of Hovey, Beach and Ward, while another American firm, Fenelon and Smith, was to construct the harbour.[68]

On 26 October, Sections 9–35 were let, and once again a number of sections were awarded to experienced American firms: Bell, Richardson & Co. were given Sections 11, 12, 15, 16, 20, 24, and 25; Joseph Beckwith Section 23; Hovey & Co. Section 35; Withy & Co., who got Sections 14, 17, 18, 19, 21, and 22 were probably also American. Others, such as Hall Davis of Thorold (Sections 9 and 10) and William Simpson of Wainfleet (Section 13) were local men, as were John Ten Broeck of Port Dalhousie (Section 13) and probably Porter & Donaldson (Section 33). William Perrine & Co. (Sections 26–32) may have come up from the Erie. The locks were awarded as a separate contract (as had been the harbour) to Beach, Hovey, Ward, and Phelps[69] – Americans all.

The records of payment tell an interesting story of over-confidence and inexperience in construction of such projects: no payments were recorded to Simpson, Beckwith, Withy & Co., or to Perrine & Co., and on 3 February 1826 these contracts were re-let. Simpson's and Withey's went to John Gooding & Co., and Perrine's to Pease & Co. The harbour contract was taken from Fenelon and given to Smith Ward and Hovey. Sections 7 and 8 do not appear to have been let until April, when 7 went to Kennedy & Co., and 8 to James Simpson. By now the lock contract was the sole preserve of the American Oliver Phelps (fig. 3.1).[70] Pease & Co. appear to have had troubles: Sections 31 and 32 were transferred to Orin Straight by 10 June (but 31 went to Davis & Simpson, and 32 to Bigelow & Jones by 17 July); and on 6 October 1826 Sections 26 and 27 were given to James Simpson, and 28 to Thomas Hannan, while 29 and 30 went to J. Hoag & Co.[71]

With the exceptions noted, the contracts on the main line remained as awarded until 13 April 1827, at which time Hovey & Ward relinquished their contract for Sections 1–6, and their sub-contractors agreed to carry on the sections they had been working on: that is, John Hartwell (1, 2, 3), Jarah & Andrew Rowley (4), and S.R. Hatheway and Love Newlove (5). Hovey & Ward retained Section 6.[72] All these sub-contractors were American, by the way, but on 24 August Hartwell sub-let the lock-pits on Sections 1 and 2 to G.W. Harris of Thorold.[73] These arrangements, like earlier ones, did not remain in place for long: on 26 May, Phelps took over the whole Deep Cut.

As we have noted, engineers went from job to job, often working on more than one at the same time. Contractors, too, followed the work, not only from the Erie to the Welland, but also, as the cases of James Clowes and Walter Fenelon show, to the Rideau as well. James Simpson may also have done some work on the Rideau. Apparently two contractors from the Welland were interested in the construction tactics of Colonel By on the Rideau, especially at the dam at Hog's Back, which they visited around 1826.[74]

Despite their practical knowledge, many contractors were illiterate, or semi-literate at best. For example, when questioned by Mackenzie in the process of the 1836 inquiry, William Orderly confessed, "I can neither read nor write."[75] Such men, like most common labourers of the time, simply made an "X" when signing documents. Others, if not actually inexperienced, seem to have been over-confident. Still others may have been confused by the haphazard way in which the directors managed the enterprise. Whatever their experience in the United States, working and building conditions on the Niagara peninsula were not identical to those elsewhere and that difference could also have played a role in the First Welland's faulty lock construction.

While we found undoubted similarities between awarding of contracts on the Erie and Welland, significant differences appear. One has already been noticed – the small number of local firms involved, no doubt due to the lack of experienced contractors available. Moreover, on the Welland a number of firms were awarded multiple sections. More important (and perhaps a function of sheer distance) was the fact that, while on the Erie separate contracts were let for various structures such as culverts, bridges, locks, aqueducts, bridges, and towpaths, for jobs such as building and removing fences, sinking shafts, weirs, and dams, as well as for the provision of timber, stone, lime – even labour – on individual sections, very few such separate contracts were awarded on the Welland: timber for the tunnel, the harbour, bridges, and locks were the exceptions. While timber was readily available in the area, metal casting for the lock gates had to be obtained elsewhere, from the firm of J. McIntosh & Sons of Montreal, for example.

Decreasing American Presence

The foregoing description pertains only to the main line. The route of the Western Section from the Welland River to the Grand River, although projected by Merritt as early as 1823, had, as we have seen, entailed considerable debate, and only in late 1827 was a contract

Table 1 Feeder Canal: Contracts let by 9 February 1829

Section(s)	*Contractor(s)*
1–5	Lemen, Ayres & Co.
6–14	T. Merritt (a cousin of W.H. Merritt)
15–21	Peter Keefer & Co.
22, 23	T. McMahon
24, 25	McGill & Co.
26, 27	J. Berger
28, 29	Scott & Galbraith
30–34	Trotter & Co.

signed. The firm of Horatio Nelson Monson, James Simpson & Co., began work almost immediately, from a point on the Welland River to Broad Creek. This line was still being excavated when the disastrous land slips occurred in the Deep Cut in late 1828, making it impossible to feed the canal from the Welland River. Instead, the Grand River would be used as the source of water, and a separate feeder constructed. On 1 January 1829 the board resolved that the Feeder would be "conducted to the bank of the Welland, at or near Helm's Creek" and issued instructions to "construct an aqueduct over the Welland at that point, and dig a Feeder from thence on the North side of the Welland to the Deep Cut."[76] A dam, lock, and embankment at the Grand River would be required, as well as excavation at the mouth of the Welland River. Apparently the Western Section was not considered suitable after all, since it did not connect directly with the main canal, and ended at Broad Creek. Also, there may have been a problem with its depth, since damming the Grand would have raised the water level of the Feeder. We found no reference to this question in contemporary records.

At any rate, the new Feeder Canal was divided into thirty-four sections, and a call went out for tenders to be submitted by 19 January 1829. By 9 February the contracts had been let. The brush dam (to cost £2,625), was let to an American, Judge Wilkeson (Wilkinson); the lockpit, embankment and puddling to Wilkinson, Simpson, and to H.N. Monson & Pratt; the mouth of the Grand River to Robert Campbell & George Rowe; the aqueduct to Phelps, Brundage & Lewis. While the practice of awarding multiple sections continued, as can be seen from table 1,[77] very few of the firms can be identified as American.

As we have seen, the Royal Navy had objected to locating the dam at the mouth of the Grand River, so on 8 May 1829 the Welland Canal

Company directors accepted a proposal from Wilkinson & Co., to build a dam at the new location for $12,500, on condition that Wilkinson personally supervise the work and have it completed by mid-July.[78] (Wilkinson's "roguery" in this connection will be discussed in chapter 6).

When it was decided to "complete" the Welland with a direct link from the main line to Lake Erie, a distance of about 12 miles (7.45 km), divided into nineteen sections, the new preponderance of Canadian over American contractors was confirmed.[79] A new pier at the Grand River and the harbour at Gravelly Bay went to Lewis, Garrison & Little (a merchant of Seneca, on the Grand River), who also got Sections 15, 16 and 19; Sections 1 and 2 went to Buchanan, Ewen & Armstrong; Section 3 to W.M. Doty; 4 to M. & S. Sixsmith, Bradley & Saunders; 5 to Moore and Walker; 6 to Craig & Boyle; 7, 8, 9, 17, 18 to H.N. Monson; 10 and 11 to Love Newlove; 12 and 14 to G. Hexson (Hixon); 12 to F. Galbraith.[80] Lewis and Newlove, who had come from the Erie, had by now settled in the area, as had Oliver Phelps.

Another development was that, unlike the situation requiring frequent re-assignment of contracts on the original main line, much greater stability now prevailed. Many of the first contractors had run into financial trouble, perhaps on account of excessive confidence based on the success of their contracts south of the border, as well as unfamiliarity with the different terrain in the Niagara Peninsula. For their part, the directors of the Welland Canal Company had lacked experience, and were chronically short of funds. This combination of over-optimism and inexperience took its toll, but some lessons were learned, and both the Feeder and the Lake Erie extension were accomplished with far fewer troubles than had occurred on the main line. That is not to say that there were no problems at all. Growing confidence could also lead to superficial methods and lack of attention. William Hamilton Merritt's cousin, Thomas Merritt Jr, for instance, was taken to task by engineer Barrett in 1829 for leaving "several very bad bars" in his section of the canal. "I must set a company to go through each job and remove every bar," the irate engineer scolded.[81]

During the 1830s numerous contracts were awarded, such as the deepening of the Feeder, additional work on the pier and harbour at Gravelly Bay, repair and rebuilding of various locks, culverts, new bridges, waste weirs, lock gates and guard gates, raising of embankments and towpaths. We have gone into considerable detail regarding these contracts on the First Canal, and those who received them, in order to make clear the changes that would occur as the century moved forward.

Table 2 Second Welland Canal: Early Contracts

Contractor	*Contracted for*
Thomas Merritt	a culvert at Cranberry Creek
John Betty and George Stewart	excavate passing places at Ramey's Bend and at Hardison's
John Toyne	a passing place at Thomas Merritt's
Henry Doushon and T. Merritt	widen the canal from Stonebridge to the Guard Lock (re-let to Merritt alone on 8 February 1841)
Archy Craig	deliver 25,000 cu. ft. of square timber
James Little	deliver 100,000 cu. ft. of square pine

Contracting on the Second Canal: Growing Local Expertise

By the time the directors ordered a start to reconstruction of the decaying wooden locks in stone, the pattern for contracting on the Welland was well established. On 3 January 1839 the company ordered H.H. Killaly to "lay out the work from Lock 37 to 7 in such sections as would be adapted for letting." In view of the impending government buy-out of the private shareholders, nothing major could be undertaken, but on 23 June 1840 the company sent out notices calling for specifications for the new locks, and on 6 July these were received for the excavation of 18 locks and ponds for Locks 31 to 7, the "Mountain Locks." On 18 July the company engineer, J.S. Macaulay, referred to estimates submitted the previous April by Killaly for enlarging passing places and for widening and deepening the Feeder, and the estimates for August include certain expenses attributed to "New Works" for the first time.[82] Such entries become a regular feature, and include expenses for engineers employed on the work.

On 8 August 1840 the company decided that all proposals for rebuilding the locks, as well as for supplying stone, were too high. Nevertheless, they ordered that quarries should be opened to provide stone. In October new offers were called for, and on 1 December some contracts were approved. Most of the contractors were now Canadian, not American (table 2).

When these contracts were approved on 11 December, the company secretary asked which should be entered under "New Works" and which under "Old." The directors decided that only the stone excavation and the timber should be considered "new."[83] In a querulous tirade to the provincial secretary, S.B. Harrison, on 11 January 1841,

Engineer Macaulay strenuously objected. Having just learned the board's decision (via a letter from his assistant, James Lyons), he shot back: "The culvert proposed to be built is clearly a 'new work' and ought not therefore to be undertaken without consulting the Engineer." He went on to question plans for the culvert on several grounds: that an "irresponsible person at Dunnville" was to select the site; that the dimensions should be other than those chosen; that the contractor had not been required to place the excavated earth where "it would be advisable"; and finally: "The means of bringing the water to the site selected ... and taking it from the same are treated of as extraneous matters hereafter to be provided for."[84]

Unfortunately, contention over the Cranberry Creek contract continued to escalate. Assistant Engineer Lyons complained to Macaulay on a number of occasions in the next few weeks, as Thomas Merritt proved increasingly obstreperous: he "persisted in heaping promiscuously on the Banks, both Rock, and Earth" and was "extremely self-willed and obstinate." Two weeks later Lyons reported that Merritt & Co. intended to have their own way and would not stack stone as ordered for any compensation, and that they had abandoned the feeder culvert. After Merritt took over sole responsibility for the contracts on 9 February, Lyons continued to complain. As of 2 March Merritt had threatened to block up the canal entirely, and Lyons did not doubt that he might do just that! In fact, on 27 March Macaulay told Lyons that he had written to the board detailing some of Merritt's misdeeds, including the fact that his men had filled in a back ditch and flooded the Stone Bridge distillery.[85] That appears to have been the last straw, and the contract was terminated.

These preliminary "New Works" were soon to assume a more structured form when they were taken over by a Provincial Board of Works established on 17 August 1841. Killaly, as the chairman, presented a memorandum to the governor general on 12 August, "Respecting Various Public Works," which stated: "Of the Works which are indispensably and immediately necessary to the advancement of the general interest of the Country at large, the Welland Canal unquestionably stands foremost." On 18 August the Legislature allocated £450,000 to complete the Welland Canal *"in a permanent and fully sufficient manner*, with cut stone locks."[86] Killaly, who was to oversee the rebuilding of the Welland, was also instrumental in organizing the Board of Works. In so doing he set policies that would shape a nascent Canadian civil service, including many related to contracts: the forfeiture of drawback on failure of a contract; a ban on government interference between contractor and labourers; and labourers' responsibility for damage on

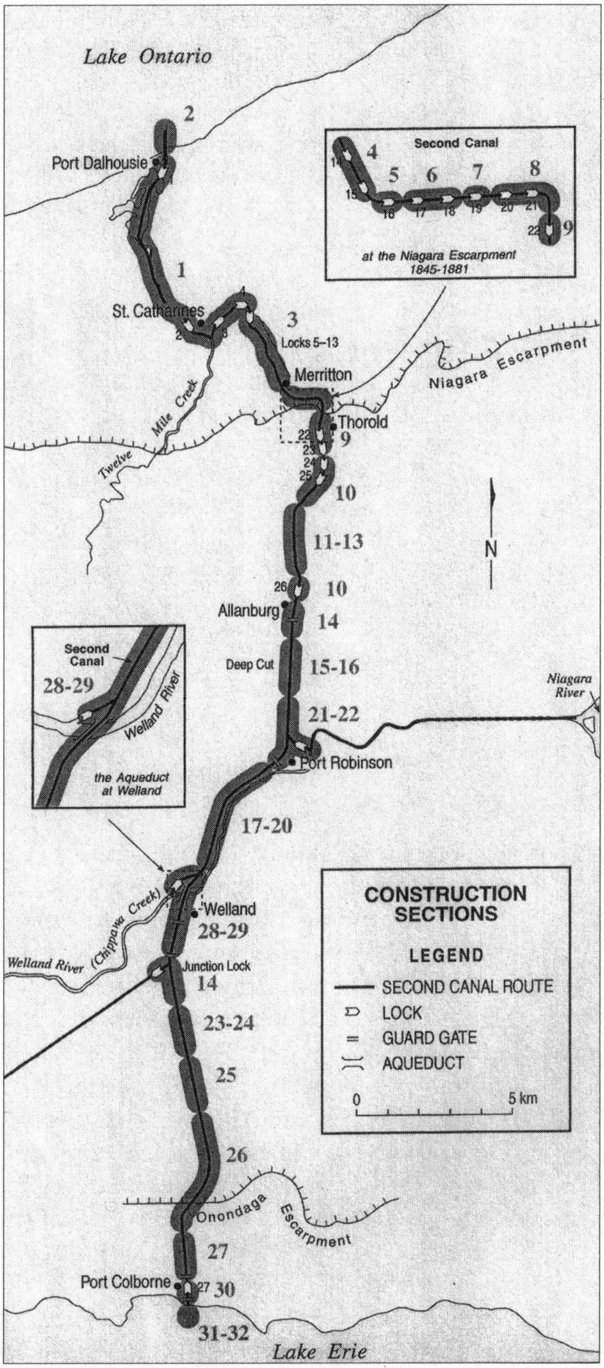

3.2 Construction sections for the Second Welland Canal (Loris Gasparotto, Department of Geography, Brock University)

Table 3 Second Welland Canal: First Major Contracts

Section(s)	*Contractor(s)*
1–7	Sherwood & Tench
8–21	Cotton (elsewhere, Collier and Haight)
22–42	Lovejoy & Case of Hamilton

Source: LAC, RG 43, vol. 2439

Table 4a Second Welland Canal: Contracts re-assigned in December 1842

Section(s)	*Contractor(s)*
10	Samuel Buchanan
11	W. Maloney
13	A. & J. Maloney
14–16	John Russell
17	F. Foley
18	John Coyle
19–21	John Cameron
12	Thomas McMahon

Source: LAC, RG 43, vol. 2539

construction sites.[87] The form of the contracts and the methods of payment were also to be more tightly controlled.

Shortly after the institution of the new regime, contractors were notified (14 October) to submit tenders for widening and deepening the Feeder, and a total of thirty-one tenders were received, for forty-two sections (fig. 3.2). The first contracts were awarded on 2 November as indicated in table 3.[88]

Ditching on some sections of the Feeder was separately contracted in May 1842: Stephen and Andrew Boyle (recent immigrants from Ireland), Sections 8–13; James Harper, Section 4. On 12 September 1841 Haight and Collier were contracted to do all work on a Guard Lock at Dunnville. However, by late 1842 it was clear that at least two firms were over-extended, so in December 1842 a number of alternative awards were made (table 4a).

Then, in January 1843 yet another major re-assignment took place; this time, twenty-four sections were implicated (table 4b). Perhaps we can assume that these new players, Sharp & Larkin, William Benson,

Table 4b *Second Welland Canal: Further re-assignments, January 1843*

Section(s)	*Contractor(s)*
8, 9	Sharp & Larkin
12	William Benson
22–42	Van Norman

Source: LAC, RG 43, vol. 2539

Table 5 *Second Welland Canal: Contracts awarded on the main line, April 1843*

Section(s)	*Lock(s)*	*Contractor(s)*
3 & 4	10–15	E.W. Thompson & Co.
5	16	Andrew Boyle & Co.
6	17, 18	Samuel Zimmerman
7	19	Boyce & Cartwright
8	20, 21	S. McCullough & Co.
9	22, 23	Oswald, Wynn & Kingman
10	24–26	Daniel Sharpe & George Quinn
1 & 2	4–7, 8 and 9	George Barnet of St Catharines and Milton Courtwright & Co. respectively

Source: LAC, RG 43, vol. 2539

and Van Norman, had been among the earlier tenderers. To the best of our knowledge, they were mainly local men.

When it came to rebuilding the main line, a new policy was followed: the harbours were awarded separately but most of the locks were included in the twenty-nine sections (fig. 3.2). In November 1842 a total of eighty-seven tenders were received for Sections 3–10, including locks 10–23. Between then and the awarding of contracts in April 1843, two of the firms (Vanderbugh & Kerr for Section 4, and Cummings & Co. for Section 6) had been replaced (table 5).[89]

The number of tenders submitted later in the year for excavation of earthwork is unknown, but table 6 shows successful applicants. As had been common on the Erie, a number of separate contracts were awarded in 1844 for specific jobs (table 7).

Contracts were also let for a number of waste weirs, back ditches, and culverts, as well as excavation at a number of points. Various firms

Table 6 Second Welland Canal: Contracts awarded in later 1843

Section(s)	*Contractor(s)*
11	O'Neill & Co.
12	Larkin & Sharpe (later McKenney & Williams)
13	Cook & Co (later McKenney & Williams)
19, 21 & 22	Cook & Co.
15 & 16	Carmichael & Co.
17	Sharpe & Haughey [no security] (later Cook & Stuart)
19 & 20	Moore & Cromwell (of St Catharines)
23–26 & 29	Higham, Farrell & Hayes
27	Wood, Barker & Clark (later John Brown)
28	McManus [declined] (later Sherwood & Buell)

Source: LAC, RG 43, vol. 2539

Table 7 Second Welland Canal: Contracts awarded in 1844

Contract	*Contractor(s)*
Excavation and lock masonry, Lock 1	Sherwood & Buell
Excavation and masonry, Allanburgh and junction locks	Wm. Buell, Jr
Dredging of the harbour at Port Dalhousie	S. Smiley (Port Dalhousie)
Section 30, including the Guard Lock at Port Colborne	C.J. McDonagh
Section 28, including aqueduct	Zimmerman & McCullough
Gates for locks 1, 27, 29 & for 26 smaller locks	J.L. Wilkinson
Bent bridges	Osterhaus & Mead
Swing bridges	Moses Cook
Piers at Ports Colborne, Dalhousie & Maitland	James Russell

Source: LAC, RG 43, vol. 2539

were asked to supply materials, usually for a specific location, and Louis Shikluna, a Maltese shipbuilder based in St Catharines, was to build a drydock at new Lock 3. In 1845 further work was done on the Feeder, as well as more dredging at the mouth of the Grand River and the harbours at the ports. Locktenders' houses were constructed, the one at Broad Creek to double as a toll collector's office.

The following year, Cotton & Rowe were given the task of erecting lighthouses at all three ports, and C.H. French began excavation on the Deep Cut, in the first attempt to achieve the supply of water from Lake Erie instead of the Grand River. In addition to the many minor jobs undertaken, contracts were let for a new line between St Catharines and Port Dalhousie, with Stephen and Andrew Boyle prominent among the firms employed. Considerable work was undertaken to bring the line to Port Colborne into full use, and this was accomplished in 1850.

The attempt to achieve the Lake Erie level was to continue for many a year, with John Brown of Thorold becoming the main contractor for the purpose in the 1850s. Success in reaching that level did not occur until the summer of 1881, as part of the work on the Third Canal. Not that there was any hiatus in the awarding of contracts for repairing or improving the canal, or delivering all manner of supplies. New bridges and culverts were needed, embankments raised, new lock gates built, balance beams replaced and – in 1851 (and a sign of technological progress) – "crabs" (winches) to operate the gates ordered (from Andrew Heron). The number of contracts awarded annually reached a high of fifty in 1855, then decreased through the late 1850s and '60s.

As we have seen, the expectation of Confederation was responsible for a reluctance to proceed with any major work until the new government had a chance to assess the situation. One of that government's early actions was to establish a commission to study inland navigation, and its 1871 report provided an impetus for beginning the Third Canal (already much in demand). The first contract for that canal was let on 26 December 1871 to George N. Neilson & Co. of Belleville, to enlarge and deepen the harbour at Port Colborne (as Section 36 it was re-let on 17 July 1875 to C.F. Dunbar of Buffalo, New York).

We have only occasionally mentioned the origin of the Second Canal contractors, but the majority appear to have been located in the Niagara area. True, a few American firms were still involved, such as Carmichael & Co. of Brooklyn, and Higham & Veeder of Canandaigua, both in New York; and Samuel Zimmerman had emigrated from Pennsylvania in 1842. But the Collier, Vanderburgh, and Kerr families from St Catharines, the Larkins, Sharps, and Oswalds from Thorold, John Russell from Marshville, and the Thompsons from Dunnville typified the growing presence of local and regional involvement in canal construction. The two Third Canal contractors mentioned above exemplify the further evolution of the profession, as firms from other parts of the country tendered for public works contracts.

Contracting on the Third Canal: National Contracting Firms

Records give us far more information about the contracts for the Third Canal than is available for the earlier period (fig. 3.3). To begin with, an Order of the House of Commons of 13 March 1873 led to the publication of copies of all tenders (including those that were withdrawn, as well as the contractors' home bases and the names of their sureties, and all correspondence regarding such tenders), in the *Sessional Papers (No. 6) for 1873*.[90] There were ten tenders for Port Colborne and, with the lowest being withdrawn, the field was left to George Neilson of Belleville. The next lowest was from the firm of F.B. McNamee of Montreal who, on 9 February 1872, having submitted the lowest (of eight) tenders, was given the contract for similar work at Port Dalhousie.

The tender for excavation at the Deep Cut, submitted by Robert Mitchell & Co. of Bic, Quebec, was accepted on 23 January 1872. According to the contract, his residence was in Toronto, while his partner, James Cotton (a contractor on the Second Canal), was from Ottawa – a further example of firms based well beyond the Niagara area becoming involved in Welland public works projects. Here, Mitchell's bid was actually the fifth-lowest (of twenty, including those of Neilson, McNamee, and John Brown), but the others withdrew one by one. The third lowest, Michael Fitzgerald & Co. of St Fabien, Quebec, was told that his securities (John D. McCormick and John Hoban, both of St Fabien) were "not known to the Department" and would have to be replaced. Perhaps it was more than coincidence that Fitzgerald withdrew on the grounds that, having visited the Deep Cut, he was deterred: "Wages [are] so high it is impossible for me to carry it through."

The fourth of these early contracts for the Third Canal was for deepening and clearing out the Feeder. The eight entries (including those of McNamee and Brown), tendered sums ranging from $90,000 to $211,000. The third lowest, Henry W. Manning of Cookstown (also in partnership with James Cotton), was given the job on 11 October 1872 at $126,900, after Joseph Cairns & Co. of St Catharines declined, claiming that they had been unable to procure the necessary plant. George Harvey, of Walkerton, who put in the lowest offer, had been disallowed by the minister, on the grounds that he was already a contractor for extensive harbour work at Goderich, and was not felt to have sufficient means to handle both jobs.

Altogether, a total of forty-six offers for these four contracts were made by only twenty-five different individuals or firms, of which only John Brown (aside from Cotton) had been active on the Second Canal. The contractors' home bases were dotted all over southern Ontario.[91]

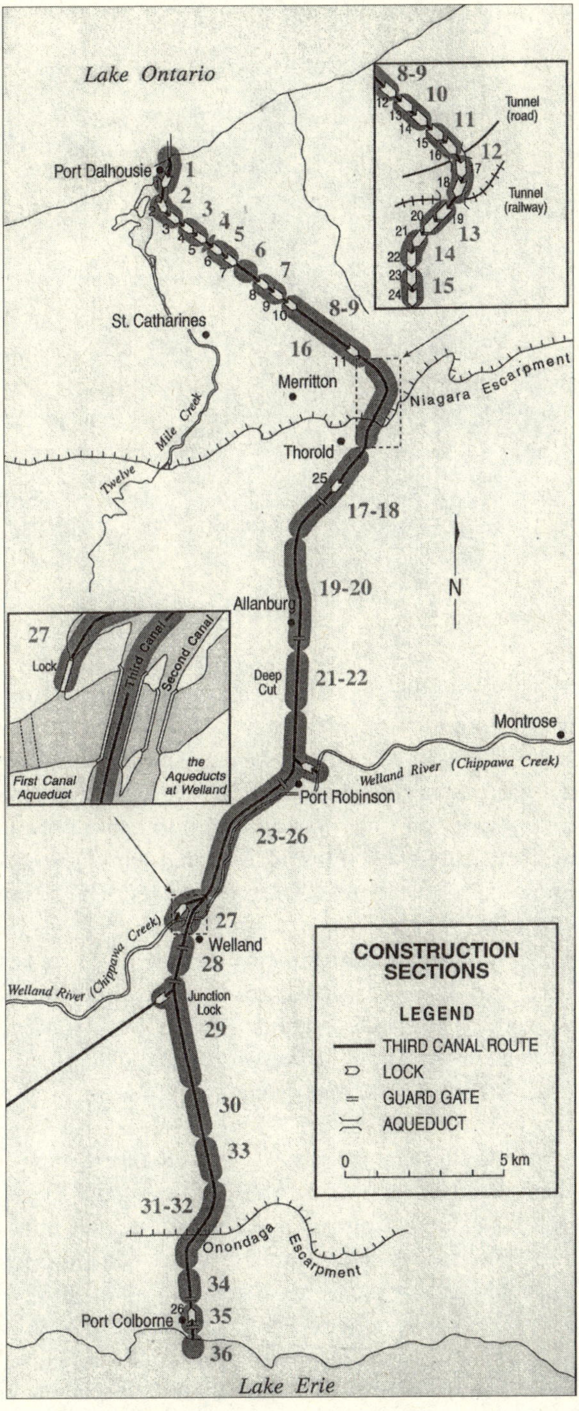

3.3 Construction sections for the Third Welland Canal (Loris Gasparotto, Department of Geography, Brock University)

3.4 John Brown (1809–1876) (H.R. Page, *Illustrated Historical Atlas*, 48)

There were only two American entries, both from Buffalo, and neither was accepted.

The next batch of contracts, for Sections 8–11, 15, 16, 21, 22, and 29–32 (out of 35), was awarded in the summer of 1873 (fig. 3.3). Unfortunately, no information was published regarding the tenders, and we have only the names of the firms – including some by-now familiar ones – and the dates of the contracts. The experienced John Brown was given Sections 15, 31, and 32 on 17 July. That same day Robert Mitchell got Section 29 (transferred to John Ferguson on 4 December); and John Ferguson got Section 30. The following day, Section 10 went to John Ginty, and Section 16 to John Elliott (transferred to Brown on 15 March 1874); on 21 July Cairns, Morse & Hart got Sections 8 and 9; Section 11 went to Paul Ross, and Sections 21 and 22 to Brown on 24 September.

Of all these men, Brown was extraordinary – probably the most active contractor during the period of the Third Canal construction (fig. 3.4). According to an obituary[92] he was born in Scotland in 1806, and apprenticed as a stonecutter in Glasgow. He emigrated to New York when he was twenty-three, but soon moved to Lockport, on the Erie Canal, where he received a contract to build the Niagara Flouring Mills. His next move was to Niagara Falls, New York, where he built several houses. In 1838 he moved to Canada and built the first railroad in "Western" Canada, between Niagara and Chippawa. He also got a contract to furnish stone for Fort Niagara and barracks in Toronto. In 1844 he began his long association with the Welland Canal when, in partnership with Alex McDonnell, he received a contract for Lock 2 of the Second Canal. The firm's last contract on the Welland was in 1850, but Brown himself had contracts from 1847 through 1874.

Another aspect of Brown's work came with contracts for six lighthouses on Georgian Bay and Lake Huron. He was obviously highly regarded by the Department of Public Works, for he also worked on a number of railways, including the Great Western, as well as the Suspension Bridge at Clifton, the St Catharines jail, several of the macadamized roads in the area, extensive improvements of the harbours in Montreal and Quebec, and deepening the harbours at Saginaw, Michigan, and Sault Ste Marie, as well as Kincardine, Goderich, and Rondeau. His canal works were not confined to the Welland, as he also built the Lake St Clair Canal. He was obviously the largest contractor on the Third Welland. (It was fitting that he met his death near Section 15 of that canal, having been thrown from his buggy.) The Thorold *Post* estimated that these contracts were worth about $2,000,000. Not bad for a boy who had had little formal education! Perhaps the highest tribute was that "he had in his employ men who had been with him for thirty and forty years steadily." His contracts were not re-assigned, but continued under the direction of his executors.

Before Brown died in 1876 another group of contracts, for Sections 2, 3, 5, 6, 7, and 12–14, had been awarded in the summer of 1874. Tenders had been received in October, but the Department was not happy with them, and Chief Engineer Page suggested that new ones be called for. George Neilson, James Cotton, John Elliott, and McNamee were familiar names on this list, but newcomers were Patrick Shannon, and the firms of Ferguson, Mitchell & Symmes and Helliwell & Hartwell. The second tenders were received in January 1874, but only the names of the six lowest offers (and the amounts) for the two submissions were published. Correspondence regarding the awards reveals little else, except that Denison & Belden, who were given Sections 2 and 3, were from Syracuse, New York, had been known to the state engineer surveyor for twenty years, and were each worth a million dollars.[93]

Denison & Belden also tendered for the other sections, their unsuccessful bid for Section 6 being the lowest in 1874. Helliwell & Hartwell were the lowest for Section 6 ($67,880) but, interestingly, the contract went to Patrick Shannon (of St Thomas) for $68,290. The firm of Buck, Flood, Cooper & Barnes were lowest for Sections 7 and 12 ($283,935 and $327,415) but – again without a given reason – the former went to Eli Higgins & Timothy Sullivan (fourth at $327,580) and the latter (not awarded until 27 July 1875, when new tenders were again called for) went to the lowest, Lobb, Dawson & Murray. No explanation has been found for skipping the first three bids, those by Helliwell & Hartwell, and Denison & Belden. Helliwell & Hartwell's lack of success may well have been due to their haggling over surety for Section 13, for which theirs was the lowest offer. The government wanted 5 per cent of the value in Dominion bonds; the firm offered $20,000 in real estate. They were asked for details, which seem to have been inadequate, and Hartwell apparently offered his claim to the contract to John Brown through a third party, but Brown refused.[94] The contract for Section 13 was finally awarded to Ginty & Dickey on 29 June, for $325,490. Their name does not appear in the list of tenders, which ranged from $313,160 to $338,590. They had, however, been sixth-lowest for Section 12. Section 5 went to Alex Manning & S.D. Merrick (of Toronto), whose bid had been fifth-lowest, at $352,000 (the low was from Denison & Belden, at $312,265). John Brown, who had tendered for only Section 14 on both occasions (fourth-lowest in October, second in January), won out over Thomas L. Helliwell and J.K. Hartwell (for $321,972).

When further sections were given out in 1875, Public Works correspondence reveals another aspect of the process – that the government could act speedily on occasion. On 17 June Page sent copies of the printed specifications and form of tender to the Department for advertisement; by the 26th submissions had been received from thirty firms, and telegrams were sent to them acknowledging receipt, stating that results would probably be announced "next week." On 5 July telegrams were sent to certain firms to come to Ottawa to discuss their tenders. (See table 8 for invited firms.)

The contract for Section 1 was the subject of considerable discussion, showing that, not only were American firms still interested in work on the Welland but also that they had local supporters. The government had accepted the tender from the Americans Denison & Belden, but on 4 August the St Catharines *Daily Times* broke the startling news that the Canal Investigation Committee of New York State had determined that repairs undertaken by these contractors, which should have cost no more than $20,000, had cost five times that amount. A week later the firm was advised by telegram: "You will please bear in mind that contract for Section 1 is not to be considered as closed before it is signed by the Minister and that you must not make any preparations for proceeding with the work before you are instructed to do so by the Department." The *Daily Times* then carried a series of

Table 8 Third Welland Canal: Contractors invited to tender in 1875

Section(s)	*Contractor(s)*
1	Denison & Belden
4	Campbell, Blake & Blake (of Chicago)
12	Lobb, Dawson & Murray
23 & 26	John Carroll
24, 36	C.F. Dunbar (of Erie, Pennslvania)
25	Ferguson, Mitchell & Symmes (of Toronto and Welland)

Note: Contracts were awarded later that month for Sections 4, 12, 24 and 36, and 35. Those for Sections 1 and 23 were not awarded until the fall, when Carroll got 23 only. (He got Section 26 on 18 August 1876.)

Source: LAC, RG 43, vol. 2539

editorials and articles concerning the matter, noting that the American firm had "faithfully carried out their contract on Sections 2 & 3, and we know no reason why the public treasury should be invaded to reward a political supporter" – and in addition, that the local firm of Larkin, Nihan & Co. had "strong claims on the party in power."[95] Apparently the charges against the Americans were substantiated, as an Order-in-Council of 3 September noted that the Commission had found "serious frauds," and that the second lowest tender (that of Larkin & Co.) should be accepted – as it was, on 16 October.

Not all local voices were as ecumenical with their support as the *Daily Times*. As more non-local, but Canadian firms competed for contracts on public works, opinion critical of American involvement was voiced. The emergent nationalism of Killaly's 1841 memorandum was fully fledged now. The aforementioned controversy aroused anti-American feeling, which, when publicized in the local press, prompted the American contractor Charles F. Dunbar to write to the Thorold *Post*. His letter, appearing on 3 September, pointed out that, while he was an American, his wife was a Canadian; furthermore, the Canadian Shanly brothers had contracts on the American Hoosac Tunnel, and John Brown had also had contracts from the American government. Large-scale construction sites were becoming big business on both sides of the Canada–United States border, attracting ambitious professionals wherever located.

The next major awarding of contracts, for which once again we have considerable information, came in 1877. The date for receiving tenders

Table 9 Third Welland Canal: Contracts awarded in September and October 1877

Section(s)	*Contractor(s)*
27, 35	Hunter & Co. (27 later to H.J. Beemer)
7, 18	Robert Campbell
28	Ferguson & Co.
19, 20	Haney, Haney & Parry of Dunnville
33 & 34	Ambrose Clark

Source: LAC, RG 43, vol. 2539

was originally set for early June, but protests that contracting firms had too short a time to respond led to an extension to 3 August. As a result bids came forward in unprecedented numbers – between fifteen and eighteen for each section offered. Eighteen offers came in for Sections 17 and 18, ranging from $477,079 (John Hunter, Captain James Murrary & Merritt Andrewes Cleveland, all of St Catharines) to $692,158 (Buckner & Buckner); sixteen for Sections 19 and 20, from $244,253 (also Hunter, Murray & Cleveland) to $423,903 (John D. McDonald); eighteen for Section 27 from $8,674 (Hunter & Co.) to $1,273,476 (Stanton & Balch); sixteen for Section 28, from $105,086 (Hunter & Co.) to $215,650 (Buckner & Buckner); seventeen for Section 33, from $276,238 (Clarke & Jones) to $523,841 (Buckner & Buckner); sixteen for Section 34, from $318,383 (Clarke & Jones) to $650,821 (Sutton, Rousseau & Rousseau); and fifteen for Section 35, from $446,251 (Hunter & Co. again!) to $728,112 (Ferguson, Mitchell & Symmes).

After due consideration the contracts were awarded in September and October (see table 9). Ambrose Clark's contract was granted only after acrimonious correspondence regarding sureties with his sometime partner, Ralph Jones.

Several American firms tendered, among whom were Clarke & Jones – the sureties named by Clarke on 12 September were from Buffalo. Clarke died, intestate, on 12 August 1878, and on 5 December 1879 Section 33 was transferred to Bannerman & Co., and 34 to McNamee on the 23rd. With the addition of the agreement with Thomas B. Townsend for construction of the lock gates on 17 July 1880, the main work on the Third Canal was now completely under contract.

The sections between Thorold and Port Dalhousie had all been awarded for a depth of 12 feet (3.65 m). On 30 April 1875 Page was instructed that henceforth all work should be done for a depth of 14 feet

Table 10 Third Welland Canal: Contracts awarded for the Deepening, March–May 1886

Section(s)	*Contractor(s)*
A	Cook & Shields (later Murray & Cleveland)
B, C	Smyth (sometimes Smith), Leonard & Mumford
D	McDonald & McFarlane
E	Smyth, Leonard & Mumford (later Carroll & Shields)
F, G, H, I	Charles Raynor & Co.
J	William Gibson & Co. of Beamsville
K-South	John Conlon of Thorold
K-North	R.H. Sutton of Toronto
L, K, N	J. Isbester & Reid, of Ottawa
O, P	McNamee
Q, R, S, T	C.F. and H.T. Dunbar of Buffalo

Source: LAC, RG 43, vol. 2539

(4.26 m). Deepening of the northern part of the canal was not undertaken until the spring of 1886 but once again many firms contended for the job. Among them were Fraser, Conlon, E.D. Smith, and H. Keefer of Thorold, who confidently trooped off to Ottawa, only to be told that contracts would not be let at that time, but that new tenders would be called for, to be submitted by 9 March. This time the sections were designated by letters A to T, and work was soon begun, with contracts being awarded between 20 March and 28 May (table 10).

An interesting aspect of at least some of the partnerships tendering for contracts is that while one or more members of a group might identify themselves as contractors, one other member was often a merchant, or at least someone with money and/or real estate to invest. An early example is the firm of Marshall Lewis, Louis W. Garrison and James Little, who had contracts for the piers at the Grand River, and for Sections 15, 16, and 19 on the Gravelly Bay line in the 1830s. Lewis was originally from Elbridge, New York, had worked on the Erie, and was variously described as a millwright and architect. He designed dams, waste weirs, and a lock model, and was awarded a contract for the bridges required on the First Canal. When the partnership was dissolved, he was retained by Little to superintend the completion of the Gravelly Bay lock. While Little described himself as a "contractor" at that time, he is elsewhere identified as a merchant of Seneca (on the Grand River). Lobb, Dawson & Murray (1870s) are another good example: Charles Lobb of St Catharines, was a contractor, as was George Dawson of "North East in the State of Pennsylvania," while Thomas Murray of Clifton was identified as Baggage Master of the Great Western Railway.[96]

Of course, contracts were awarded during these years for repairs and improvements on the Second Canal and for materials of all types for both the Second and Third canals. Many of these secondary contracts went to local, or at least area firms. This was especially true of the timber and lumber of different types and sizes, but at one point (in 1876) oak timber was ordered from P.G. Brown of Ingersoll. Thus, a positive infuence on the local economy continued, both through employment, and through the provision of goods and services. Businesses were also encouraged to develop products and accommodation of use to canal staff as well as passing sailors and travellers.

We make only occasional reference to sub-contractors, although scores of them must have been employed on the Welland Canals over the years. They make their way into the records only rarely, usually when trouble has occurred with the primary contractor. The government made its hands-off policy clear as early as 1842: "The Board [of Works] in no wise recognizes sub-contractors, therefore cannot interfere."[97] Despite their general anonymity, sub-contractors doubtless made an important contribution to the history of the canal.

The many engineers and contractors on the First Welland who had come from the United States were examples of the tendency of both professions to be peripatetic. The expertise of local firms also saw wider horizons. The Clowes family were also involved with the Rideau, and Walter Fenelon, who worked on the Welland's harbour, was given the Rideau contract for the Hog's Back dam early in 1827, as well as building a railway to carry stone from the quarry. (Unfortunately, a flood early the next year swept away his works, and the contract was reassigned.) Similarly, on the Third Canal, some builders, notably John Brown, were involved in government contracts outside of Ontario.

Work on the Soulanges Canal, in Quebec,[98] began in 1892, under the direction of Thomas Monro, who had supervised the northern section of the Third Welland. When the authorities decided to use concrete in the lock floors (except for the sills) as well as the bridge abutments,[99] Monro perhaps understandably chose the firm of Joseph Battle of Thorold to supply natural cement. In addition Randolph Macdonald, who tendered unsuccessfully for work on the Welland in 1874 but was successful in 1890, received two contracts on the Soulanges, for Section 13 in November 1892, and Section 9 in January 1893. John O'Brien of Cornwall, contracted to make a road along the Welland in 1890, was probably part of Denis O'Brien & Sons, who were given the first contract on the Soulanges, for Section 12, in April 1892. Charles H. Raynor & Co. were given Section 8 on the Soulanges in December 1892, having already completed Sections F, G, H, and I of the Welland deepening in 1886. Five large swing bridges, as well as the sluices in the lock gates, were built by Dominion Bridge of Lachine, who would be one of the contractors for Fourth Welland Canal bridges.

When it came to construction of the Canadian lock at Sault Ste Marie (1889–94), only one general contractor was employed: Hugh Ryan & Co. of Toronto, who in turn sub-contracted the work to the Miller brothers of Ingersoll, Ontario. In 1894 the eight steel butterfly valves were contracted to Ryan "with the work being done by the St. Lawrence Foundry Co. and the Bertram Engine Works Co. of Toronto." Allan & Fleming of Ottawa did the upper river channel dredging and the entrance piers, while Beatty & Sons of Welland provided the dewatering pumps. Canadian General Electric of Toronto supplied electrical equipment, and Canadian Locomotive & Engine Works of Kingston had the contract for the electric-powered lock gate.[100]

Similarly, construction of the Trent-Severn Waterway attracted contractors who had worked on the Welland. Larkin & Sangster of St Catharines, for example, held contracts there from 1900 to 1919.[101]

As the nineteenth century was nearing its close, the contracting pattern of earlier years on the Welland Canal continued. The length of individual contracts was generally between one and two miles, and of a total of thirty-two awarded, only eight firms were given more than two contracts between 1872 and 1886. Of those, John Brown of Thorold tied with the Dunbars of Buffalo, with seven apiece; McNamee of Montreal, Ferguson & Co. and Rayner & Co. had four each; while Hunter & Co. of St Catharines, Campbell & Co., and Isbester & Reid of Ottawa each had three. American firms still bid successfully, although they were now outnumbered by Canadian individuals and partnerships, and specialization had become more common. In addition, many of the firms were now bidding on large-scale projects virtually anywhere in Canada.

All the surveys, the engineers' plans, and the intentions of the contractors as laid out in their tenders would be tested by actual conditions "on the ground" when the labourers began the arduous process of excavating a trench to channel water, the canal's essential power source. "Digging the ditch" will be the subject of the next chapter.

CHAPTER FOUR

Digging the Ditch

Anyone reading the letters, memoranda, and reports relating to the building of the First Welland Canal cannot help being struck by the optimism of William Hamilton Merritt and the Welland Canal Company. Time and again they expressed great confidence in the success of the Welland, echoing and reinforcing Merritt's own faith in the future of the enterprise.

"Gentlemen," said George Keefer on 30 November 1824 at the ceremonial sod-turning near New Holland (now Allanburg), "it is with pleasure that I remove the first earth from the Welland Canal, and ardently hope that the work may continue uninterrupted until the whole is completed."[1] And on 18 December 1824 the directors reported: "There seems every reason to anticipate that the work will be completed, or certainly very nearly so, during the next year."[2]

Unfortunately, the work rarely proceeded as smoothly as Keefer and the directors so ardently hoped! They seriously miscalculated the magnitude of the challenges facing them. Wishful thinking and a desire to please stockholders were probably at play here. Such excessive optimism no doubt led to the underestimation of costs, often on the part of American contractors. Of course, the company soon became aware of their difficulties. As we have seen, Merritt himself faced much pessimistic criticism from his contemporaries, some of it well founded. His optimism may, in fact, have been a reaction to the negative prognostications surrounding the project. While later generations have marvelled at his daring and vision, they have noted the obscurantism and disingenuousness of his and the company's public statements as they walked a tightrope between technological and financial success and bankruptcy in disgrace. Perhaps Merritt and company officials really believed their brave words. Certainly, long before the profession of "public relations" was invented, Merritt appreciated the necessity of instilling confidence in the "product."

4.1 A stump-puller used during construction of the Erie Canal c. 1820. We have no evidence that such devices were used in the construction of the First Welland, but the American backgrounds of many of its engineers and contractors suggest the likelihood. If such is not the case, how were the stumps of large trees in Niagara's still primeval forests removed? (R.M. Styran)

"ONE OF THE MOST WONDERFUL HYDRAULIC CONTRIVANCES OF MAN"[3]

No actual construction of the First Canal could begin before the ground was cleared of trees. Then the earth had to be ploughed or scraped, with four to six – sometimes as many as ten – oxen pulling each plough or scraper. Men with picks and axes tackled obstacles such as larger tree stumps (fig. 4.1). This "grubbing" involved digging beneath, lifting, and hauling away stumps. Much of the actual ploughing, grubbing, and digging was done by local sub-contractors, often farmers who lived along the line of the canal and who owned ploughs, wagons, and teams. Not a problem for most of the line of the Second or Third Canals, this was an essential first step in the construction of the First. Only after it was accomplished could actual excavation begin.

The scene of such activities would have been impressive even to twenty-first-century eyes. One of Merritt's sons wrote: "Where the forest stood a short time ago, was now a scene of life and bustle. The sharp rattle of the axes hewing and carving their way through the old woods; the unceasing hammering of the pick on the clayey banks, and occasionally the crash of a falling tree, mingling with the loud gunpowder explosions when a blast was discharged, all lent a charm to the work."[4] The workers "on the ground" of course had a different view of such "charm," as we shall see.

A Subterraneous Passage or Mine

In predicting the success of construction of the First Canal, the company directors announced in 1824: "We can confidently assert that no serious obstruction will intervene."[5] Neither did the canal engineers consider the Niagara Escarpment a great problem. On the other hand, the topography that would prove especially troublesome was the height of land – the "Grand Summit Ridge" – between Allanburg (New Holland) and Port Robinson. The original plan was for a tunnel, not an unusual feature of canals at the time. James and Samuel Clowes recommended a tunnel in 1824 and Nathan Roberts's report of that year approved of the tunnel concept, "a subterraneous passage or mine."[6] A tunnel 2 miles (3.2 km) long, 9 feet wide (2.7 m), and 8 feet (2.4 m) high was proposed, which would carry barges similar to those on the Erie Canal. In late 1824, a number of American stockholders wrote that they approved of "increasing the Tunnel to 15 feet wide, (15 feet is the clear of the Erie Canal in this State) as we ought to keep in view Sloop, as well as Boat navigation."[7] They went on to recommend consideration of "how far it is practicable (*now*) to make the Canal large enough for Sloop navigation over the ridge from the Chippewa River," adding: "Should this not be deemed prudent at present ... we think it would be advisable to have an *open cut* instead of a Tunnel."

Contractors' bids for the tunnel were received by 15 November 1824. Alfred Hovey of Montezuma, New York, received the contract, while Kennedy and Simpson were to excavate the remainder of the summit level. Work began on 29 November at New Holland – one day before the sod-turning – and continued throughout the winter. Much timber was required to shore up the tunnel's ceiling and walls, and in early December twenty-one bids were received from contractors wanting to supply lumber for the purpose.[8] By the first of February buildings and machinery had been set up, all equipment was at hand, both entrances to the tunnel had been taken out to bottom, and a shaft to bottom level in the centre of the tunnel had been sunk to test the soil. The company's Annual Report proudly stated that the whole work would be completed before the end of 1825. The board was further encour-

4.2 The Deep Cut on the Third Canal in 1892. A steam tug (no longer tow-horses) pulls two schooners through what was the most difficult construction terrain for each of the two nineteenth-century reconstructions of the Welland. Note the high berms, evidence of the masses of spoil excavated between Thorold and Port Robinson. (*Scribner's Magazine*, vol. 11, issue 3, March 1892)

aged by the prevailing good weather and the fact that "no water is met with at either end or centre until below water level." The Welland Canal, which critics assumed would be an undertaking of great magnitude, gave every sign of being "simple and easy" in construction.[9]

What was it, then, that led one historian (with a century's hindsight) to call this tunnel project "an ill-digested scheme"?[10] Merritt himself had not been sanguine about the prospect of its success. Describing the Deep Cut itself as an "expensive job," he ruminated: "I have a great aversion to the Tunnel in consequence of the Timber which I fear will decay sooner than we anticipate."[11] Indeed, the work did not go well. Timber for shoring up the roof and walls was promptly delivered to the site, but the excavation ran into stiff clay with streaks of hardpan and stones and rock that had to be blasted with gunpowder. Oxen died in accidents and horses became ill. The labourers, who worked in long shifts deep underground, soaked with water, breathing bad air, fell ill with the "ague," likely malaria. Unexpected artesian water erupted so that the workers were "obliged to retreat as fast as possible."[12] Although £3,000 had by then literally been sunk into it, the directors gradually began to have doubts about the effort.

In April 1825 the tunnel was abruptly abandoned and Hovey, the contractor, gave up the project. The company would instead excavate a deep trench cut down through the entire ridge (fig. 4.2): 2 miles (3.2 km) long to a depth of nearly 60 feet (18.2 m).

What was it that forced their hand? The New York stockholders, as we have seen, had been having second thoughts of their own: a tunnel would have size limitations, and this no longer seemed practical to them unless it could accommodate sailing ships. A larger canal would be able to take larger ships with heavier cargoes, which would be directed to the Welland – otherwise, trans-shipment of cargo would be necessary, as happened at Buffalo for the Erie. Of course, the enlargement seemed to offer higher profits, too. Moreover, Francis Hall as well had recommended increasing the size of the tunnel to accommodate sloops and, if this was not possible, then an open cut should be excavated. William Lyon Mackenzie also claimed to have encouraged the enlargement of the canal to accommodate schooners, a procedure that would have entailed abandoning the tunnel concept.[13] In view of these objections, the directors decided to enlarge the dimensions of the entire canal, and to give up on the tunnel in favour of a deep cut through the Grand Summit Ridge.

The Only Formidable Obstacle

By the fall of 1825 work was well underway on excavating the entire cut; it would continue through the winter of 1825–26. Ultimately the Deep Cut would be 2 miles (3.2 km) long, with a depth of from 30 to nearly 60 feet (9.1–18.2 m). The depth of the cut was to be 7.5 feet (2.2 m) below the bottom of Chippawa Creek, so as to allow water from the river easily to enter the canal. Characteristically, the directors began the project with high hopes – and an excess of confidence. Their report of 1826 announced: "It is impossible that earth more favorable for such an operation could have been met with. There is no rock to impede the excavation, and, though the soil a stiff clay, is more expensive to remove than lighter earth, that difficulty is amply atoned for by the solidity and tenacity of the banks and the assurance there seems to be that they will sustain without material alteration, the influence of the weather."[14]

Merritt described the cut well: "It commences with an almost abrupt height, of thirty feet above the canal bottom, then gradually rises to fifty-six feet six inches in a distance of one hundred and six chains, then gradually descends in a distance of twenty eight chains to thirty feet, when it as abruptly breaks off in another ravine. The entire distance through this cut is one mile fifty four chains, averaging about forty four feet cutting; to the depth of from twelve to eighteen feet from the surface, it is composed of clay with a small mixture of sand, and below this, a tenacious blue clay."[15] By 1827 he had realized (as he wrote to his father-in-law): "The Deep cut is the only formidable obstacle we have to contend with on the line of our Canal."[16]

Embarrassing Difficulties

Two years later Merritt acknowledged that they had run into "embarrassing difficulties."[17] Thousands of tons of earth had to be removed from this man-made canyon, carried in scows or workboats, and deposited in Chippawa Creek or in a large reservoir below bottom level at one end of the cut. Alternatively, the spoil was removed with wagons and carts and laboriously deposited on the banks of the excavation. "The bottom of the canal was ... a scene of great life and industry – hundreds of men and of animals were busily employed in the most active industry." So wrote an American journalist about the excavation on the Deep Cut in the fall of 1827.[18]

As the project proved more expensive than the contractors had expected, Beach, Hovey and Ward went bankrupt and by 1827 were compelled to relinquish the contract. Aware that the work at the Deep Cut was proving to be more demanding than expected, the directors realized that new methods were needed to expedite the work. After Beach, Hovey and Ward withdrew, the board reported that, before entering into new contracts, they would offer a reward of £125 to the person who would construct a machine that would remove the greatest quantity of earth in a given time, at the least expense. Many designs were submitted,[19] and Oliver Phelps (fig. 3.1), won for his "machine," which is illustrated and described below (fig. 4.3). Phelps then took over the abandoned contracts. Mechanical ingenuity, however, was not sufficient to meet the demands of the Deep Cut excavation.

Nevertheless, the engineers proceeded methodically with the work of digging the channel from Lake Ontario to Chippawa Creek. The project had, as we have seen (chapter 3), been divided into thirty-five sections, with contracts given to a number of contractors or contracting firms. At first the company had great confidence in its contractors:

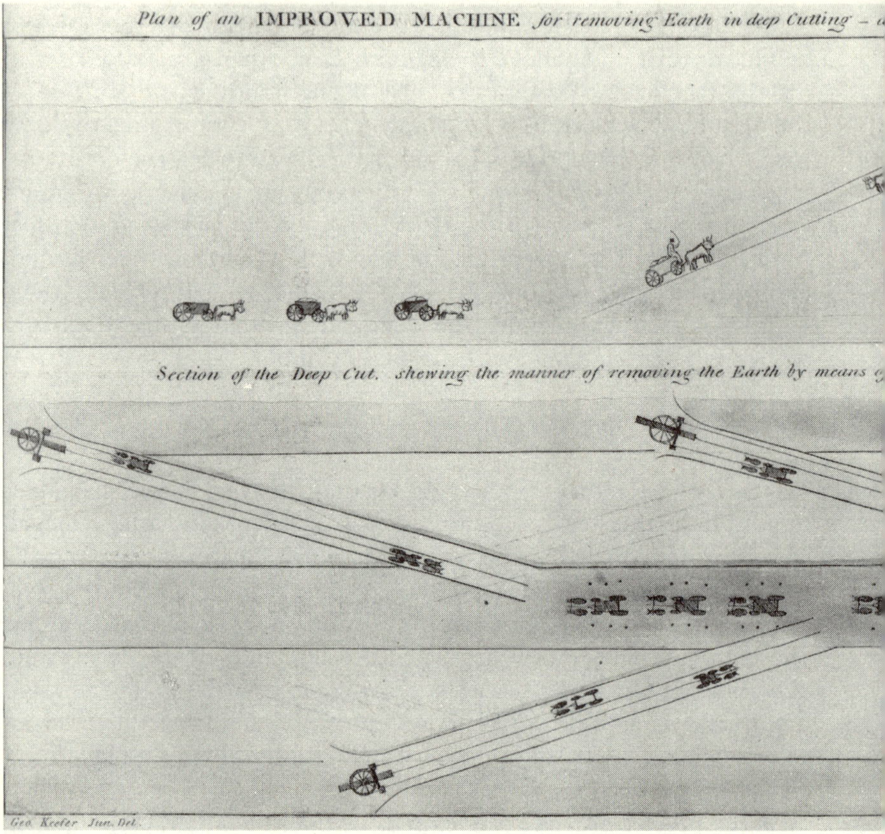

they were, said the directors, "persons as eligible in all respects as they think the Board could have met with ... They have exhibited a knowledge of their several descriptions of work and have practised to this time a regularity, economy and a persevering industry in the conduct of it which it is believed have not often been excelled."[20]

On the other hand, as we have seen, the execution of First Canal contracts occasioned much controversy, not to say scandal. Some contemporaries criticized the awarding of the initial contracts in 1825 as extravagant – too much was being paid for the work. But the directors countered that "no part of the Erie canal [had] been executed as low as the present contracts for this work."[21] Furthermore, the abandonment of the tunnel and the ensuing difficulties with the Deep Cut and many of the locks (chapter 5) still arouse debate among historians. Given the company's many financial restraints, the search for the root of these problems has often led to criticism of the excavation contracts. A particular target was Phelps, described by one researcher as "an Erie

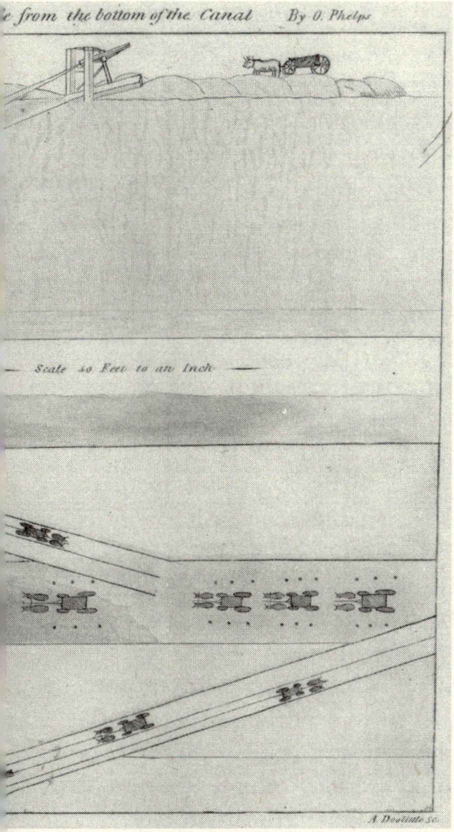

4.3 Oliver Phelps's Excavating "Machine" c. 1827. Phelps exploited gravity (the weight of oxen, cart, and driver) and brute animal strength to lift spoil from the First Canal's deepening prism. Despite improvements such as these, men and beasts occasionally careened to injury or death down such muddy, slippery slopes. (LAC: C-101265)

Canal contractor of dubious repute."[22] For example, timber delivered for the (never-finished) tunnel was used instead to construct part of the towpath and several locks, and Phelps seems to have used some of it for his store and for a Presbyterian church in St Catharines. One of Mackenzie's later accusations, moreover, was that George Keefer, president of the Canal Company, had dishonourably sold the timber to Phelps at considerable profit.

At a distance of nearly two hundred years, the truth about Phelps's actions is difficult to ascertain. At the very least, he seems to have been a canny operator. In his defence before the 1836 investigating committee, he maintained that, during his work on the Deep Cut, other contractors tried "to throw obstacles in the way against the progress of the work." He described himself, on the contrary, as diligent and conscientious: "Whenever I saw a stick of timber worked into the lock, or attempted to be, that was at all unsound, or any tie that I thought was too small and inefficient, my invariable rule was, not barely to tell them that that would not answer, but take an axe and with my own hands cut it to pieces so that it would not be worked in." This sounds self-serving, for it is not hard to imagine other contractors of the time also having such a "hands-on" involvement in the work. His account of losses on the contract (to which poor weather conditions contributed) is more compelling: "Many of the oxen got killed by running off the bank – many died otherwise – the horses mostly all of them had the glanders when I took the work ... the waggons ... were broken to pieces."[23]

Yet sub-contractors who worked for Phelps on the Deep Cut complained that he defrauded them. John J. Lefferty, MPP, believed that "too large contracts [were] given out to one individual," which may have been a veiled reference to Phelps for his taking up the recently relinquished contracts. Lefferty indirectly suggested that large contractors were compelled, because of the size of their jobs, to let out parts of the contract to sub-contractors, to whom they paid a lower price than their own estimate. "These sub-contractors," he maintained, "frequently run away with the money."[24] He also stressed the harm done to labourers who were left unpaid by absconding contractors. One sub-contractor claimed that Phelps never allowed his employees "extra allowances," and that "he broke them all down but David Thompson." Mackenzie claimed that Phelps "contrived to get his partners in the locks contract out of his way, so that he got the Deep Cut job to himself." Yet the fact remains that, in its final judgment the 1836 Committee found only that Phelps received "advantages" in his contract.[25] In addition, since many of the contracts were re-allocated several times before the work was finished, and most of the main contractors let out parts of the work to sub-contractors, we cannot determine how many "contractors" were actually at work on any contract at any one time.

Some of them may have wished they had never heard of the Welland Canal. Beach, Hovey and Ward, for example, had relinquished their contract for the Deep Cut on April 1827, apparently at a considerable loss. In July 1827 Smith Ward wrote in desperation to Merritt, "Alas! ... I have a tender and affectionate wife, with her little ones, who look to me for their support; for whom I was blessed with a comfortable living previous to my present disaster ... My creditors must prey upon my effects so long as there is a crumb to feed their gorgeous appetites; not only so, but looked on with contempt and disgrace. I must be looked upon as unfit or incompetent, lacking energy or judgment, or both, and not worthy to be entrusted with any work of importance hereafter ... I have acted in good faith, discharged a clear conscience, for which I can answer to my God. Adieu."[26]

It seemed that the company would make no recompense in such cases. It was not until 22 November 1828, Ward meanwhile having died, that the company's Minutes included the following: "Application having been made on behalf of the widow of the late Smith Ward, who is left in very destitute circumstances, and is therefore unable to pay the arrears due on 10 shares of Stock held by him, Resolved, That the said shares be forfeited, and the amount paid on them, £95 5s, be presented to the widow."[27]

Even then, the story continued, for some years later, in 1852, E.T. Ward, Smith Ward's son, wrote to Merritt concerning "a considerable sum of money [which] still remains due the contractors." Ward was also writing on behalf of Hovey, who was "very desirous of applying immediately, as he is getting old and would be glad could anything be obtained to derive some benefit from it himself." The younger Ward had inherited the eloquence of the elder:

> My Father upon his deathbed told my Mother that in all probability there would be at some future period a considerable amount due her or his children in Canada, and directed her in case of our attempting to get it, to apply to you for aid; he evidently regarded you as his best perhaps his only friend in Canada, and it is to you my dear sir, that I look now for help. I was four years old only when my Father died. I remember none of the circumstances as they transpired before his death. But this I do remember, that my Family were driven from the home of my infancy, that they were stripped of every thing they possessed, that the property which my Father worked for, which was his and which should now be mine, has from my earliest recollection, been in the hands of the stranger. I remember too that at the age of fourteen years my Mother being too poor to support me I left her and from that time threw myself upon my own resources.[28]

We cannot determine whether the elder Ward's problems were due to his own inefficiency, the Canal Company's unorthodox practices, or the intractability of Niagara's geology. This correspondence, however, offers a poignant glimpse into the difficulties of the contracting profession.

One Railway May Be Formed

If the Welland Canal Company's method of granting of contracts was perhaps ill-judged, their optimism on technical matters was certainly ill-founded. For example Merritt, the company, and their engineers anticipated no difficulties with the topography of the canal's route, an attitude that proved to be quite erroneous. To be fair, the impressive Escarpment did not in fact present any real problem to the surveyors and engineers who submitted plans for the proposed canal. Familiar with American and British canal-building methods, they understood the traditional ways of taking a canal up a rise of land: a series of locks following the slope, or an "inclined plane" or railway for raising and lowering boats. This sort of "rail-way"[29] was the method originally suggested for taking the Welland over the Niagara Escarpment. Canals through the Appalachians made use of inclines, and plans were afoot to use inclines on the Morris Canal in New Jersey (built 1824–31) at the time when the Welland was under construction. American engineers working on the Welland may have been aware of these projects. However, a closer example would certainly have been familiar: a "railway" had been built in 1764 at Lewiston, New York, to haul goods up from the river. And in 1788 the British military engineer Gother Mann (1747–1830) had described British incline railways in an official report.[30]

In May 1823 the American Hiram Tibbett(s), reporting on his survey, recommended a "railway" for the Twelve Mile Creek route: "From Mr. Decoe's [sic] Mill dam, it will be necessary to carry the water through the farms of Messrs. Burneston & Cooper, where nature has formed a ravine, or cut to the top of the mountain ... From this to the waters of the west branch of 12 Mile Creek ... nature has continued her favours; the ravine extends with a gentle descent ... the whole way, and one railway may be formed to take up boats at once, or two can be constructed if necessary, or more convenient."[31]

The railway project was by no means universally popular. Some locals feared that rafts and timber could not be sent down an inclined plane, whereas logs could be transported through a series of locks.[32] Such opposition may have contributed to abandonment of the idea. Although no incline was built on the Welland, Samuel Power noted in 1846 that one of the contractors on the Second Canal had used an incline to transport materials.[33]

Slides and Their Aftermath

Despite bankruptcy among the contractors and the financial setbacks endured by the company, the Deep Cut work pressed on vigorously throughout later 1827 and 1828.

But even the best-laid plans can go awry: toward the end of October 1828 a series of landslides began, which were reported as "a great disaster."[34] A more overwhelming calamity occurred in November: landslides swept tons of clay, sand, and gravel down the slopes of the cut into the prism, wiping out months of work – "the catastrophe of the slides," as Mackenzie later described it.[35] Testifying at an 1830 Select Committee inquiry, David Thompson (an MLA who had, with Love Newlove, taken over a sub-contract on the Deep Cut in September) was asked if it was "generally apprehended that the Deep Cut would slide in before it did give way?" To which he replied: "From the time of the first slip, I was of opinion that if the excavation was persisted in below the surface of the Welland, it would give way – I advised Mr. Merritt and the engineers that there was no probability of it continuing to stand, because the clay below that surface absorbed water quickly, and was therefore unable to support the weight of the Banks."[36]

Generally speaking, Thompson was correct. When the workers got to the bottom of the Cut, they reached a bed of loose sand and, when water entered the Cut, it carried away the sand, weakening the banks.[37]

Could this problem have been avoided? Was the colony's dearth of engineering talent the cause? In 1830 Commissioner Robert Randal, reporting to the Upper Canadian Legislature on the wisdom of another grant to the company, thought: "Had more pains been taken to ascertain by deep borings at short distances, the nature and quality of the sub-stratum ... a vast saving would have been afforded to the colony."[38] Wiilliam Lyon Mackenzie was more direct in his accusations of 1836: "Many thousand pounds were lost by the neglect and carelessness of the Engineers, Directors and Managers of the Canal Company in not taking proper precautions to prevent the catastrophe of the slides."[39]

In fact, some thought *had* been given to soil quality. As early as 24 June 1824 Francis Hall referred to "borings" between the Chippawa and the first lock, and several of the contractors tendering for the Deep Cut on 1 July 1825 had either excluded quicksand (as well as hardpan!) from their offers, or had specified an additional cost. In his 1836 testimony Mackenzie said that Beach, Hovey and Ward had told him that, after a shaft had been sunk, "when the men who were working came down to the quicksand, the sand and water rose so quickly upon them, that it was with difficulty they escaped with life. The water nearly filled the shaft; this was before the excavation."[40]

The problem appears to have been aggravated by the fact that spoil had been deposited directly onto the banks, making them heavier, especially when worked upon by the effects of ice, snow, and rain. Mackenzie also testified that Thompson had written from the Deep Cut on 10 November 1828: "From the last slip to Chippawa the clay below its surface is such that water reduces it to a soft substance that cannot resist the heavy banks." James Geddes, in his report of 27 December 1828, had also noted: "The soft substance at the bottom of the Deep Cut ... was insufficient to support the superincumbent banks of clay." He further explained that "[while] attempts to bore below the level of the bottom of the Deep Cut were made ... the substance found was loose sand; and the difficulty of boring was such that the Auger was not made to penetrate more then eight feet below the level of said bottom." The contractor Newlove testified at the 1836 enquiry that he thought "Mr. Phelps laid the dirt too close to the edge of the Canal."[41] Further support for this view was received in 1838 when Killaly and Baird suggested that the Deep Cut had collapsed because of "the improper manner in which the immense excavation ... was disposed of on the very edge of the Canal."[42]

In its final judgment, however, the 1836 Committee (which heard considerable testimony on the subject) found the evidence "contradictory" and blamed, not human error, but the "nature of the soil at the bottom" of the cut, that is, the layer of quicksand.[43] Some twenty years later another noted engineer, William Kingsford, gave his diagnosis: the problem was "caused by want of knowledge. Any engineer knows, that by the help of good drainage and with banks of sufficient slope protected by sods, any cut may be secured; and so much heavy excavation would have occurred here, that it could have been done at a very low rate."[44] So much for hindsight.

Whatever the cause of the disaster, the directors had once again to change their plans, giving up the idea of supplying the canal from Chippawa Creek. Another solution to the supply problem was necessary and, as we shall see in chapter 6, the directors turned to the Grand River, via a feeder canal dug across Wainfleet Marsh, and an aqueduct across Chippawa Creek to connect the Feeder with the main channel.

Another change was also necessary. From the beginning, the canal builders had recognized the inconvenience of the lengthy and circuitous route via the Niagara River to Lake Erie, and by early June 1831 they had decided to "complete" the First Canal by a direct link. Contracts for "the termination of the canal into Lake Erie"[45] at Gravelly Bay were signed on 3 June, with the intention that the new line would be complete by January of 1832. H.N. Monson and the company of Marshall Lewis, James Little, and Louis W. Garrison were to do most of the work, with Lewis, Little, and Garrison building the harbour in Gravelly Bay. The challenge on this stretch, the Onondaga Escarpment or "rock cut," was successfully met, and the first vessel passed through the "Lake Erie Extension" at Port Colborne on 1 June 1833.

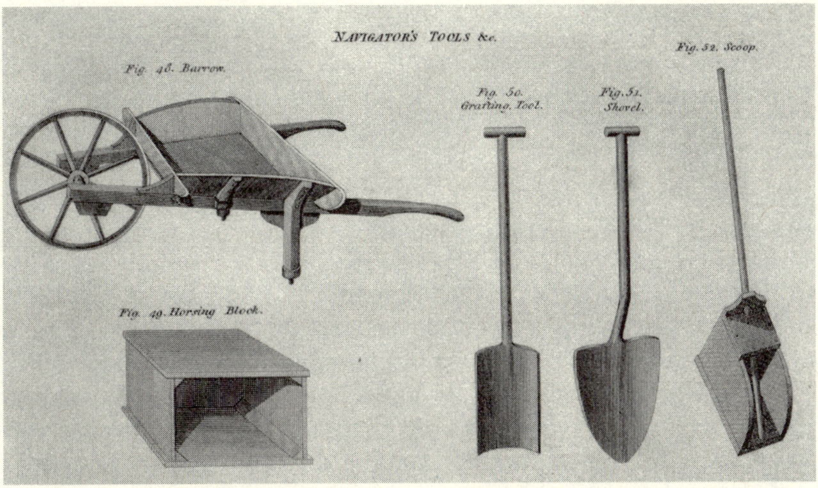

4.4 Canal labourers' tools c. 1820. The term "navigator" – meaning a builder of water navigation systems – became shortened to "navvy." Not shown are the pickax and saw needed to hack away at Niagara's hardpan and still dense forests in the 1820s. (Abraham Rees, *The Cyclopædia*, Plates, vol. 2, Plate VII)

Carting Up the Muck: Tools, Equipment, and Machinery

So far our description of "digging the ditch" has tended to be at arm's length. But a reader might justifiably ask "how did they actually excavate the trench?" Unfortunately, we have found only one contemporary illustration, and few scattered references by contractors to the methods of work of construction of the First Canal. The traditional view is of men working with picks and shovels, transporting soil in wheelbarrows or in horse- or ox-drawn carts – rightly suggesting a great deal of back-breaking labour. Yet even such simple tools were not at first readily available to the Welland project. In the early 1820s the fledgling colony lacked sufficient quantities of the picks, spades, shovels, scrapers, carts, and wheelbarrows needed for "carting up the muck" (fig. 4.4).[46] Upper Canada was still sparsely populated and large contracting firms were as yet unknown. In 1824, before construction of the First Welland had begun, the surveyor Rheddy Cusack for one complained that he had not been "furnished with the proper implements to ascertain the quality of the earth."[47] We know, therefore, that equipment was borrowed or imported from the United States, both for the First Canal and for the subsequent reconstructions.

Fortunately for Merritt, completion of the Erie Canal released not only contractors and labourers but also some of their equipment.[48] Certain items, however, still had to be borrowed. In June 1825, for instance, Merritt sent a request to J. Macaulay at the Royal Navy station at Kingston: "We find ourselves at a loss for some cordage, say ropes and pully blocks, one or two small anchors two or three large boats, or small craft of some discription for the construction of our Harbors."[49] Other equipment had to be obtained from abroad. Later in 1825 Merritt complained to a Select Committee of the Legislature about the dearth of basic equipment.[50] The Welland Canal Company, he said, "had already paid somewhere about $200 for [import] duties, principally on waggons and horses brought in to work on the Canal, and on scrapers, ploughs, shovels, and spades, or rather the contractors have paid it, but with the understanding that the Company will repay it if not remitted."[51] Explaining why the company needed a remission of such duties, he continued: "The proper Spades and Shovels are ... made in the United States ... Waggons could not be procured in this country at a reasonable price, or in sufficient number."[52]

Despite the paucity of contemporary visual evidence, a reasonable picture of the excavation of the channel and construction of the original thirty-four wooden locks can be pieced together (chapter 5). The testimony and documents presented at the 1836 enquiry into Mackenzie's charges (already quoted extensively) included a number of inventories of equipment.[53] In addition, a drawing of Phelps's earth-moving machine (fig. 4.3), and an 1830s sketch of work on the Erie Canal give valuable information.

Excavation of the ditch itself was the most labour-intensive aspect of a canal project, a job for the unskilled "navvies," supervised by contractors or their overseers (chapters 9 and 10). The navvies cleared the ground of brush, trees, and/or surface rocks, in itself onerous work through what was for the most part uncleared land. As a measure of its difficulty, prospective contractors bid for that work at from $15 to $60 per cubic yard, as compared to earth excavation, the price of which ranged from seven to fifty cents per yard, depending on the terrain.[54] For example, on 5 May 1825 the board minutes record that three contractors had been paid the following for excavation work: $490 for 3,921 yards @ 12 1/2¢, $376.30 for 2,090 yards @ 18¢, and $3,897.30 for 25,982 yards @ 15¢. The contractors for the tunnel (Beach, Hovey and Ward) had been awarded their contract at 56¢ per yard. Recorded payments show an interesting range: Hovey and Ward were paid 25¢ for excavation above water, and 50¢ under water in 1826; and in 1828 the contractors for the Western Branch received on average 13¢ per yard for excavation, \$40 to \$60 for grubbing, and \$12 to \$16 for chopping and clearing. For the Deep Cut, excavation rates varied: contractor David Thompson got 33¢ for excavation with a team, 35¢ with a scow in 1827, while Hall Davis got 36¢ for mud.[55] In contrast, James Clowes was hired at 7/6 per day for surveying, and the American engineer Nathan Roberts was engaged at £500 per year plus lodging and expenses.[56]

Stiff clay, hardpan, and rock excavation would, of course, demand higher prices than ordinary soil, hence the variations (tenders for rock ranged from 75¢ to \$1.44). At some stage, access roads had to be cleared and more or less levelled, to allow the men and their ploughs, wheelbarrows, and carts to approach the site. The soil had to be ploughed to break up the earth for easier removal. For example, Phelps noted that soil conditions in the Deep Cut made for extremely adverse working conditions: "There were many streaks of hard pan that could not be ploughed, but had to be picked [that is, broken up with picks] – there were many large stone and rocks which took from 4 to 12 yoke of oxen to draw out of the ditch – there were some so large that they had to be blasted ... When I began [in 1827] the usual number of yoke of oxen to each plow team was from 4 to 6 – not long after I was compelled to increase the number to 10 to each team, and I had from 9 to 10 teams engaged at one time, and they all had as much as they could do."

Phelps also commented on the delays caused by rain: "The soil being of such a slippery clay nature that instead of losing two days in a month by wet weather according as I had calculated, the roads were so slippery ... that an average from 4 to 5 days per month were lost." It was such harsh weather conditions that led to many of his oxen being killed "by running off the bank,"[57] as noted above.

A close examination of inventories of property taken over by Phelps from Hovey and Ward and other contractors on the Deep Cut reveals that, even in June 1827, four major contractors possessed only a limited amount of equipment. Shovels do seem to have been plentiful among the American contractors (321 listed, but 127 of these were described as "old" or "very bad"). Only five "picks" (of which two were old), eight axes (half were old), and six ploughs (one old, one with a cart), and a grand total of three wheelbarrows were mentioned. Incidentally, the inventory also included three pumps (two at \$5, one at \$15), and a total of five "machines" (one "with rope"), as well as 45 wagons and 18 carts of various kinds (two without wheels). One 6½-foot pit saw (value \$4), one wooden scoop (\$1), one powder canister (\$0.75), just over 500 pounds of assorted qualities of iron, 91 pounds of crowbars, and one large wheel for a cart to plough near the banks, are among the miscellaneous property items noted.

These inventories provoke several questions. If picks were so necessary in dealing with hardpan, why only three of them, and why only eight axes? Were labourers expected to provide their own? Robert Passfield, in depicting an Irish labourer on the Rideau Canal, noted that "an axe was a constant companion of any settler travelling through the bush in Upper Canada."[58] Conceivably, many of the local residents employed on the canal provided their own tools. The wise immigrant labourer would try to equip himself with such devices. The virtual lack of wheelbarrows is also intriguing. Some excavated soil was probably removed from the site in bags or sacks carried by the men. Certainly the necessarily small capacity of a wheelbarrow compared to a cart suggests that the latter would be preferred – and the inventories bear out this supposition, although the average cost of a wheelbarrow appears to have been $2, while a good cart, although able to handle a much larger volume, would probably have cost at least $15 (a wagon would run to about $50) – and would require at least one horse or, more likely, a span of horses or a yoke of oxen. The price of animals would vary from about $50 to $60, while a yoke of oxen would have cost at least $60. Phelps claimed that he had brought 25 yoke of oxen, 44 horses, 150 carts, and 55 wagons with him from the States.[59]

In the 1820s "horse gins" (crude augers or drills) were used in Britain for boring in tunnel work and simple steam-powered inventions were already in use there in that decade for building railways and canals. In Upper Canada, however, muscle power prevailed because, while some types of machine were being used on the First Welland, labour was often plentiful and cheap. We assume that simple cranes, such as were used on the Rideau, were in operation here. Stump-pulling machinery similar to that found on the Erie was also probably employed (fig. 4.1). In both cases these were powered by human and/or animal energy. It was the evident necessity of finding effective machinery that typically led to the invention of new types of equipment, as we have seen in the case of Phelps's machine.

We find a number of references to "machines" used by contractors, including one that Hovey and Ward set up at the tunnel in 1825 (for which they were paid $50).[60] On 26 May 1827 the directors inspected the line of the Deep Cut and "the various machines of the contractors and of Mr. Phelps, for the more expeditiously completing the excavation." Phelps's machine seems not to have been a favourite, however. Two days later the company secretary wrote to the president: "All the contractors on the Deep cut use Pratt & Simpson's Machinery in preference to Phelps."[61] In July of that year, John Donaldson was paid $75 for his machine in use on the Deep Cut.[62]

Unfortunately, the only "machine" for which we have any description is the one devised and used by Phelps. In May 1827 his proposal to excavate the Deep Cut with his own machinery was accepted by the Welland Canal Company and, as already mentioned, won the prize of £125 offered by the company for the most efficient and economical earth-removing machine (fig. 4.3). Phelps had worked out an ingenious way to efficiently carry tons of earth out of the canal prism:

> A common wagon wheel, fixed on an upright post, about seven feet from the ground on the top of the bank; a rope, with a hook on each end reaching from the bottom of the canal to the top, is fixed round this wheel which hooks on the back of the descending cart and to the tongue of the one below, so that the return team assists in pulling up the loaded one, thereby, in effect, reducing the ascent to a perfect level, as the loads are drawn up with more ease than they are removed from the level to discharge.[63]

Even American observers were impressed with "the simplicity and efficiency" of Phelps's machines,[64] fifty of which were ultimately used on the Deep Cut.[65] He may have heard of their use on the Rideau Canal construction site, or he may have known about the use of similar devices for wheelbarrows, men, and horses on English railway building sites and adapted the concept to the Welland scene.[66]

The heavily wooded nature of some of the terrain necessitated tree- and stump-removal equipment. We have descriptions of tree removal from both the Erie and Rideau canals, which suggest that many trees were under-dug, then hauled down using ropes or chains. John MacTaggart described such dangerous labours on the Rideau, where men had to "dig beneath the roots of trees, which not infrequently fall down and smother them." Ingenuity from south of the border developed a machine for dealing with stumps: a pair of sixteen-feet high wheels connected by a thirty-foot axle "into which a fourteeen-foot wheel was spoked and around which a rope was wound several times to produce an eightfold gain in power for grabbing" (fig. 4.1).[67]

Another useful piece of equipment was the scow,[68] which could be used for carrying any sort of material, as a base for dredging equipment, and especially for hauling away excavated earth and rock. When excavation began at Chippawa Creek, engineer Hiram Tibbett(s) noted: "Boats can follow every foot of the way, and be so constructed that one man can unload them without loss of time ... construct at each end a box similar to a cart body, which will be filled and discharge any quantity in the stream."[69] One scow could be loading spoil in the cut while another unloaded at Chippawa Creek.

Since the "expense of hauling or carting out the earth with Teams proves by experiment to be great,"[70] cheaper alternatives were sought, and by 1833 an ingenious type of scow had been developed – a "dirt boat" with a trap door bottom. "Re-cycling" is by no means a modern phenomenon: excavated soil was raised by one means or another to a nearby or distant site for use where an embankment was required. For example, the Annual Report for 1828 referred to a decision made the previous summer to use scows to carry earth to Chippawa Creek to be used for the towing path.[71] Another possible use for a scow was as a base for a piling machine, as referred to at various locations after 1834.[72]

Apparently the Deep Cut was divided into "a certain number of runs where the machines were fixed for carting up the muck – [Phelps] was to have the earth ploughed for them." When Phelps had taken over the Deep Cut from Hovey and Ward and others, a number of problems were revealed: some work done by a previous contractor was found "cut full of holes here and there, filled up with muck, and a great portion cut out of line altogether."[73] In addition some parts of the line were found to be "overflown" with water – drainage was to be a persistent problem and pumping was required. For example, in 1827 MacTaggart, having visited the site, mentioned that using a pump "either wrought by horses or steam, probably horses would answer best." The Welland Canal Company records show that £1.15.3 was paid to E. Wright for a pump in 1824, and that one American contractor (John Hartwell) was paid $69.12 for making two pumps (plus $75 for pumping) in July 1827. Each contractor was probably expected to be responsible for whatever pumping might be required on his section of the work.[74]

The "cordage and pulleys" requested from the naval authorities in Kingston in 1825 may well have been used in dredging operations. In the 1820s steam-powered engines for construction and transportation had already been introduced in Europe and the United States, but they were still rare in Upper Canada. Suspicion of new-fangled contraptions may have inhibited their use. The respected American engineer Benjamin Wright certainly thought horsepower just as efficient as steam, and MacTaggart was of a similar opinion: "For all the work required [on the Deep Cut], I think a steam-engine not necessary, but a good horse-pump and a reservoir, which will contain about an acre of water three feet in depth."[75] We know that, at least by 1829, the company possessed some form of dredge, and in October 1830 the Welland Canal Company directors voted $500 for a dredging machine

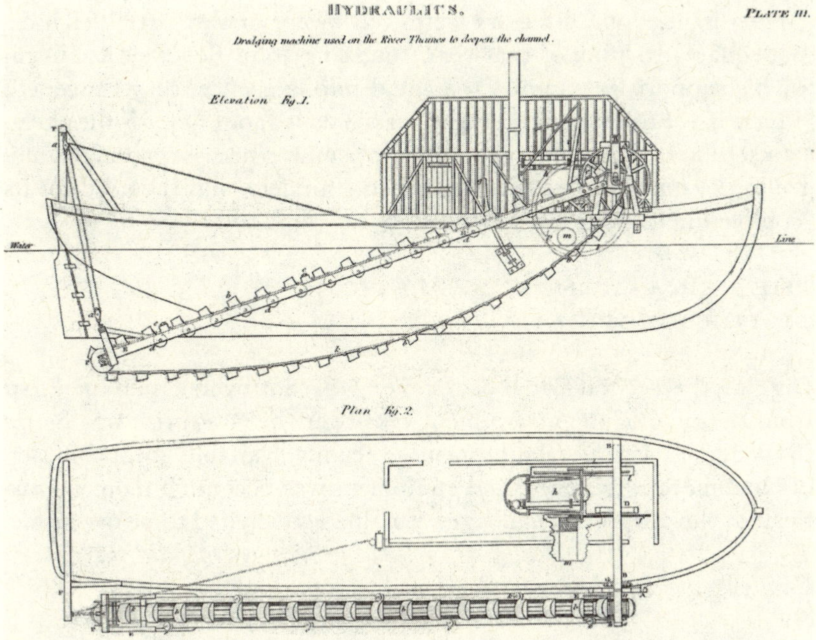

4.5 A typical steam-powered "dipper" dredge of c. 1820, using a belt of small scoops to lift material. Similar machinery was used on the First and Second Canals to deepen the channel. On Third Canal construction, dredges had huge shovels operating from their prows. (Abraham Rees, *The Cyclopaedia*, Plates, vol. 3, Plate III)

"similar to the one in operation, with any improvements."[76] These were probably horse-powered, but by late 1834 the directors were in correspondence with the firm of Elam Lynd(s) of Syracuse about acquiring a steam dredge (fig. 4.5).[77] However, after spending at least $2,874 and trying every means possible – even having an engineer sent up from the firm – Merritt informed the firm on 1 June 1835 that it did not suit the company's purposes: "It is perfectly useless to us, we have never been able to do one day's work with it ... unless we can obtain something like equity we will give you $1000 and return the whole concern."[78] In despair of ever getting any satisfaction, the company then applied to use the Provincial Steam Dredge, and also set about converting the steamer SIR WALTER SCOTT for use (see below).[79] Luckily for the investigators, the new steam technology had already reached Upper Canada. They were able to interview Amos Norton, a pioneer iron founder and builder of steam engines in York.[80]

Even in 1833 the directors were well aware of the First Welland's inadequacy. In June of that year, thanking John Beverley Robinson for his support in bringing the canal into existence, they conceded: "Much is yet to be done to make it such as it should be for the greatest usefulness."[81] Enlargement of the prism was necessary, the disintegration of many of its locks was causing anxiety, and the need for its "completion in stone" was evident.

THE PERMANENT COMPLETION OF THE FIRST CANAL[82]

Digging the Second Canal occasioned less controversy than the First: from the time of the government take-over the enterprise was better funded, engineering talent was more readily available, local contractors had more experience, and equipment was becoming more sophisticated. Nevertheless, challenges remained which had to be overcome.

Challenges Old and New

The notorious Deep Cut remained a problem. In November 1846 the contract for deepening and widening the channel at this point was awarded to C.H. French, with the aim of achieving the level of Lake Erie and supplying the canal from that body of water. At bottom the channel would generally have a width of 26 feet (7.8 m), but where slides were possible it was to be made 45 feet (13.5 m) wide. The work (mainly dredging) started in 1847, but when more slides occurred the following year, the contract was suspended. The engineers intended that the Grand River (via the Feeder) would cease to be the source of water. Although work continued into the 1850s, however, the Lake Erie level was not reached, and slides continued here in the 1860s. Dredging was also carried on between the Feeder and Port Colborne.

Local shortages of necessary construction supplies continued into the 1840s. Gunpowder for blasting still had to be obtained from the British Ordnance Department, sometimes at Fort George, although it was available in New York State. In 1842 Thomas Begly (Board of Works secretary) expressed thinly concealed irritation at the bureaucracy involved in getting gunpowder in a letter to W.B. Robinson, superintendent of the Welland. The order, he wrote, "has to go the usual rounds of the Military Depts, [and] it will be some days before the order can be had, and … there has to be a new application whenever an additional quantity is wanted."[83] In 1843 one Israel Pierce was charged with smuggling gunpowder into Niagara from the United States. The Board of Works rationalized the illegality by pleading that, when gunpowder was needed immediately, going across the border saved "a great deal of expense and loss of time."[84] Tools, iron, and larger construction machines such as steam dredges still occasionally had to be purchased in Buffalo during the construction of the Second Canal.

Cranes, Scows, and Excavators of Increased Power

Given the technological inventiveness of the nineteenth century, some development in the machinery used on the Second Canal's construction would have been expected. Devices such as hoists and cranes, although possibly in use on the First Canal, are not mentioned until the 1840s. Some machinery of this sort was necessary to lift the large blocks of stone required for locks on the Erie and Rideau, although perhaps not for the large timbers of the wooden locks of the first Welland. Our conclusion is that even when the Second Canal was in process, much of the equipment was still relatively primitive, as indicated by instructions from Killaly, the Second Welland's engineer, to one of the overseers: "It is very necessary that you should ... ascertain what tools such as blasting tools, quarry picks, bars, barrows &c., pumps or scoops (the property of the Government) are on the works and available."[85] When government engineers were building the Second Canal, moreover, human energy was still plentiful (chapter 9), and fewer examples of "the latest" machinery are found than one might have expected.

Although in the 1840s the great cost of mechanical diggers or steam excavators limited their acquisition, steam power, particularly in dredging machinery, cranes, shovels, and draglines, was gradually supplementing human and horse power. For example, in June 1845, Samuel Power, the Welland's engineer, wrote to the Niagara Dock Company complaining that their tender for a new dredge did not "include the propelling screw." What he wanted was: "a Dredge Vessel 56 x 24 the Vessel to be framed & built in the strongest & best manner ... so as to move easily thro the water. The dredging machinery to be similar in plan to that of Randik but stronger as the machine must have eight″ cylinder & 30″ stroke. There must also be a propelling screw 6 ft diameter with the required machinery to apply the force thereto & also 2 scows for carrying mud with sloping bows."[86]

By this time some enterprising contractors had begun to specialize in dredging and/or harbour construction, or in the construction of lock gates, while others (and their suppliers) were improving their equipment. In May 1845 boatbuilders were asked to tender for a "good decked scow, capable of containing 20 cubic yards of earth." In 1844 the firm of Carmichael & French, who specialized in dredging, had a "Steam Excavator" working ten feet below water level, which could remove 250–300 cubic yards of soil per day. By 1845 contractors Sampson Smiley, as well as Cotton & Rowe, specialized in harbour work and they, too, owned (or were able to lease) dredging equipment. Engineer Power had approached the Niagara Dock Company in May 1845 with a suggestion that additional machinery might be provided for the two scows on order for the Welland so that, when horses were not engaged in dredging, the vessel could be propelled from place to place "by a screw or paddle wheel situated at the stern." He had also requested that the dredges be increased from four to eight horse-power.[87] Yet in February 1849 Samuel Keefer (then the Welland's engineer) was still complaining in his "Annual Report" that the old scows could handle only 15–25 yards, and that he urgently required scows of 50–100 yard capacity.

During the construction of the Second Canal, cranes were frequent sights at the lock pits and were becoming more sophisticated. When the stone lock at Broad Creek on the Feeder was being built in 1843, Power reported: "Four cranes have been provided each of which … can lay 2000 yards per month." The following year he noted that three cranes had cost £45.[88] In an 1849 memorandum Merritt wrote that the contractors Brown & MacDonnell had proposed and agreed: "to have another Crane erected and fully ready for work at the south end of the aforesaid rock excavation … with the crane now in use at the north end of the Rock Excavation, or with such machinery as may be found necessary."[89]

By 1846 the contractor for the lock-gates could make use of special machinery for lifting the heavy timber gates (at a cost of more than £2,000), and Keefer indicated in 1848 that he needed "a lifting scow with a moveable crane" for "raising and placing the gates." The following year, Louis Shickluna of St Catharines got the contract to build this specialized crane, a machine that was the forerunner of the larger, steam-driven gate-lifters of the Third and Fourth canals.

After mid-century, steam-powered machinery was also becoming more common on the canal. The Annual Report of the Welland's superintendent for 1860 referred to the "usual number of steam dredges or excavators" in use, and mentioned that "another dredge, of increased power" was being provided for the coming season.[90] By this time the Thorold contractor John Brown[91] was engaged in the attempt to deepen the Deep Cut to admit water directly from Lake Erie, dredging being almost continuous. Needless to say this effort required ever-more powerful dredges of increasing capacity.

Strangers to Every Principle of Honour

The Department of Public Works was occasionally irritated by the slow completion of the Second Canal excavation. One can sympathize with Killaly's situation when two or three partners in a contracting firm fell out, delaying construction, plunging one of them into financial embarrassment or worse, and retarding the canal's construction. And Power was obviously enraged when he condemned certain contractors as being "men strangers to every principle of honesty, and honor, regard to justice and prudence."[93] More serious was the fact that a contractor's personal idiosyncracies could result in damage to the canal and to the navigation. Explaining the delay in opening the new channel in 1850, Killaly reported to Merritt that it was blocked by "a lump of rock just at the upper end of the Port Colborne lock" but that the responsible contractors were at loggerheads: "McDonnel <u>most improperly</u> without any reference whatever to me or without seeking any authority, allowed himself to be humbugged by Cotton and cut the dam last summer & let in the water without having <u>first</u> taken out this little lump of rock excavation which should have been done" [Killaly's emphasis].[94]

Such contretemps with contractors may have partially explained why reconstruction continued beyond the date normally taken to represent "completion" of the Second Canal (1845), but they did not deter the Department of Public Works from deepening the whole canal to a depth of 10 feet (3.04 m) of water on the sills, beginning in 1853. Moreover, in 1854 the Department embarked on a widening of the bottom of the summit level to 50 feet (15.2 m) by dredging, work that continued until Confederation.

Improvement of the canal was undertaken in other ways, as well. In order to facilitate night navigation, certain parts of it were illuminated with gas in 1853, replacing the oil lamps in use since at least 1851. The St. Catharines and Welland Canal Gas Light Company, of which Thomas Rodman Merritt, a son of William Hamilton, was a director, and which was located near Lock 4 of the Second Canal, received the contract.

THE ENLARGEMENT

Looking back after the opening of the Second Canal in the 1840s, Kingsford wrote, "a wilder, more ill considered scheme than the one ... put forth, one shewing more ignorance and recklessness on the part of the projectors, it is scarcely possible to conceive."[95] Equally critical, a Toronto journalist visiting the canal in 1875 asked, "What reason can there be for spending ten million of dollars more upon it?"[96] His stay in Niagara must have been short or superficial, because he missed the vital fact that vessels transitting the waterway were increasing both in number and size. Already in 1870, concerned to enforce its control over the Northwest Territories and Rupert's Land, and to stimulate trade within the new Dominion, Ottawa had struck a Royal Commission "to investigate the improvement of Canada's canal system by the enlargement of the Welland and Great Lakes–St. Lawrence route."[97] Among its recommendations was that the Welland indeed be enlarged and improved. John Page's surveys and his report on the practicability of enlargement followed. (The authorities used such terms as "enlarging" or "enlargement" when, in fact, an entire reconstruction was intended.) Surveys began in September 1870 and were still being carried out in December 1873. The engineer in charge of the northern section, from Port Dalhousie to Allanburg, was Thomas Monro, who had surveyed the "loop line"; he set up headquarters in Thorold. In charge of the southern section was W.G. Thompson, with an office in Welland. For contracting purposes the line was divided into thirty-six numbered sections (fig. 3.3). (The later deepening saw the route divided into lettered sections "A" through "T".) The first contract was awarded on 26 December 1871 to George Neilson & Co. of Belleville.[98]

By the end of July 1875 most of the contracts for the great new ditch had been awarded, and many American contractors were still in the running. Some local observers approved of this: the St Catharines *Daily Times*, noting that Section 1 (Port Dalhousie) was a "very heavy section," was confident that Dennison, Belden of Syracuse could do a good job: "[They] know how to build canals. They have done that thing in the States." On the other hand, the contract for Section 12 – "the heaviest" (said the *Times*) – where the "loop" curved to ascend the Escarpment, was awarded to the Canadian firm of Lobb and Company, based in St Catharines. In this section the builders would have to dig the prism and also create two lock pits (and later the locks themselves), excavate the basins for weir ponds, and build a tunnel for the Great Western Railway.[99]

Gross Slanders and Base Falsehoods

This second rebuilding of the canal was almost as controversial as the building of the First, particularly the thorny issue of granting contracts. For example, the specifications for Sections 17 to 20 (from Thorold to Allanburg) were announced on 25 June 1877 with a 5 July deadline for tenders, giving the tendering contractors only eight days to make their estimates. This situation, and some of the contracts given grants, occasioned suspicion and accusations at the local level. For the Thorold *Post* the short turn-around time for submissions amounted to "something strange." Was it designed to favour certain contractors? Did the MP (Federal Member of Parliament) for Welland lobby the Minister of Public Works to grant contracts to his political supporters? Were some of the contract tenders actually fraudulent? We have no way of knowing the answers. In 1877 one contractor urged a meeting with others to discuss a number of issues: what he believed to be the apparently low estimates of some of the tenders that were accepted by the Department of Public Works, the relatively short time allowed for tendering, and the possibility that the successful bidders belonged to a "charmed circle."[100] While patronage was indeed still an issue, part of the problem was the government's Depression-induced penny-pinching, which led the Department to cut corners and which, in turn, led contractors whose bids were accepted to cut further corners with their sub-contractors.

Eventually the issue reached the floor of the House of Commons. The spring of 1878 saw a long debate on the matter after Josiah Burr Plumb (MP for Niagara) rose to express his consternation over the slowness of the work. Alexander Mackenzie, Minister of Public Works and prime minister, defended the project, noting that Chief Engineer Page spent almost all of his time on matters relating to the Welland reconstruction.[101] Mackenzie had to fend off charges of favouritism and accused his predecessor in the public works portfolio, Conservative Hector-Louis Langevin, of the same! Mackenzie declared that the charge amounted to "gross slander" and lambasted the Opposition for making it "in all their picnic speeches." He noted that John Brown, a well-known Conservative supporter, had received several contracts.[102] The Toronto *Globe* continued accusations of favouritism and mismanagement in 1880.[103] And so it went, with little or no resolution.

Controversies again dogged some contractors and engineers in charge of construction. Throughout 1874 one contractor, J.K. Hartwell, nagged the Department of Public Works to grant him a contract, preferably for Section 12. He could not provide the securities required and denied the "base falsehood" that he was conniving with other contractors.[104] In 1880 F.B. McNamee, contractor for Section 34, had "languished in Montreal jail [for ten days] for contempt of court," having inspired a newspaper article that suggested another contractor had something to do with the mysterious disappearance of a colleague on the Lachine Canal.[105] (McNamee was plagued with bad luck. In

April 1880 his paymaster had been robbed of $15,000 while on his way to pay the navvies.)

On a more positive note, a pool of Canadian-trained engineers was now available, and civil engineering was fast becoming professionalized. Canadian-based contracting firms were more numerous, too, and operated more efficiently. The number of men practising engineering – usually civil – had expanded greatly after mid-century, and there was much work for them. Railways were under construction, municipal sewer and waterworks systems being built, and rivers and harbours being improved. Many began to believe that a professional society was needed in order to regulate their practice. Such a society could also facilitate the exchange of ideas, and raise the status of engineering to that of other professions. Consequently, the Canadian Society of Civil Engineers was established in 1887. Admittedly, the members' growing professional confidence also had less constructive results, as some tried to bar admission of foreign engineers to the profession in Canada.

The more advanced construction methods and greater professionalization of its builders did not make the Third Canal construction site immune from natural catastrophes. Excavation of its prism was interrupted by a huge freshet similar to those that had bedevilled the First Canal's builders. On 13 September 1878 Superintendent Bodwell telegraphed the Department of Public Works to report heavy rain, resulting in severe flooding, which swept away the waste weir at Port Dalhousie.[106] As usual, the Thorold *Post* gave a vivid account of the disaster: the previously dry bed of the new canal filled with a "rushing roaring torrent" of water, the result of heavy rain in the previous three days; several boarding houses were washed away, while the stables of the contractor Lobb were flooded; the horses had to swim to escape drowning. Page visited the canal and was "appalled at the amount of damage." "This is the worse accident that has befallen the canal since the commencement of the work," said the *Post*, "and will cost the country a considerable amount of money."[107] Such problems contributed their share to the delay in opening the new waterway.

The authorities had hoped to open the Third Canal to navigation in the spring of 1880, and contractors were given until 26 April to finish their work. The Feeder Canal could be used after 15 April for vessels drawing 7 feet (2.1 m) of water. The southern part of the enlargement (from Welland to Port Colborne) would open – it was hoped – by 1 May. While the contractors' cross dams in the enlarged channel were the main cause of delay, the lock gates had not all been hung and the aqueduct was not finished (chapters 5 and 6). The Department's deadlines were not met and the Feeder had to be used again in the navigation season of 1881. On 28 September 1881, when the first ship passed through the northern length of the new canal, the Thorold *Post* reported with a certain sense of triumph: "Our townspeople were treated to the long-expected sight of a vessel passing through the New Welland Canal ... The locks being still in an unfinished state, considerable difficulty was met with, though on the whole she made very good time, making the trip from Port Dalhousie to Lock 24 in twelve hours, arriving here at half past five in the evening."[108] Nevertheless, vessel owners complained of the dangerous southern stretch of the waterway and urged its completion, especially Section 34 (Humberstone), as soon as possible.

Plus ça change ...

We have seen that when the First Canal was opened for navigation via the Chippawa work began almost immediately on a line to Gravelly Bay. Similarly, although the Second Canal was "completed" by 1850, a project to deepen it started at virtually the same time. So it was with the Third Canal. In 1885 the Department of Railways and Canals decided that the banks of the channel should be raised, the summit level deepened, and the walls of the locks raised, to give the canal a depth of 14 feet (42 m). Tenders were called for in December, with the work expected to cost $1,125,000. Contracts for the dredging were allotted but all other tenders were rejected because Page considered the prices too low and in February 1886 new tenders were advertised.[109]

In fact much of the 14-foot depth had already been accomplished, as ports Colborne and Dalhousie could receive ships drawing 14 feet of water and the foundations of all the permanent structures of the canal were adequate. Deepening was needed only between Locks 2 and 24 and continued throughout 1886. Typically, the work was observed carefully by shipowners and by the ever-vigilant Thorold *Post*. The latter noted in March 1887 that some sections of the winter work were proceeding slowly and that the opening of navigation might be delayed, a possibility that caused "considerable uneasiness" among shipowners: "It will not permit of the fleet getting down from Chicago with grain in time to reship it for Europe by the first ocean steamers of the season. Strong representations are being made to the government to urge on the work of enlargement, so that the canal may be opened at the usual time."[110]

From the days when the Deep Cut was first being excavated and, throughout the history of the First and Second canals, the banks of the waterway were subject to slippage and landslides. Accordingly, the slopes of the prisms of the first two canals were carefully sodded. As the Third Canal was being completed, the engineers again sought to secure the banks. By 1883 the sides of the channel were being graded and "faced" or covered with stone, and wild clover was planted as further security. As well, trees were planted on both sides of the channel between Port Dalhousie and Lock 25 at Thorold to serve as windbreaks to protect ships from being blown against the lock walls by the prevailing westerlies.

Under Their Own Steam

By the time the Third Canal was being built great strides had been made in construction machinery as steam-powered equipment revolutionized construction sites (figs. 4.5–4.8).[111] Niagara residents were understandably fascinated by the arrival of such giant new contraptions, and the Thorold *Post*, always alert to novelty, obliged with several detailed articles on these marvels. One of these deserves to be quoted at length, since it reflects the fascination both with the construction itself and with the equipment used. As well as introducing some of the new types of machinery now available to engineers and contractors, it showcases the relatively high quality of Ontario journalism at the time. In the early summer of 1875 the *Post* described work on Sections 15 and 16 (on the brow of the Escarpment) as scenes of "extraordinary bustle and activity." The article continued:

> Huge cranes and derricks are engaged in swinging the ponderous roughly hewn stones in their resting places in the reservoir walls. Here is a Burleigh steam drill cutting rapidly into the massive layers of rock which lie in what is to be the center of the canal. Four horse teams are dragging narrow deep cutting plows through the stiff clay; at another point a quarry is yielding both building and "cement stone" in different strata. Here the "churn drill" and "plug and feather" are in requisition, and the ringing strokes of a couple of dozen drills resound all along the cut. Here too are the huge kilns or furnaces in which the stone for the famous Thorold cement is burned. Just on the verge of the embankment stands a "Black Stone Breaker," whose iron jaws are crushing up blue limestone at the rate of three or four tons per hour, to be used in making concrete for the bottom of the locks. At another point a tramway runs off to the east and following it as it skirts along the edge of the mountain you come

4.6 Steam-powered dredges on the Third Canal, each using one large bucket. (*Canadian Illustrated News*, 15 January 1876, 44)

> to one of Mr. Brown's stone quarries some three quarters of a mile away from the line of the canal. This is one of the quarries that furnished stone for the present canal when it was building [the Second Welland Canal], and from its appearance just now one would suppose that it might furnish all the stone that will be needed in its vicinity for generations to come. Here the quarrymen are swarming over the ledges of the rock, prying up great blocks of stone weighing sometimes seven and eight tons, working them down from ledge to ledge till at length they are loaded on the heavy trucks at the bottom of the quarry from which it often takes six stout horses to draw them up.[112]

That same article noted that John Brown, who was enlarging the Second Canal at the Deep Cut (Sections 20 and 21) by doubling its width and increasing its depth to twelve feet, employed "dredges below the water line and ... a land excavator, and a large number of men, teams, plows and scrapers above it." On land, in addition to four dredges, a steam derrick operated and, when the excavated material

4.7 A steam-powered shovel on the Third Canal, c. 1875, moved on skids as earth was excavated. The swinging metal scoop, clanging chains, chattering gears, and bellowing engine made for a noisy workplace. (Koudys Collection)

was transported by scow to a point near Port Robinson, a clam-shell derrick lifted it from the scows up over the bank for deposit. Brown also had three dredges and three derricks at work on Sections 31 and 32. On Sections 29 and 30, Ferguson and Mitchell had a number of "patent scrapers" as well as two dredges and two derricks.

On 16 July 1875 another descriptive report appeared in the *Post* (this time quoting the Toronto *Mail*):

> The old fashioned pick and shovel, "with a man at the end," as the navvies say, are superseded in many kinds of work by machinery. On several sections were seen "excavators" or land dredges, which scooped up an enormous quantity of clay and deposited it into trucks, which ran along a moveable track and which were dragged up the hill by chains, worked by an engine ... Ferguson, Mitchell & Symmes have in use a very large water

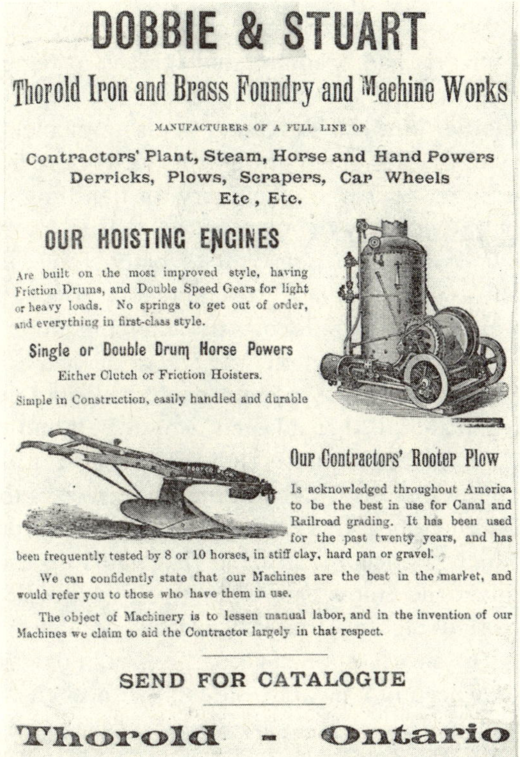

4.8 A Niagara manufacturer of canal construction equipment. Local businesses were stimulated by canal construction and maintenance. (Ontario Gazette 1892–93)

> dredge, the dipper of which scoops about two and an eighth cubic yards – more than any other dredge on the canal. It deposits the clay in a wooden box, which is lifted to the bank, 150 feet away from the canal, and emptied by a derrick having the longest boom ever tried ... it being ninety-five feet in length. Each load weights about three tons and a half ... The dredge and derrick keep excellent time, and get out on the average forty loads an hour. Another labour-saving machine, worked by the same firm, is "Slusser's Excavator," or self-loading apparatus. It is a wagon with a spoon-shaped shovel in front, which scoops up the clay, while an endless rubber band with slabs of wood across receives it and deposits it in the wagon. It is self-dumping as well as self-loading.

This article also noted that, despite all the machinery, there were employed about 300 stonemasons and cutters and nearly 3,000 navvies, as well as 300–400 horses and teams.[113]

Not only had equipment become more sophisticated over time but contracts had become more specific in regard to its provision. While a contract of 1842 contained a vague requirement that the contractor should "find all necessary tools implements and materials whatsoever," by 1875 the requirements were more detailed: "Suitable derricks or other approved machinery for handling and laying the stone must be provided by the Contractor ... The Contractor must provide at his own cost and expense all ... plant, tools, implements, derricks, machinery, and labor."[114] By now, too, almost all land-based equipment was run by steam locomotives moving along tracks.

In 1876, for example, the *Post* described a "steam shovel" at work on Section 16: after a "patent steam drill" had drilled 90–100 yards a day, the material, then blasted, would be handled by the "shovel" which "lifts the broken mass right up and desposits shovelful after shovelful on the wagons which are run on tramways to the bottom of the hill ... On the top of this embankment is stationed a 12 horse power engine, which propels the gearing that hauls up the loaded wagons and lets down the empty one."[115] With this "shovel" eight men could do the work of eighty – that is, 100 yards per day.

The new equipment on the Welland was a source of fascination well beyond Niagara residents (witness the quotation from a Toronto paper). In 1876 the *Canadian Illustrated News* published a full page of illustrations including a steam engine used at the new Lock 7, which, the accompanying article noted, "easily lifts and places in position blocks weighing four tons" (fig. 4.9).[116] The *News* also referred to a steam dredge consisting of "immense iron scoops used a great deal instead of shovelers, each removes about sixty yards a day." Such a concentration of powerful modern equipment had never before been seen in the area.

Canal-side communities continued to marvel at the large machinery on the deepening channel and lock pits, some of it doubtless exceedingly loud. Specifications for the 1877 re-letting of the contract for Section 27 (which included the aqueduct) give us a sense of the type of pile-driver available by this time: the bearing piles were to be driven "by a ram weighing not less than 2,000 pounds, falling through a space of at least 30 feet, until the pile does not drive more than one inch at a blow."[117] This driver was presumably operated by steam, as were most of the pumps now in use, one of which was praised by the Thorold *Post* in July 1876 for being "no larger than a man's hand which was pumping a tremendous volume of water."[118]

The *Post* is our best source of information on Third Canal construction, as it regularly sent its journalists to "cover" the work. On one

4.9 Derricks lifting stones onto the wall of Lock 7 of the Third Canal, north of St Catharines, 1876. The derrick is on skids or tracks and can be moved with animal power. Construction has just begun on the south wall. The gates are still absent but the mitre sill and the gate recess in the north wall are clearly shown. The public is obviously interested. (*Canadian Illustrated News*, 15 January 1876, 44)

occasion in 1878 it noted that on Sections 17 and 18 (south of Thorold) "the steam shovel on this section does great execution" and that "Judd's Patent Excavator" was in use on Sections 19 and 20 near Allanburg (but offered no description).[119] The latter was being employed by Peterson and Blakesy, who had sub-contracted excavation from Haney, Perry & Co. of Dunnville, the major contractor for Sections 19 and 20. Masonry on several sections was being done by John Esson – just one example of the degree of specialization among contractors at this time. Another indication of the variety of equipment now in use was a list of plant sold in 1881 by the firm of F.B. McNamee & Co. to the Department of Railways and Canals: five steam derricks, three steam pumps, two building derricks, two blacksmith shops and forges, anvils and tools, and seven tons Dualine (an explosive).[120]

By 1886 the new dredge CITY OF TORONTO (in use by contractor Beemer at the aqueduct) marked another development; it was touted by the *Post* as the first ever made in Ontario of all-Canadian manufacture. The local firm of Matthew Beatty in Welland had built the machine, which cost only $13,000, or $5,000 less than a Lockport company would have charged.[121]

The references to "Burleigh steam drill," Black Stone Breaker," "Judd's Patent Excavator," and "Slusser's Excavator" indicate that the development of new and improved equipment was fairly widely dispersed by now. Also, other local firms, such as Dobbie & Stuart (fig. 4.8) and Townsend in Port Dalhousie, were now manufacturing equipment that could compete with the best made elsewhere.

The usefulness of scows for various purposes in construction has already been mentioned. In September 1881 the *Post* published a communication from "Observer" describing the equipment used in hanging lock gates:

> The gates are made at Port Dalhousie by T.B. Townsend and floated up eight at a time. A double pontoon with heavy framework, also made by Mr. Townsend, is used for the purpose of hoisting the gates. The pontoon is placed between two gates floating in the water, and upon each side of the framework are suspended two steel cables. These cables are attached to the upper end of the gates, then by machinery the gates are gradually drawn out of the water and hoisted to the perpendicular, where they remain suspended one on each side of the pontoon. The pontoon is then floated into the lock and the work of stepping the gates is commenced ... When one gate is hung, the balance of the pontoon is kept by water let in through valves into a water-tight compartment on that side.[122]

Unfortunately for the Department of Railways and Canals, Townsend was, according to Chief Engineer Page, not only "more than ordinarily skilful" but also "inordinately grasping" and was apparently unwilling to sell this double pontoon equipment even for $1,800. Earlier in 1882 William Ellis (now in charge of both Second and Third canals) had recommended to the Department the purchase or construction of a scow to lift lock gates into place, "there being nothing whatever at present on the Canal belonging to the Department that could lift one that might be displaced or that could replace one anywhere where needed, the stoppage of navigation would be the result of the absence of such an indispensable appliance."[123]

It would seem that negotiations to purchase Townsend's equipment fell through, for in 1885 the Port Dalhousie Gate Yard, which repaired and produced various items of equipment as well as lock gates, built a "first-class strong crane scow for lifting lock gates and fixing heavy

4.10 Temporary rail line on Third Canal construction at the Escarpment. Despite the introduction of steam power, horses and mules still pulled loaded "stoneboats" on temporary wooden rails, as here. (SCM: N-1005)

repairs, 50 foot keel, 23 foot beam, and 7½ foot hold."[124] This was a modern steam-powered version of the Second Canal gate-lifter – and the predecessor of the huge gate-lifter of the Ship Canal era. In operation in the same year were also a lifting scow (the RED ROVER) converted into a ferry, and another crane scow (the HERCULES) removed to Welland.

The steam locomotive was also of immeasurable help in the construction of the Third Canal. The Welland Railway, opened in 1859 and running north-south on the east side of the canal, was of service to builders, as was the Great Western (opened in 1853) on its east-west line. There were also special "construction railways": one ran from the Queenston quarries carrying stone to the lock pits. As well, the Great Western Railway laid out track connecting to a Beamsville quarry that provided some of the stone for the Third Canal aqueduct. In addition, temporary lines (or tramways) were set up alongside excavation sites to transport men and spoil to and from the cutting. These tracks could be moved at will, and they served to carry lathes, workbenches, and other smaller machinery from site to site for setting up temporary workshops (fig. 4.10).

Even the most sophisticated technology is subject to breakdown. We have seen how First Canal engineers simply could not get a new steam-

4.11 Mule-drawn "stoneboats" at a lock of the Third Canal near the Escarpment, c. 1875. These low-slung carts eased the lifting of large limestone blocks. Derricks were operated by hand-powered winches. The finished stones arrived on site by a purpose-built railway (fig. 4.10) and could be pulled through the prism on mule-drawn carts. (Koudys Collection)

powered dredge to work, and machines were as much the victims of chance and accident as were humans. During Third Canal construction, powerful steam shovels became mired in Niagara's mud. The traditional motive force – animal power – was also subject to failure: we have already mentioned ox teams slipping into the Deep Cut in the 1820s. For reasons that are not completely clear, horses were especially subject to accident during the building of the Third Canal, most often being drowned after falling into the waterway. In 1875, for example, Battle, Corcoran & Kinneth made a claim to the Department of Public Works for the loss of a team at Port Dalhousie harbour. The Department refused the claim; a similar claim the following year was also rejected – as were others later. Another accident, which occurred in 1887, was reported by the ubiquitous Thorold *Post*: "Mr. Ed. Doyle on Monday last lost a valuable team, which in some way got into the new canal while working on section 10. It is supposed the new built earth, being loose, gave way, and that the horses lost their footing and slipped into the water, being drowned before they could be rescued."[125]

It is possible that the increased number of teams at work and the project's greater expense to contractors account for the more frequent mention of loss of horses. The growing public concern with the humane treatment of animals, moreover, may explain the complaint voiced in the Thorold *Post* in 1877 that a sub-contractor was mistreating his horses on Section Twelve.[126]

Despite the advantages of steam-powered mechanical diggers and other new equipment, they were least effective on heavy clay – so abundant in Niagara. Human energy was still necessary for wielding picks and shovels, and horses and mules would provide motive power on Welland Canal construction until even after World War One (fig. 4.11). The work site was as dangerous now as earlier – for animals as well as men.

After the Third Canal was completed, the Second Canal continued to operate until about 1915, but Merritt's original waterway and its locks virtually disappeared. In several places, such as northwest of Chippawa Creek, excavated spoil was dumped into the original prism, obliterating it. By 1887, the "new" (or Third) Canal was fully operational and impressed observers with its size. For local historian Ernest Cruikshank, its "long lockless stretch" between Allanburg and Port Colborne, with its "perceptible current" resembled "a river rather than a canal."[127] More spectacular was the series of locks that allowed ships to negotiate the 362-foot difference between lakes Erie and Ontario. To this crucial element of the canal we now turn our attention.

CHAPTER FIVE

Creating the Lifts

Once the land was clear and a route at least provisionally accepted, excavating the channel became the Welland Canal Company's next priority. Most canals are more than just man-made ditches, however, because the terrain they cross is seldom all on the same level. So once "Mr. Merritt's ditch" was underway, consideration had to be given to the important question of how to get ships up and down the change in elevation between lakes Ontario and Erie – especially the steep rise of the Niagara Escarpment. There were a number of possibilities, among which were tunnels and inclines, discussed above. The more common solution was to build locks – or series of locks – or, one might say, "big bathtubs for boats." These structures are referred to as "lift locks" – although there are other types of lock.[1]

The locks of nineteenth-century canals illustrate the progress of mechanical devices over fifty or sixty years. Their construction on the Welland also documents the growth of Great Lakes trade, the development of technological sophistication, and, as we shall see in chapter 10, the emerging organization of skilled labour in Canada.

GOOD STRONG WOODEN LOCKS

We have no contemporary drawings of the original Welland's locks but we know that they were little different from those of other canals in Europe or North America in the early nineteenth century. They were similar to those designed by Francis Hall for the Shubenacadie Canal in Nova Scotia or those built for the Rideau Canal by Colonel John By (figs. 5.1, 5.2). The principle of operation is simple: the weight of water – or the force of gravity – is harnessed to fill and empty each chamber. To prepare to fill a lock with water and lift the ship, the downstream or foot gates are closed behind the entering vessel. Valves (sluices or paddles) in the upstream or head gates are then opened to allow more water to flow in (fig. 5.3). As the water level in the lock chamber rises, so does the ship. When the water level in the lock attains the height of the water in the upstream reach (or stretch of the canal), the head gates are opened and the vessel proceeds out of the lock: the ship has been lifted from one level to another, hence the term "lift lock."

On the First Canal, locktenders operated the gates by hand – or rather by body – leaning on balance beams built into the top of gates, pushing them into position. The beams extended out over the ground beyond the wall of the lock, helping to "balance" the weight of the gate.

Forty locks were built on the First Canal and, as would be expected, the major lift locks (21 to 29) "climbed the Mountain"; that is, they carried ships over the Niagara Escarpment. The lock at Port Colborne on turbulent Lake Erie was more of a "guard" lock, maintaining the depth of water in the canal at the lake level, but it did function as a "lift" lock on occasion, although the "lift" was usually only a few inches. (As a safety measure, it had two sets of gates.) Elsewhere on the channel the Welland had several "guard" gates, which were used to control the flow of water during times of emergency, flood, or very high lake water levels. These were sometimes referred to as "guard locks," but in fact consisted of only a single set of gates, as at Dunnville or Port Robinson. According to the Annual Report of the Welland Canal Company for 1835, three of these operated on the canal.[2]

The Welland's locks were different in one respect from locks built elsewhere in North America in the early nineteenth century. Most locks elsewhere had smaller upper (head) gates, resting on higher sills or breast walls. Moreover, culvert sluices were often built into the lock wall rather than into the gates. As with the locks of the St Lawrence canals, however, the upper and lower gate sills on the Welland were often on same level. The head gates extended down to the level of the lock chamber floor and were the same height as the foot gates. This construction method created less danger of flooding ships and drenching sailors or passengers travelling upstream when the water was let into the lock through the head gate sluices, because the sluice was more likely to remain underwater.[3] Nevertheless, not every lock on the Welland was so constructed; the 1987 excavation at Lock 24 revealed a set of head gates resting on a breast wall.[4]

The locks were all the same size except the three between Port Dalhousie and St Catharines, which were intended for "pollywogs" (paddle-wheel steamships) and the servicing of certain stockholders' mills. These were 32 feet (9.6 m) wide and 125 feet (6.5 m) long, with lifts of between 5 and 9 feet (1.5–3 m). The directors considered making all the locks this size, but found the project too costly. Moreover they believed that such locks would have to be combined on the Escarp-

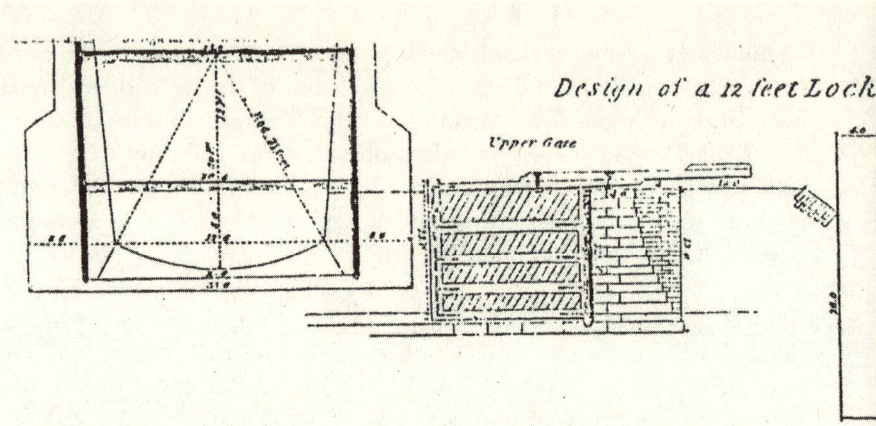

5.1 Francis Hall's design for the locks on the Shubenacadie Canal, c. 1828. Similar plans for the First Welland Canal are lacking, but designs such as Hall's give us an idea of how Niagara locks were built. (PANS: MG 24, vol. 1)

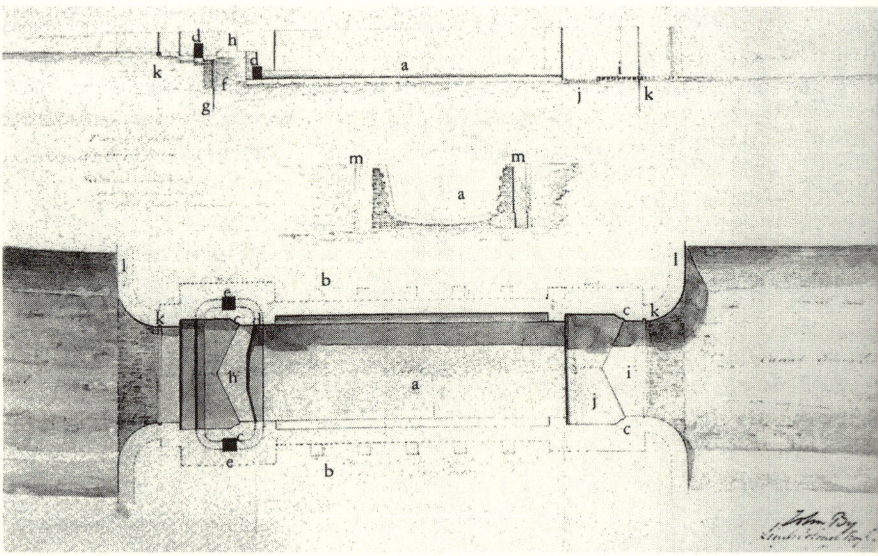

5.2 John By's plan and section of a Rideau Canal lock, c. 1828, similar in design to the locks of the First Welland Canal: (a) lock chamber; (b) reinforcing piers behind each wall; (c) hollow quoin pier where the gates pivotted; (d) tunnel sluices; (e) manholes; (f) breast wall; (g) sheet piling; (h) sill for the upper gates; (i) sill for the lower gates; (j) gate recess floors; (k) stop-log grooves; (l) wing walls; (m) clay puddle. (Robert W. Passfield, *Building the Rideau Canal: A Pictorial History*, 117)

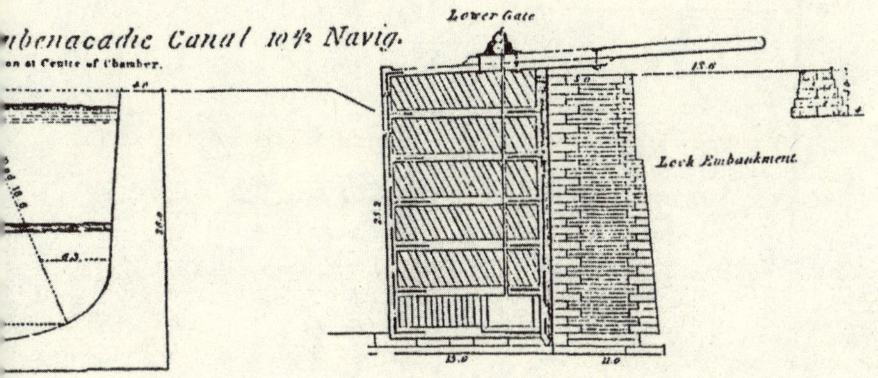

ment, thereby adding to the complexity and expense of the undertaking.[5] By the early 1830s, however, ship dimensions had increased so that even these three locks were too small for many ships.[6]

The influence of American interests in the construction of the First Welland emerged again when the size of the locks was under discussion. The New York stockholders believed that the originally projected dimensions, with locks of 72 by 12 by 4 feet (21.6 by 3.6 by 1.2 m) were too small. Consequently in September 1825 the Board decided on lock dimensions of 100 by 22 by 6.5 feet (300 by 6.6 by 22.5 m), with the harbour lock to be 125 by 32 by 10 feet (36.5 by 9.6 by 3 m). J.B. Yates, speaking for the New York stockholders, was the prime mover of this decision.[7]

In a Great State of Forwardness

In July 1825 the directors advertised a contest for the "most perfect model of a wooden Lock." The winner, multi-talented millwright and architect Marshall Lewis, was awarded the prize of £25 and went on to design all the locks and supervise their construction.[8] (The reason for building a model is not clear; nor is its fate known. Conceivably the directors wanted an item to show to prospective investors or interested local businessmen.) Alfred Barrett later made improvements to the lock design.

There is no record of the company directors' decision to have the locks built of wood rather than stone. (See below for a discussion of this question.) Lack of funds in company hands (and in the colony

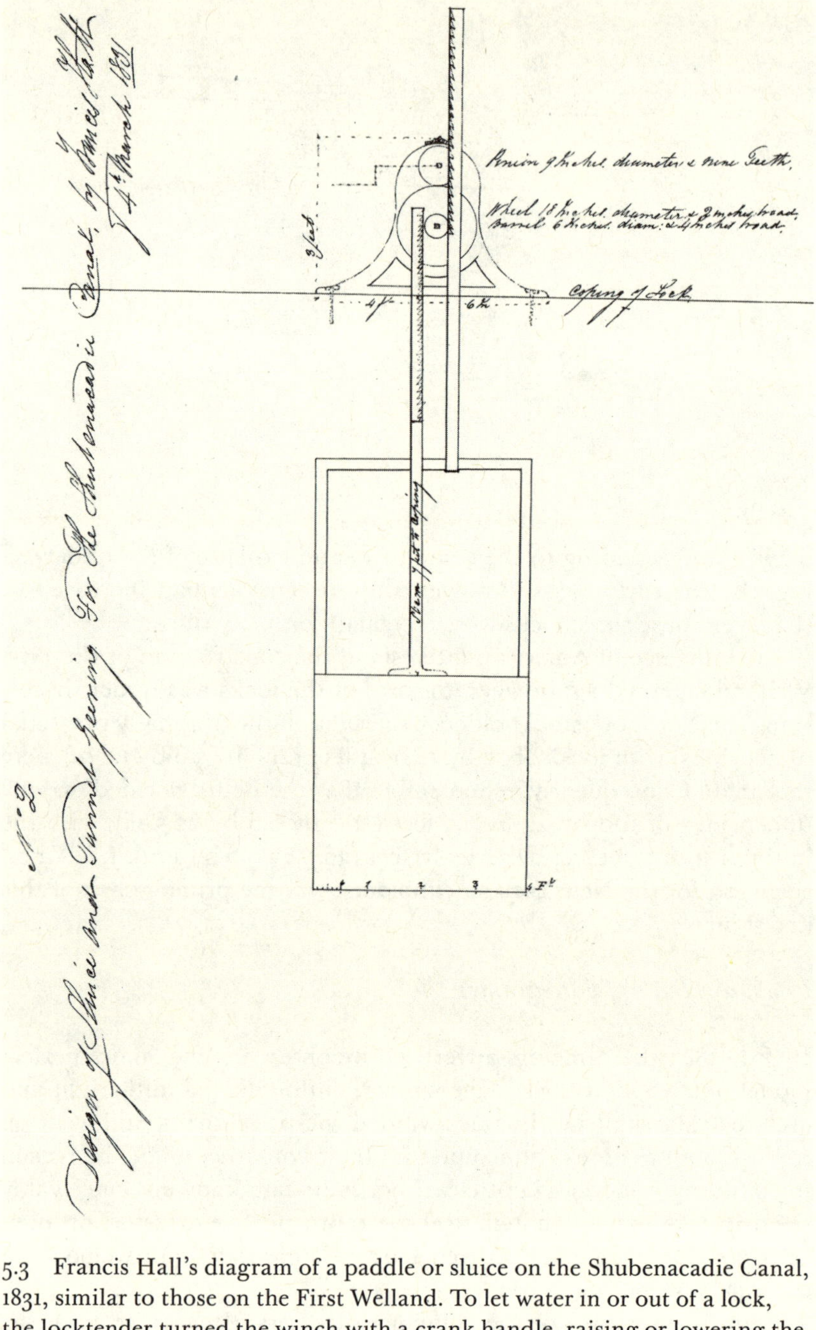

5.3 Francis Hall's diagram of a paddle or sluice on the Shubenacadie Canal, 1831, similar to those on the First Welland. To let water in or out of a lock, the locktender turned the winch with a crank handle, raising or lowering the paddle in the gate. (PANS: MG 24, vol. 4)

itself!) may have dictated the choice. For whatever reasons, wood was chosen, and the first contract for locks was awarded on 26 October 1825 to the American firm of Beach, Hovey & Ward and Oliver Phelps, who were to build all the locks in the thirty-five sections at a cost of $2,200 each.[9] Actual construction started soon thereafter and on 16 March 1826 Merritt made a notation that "Mr. Phelps wishes the Lock Pits on Section No. 25 finished by the 1st April."[10] The following July the lock at what would become the Lake Ontario terminus, later Port Dalhousie harbour, was begun. While heavy summer rain and Twelve Mile Creek's consequent overflowing delayed construction that year, the terminal lock and the two similar locks between the lake and St Catharines were finished by late fall. So too were four other locks between St Catharines and the Escarpment. At the end of 1827 the directors reported that the locks in this stretch were "in a great state of forwardness."[11]

Two locks, however, were not yet even started. The collapse of the Deep Cut's walls and the necessary change of plans necessitated the construction of two more locks than originally planned (to connect the main channel with the Feeder at Allanburg). Significant mistakes also delayed completion. For example, Marshall Lewis miscalculated the amount of timber that each lock required, originally estimating 24,000 feet of lumber for each lock whereas 38,000 feet were required. Lewis was also wrong in assuming that an earthen floor would suffice for each lock because plank flooring ultimately proved to be necessary.[12] It was not until October 1829 that all were finished, more than two years after the projected completion date.

Phelps's role in the construction of the locks was (and remains) controversial (see below). According to the *Farmers' Journal* of 5 April 1826, he had taken over the contract from Beach, Hovey & Ward, and it appears that he sub-contracted much of the work at a considerably lower price than his own contract price (making, of course, a profit for himself). He had contracted to have the locks finished by April 1827 but only about one quarter of them were ready by that date.

A Variety of Opinions

In the event, the locks on the First Welland proved to be "a fruitful source of declamation and misrepresentation."[13] So wrote J.B. Yates in 1833 – and he was not exaggerating. In 1830 Lewis had confidently announced to a legislative committee: "The work [on the locks] has been well done, and ... it will be permanent ... There is not the least danger of their giving way."[14] Unfortunately, even though they had not been exceptionally difficult to build, they began to decay and fall apart within a few years of completion. Frequently in disrepair, they caused the canal to be shut down temporarily from time to time, a situation that understandably led to complaints from shipowners. A shower of criticism ensued.

Why did they tend to rot or sink inward or leak water? Should they have been constructed in stone rather than wood? Was a mistaken choice of building material the fundamental problem? Was the workmanship at fault? Valid and thought-provoking questions, but not at all easy to answer.

Among the stresses that the walls of a lock are subject to are the weight of the earth behind them and pressure of the water within the lock. Ground water outside the lock also adds to the weight pressing the sides inward. Moreover, emptying a lock of water in winter or for repairs removes the weight of water that counterbalances the weight of earth behind the walls and can lead to them buckling inward. Consequently, the material used in construction and the method of construction itself are vital to the durability of the structure.

Whereas the locks of the Rideau and the Erie canals were built of stone, the contemporaneous locks of the First Welland were made of wood – specifically, oak, pine, and hemlock timbers. White oak was used for the gates and the associated hollow quoins and mitre sills; pine for the floors and chamber walls as well as the gate planking. The Welland was not unique in this regard, for wooden locks were built on some American canals of the time, such as the Potomac Canal near Washington, DC (1795) and the Middlesex Canal between Boston and Lowell, Massachusetts (1795–1803). The North West Company had built a wooden lock at Sault Ste Marie in 1797–98, and one was constructed at Bobcaygeon (on what would become the Trent-Severn Waterway) in 1832. While cost may well have been a major factor for the Welland, other good reasons for using wood existed.

The choice of wood must have seemed obvious to the Canal Company. Wood (especially pine) was in great supply in the still largely forested Niagara Peninsula, while stone, although available, was more expensive to quarry, prepare, and deliver. Wooden locks could be more easily repaired in the non-navigation season, whereas stone was harder to work with in the winter.[15] If totally immersed in water, wooden locks and their gates could endure for decades; above water level, they were anticipated to last only for ten to fifteen years.

Contemporary experts thought wood was adequate. Surveyors James and Samuel Clowes recommended wooden locks to the directors in 1824; the exposed parts, they predicted, would last ten years.

In a report of the same year the American engineer Nathan Roberts also strongly approved of wooden locks. Thomas Proctor, the company's agent in New York, wrote in 1825: "the locks ought to be of wood ... a good strong wooden lock will remain in good order with as little or less expensive repairs than a stone lock, will last from ten to twenty years and be built at one-tenth the expense, that is for the corresponding parts built of stone or wood ... To construct stone locks therefore on this canal would be uselessly wasting the money of the Stockholders."[16]

J.B. Yates, Merritt's friend and contact man in New York State, wrote after the fact: "*In no one instance, has the delay in navigation of the Welland Canal been owing to the Locks having been made of Wood, but the same causes would have produced the same accidents with Locks of any other construction*" [emphasis in original].[17]

Others agreed. Oddly enough, even John MacTaggart, critical though he was of other aspects of the First Welland, noted: "As to the wooden locks, I conceive few engineers could have cause to complain of them."[18] The American engineer Benjamin Wright believed that wooden locks, properly constructed, would be adequate even for any contemplated rebuilding of the canal.

Wooden locks were defended by the government-appointed commissioner, Robert Randal in 1830. Having inspected each lock and asked the advice of a professional carpenter, he found the locks "*on the whole* [Randal's emphasis] as fine a specimen, both in design and workmanship, as any other which have come under my observation on this continent." The timber had been cut down at the correct time and hence was not full of sap. It had been properly seasoned. His only criticism was that the lock gates should have been made of "sunk oak or timber that had been immersed some time in water, and afterwards thoroughly dried."[19]

In one respect, timber was an ideal building material in a pioneer society where the future might see rapid economic development. Locks built of wood could be easily taken apart and rebuilt on a larger scale. But what if the economy faltered? Investors preferred locks of inexpensive wooden construction rather than the more costly stone because, if the waterway enterprise failed, their losses would be minimized.

Nevertheless, despite all these protestations, the locks of the First Welland Canal proved to be exceptionally faulty. Wright gave the following diagnosis: "The plan of block work for the sides of the locks is very objectionable and more particularly the plan of securing the ties by dovetails not passing through the front or face timbers; and for this reason, a little bad workmanship, or decay in the timber, makes a weak place in the work; and this with a clay puddle behind it, a substance that with the common operation of severe frost, will certainly cause these ties to lose their hold upon the front timbers, being only let in."[20] Similarly, MacTaggart judged that the piling holding the locks in place was not secure and predicted, therefore, that the locks would "evidently give way to the pressure coming against them."[21]

Both of these engineers were sophisticated, knowledgeable, and experienced in canal building, so it would appear that design and workmanship may indeed have been the source of the locks' weakness. But here a difficulty presents itself. Probably for the first time in our study, the question of the personality and character of the Welland's consultants arises. Can we believe Wright? While his reputation as a pre-eminent American civil engineer has been generally accepted, his remarks quoted above may bear out D.H. Calhoun's view of him as "a skillful hypocrite ... more responsive to organizational demands than to whatever vague professional standards may have existed for the engineer of the period."[22] Moreover, Wright did not seem to have had any great objections to the workmanship when consulted by the Welland Canal Company. Perhaps he should have. As for MacTaggart, he paid only one brief visit to the Welland.

The locks had other weaknesses. The wooden cribs (frames supporting the lock walls) were filled partially or entirely with "puddle," a compound of clay and water, designed to make them watertight. Subject to frost action, however, puddle could shrink, weakening the timber construction. In his report quoted above, Wright suggested that this was a major cause of lock deterioration. He also believed that simple planking would have been a better guarantee of watertightness than Lewis's use of caulking to hold timber joints together. He also would have used oak instead of pine in the gates.[23]

Our considered conclusion is that the decision to construct the First Welland's locks of wood (whatever motivated it) was not unwise, but that the methods of the contractors and the skills of carpenters were questionable, as MacTaggart had intimated in his remarks about piling. Francis Hall summarized the problem best when he wrote in 1836 that the timber framing in most of the locks was "comparatively sound" but the "workmanship in all is defective."[24] He did not approve of the design of the locks but believed that, when locks failed, the contractor was usually to blame.[25]

Despite their durability under water, wooden locks can undergo decay above the water line or when water is removed from the chamber. Frost and repeated wetting and drying from rainfall can cause deterioration. Significantly, some of the locks lay empty for months during the construction period, so that even the parts intended for immersion began to rot. The heart of the matter would seem to have been the financial difficulties of the Welland Canal Company. The contractors' attitudes "on the ground" were also largely to blame. These men likely felt obliged to work speedily because each was paid only from the funds the company had on hand, the balance to be forthcoming after the government came up with another new loan. Contractors could not fail to be aware of this and must occasionally have wondered how they were going to pay their navvies or even support their own families. It was unfair to accuse them of "fraud," as Yates did in 1833.[26] Many of them were experienced canal-builders, often veterans of Erie Canal work but, under the circumstances, even the most upstanding of them must have felt obliged to "cut corners." Jedediah Merritt was probably correct, therefore, when he referred to the "hurry in which the contractors went on with their work."[27]

When they were finished, the First Canal locks cost the company $116,412[28] or $3,423 each, a sum that was more than half as much again as the original estimate of $2,200. Why the difference? Changes to the initial design added nearly $800 to the cost of each one, while no one seems to know what occasioned the remaining $400. Of course it is possible that Oliver Phelps, the contractor – and sub-contractor – knew ...! His role in the inadequacies of the First Canal remains central, if vague.

As we know, repairs to the First Canal were continually needed, but the company also tried to improve the waterway, building and rebuilding the locks of the First Welland even into the 1840s. One additional lock was planned – but never built – in the First Canal era. In 1827 Barrett had recommended construction of a lock at the Dunnville Dam to obviate the necessity of trans-shipment of goods from the Grand River to the feeder and, when the dam was being built, Phelps's proposal for a lock at that point was accepted by the directors.[29] But when Randal inspected the waterway in 1830, he reported that "neither ark-gap, lock nor apron [had] been constructed" at Dunnville.[30] In 1831 Barrett again recommended a lock here and, in his 1836 testimony, Hall stated that a lock at Dunnville would be "useful."[31] A set of guard gates (not a genuine lock) does seem to have been constructed in 1829, but this feature would not have permitted ships or barges to move smoothly from river to canal. In 1836 the board finally decided to build a genuine lock at the dam, and in November of that year Murray and Camp were awarded the contract.[32] Unfortunately, that work was discontinued on 27 April 1837.

From the record, it is not clear why this should have occurred, but the composition of the board had changed on 18 April. It was now dominated by government-appointed members, with J.S. Macaulay –

5.4 Lock 6 of the First Canal, showing the cribbing used to buttress the lock's unreliable wooden walls. The lock is now buried in Centennial Park, St Catharines. (LAC: C-140741)

a man who would soon recommend that the canal be abandoned – as president. Progress was probably also slowed by the deflection of attention to the political turmoil of 1837. Nonetheless, in 1839 the board again decided to prepare specifications and working plan for a ship lock at Dunnville, and Killaly was asked to prepare plans and estimates for this lock (which would be associated with a graving dock) in May of that year.[33] The lock seems to have been built, for there is a reference to it on 4 October 1839, when it was said to be "now used a Dry Dock by Capt. Sandon."[34] Only in the late 1840s, however, was it completed.

Although the locks of the First Welland were largely wooden, the canal builders did not entirely reject stone. For example, rubble-stone (broken stone) (fig. 5.4) was used to fill some of the wooden cribs at the sides of the locks and the Port Colborne lock was built of stone above the water level. In addition, the directors judged that, for making repairs or improvements, stone was cheaper than wood. Accordingly, in 1835 the board decided to buttress the lock approach walls with stone.[35] Such exposed stone was "dressed" (faced and smoothed). In the same year an experimental stone waste weir (a dam with a spillway) was built at Lock 18 on the Escarpment. In 1836, moreover, masonry was installed at the aqueduct, presumably also at the approach walls. In addition, the aforementioned Dunnville lock was originally to be built of stone. Reporting to the lieutenant-governor in 1837, the company included estimates for the cost of a stone lock to be built on the Grand River to connect with the Feeder Canal.[36] Company records occasionally use the expression "stone locks," a puzzling phrase since none of the First Welland's locks were ever built entirely of stone. However, Barrett noted: "we have seven rock foundations" between the Escarpment and St Catharines.[37] Presumably these locks, resting on the solid limestone of the Niagara Escarpment, were the chambers in question.

The Lock Gates

No lock was complete until the lock gates – which sealed the ends and allowed the water levels to be raised or lowered – were hung. Like the locks themselves, the First Canal's gates were made of wood. As we have seen, building materials such as timber, charcoal, and lime were plentiful in Niagara but other supplies, such as iron for hinges and other lock features, had to be brought in by water. Iron was costly and rare in Niagara; hence, contractors tried to keep ironwork to a minimum, preferring, for example, to substitute treenails (wooden plugs) for iron spikes. Nevertheless, some iron was essential in the lock gates to guarantee strength and durability. Although specifications required cast iron paddles in the gates, the excavation of Lock 24 revealed wooden sluices, suggesting – on this site at least – either the contractors' economy or a rebuilding in wood at a later date. Cast iron was used for gate pivots and, as noted, in the paddles. The pintle upon which the gates swung was also of cast iron. Wrought iron was used to make bolts, spikes, and nails, in the mitre sills and gates, and in the paddle rollers.

The source of the iron is a matter of conjecture, since the only iron foundry in Upper Canada in the early 1820s was the Normandale Furnace near Long Point on Lake Erie. Benjamin Chadwick's foundry at

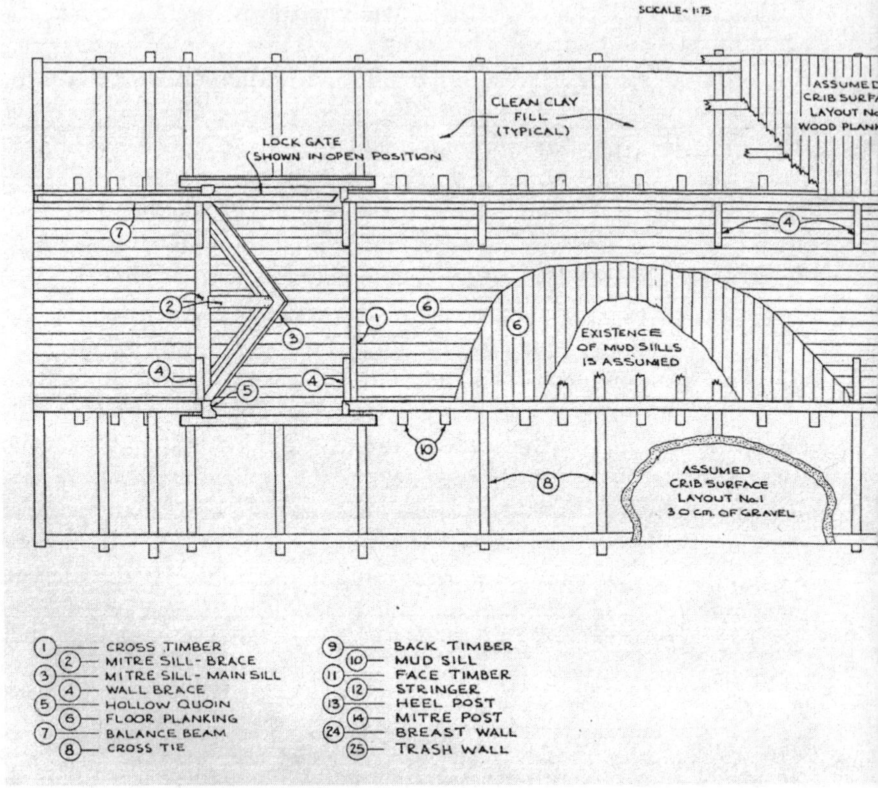

Lock 2 on Twelve Mile Creek was established only in 1828, when most of the locks were already completed. The Lock 24 excavations uncovered iron "T" bars with marks suggesting they had been manufactured by Uriah Seymour in Wolcott, New York, at his furnace which operated between 1824 and 1836.[38] Again, the company found the American connection fruitful.

The lock gates on the First Welland operated in much the same way as gates on canals elsewhere in North America at the time. Indeed the present Welland's gates operate on basically the same principle, except that water enters through sluices in the lock walls, whereas on the first three versions of the canal it passed through paddles or sluices in the gates themselves. All these gates consisted of two "leaves" and were "mitred"; that is, when closed, the leaves pressed against each other and against the "mitre sill" – a ridge of wood on the lock floor in the shape of a "V" that pointed in the upstream direction and provided a watertight seal (figs. 5.1, 5.2, 5.5–5.7).[39] The sluice or paddle in each

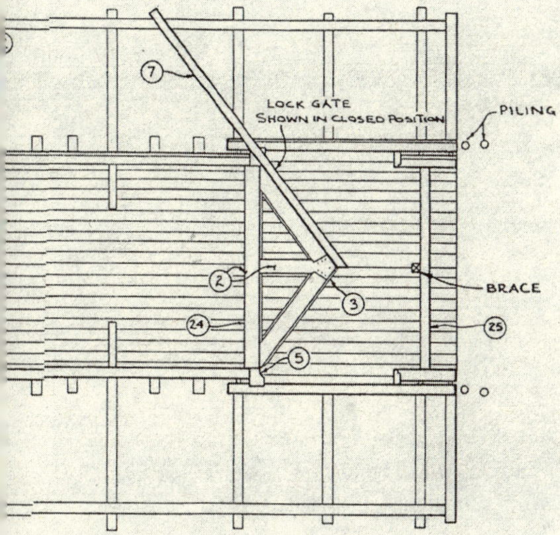

DIMENSION	PER SPEC.	TAKEN 1837	TAKEN AT FLOOR LEVEL 1987
LIFT	10'-0"	10'-4"	N/A
LENGTH OF CHAMBER	110'-0"	110'-9"	N/A
WIDTH AT UPPER GATE	22'-0"	21'-5"	6.37M 20'-11"
WIDTH AT LOWER GATE	22'-0"	21'-0"	6.6M 21'-8"

5.5 Reconstructed plan of Lock 24 on the First Welland Canal in Merritton, delineated by Robert Barnett. (Located on the Niagara Escarpment, this lock was excavated in 1987, then reburied to protect it from deterioration.) (Christopher Andreae, Lock 24, First Welland Canal, 178; reproduced with the permission of Robert Barnett)

gate slid up and down in grooves reinforced with iron. The paddle was lifted or lowered by levers attached to the balance beam. Excavations at Lock 24 suggest that weaknesses in the lock gates were addressed over time. Repairs seem to have been made in oak, replacing the more unreliable pine. In fact, entire gates were replaced in the 1830s.

Even then, parsimony and usage elsewhere favoured the use of wood. Still, innovation in lock building was not entirely excluded. In 1827, the *Farmers' Journal* gave a description of a gate that had a cast iron valve instead of a wooden paddle, and which was installed on a gate in a lock near St Catharines "by way of trial." The article suggested that Marshall Lewis, "well known in many parts of the country as a most able and ingenious mechanick," might have "invented or rather made some very important improvements in the common 'paddle gate.'"[40] Although the experiment was successful, financial restraints may have militated against the use of iron valves because lock gates of this type do not seem to have been installed on the First Welland.

5.6 Excavation of First Canal Lock 24 showing mitre sill (the triangular shape on the lock's floor, used to brace the closed lock gates). (Photo: R.R.T.)

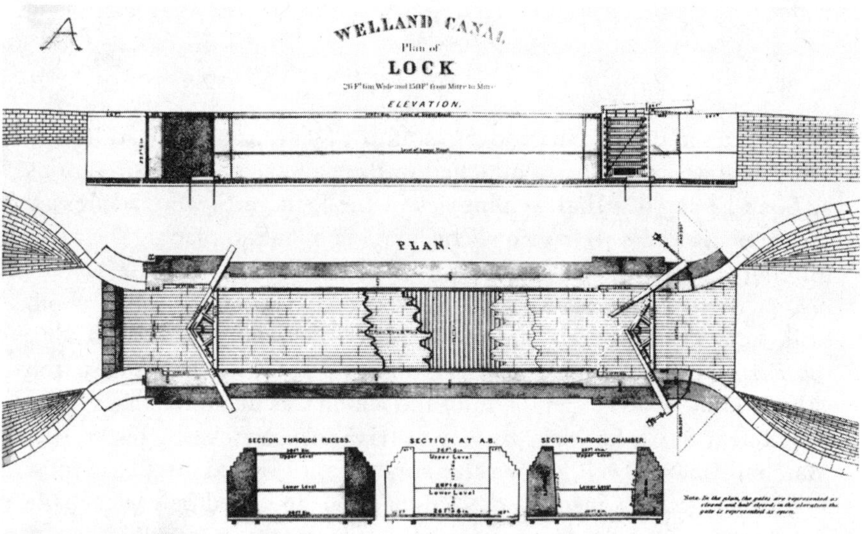

5.7 A stone lock of the Second Canal, showing the wooden flooring, the balance beams on the gates, and the flared, sloping wing walls. (LAC: NMC-3378)

Much Is Yet to Be Done

When the Welland was opened to Port Colborne in 1833 the company was justifiably proud of its accomplishment. But, as they had then acknowledged, "much is yet to be done."[41]

Whatever the workmanship, even well-constructed locks were prey to the effects of ground water, which made the surrounding soil heavier and caused it to exert additional pressure on the chamber walls. Some walls had settled inward, reducing the width of the chamber to as little as 20.5 feet (6 m). It was not unknown for part or all of a lock wall to collapse. Francis Hall's report of April 1836 is indicative. He informed Merritt what was needed despite the work that had been done during the previous winter: "A great many repairs must still be contemplated after the canal is open, as, 13 setts of new Lock Gates; new waste wear [weirs] in many places must be built; which the return of spring has shewn to be defective, slides in several places must be removed, and guarded against, and material provided and deposited at those Locks and works that appear most defective."[42]

That year alone the canal was closed for 93 days out of the 184-day navigation season.[43] Late in that year the company directors pessimistically acknowledged: "The locks are now from the decay of their materials, and the position in which they are placed, far more expensive to keep in a state of temporary repair than the increasing business of transportation will warrant."[44]

As we have seen, in 1837 the Legislature voted to buy out the private shareholders and the composition of the board of the Welland Canal Company was changed, so that the majority of the directors (three out of five) were York-appointed, giving effective control to the government. At their meeting of 15 June the new board decided to employ Killaly and Baird to "examine into the state of the Welland Canal" and to suggest how to make "the same a permanent work." In the map accompanying their report of 23 February 1838, they noted that of the forty locks, six were in "partial" or "bad" repair and seventeen were "out of repair." Only nine were "in good repair," no comment was made on three, and the comments on another four are illegible.[45]

By 1839 the situation had worsened, as the walls of the locks had continued to settle inward. In the navigation season of that year, the canal had to be closed on at least two occasions for ten days each time. In addition, ships were increasing in size, rendering even stable, secure locks too small. The schooner-size locks could not accommodate the growing number of broad-beamed steamers on the lakes. While the locks varied in size, it was the smallest lock on the waterway that determined the maximum size of ships that could use the whole canal.

As early as 1834 the shareholder-controlled board of directors had determined to widen to 21 feet (6.4 m) those locks which required it. Then in 1838 the new board decided to build a new lock at Port Dalhousie, big enough to accommodate the newer steam boats. The other locks would necessarily also be enlarged. Perhaps the directors had heeded Baird and Killaly's suggestion (made the same year) that stone locks large enough to admit steamers should be constructed. Nothing, however, was done, on account of the political changes at the time.

As we have seen, by the early 1840s the political turmoil had settled and unfinished business could now be attended to. Following the union of the Canadas in 1841, Killaly (as chair of the new Board of Works) took up the cause of enlargement, urging on Lord Sydenham the need for "the completion of this work," and urging the authorities to build to the following specifications: "Cut stone Locks of 120 feet in length, 26 feet wide, and 8 feet 6 inches depth of water on the cills, together with the required weirs, waste-gates, stone aqueduct over the Chippawa, a Steamboat lock and a capacious and safe Harbour at each of the terminations, widening of the deep cut, widening and deeping [sic] of the feeder throughout."[46]

THE SECOND CANAL

The main difference between the First and Second Welland was the locks. The route was virtually the same, and Port Colborne and Port Dalhousie were retained as the main harbours, but the size and material of the lifts was changed (fig. 5.7). Initially the new structures were intended to be the same size as the existing ones but, when plans were changed, the locks were enlarged to 150 feet by 26.5 feet (45 by 7.9 m) with 9 feet (2.7 m) of water over the sills. The locks at the entry ports were larger at 200 by 45 feet (61 by 13.7 m), with 9 feet (2.7 m) of water. These measurements applied at Port Dalhousie, Port Colborne, Lock 2 at St Catharines, and the new lock at Port Maitland on the Broad Creek branch (linking the Feeder with the estuary of the Grand River).

Stone Replaces Wood

This "permanent completion"[47] was not only to be larger but also to be "permanent" in the sense that the locks were to be built of stone. Each wall was to be faced with dressed stone and backed by a rubble-filled crib. We have already mentioned that every lock bore its number elegantly carved into a stone near the top layer of masonry at its entrance,

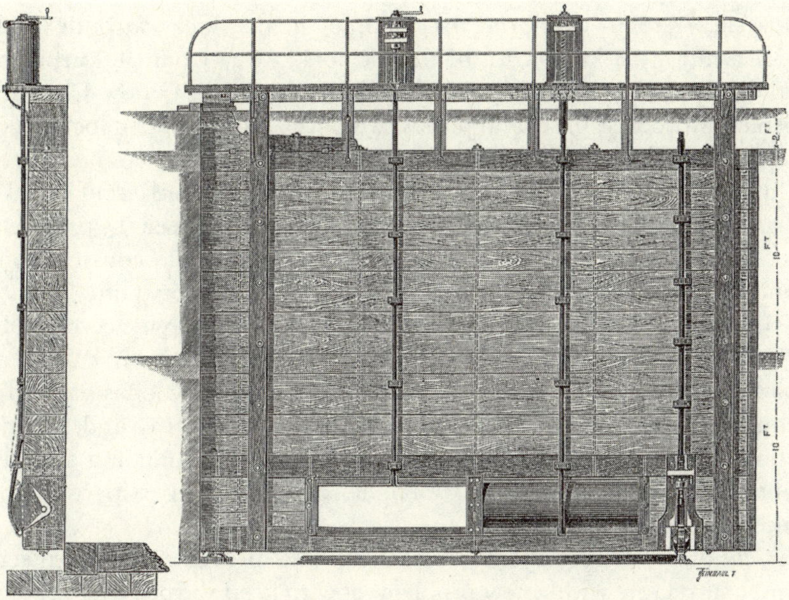

5.8 A Second Canal lock gate, c. 1870, with paddles or sluices similar to those on the First Canal. (See also fig. 5.3.) (*Engineering*, 25 February 1870, 130)

and that some of these numbers may still be seen on the "Mountain Locks" along Bradley Street in St Catharines (fig. Int.4). In order to relieve the pressure of water on the walls, they were now made to slope almost imperceptibly back from the lock floor to the wall copings at the top.

The lock gates were of red or Norway pine, covered with planks of the same wood. Their balance beams were 32 feet (9.6 m) long. Sluices in the gates were operated by a lever system similar to those in First Canal locks. Although Samuel Keefer recommended making the head lock gates smaller than the foot gates, resting on a breast wall,[48] the practice was not carried out in most of the new lock chambers (fig. 5.8). Slots in the walls for stop logs were installed at the upstream end of each lock.

Although the route of the First Canal was in general followed, the new locks were not built on exactly the same sites as those of the First Canal. The changes were necessary in part because construction at or near the old sites would have inhibited ship traffic and in part because, in certain cases, the engineers deemed it expedient to choose entirely new sites. At Port Colborne, for example, the new lock was built about half a mile (0.8 km) north of the old lock, away from the turbulent lake.[49] Here the lock may still be seen, near what is now Clarence Street. Moreover, in several places two of the older wooden locks were replaced by a single one of stone – as at Port Robinson, connecting to Chippawa Creek. At the new stone aqueduct "a double circular lock" was to be built to connect the canal with Chippawa Creek. Department records make several references to this lock "of peculiar construction" but, in the event, the lock that was built was a traditional one.[50]

In the narrow valley of Dick's Creek and Shaver's Ravine connecting Twelve Mile Creek to the Escarpment, the locks of the First Welland had been built at the most low-lying sites, but the new locks had to be constructed on the west side of the operating waterway and slightly above it. On the Escarpment the new locks were built in a straight line to the south of the First Canal, closer to the steepest part of "the mountain" (fig. 5.9).

Obviously the rebuilding of the Welland provided the engineers and contractors with a new problem: how to keep the old channel and locks operating efficiently while new construction took place, often cheek by jowl with the functioning canal? Contractors were repeatedly told that nothing must interfere with "the navigation." Hence, even while the Second Canal was under construction, improvements to the First Canal's rotting locks continued. For example, in 1846 the old Locks 1 and 2 (in Port Dalhousie and on Twelve Mile Creek, respectively) were lengthened.

Because the control of water flowing through the channel remained crucial, guard gates were installed south of Lock 25 (Thorold) and at Allanburg. At Port Colborne guard gates were set at each end of the new lift lock. The locks at Dunnville and the Junction were also essentially guard locks, controlling the waters of the Grand River and the Feeder. Meanwhile, a new guard lock at Dunnville (planned much earlier – see above) was now to be built, and tenders were called for in 1842.

The order of the day, of course, was total reconstruction. Contracts for the first twenty-one locks (that is, from Lake Ontario to the top of the Escarpment) were awarded in 1842, with a projected completion date of 1 December 1844. Tenders for the lock gates were called for in November 1843, and by May 1844 Samuel Power (the engineer in charge) could report to the Board of Works that construction of the locks was well underway. In September of that year the St Catharines *Journal* admired "the most unexampled activity" observable at lock sites: seven locks were finished between St Catharines and Thorold,

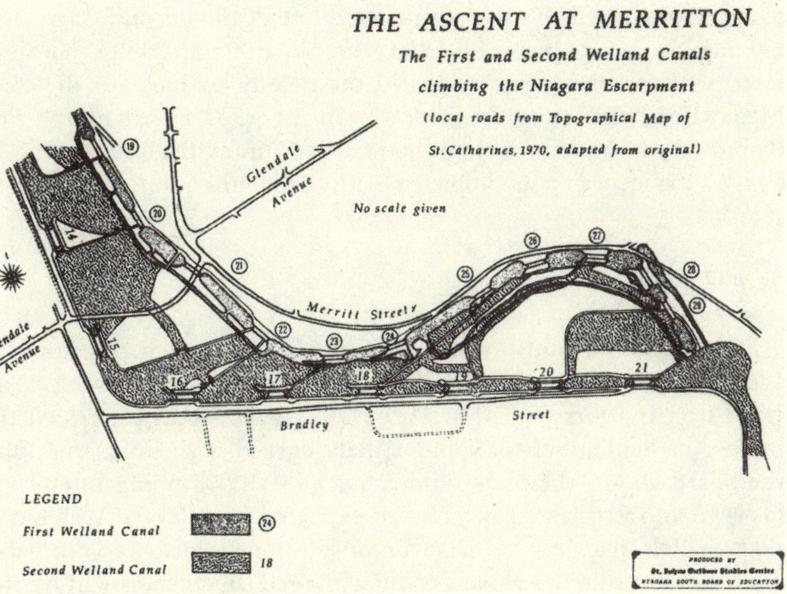

5.9 First and Second Canals at the Niagara Escarpment. The difficulty of building the Second Welland on virtually the same constricted route as the First is clearly shown here. Shown also are the vast ponds necessary to store the water and its power. The waterway's route rises from left to right, up the Escarpment. (See also fig. 5.11.) (Colin Duquemin, St John's Outdoor Study Centre, District School Board of Niagara)

and twelve others would be finished by the end of the month, leaving only four more to complete.[51]

Not surprisingly, the board's completion deadline was not achieved. The excavation of the pit for Locks 1 and 2, the most northern locks,[52] was slow so that in January 1844 Power had to threaten to take the work out of the hands of the contractors (Higham, Parnell and Hayes). By the spring of 1845 several locks, such as those at Port Colborne, Broad Creek, and Dunnville, were still unfinished, as was the northern harbour at Port Dalhousie and its new lock. Winter work was undertaken in both 1844 and 1845 in an effort to speed up construction, but delays could not be overcome.

In the early winter of 1847, it was flooding that slowed work on Lock 1 at Port Dalhousie (including the hanging of the gates). A further complication here was that the old line – the First Welland Canal and its lock – was still in operation. Ships passing through old Lock 1 had to be manoeuvred across the projected line of the Second Canal connecting it to a new outlet on Lake Ontario, an undertaking that interfered with dredging operations in the new outer harbour (fig. 6.8). Meanwhile, work progressed slowly on the locks at Allanburg, Port Robinson, the aqueduct, the Junction, and Dunnville. The new lock at Port Colborne was not completed until 1848 and not operational until 1849.

At the Eleventh Hour …

The delay in finishing the new, larger locks bothered the Board of Works to such an extent that they authorized the lengthening of old Lock 1 on the First Canal at Port Dalhousie. Merritt suggested this project in September 1845 and Killaly agreed with him, reminding the board about "the preparations made by the Shipping Interests of Oswego and Rochester," which had expected an enlarged Welland by 1845. Killaly had learned that, because the new lock was not yet in use, "eleven propeller vessels of the enlarged dimensions will be shut out" of the canal.[53] Eventually the Board concurred, but the Order-in-Council authorizing the enlargement of the old entrance lock did not come down until 21 January 1846. Always frustrated by the snail's pace of bureaucracy, the emotional Killaly wrote to Merritt: "You will be glad to know that at the eleventh hour the work of enlargement is ordered by the Committee. The Govt. have agreed to advance the sum – not to exceed £2,500. I was truly sick of the whole business. The benefits were admitted, but the question as to whether they would not advance the paltry sum or was [sic] about to deprive the country of them."[54]

Old Lock 2 was also lengthened at this time and the work on both older locks was finished by mid-March 1846. The two First Canal locks at Allanburg were also refitted in the winter of 1845 in order to keep navigation moving during the construction of the new stone one, already in progress. In April 1845 one of these older locks developed a leak, delaying opening of the canal for five days.

Part of the reason for the delay in completing the locks was the Board of Work's decision to enlarge them – *after* construction had begun! Typically, it was only petitions from commercial groups (such as one from the Quebec Board of Trade in May 1843) that goaded the authorities into action. At a special meeting on 5 April 1843, the board decided to make Port Dalhousie and the Broad Creek locks accessible for steamboats – "to meet the views of the trade."[55] Of course this complicated matters for contractors already at work on those lock

5.10 Lock 1, Second Canal at Port Dalhousie. The name of a Montreal iron foundry can still be seen on the lock gate hinge. Construction of the Second Welland acted as a catalyst to industrial development throughout the Canadas, where railways were also being developed. (Photo: R.R.T.)

pits. Then in January 1844 came the decision to enlarge Lock 2 at St Catharines as well. In another instance, the board in 1848 ordered the raising of the walls of the Allanburg lock, making the work of the contractors (Brown and McDonnell) more difficult and provoking a "most uneasy" Killaly to nag them about their "unnecessary delay."[56] For their part, contractors wanted compensation for the added expense involved in the changed specifications, which in turn complicated the finances of the board.

Perhaps inevitably, misunderstandings arose between contractors and the Board of Works. For example, on 29 January 1849 Moses Cook (who had the contract for the gates of Lock 1) seemed to announce his wish to be released from the work. Killaly regretted this for he thought Cook "an intelligent and experienced Contractor." Barely a week later, however, Cook arrived at Killaly's office to say that he wanted to take up the work again![57] In other cases contractors resigned their contracts without finishing the work, turning them over to other firms. The company of Gartshore and King of Dundas, for example, relinquished their contract for lock gates to J.L. Wilkinson of Montreal in 1844. One can appreciate the contractors' frustration with the changing policies of government bureaucrats, but such shifting of responsibilities only added to the mountains of paperwork at the board headquarters and added to the delays in completing the Second Canal.

As on the First Canal some parts of the locks were made of iron, most of which was still manufactured outside Niagara. For example, on the upper walls of Lock 1 at Port Dalhousie one can still see the iron pintle embedded in the lock wall bearing the words "J. McIntosh and Son. Montreal" (fig. 5.10). While Anderson, Auldjo, Evans and Co. (also of Montreal) provided cast iron, foundries closer to the project (such as that of Thomas Towers in Dunnville and Gartshore and King of Dundas) were also employed.

Because the locks of the rebuilt canal were made of stone, caulking and treenails (as used on the First Canal) were no longer needed. The joints between stones were grouted with a mixture of cement and sand. For the foundations of locks the contractors used hydraulic cement to fill the spaces between the timbers lying beneath and supporting the floor planks, creating a solid monolith.[58] More traditionally, the mitre sills were made of pine or hemlock. As on the First Canal, the backs of the walls were filled with "puddle."

Finally, in 1849, all the locks were in working order, those at Port Robinson, Port Colborne, and the aqueduct being complete just in time for the opening of the navigation season. Despite the government takeover, advances in technology, and a somewhat more secure funding base, the rebuilding the of Welland's locks had taken as long as did the construction of those of the First!

Even now construction workers could not rest. Despite their more durable construction, the new stone locks and gates of the Second Canal were still vulnerable to damage by ships, especially as those ships became larger and more powerful. And what is more, it seems some ship captains had difficulty adjusting to the new locks. For example, in 1847 the SCOTLAND rammed the gates of an Escarpment lock. The Broad Creek and the Port Dalhousie locks were also damaged by ships in the same navigation season, and in 1859 a steamer tore away the gates of Lock 25 south of Thorold. Because it was situated close to the Escarpment and just south of several locks that powered mills in that community, this lock was perhaps the most crucial to the system. A sudden surge of water could flood property, wreck ships, mills, and other locks – even endanger human life. Therefore, in 1861 a guard gate was put in south of Lock 25. Spare gates were obviously necessary as well and the Department set about providing them.

Locktenders crossed the locks by walking along the balance beams, a feat of agility for even the most light of foot. But accidents did occur, especially in icy weather, and drenchings and even drownings were all

5.11 Second Canal Locks at the Escarpment, looking west, showing the hand-operated sluices, c. 1904. By this time, winches and cables had replaced balance beams for opening and closing the gates. In the foreground is probably Lock 21 near the top of the incline. (See also fig. 5.9.) (AO: ST-406)

too common. In 1844 the new lock gates were equipped with railings to prevent locktenders from falling into the water. The opening and closing of lock gates was also made easier over time. The first contract for the installation of winches for smoother operation of the lock gates was awarded in February 1850 (fig. 5.11).

When the channel of the Second Canal was dredged in the 1850s, the locks were deepened from 9 feet (3 m) to 10.25 feet (3.1 m) by bolting down timber on the copings of the walls and raising the banks and weirs. Eventually the lock gates were replaced with improved ones and masonry was substituted for the timber on the coping.

The 1870 Royal Commission that recommended a further reconstruction (the Third Welland Canal) envisioned the continued use of the Second Canal for smaller ships between Port Dalhousie and

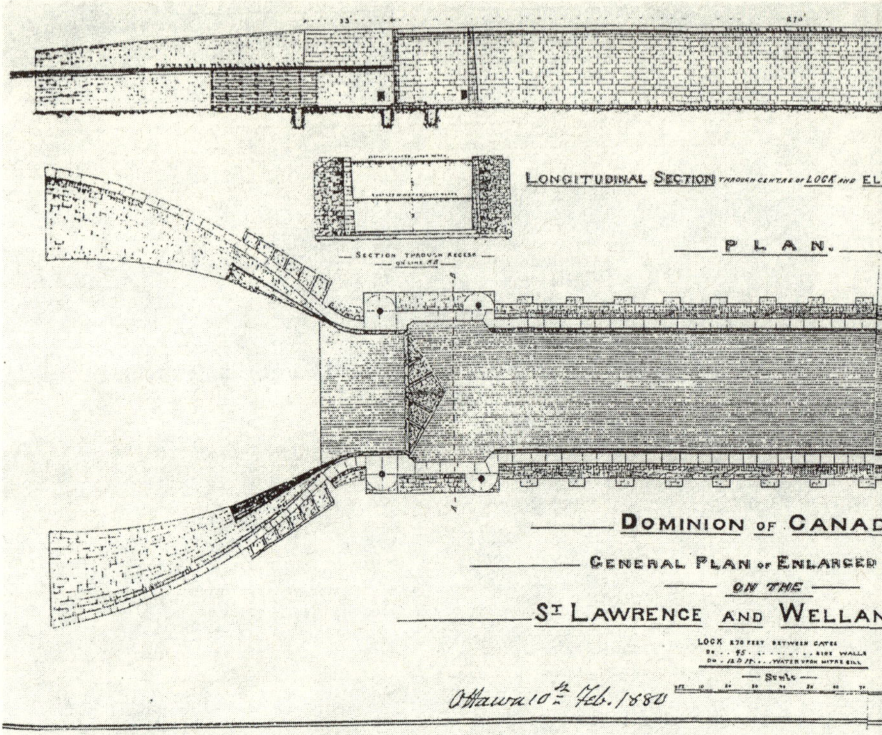

Thorold, a practice that continued, mainly for barges, until about 1915. Its weirponds also functioned as a source of water for canal-side mills right until the 1930s. In addition, Lock 1 at Port Dalhousie served the Muir Brothers Drydocks for several years after the Second Canal ceased to be the main line.

The Proportions of Noah's Ark

Plans for the reconstruction of the Welland that began in 1871 involved even bigger locks: according to Thomas C. Keefer, the builders of these locks "adopted the proportions of Noah's Ark, and made the lock chambers 6 to 1" (i.e., six times as long as wide).[59] As recommended by the 1871 Royal Commission's report, the dimensions were to be 270 feet (82.3 m) in length and 45 feet (13.7 meters) in width, with 12 feet (3.7 m) of water over the sills (figs. 5.12–5.17). The commissioners also proposed that these dimensions should prevail on the St Lawrence waterways and the planned Sault Ste Marie Canal. They added that the Second Canal lock at Port Colborne should be retained

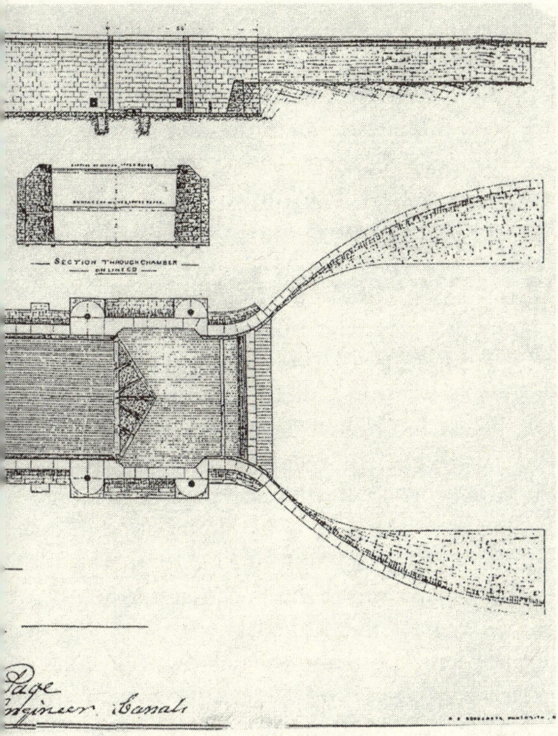

5.12 (*left*) Third Canal lock, with breast wall outside the mitre sill, c. 1880. (Compare figs. 5.5 and 5.7.) (Ottawa: *Report of the Chief Engineer of Canals to the Minister of Railways and Canals*, 16 February 1880, 42)

5.13 (*below*) Locks 23 and 24 of the Third Canal at Thorold at the top of the Escarpment, c. 1892. The locktender's shanty, gas illumination, and privy are visible. Note also the immense force of water dammed by the waste weir. (*Scribner's Magazine*, vol. 11, issue 3, March 1892, 280)

with a view to drawing more water into the canal and obtaining the canal's water entirely from Lake Erie. The lock at the junction with the Feeder (formerly a guard lock) should become a lift lock because the new channel would have a water level different from the Feeder. A new lock connecting the canal with Chippawa Creek at the aqueduct was to be built, since construction of the new aqueduct would wipe out the site of the older lock. These changes were adopted and – once again – construction took much longer than anticipated.

While the completed locks of the Third Canal ultimately resembled those of the Second Canal in general shape and operation, this was not a foregone conclusion. In 1873 a different configuration for the lifts was discussed, centring on the idea of twinning and combining some locks. John Grenville, who, as we saw in chapter 2, recommended a "double track" canal on a route through St Catharines, touted the virtues of "a double tier of combined locks" at the Escarpment. T.C. Keefer supported Grenville's concept for the sake of economy of construction and speed of ship transit.[60] On consideration, however, reconstructing the locks on the Escarpment and through St Catharines was deemed impossible because, as we have mentioned, they would be too close together. The slope of the Escarpment and the narrow valleys of Dick's and Twelve Mile creeks were too confined to support a new channel, or at least new locks beside the old, especially as the larger locks and prism would require larger weirponds for storing the greater volume of water involved. Moreover, the bigger ships of those years needed more space to pass each other in the channel. Simply rebuilding the old locks was not an option because it would entail disruption to the navigation in what was already a confined space. Hence the much-discussed "Grenville Route" was not built.

By the 1870s the new technologies of the Industrial Revolution, which had transformed the Western world, were evident on the new canal. For example, "giant water wheels" or turbines opened and closed the gates, which were moved by steel cables.[61] Another interesting feature was the new guard lock at Port Robinson. Built by John Esson, of Toronto, sub-contractor to John Carroll, this structure controlled the water in the northern section of the canal, in the event that the southern part had to be drained. Unlike the other locks, this lock had "drop gates" that were raised and lowered by chains.[62] More traditionally, both head and foot gates of the Third Canal locks were of the same height, as on the Second Canal. Other typical features of most of these locks were the vertical slots to hold "stop logs" for purposes of draining and safety during repairs.

If the growing size of lake ships influenced the dimensions of the Welland's locks, the length and width of the new canal's locks in turn

5.14 Third Canal locks at the Escarpment, c. 1928, with construction of the dike for the new Ship Canal's Lock 6 pondage and railway tunnel. The photographer is looking southwest with Thorold in the distance. The hydro poles document the electrification of the operating canal completed by 1908. (LAC: PA-172886)

influenced the design of ships and the construction of locks elsewhere! The size of the Second Welland's locks had already helped to create the "canaller," a steam-powered barge with machinery astern and wheelhouse aft over a blunt prow, with a long hold in between. By the Third Canal era such vessels were plying all the Great Lakes. Usually carrying flour or wheat, these freighters were 255 feet (76.5 m) long and 42 feet (12.6 m) wide. The new Canadian lock at Sault Ste Marie (begun in 1889) was designed to accommodate two of these ships at the same time.

The Third Canal had a more dramatic effect on the landscape of Niagara than its predecessors. Large stone weirs for holding back water for the locks in huge ponds lay adjacent to the broad reaches of the canal (fig. 5.14). Ironically, none of these supported industries, for government policy eventually (and only after much discussion and investigation, and many reports) had rejected the idea of leasing water rights on the new Welland. Some of the locks on the new "loop line" from Thorold to Port Dalhousie may still be seen east of the Ship Canal

5.15 Lock 2 of the Third Canal under construction, near Port Dalhousie c. 1875. The mitre sill and wooden flooring (features similar to those of the Second Canal) are visible. Photography was still a relatively new phenomenon and all concerned with Lock 2 have shown up to be "in the picture." Note the absence of hard hats. (Koudys Collection)

in the vicinity of the General Motors Plant. Here the "mountain locks" lie on a gently curving line, approaching the Escarpment obliquely.

Once this second reconstruction of the Welland had been announced, work began began immediately, with the contract for enlargement of the Port Colborne harbour awarded on 26 December 1871 (fig. 6.10). By February 1873 trial pits for the locks were being dug. Tenders for locks on Sections 2 to 7 (from Martindale Pond to Queenston Street at St Catharines) and 12 to 14 (the Escarpment) were called for in early September and awarded on 13 September of the same year.[63] In June 1876 the Thorold *Post* reported that John Brown (who had worked extensively on the Second Canal) "had the honour of completing the first lock on the new canal" – Lock 21 on the Escarpment.[64] Brown had several other contracts on the Third Canal, some of which were taken over by other contractors following his death (fig. 3.4). By July 1876 work was underway at Locks 1 and 2 at Port Dalhousie, and the guard lock south of Thorold was begun in the summer of 1877 (fig. 5.15).

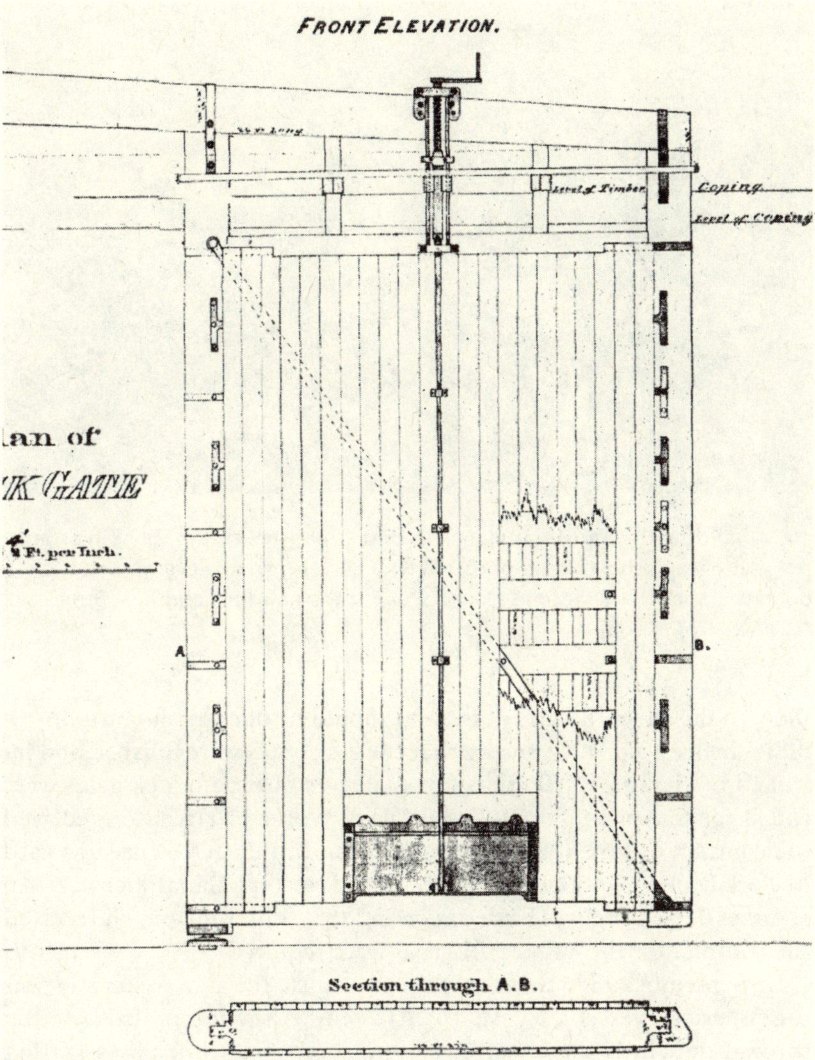

5.16 A lock gate of the Third Canal. The operating mechanism was similar to that on the First and Second Canals – but would soon be powered by electricity. (LAC: RG 43, vol. 1379, file 3730)

Although the lock gates were the last part of the canal to be constructed and installed, they were the most important parts of the waterway, for the efficiency of the canal depended on their smooth operation (fig. 5.16). This was the notion behind the message of the Minister of Railways and Canals to Chief Engineer John Page in April

5.17 Building the Third Canal lock at Port Colborne, c. 1875. Looking south, the photograph shows hand-operated winches, the grain elevator, and the operating lock of the Second Canal between the new lock and East Street. (Koudys Collection)

1880, to the effect that the new canal should be operational by 20 April 1881 – hence Page must ensure that the lock gates were finished and installed by that date.[65] Tenders for the leaves of the 110 lock gates were called for in April 1880. Townsend Tool Works of Hamilton received the contract in June 1880, and work began in July at Townsend's yard in Port Dalhousie between the First and Second Canal locks. When channel deepening was undertaken in 1886, John McDonagh received the contract for the larger gates that were required.

In September 1881 the first ship to transit the new waterway was the American vessel DON M. DICKINSON. Although pulled by a tug through much of the canal, it experienced some difficulties getting through locks that were not yet completely functional. From then on, the Second Canal locks became obsolete south of Thorold and no lock at all was required at Allanburg because of the lower level of the new canal. At Port Colborne the Second Canal lock was retained, along with the new lock to the east of it and a new partially covered raceway to the west, controlling the flow of water into the new canal (fig. 5.17).

"If something can go wrong, it will" – or so Page and his engineers might have believed. Lock 1 at Port Dalhousie proved especially troublesome. As early as 1876 construction was retarded when Connolly, the contractor, found that the bottom of the pit was not rock but hard clay, probably the same hardpan that had bedevilled construction since 1825. Dredging was as useless as underwater blasting. Eventually Connolly built a cofferdam, pumped out the water, and blasted the clay in the dry. Only then could excavation begin.[66] In March 1881 a large crack appeared in the masonry of that problematic lock, while the ground above and behind the affected stones threatened to cave in as water poured into the chamber. Repairs began immediately but Lock 1 continued to provide challenges. In May 1881 William Ellis sent a troubled telegram to Ottawa:

> The foot gates at Lock 1 New Canal were taken away by order of Mr Page Thurs. last leaving the navigation of this canal entirely dependent upon a dam recently put in at head of same which dam he is aware is somewhat weak and unreliable owing to its not resting wholly upon a good & solid foundation (unavoidably so). No one is at work so far up to this moment putting in the intended new gates. I deem it my duty to notify the Department of the present state of things & thus release myself of our present exposed condition about which I was in no way consulted. I thoroughly urge no time should be lost in putting in the new gates at Lock No. 1 to make this Canal system safe.[67]

The problems were eventually overcome and today Lock 1 still stands, its stonework, remarkably, nearly intact.

Also at Port Dalhousie, Lock 2 proved to be a headache but in this instance the contractors were unmistakably at fault. Murray and Cleveland had piled a large amount of stone, sand, and other building materials on the ground above its cribs. When water was let out of the lock in late April 1887, the cribbing collapsed, sending those materials crashing down into the canal prism. Their retrieval and the cleaning out of the channel proved a costly setback to the contractors.

In July 1881 defective valves in some of the new gates caused locktenders difficulty in opening and closing the gates. By August, the crisis was temporarily solved by the installation of turbine wheels to aid the valve operation, but not without causing "another vexatious delay"[68] in opening the new canal. The hanging of the gates had to be postponed in this case, to be resumed only in early August. By the end of the navigation season, when the turbine wheels were disengaged, the gates seemed to be working well; but by the summer of 1882 Ellis complained that the "valves, gates, tracks, gearing etc." were working in a "very threatening and troublesome manner."[69] Operating the valves by hand-operated winches (the preferred method) was difficult and time-consuming, provoking complaints from mariners – which canal authorities always sought to avoid. Accordingly, turbines were again installed in 1883 on several locks; but even then problems arose with the copper cables that actually pulled the gates into place. Their replacement by steel ones finally seemed to prevent further problems.

Rascally Outrage

As if such physical challenges were not enough, the contract for construction of the lock gates was not without controversy and sensation. Townsend Tool Works, the contractor, was run by a deputy of the Chief Engineer of Public Works. This conflict of interest led to "considerable dissatisfaction and even indignation," because the builder was a civil servant and, added the Thorold *Post*, "there are rumours afloat, even by the Conservative press, of the 'crookedness' of the transaction." It was feared that such a man would have access to information denied to other tendering contractors.[70] The St Catharines *Journal* echoed this concern, to no apparent effect.[71]

Further complications developed when in February 1881 six of the new gates stored at Lock 2 were damaged in a "rascally outrage."[72] Chief Engineer Page recommended that night watchmen be employed and perhaps also a detective hired to investigate.[73] Townsend echoed the need for men to protect his work. He told the Department of Railways and Canals that he knew of "no personal enemy," noting that his contract required him to store valuable equipment at sites along the new canal. He added that about twenty pieces of equipment had several weeks previously been "mutilated by having the brass work taken out of them."[74] No connection between the granting of the contract – alleged to be political patronage – and the damage was ever proven.

However, Townsend himself was a thorn in Page's side and the Department – or perhaps Page's rectitude – may have antagonized less punctilious men such as the lock gate builder. In May 1882 Townsend went to Ottawa to negotiate extra claims for the lock gates with Page personally, staying over a month in the capital. When Page offered about $7,000 less than the gate builder wanted, Townsend was indignant: "The Chief Engineer, with his perfect method of doing business, has not deemed it necessary to explain [his rejection of the total of the contractor's claims]." Townsend then suggested submitting the claims to Walter or Frank Shanly, or to Samuel Keefer, either of whose decision he would accept as final. Page refused and Townsend declined to appeal to the Dominion Board of Arbitrators, whom he thought ill-equipped to pass judgment: "gentlemen who are wholly unacquainted with such matters – were I to do this it would be only by accident I should get a just verdict." And so he accepted the chief engineer's "unjust amount," attributing Page's parsimony to "too much work or

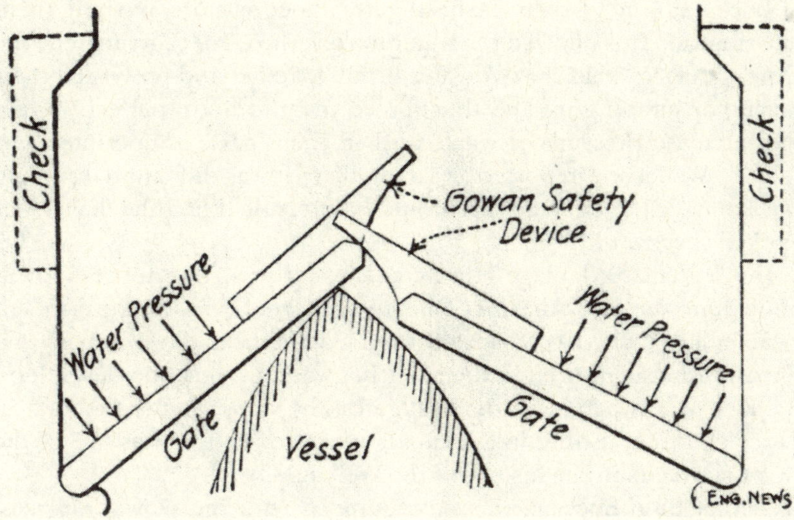

5.18 Gowan safety devices installed on Third Canal locks: two large "horn" castings, one on each gate. When one leaf is pushed back out of proper mitre by a ship, the other horn would guide the leaves back into place. (SCM: Archives, Welland Canal file, envelope 1)

personal malevolence." As for Page himself, he described Townsend as "fairly intelligent and more than ordinarily skilful – rather fawning than otherwise ... unusually opinionated and inordinately grasping."[75]

Like its predecessors, the Third Welland Canal never existed in stasis. By late 1905 electicity was replacing gas as a source of lighting, and by 1908 electric motors were used to open and close the lock gates. Now both engineers and labourers had to be warned about a new hazard – electric shock. In 1907, therefore, the authorities decided that notices should be posted along the canal, containing "information for the resuscitation of persons suffering from electrical shock and apparently dead."[76] Electrocution would become a constant danger when the Ship Canal was built in the twentieth century.

Over time, the familiar balance beams on the locks were phased out. In 1910 an experiment was tried out on Lock 24 with a new invention that was to prove invaluable: the "Gowan Safety Device." Consisting of short projections on the ends of gates, this device functioned to protect the gates from ships' prows, strengthening the gates in case they were rammed by a ship (fig. 5.18). The *Evening Journal* reported on the arrival of the "contrivances" in St Catharines on 11 June. Two years later the same paper trumpeted their worth, describing an accident involving the steamer BEAVERTON, which had run into the head gates of Lock 24, "and opened the head gates a foot or more, pushing them out of mitre. This allowed the water to rush through." Fortunately, the Gowan device "held the two gates firmly together and prevented their raising or jumping up and thus forced them to mitre perfectly when the immense pressure of water pushed them back." Superintendent John L. Weller was reported as saying that "It was difficult to estimate the extent of the damage that would have resulted had the device not worked successfully."[77]

The "extent of damage" that could result was soon to be known: on 21 June the St Catharines *Standard* reported that the government steamer LA CANADIENNE had rammed the headgates of Lock 22. The ship smashed through them, letting water in the upper level flood the lock and sweep away the headgates, the ships, and the footgates. Three children, fishing in the canal, were drowned. It was one of the worst accidents in the history of the Welland Canal.

At that time Lock 22 was not equipped with the Gowan devices. This accident may have spurred officialdom to action; aside from the tragic loss of life, the repair bills themselves would have provided an incentive: the repairs for the protected Lock 24 had cost $28.16, those for Lock 22 cost $5,479.53. Later that year a contract was signed with James Battle and N.W. Gowan to supply "20 steel castings forming the Gowan Safety Apppliances for locks gates" at a cost of $6,000.[78] Two accidents in October of 1914, involving Locks 23 and 24, show a similar pattern: Lock 23 (with no Gowan devices) $4,881.74; Lock 24 (protected) $950. L.D. Hara, acting superintendent of the Welland in June 1914, stated in his Annual Report that Locks 5, 7, 9, 10, 17, 19, 21, and 24 already had the devices on the headgates, and that the masonry on Locks 5, 7, 9, 10, 17–24, was prepared for installation on the footgates. By the winter of 1914–15 Gowan Safety Devices had been installed on the foot gates of all the locks.[79]

Thus the locks of the Third Welland Canal entered the twentieth century in a constant state of improvement and reconstruction. In fact even when it was superseded by the Fourth ("Ship") Canal, parts of the Third continued in use. The problematic Lock 1 of the Third Canal at Port Dalhousie, for example, operated until about 1969.

Third Canal Methods and Materials

At first glance a canal buff will not notice much difference (apart from size) between the locks of the Second and the Third canals. This is because building materials changed little between the 1840s and the

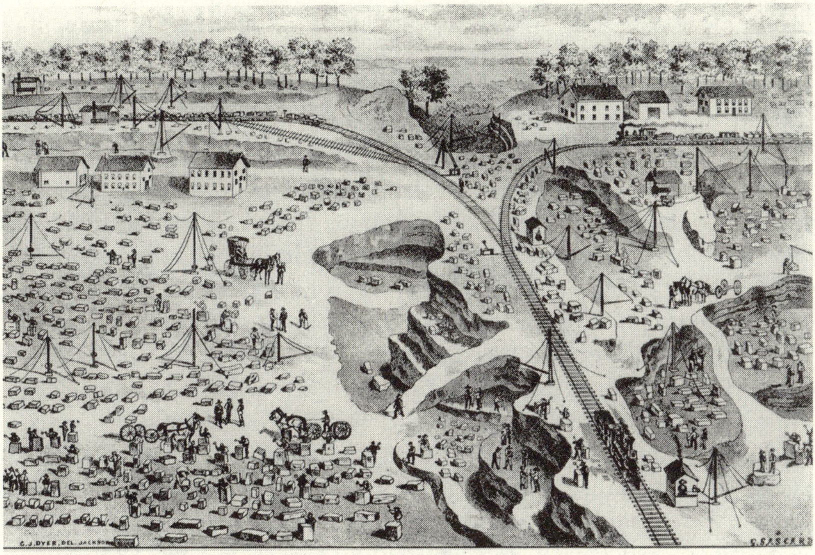

5.19 William Hendershot's Stone Quarry at Queenston Heights, c. 1876. From here, a steam train carried finished stone to Third Canal lock sites. (H.R. Page, *Illustrated Historical Atlas*, 56)

1870s, although iron, then steel and concrete, were increasingly prevalent in construction.

The limestone – notably used on the guard lock south of Thorold – came largely from the quarries of W.M. Hendershot on the Escarpment, approximately a mile west of Queenston (fig. 5.19). These quarries covered an area of about 90 acres (36 ha) and were eventually connected to the main line of the Great Western Railway by a spur line. Other shipments of stone came from Manning and Ginty's quarry (also at Queenston), and some was supplied by quarries at Beaverdams and in Pelham. Given the condition of early roads and the few railway options, builders were sometimes forced to use a circuitous route to bring stone to the sites of the new locks. Before the spur line to the quarry was built, Hendershot took stone down to Queenston, loaded it onto barges, sent it down the Niagara River, along the lake shore, thence through Port Dalhousie harbour and along the old canal to the construction sites. Some stone was brought in by barge from quarries on Pelee Island for Locks 17 and 18 on the Escarpment. New quarries were soon opened in the vicinity to meet the greater demand for stone. When Fraser and Company opened one in September 1877 on Peter Hoover's farm near Section 16, "the blast," commented the *Post*, "was a beautiful one." By August 1877 most of the necessary stone had been quarried and delivered so that local quarries were nearly idle; at Queenston Heights, the men amused themselves by racing handcars.[80]

As with other materials, the supply and delivery of stone to the lock sites was not without incident. The *Post* reported a rumour that Monro (construction superintendent for the northern section) had condemned all the stone delivered from one quarry: "If true [this] will be a considerable loss to contractors using that stone."[81] One contractor, R.J. Campbell, did not pay his supplier of stone, William Hunter. When Hunter complained, he discovered that, true to tradition, the Department of Public Works refused to intervene in disputes between contractors and sub-contractors.[82] Another contractor, Claudius Ekins, co-lessee of a Beaverdams quarry, "decamped" with almost $2,000 in hard cash, leaving his partner (David Brown) in some embarrassment. As usual, complaints were heard about too much work being given to American contractors; noting that nearly all the stonework on the Escarpment locks was being handled by contractors from the States, a writer to the *Post* urged that Canadians be given their fair share.[83]

As we saw in chapter 4, contemporary references to cranes and dredges proliferate but detailed descriptions of the actual construction of the locks are rare. However the few drawings and photographs available reveal steam-powered stone-setting machines that moved on tracks laid down in the bed of the lock pit, each sporting four derricks. Every derrick used a block-and-tackle system to raise the stones into place, after which the lock gates were installed. Some stationary cranes were powered by teams of horses or mules. In the Third Canal era, four-wheeled carts – "stoneboats" – pulled by teams of animals still removed spoil and delivered stone. The joints were grouted with hydraulic cement. "Puddle" was inserted behind the lock walls, as in the past. Cement mixers were positioned above each lock, so that they could send the liquid cement down chutes to the floor of the lock.

With its channel excavated and lock chambers constructed, a canal still lacks the vital component of its operation – water. For the Welland, the source and reliability of its water supply had been problematic from the beginning and was not fully resolved until 1881. Moreover water, although essential for the canal's success, could – by way of the stormy Great Lakes or inland floods – be disastrous for "Mr. Merritt's Ditch." This paradox and other water-related issues, are the subject of our next chapter.

CHAPTER SIX

Managing the Water

The landscape into which the nineteenth-century Welland Canals were set could best be described as "waterous," lying between two of the Great Lakes on a peninsula bounded by the wide Niagara River on the east and incised with many lesser watercourses, including Ten and Twelve Mile creeks, Lyons Creek, and the larger Chippawa Creek (Welland River). Countless other smaller streams scored this landscape – water was everywhere. Nevertheless the supply for the Welland was often problematic. William Hamilton Merritt's original idea for a canal arose from his desire to replace the erratic water levels of Twelve Mile Creek with a steady flow. Even tapping the Grand River in 1829 did not provide an adequate supply. Ensuring enough water for the great ditch, therefore, would be a constant concern of the Welland's engineers until 1881.

SANGUINE HOPES

The original idea had been to supply the canal from Chippawa Creek, but disastrous land slips in the Deep Cut in November 1828 made it clear that a sufficient depth of channel could not be obtained that way. The solution was to dam the Grand River and tap its resources through a "Feeder." The Commissioners of Internal Navigation had suggested such a dam in their report of February 1823, and engineer Alfred Barrett had also raised the idea in 1827.[1] Reporting on the matter in December 1828, James Geddes concluded that the company should consider "the expedience of supplying the Canal with Water from the Grand River instead of the Chippawa."[2] Water from the Grand could be obtained by damming it near its mouth and digging a channel through the Cranberry or Wainfleet marsh to join the main line at what became Port Robinson. In this way the engineers could get water from a higher elevation so that it could flow over the shallower parts of the Deep Cut, at which point further excavation would be unnecessary.

Ground had been marked out for the dam half a mile from the river mouth, the contract had been let, and £400 had been spent, when the decision was made to change its site, moving it farther upstream. As we have seen, Commodore Robert Barrie had wanted to see it located 18 miles (14 km) from the river mouth but Barrett (who had co-operated with Geddes on a survey for the Feeder) outlined the difficulties of building the dam upstream. In a note to the directors in June 1829, he expressed his opinion that a site farther up the Grand River would entail lengthening the Feeder by five miles, and that the dam itself would have to be built six inches higher. In addition, mill sites would need to be removed five miles farther away from the main line of the canal.[3] The directors, however, felt obliged to heed the commodore's concerns. They were perhaps influenced by the fact that the required extension to the Feeder would pass through company director (and Attorney-General!) Henry John Boulton's land – the Boulton or Selkirk tract. Moreover, Lieutenant-Governor Colborne approved of the new site.

So the Grand River Dam was built at the picturesquely named Bear's Foot Rapids, 4.5 miles (7.2 km) upstream from Lake Erie at what would become Dunnville. It was about 6 feet (2 m) high, providing an 8-foot (2.4 m) drop in the water level from the river to the Feeder. Whole trees were cut down and, with their branches still adhering, were laid lengthwise in the river. Gravel (brought up by scows from the river mouth) and stones were heaped onto them and then alternate layers of brush and gravel dumped into cribs.

Because it created the headpond for the whole canal, much would depend on the dam's stability. Finished in 1829, it was 594 feet (178.2 m) long, 18 feet (54 m) wide at the base, and 7 feet (2.1 m) high and the water supply was controlled by a floodgate. A bridge for the public road was erected near the floodgate. A retaining wall bolstered it at the western end, as well as an embankment 484 yards (442.5 m) long. Seven smaller weirs were also built on the western side in marshy land where Sulphur Creek flowed into the Grand River.

Regardless of its location, the dam fit into Merritt's plans for a great navigation system linking the Grand River to his Welland Canal. The Grand had been surveyed in 1827, and in 1832 the Grand River Navigation Company (of which Merritt was a director) was incorporated with a grant of 200 acres (82 ha) of land near each dam and lock site. The Navigation Company proceeded to build locks on the river to create a waterway system linking lakes Erie and Ontario with Brantford. Until construction of the Second Welland, however, the dam was a barrier to navigation because goods had to be be portaged or trans-shipped around it. Nevertheless, Merritt believed that the dam and improved navigation on the Grand would be advantageous to Haldimand County (for which he became MPP in 1832). In his mind, the Grand River, the dam, and the Feeder had a role to play in the great waterway which he envisioned connecting the Grand, the Welland Canal, the Great Lakes, and the St Lawrence.

Construction of the dam began in early 1829, and in late May James Black, the company secretary, wrote to a London stockholder that the directors were pleased with it: "All is now progressing to their satisfaction and sanguine hopes are entertained that the waters will be united by the end of July."[4] In fact the structure was finished by the middle of that month but on 3 October it sank several feet, preventing water from being let into the Feeder and hence into the whole canal. Merritt, as usual, took a "hands-on" approach to the crisis, writing in his journal on 4 October: "Sunday – Returned to dam. All hands at work raising the banks. Found every job so deficient that I had the water stopped at Broad Creek. Went through with the engineers, and took a rough estimate of what was required."[5] The opening of the canal had to be postponed, but by mid-November the dam was considered stable again.

Because this dam and the related Feeder were vital to the navigation on the Welland, its state of repair and the condition of the Feeder were frequent subjects of discussion at board meetings. In 1831 the Feeder sprang leaks, causing a delay in the opening of navigation. In 1834–35 the directors let contracts to improve its banks, to build a culvert at Broad Creek, and to widen and deepen the Feeder itself, installing a guard gate at the junction. In August 1835 tenders were called for raising the dam. As we have seen, no lock was built into the dam at first, but one was installed in the 1840s.

What lay behind the directors' description of the Grand River Dam in their Annual Report of 1832 – disingenuousness or genuine ignorance? They wrote that the waste weirs associated with it permitted the "discharge [of] any quantity of water, which is under perfect control." In fact the dam was a headache for both the directors and the local population, and its location and structure inspired much criticism. Engineer Alfred Barrett had doubts about its effectiveness[6] and in 1831 Commissioner Robert Randal complained: "The erection and maintenance of this great dam across the Ouse [Grand] is unauthorized by any legislative act of this Province. The lands of individuals situated on the banks of the river, for a distance of about ten miles, are overflowed without the consent of the owners, and without recompense having been afforded them ... fish are prevented from ascending the river, and neither ark gap, lock nor apron has been constructed or maintained of a sufficient width and depth to admit boats, arks and rafts."[7]

In 1835 William Lyon Mackenzie, among his accusations, charged that company directors such as Boulton (who owned property on the Grand) had encouraged Barrie to object to the original location of the dam, hoping that an extension of the Feeder to a site farther up the Grand would increase the value of their land.[8]

Mackenzie's allegations were never proven, as we have seen, but the flooding along the Grand was often disastrous. In the early 1830s, two to three thousand acres (as many as 12,000 ha) of flat land were inundated and damaged along the Grand between Dunnville and Cayuga. Often the water rose so suddenly that people had to flee in the night. Claims for compensation amounted to £4,000, a huge sum that must have appalled the directors. A board of arbitration was set up and in 1835 the amount of legitimate claims settled at £1,600. (Later claims raised that total to £3,000.)[9] Many of the afflicted residents were from the Six Nations lands – their compensation was never fully paid.

Within the company itself, actual construction of the dam provided difficulties because, in a by-now familiar vein, problems with a contractor emerged. In September 1829 Barrett wrote to Merritt about the American judge Samuel Wilkinson [Wilkeson] (1781–1848), who had sub-contracted with Simpson, Monson, and Pratt, for the dam:

> Judge W. sent down for Pratt who appeared at the dam the next day after I arrived and immediately W. took him by the arm and they went in close consultation under an umbrella arm in arm (a novelty indeed) for 2 or 3 hours he was very polite to him all day ... Pratt is very anxious to get his share of the profit as he wishes soon to leave for his farm near Lockport and from the manner that the work is conducted on the Monson Simpson & co. Marsh job he does not expect much from that quarter and his share of the money on the dam is now his only dependance, am extremely anxious to get it ... You see from this that circumstances alter cases, especially with Wilkeson in relation to his partners he has the faculty of using them as occasion requires.

After the dam collapsed, the board decided in 1830 that Wilkinson, in particular, was at fault and should be "prosecuted for his roguery." The case dragged on into 1833, when the company finally collected £1,000 from the judge.[10]

Elsewhere on the canal, less imposing dams or weirs were constructed to manage the vital but potentially dangerous water. At Port

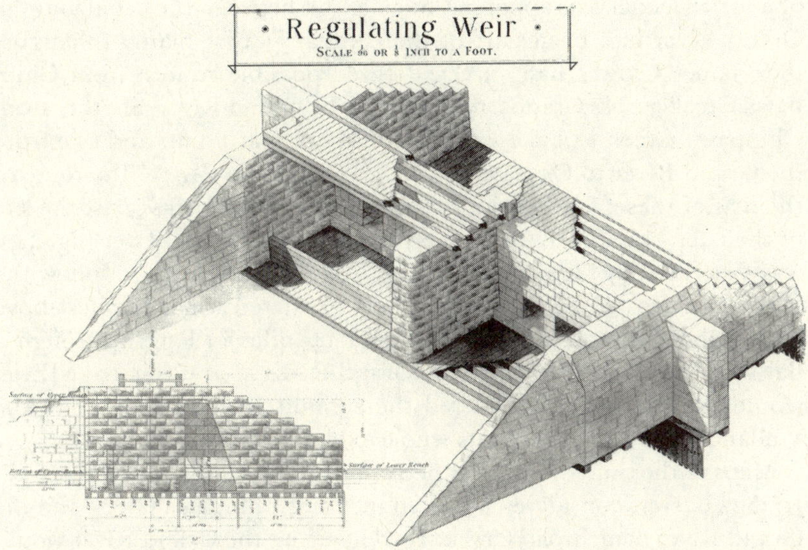

6.1 A regulating weir on the Third Canal. Over a century later, several of these structures, with their fine stonework, can still be seen below the Escarpment south of Glendale Avenue, near the extant locks. (LAC: NMC-21829)

Dalhousie, for example, a weir was built in the 1820s across the mouth of Twelve Mile Creek to control the movement of the sandbar there and to direct the flow of water out of the river into the lake. This configuration created a basin that served as a protected harbour for lake and canal vessels. It was rebuilt for the Second Canal, but farther inland, splitting the old basin into an inner and an outer harbour, connected by Lock 1 of the new canal. The Second (and particularly the Third) Canal had large weirponds associated with most locks, which acted as power storage units whose water was controlled by dams (fig. 6.1). Some of these dams are still visible at the Mountain Locks Park (Second Canal) and behind the General Motors Plant (Third Canal). Their enduring and massive stonework testifies to the tonnes of valuable water they retained.

Through a Shaking Quagmire

Even as the idea of a dam on the Grand River predated the digging of the Welland channel by several years, so the notion of connecting the Grand with the Welland Canal in some way arose before the necessity of a major feeder was apparent. Such a link between the canal and the Grand River had been part of the company's first plan.[11] In August 1824 James Clowes had surveyed three possible routes: from Chippawa Creek across Cranberry Marsh to the Grand River; another from Chippawa Creek to Lake Erie west of Sugarloaf Point; and one from the Grand River to Oswego Creek and Chippawa Creek. The route of the first of these, from Chippawa Creek near "the Forks" past the site of the later Marshville (Wainfleet) to the lower Grand River (fig. 2.3), was described by George Phillpotts: "It was ... intended to follow the Welland [River] to Forks Creek, which is situated about 11 miles above Port Robinson, and by a cut of about 14 miles in length through a flat swampy country to enter the Grand River ... and this Lake [Erie] would thus have been rendered the summit level and feeder of the Welland Canal throughout its whole extent."[12]

Maps of the time show a planned cut about 12.5 miles (20 km) long.[13] In 1827 Barrett considered a line connecting Chippawa Creek and the Grand River near Broad Creek. Feeders using the Grand River would make that watercourse the summit level of the canal and maintain the depth of the creek, securing a reliable supply of water in the Welland for the canal at the Deep Cut. As we have seen, the board decided in 1828 on a deeper Feeder, direct to the Grand River, through which water from the dammed Grand could be channeled through Cranberry Marsh to join the main line at what became Port Robinson.

Already in 1826 the company had been granted control of the "Great Marsh" in Wainfleet Township. Crown land, these 13,000 acres (over 52,000 ha) were described by MacTaggart as "a shaking quagmire, full of rattlesnakes and growing with spotted alder."[14] It was through this inhospitable tract of swamp that the Feeder would be built. One engineer, at least, was optimistic: "Although the slips at the Deep Cut have been considered a great disaster," mused Geddes, "yet as they have been the means of leading to a plan of canal altogether preferrable to the one that was prosecuting, the occurrence may be considered fortunate."[15]

Merritt was always keen on using a feeder to supplement the water supply from Chippawa Creek. In particular, he preferred a line from Port Robinson to Broad Creek (which flows into the Grand River near its mouth) and he persuaded the reluctant directors to begin excavating before the canal itself was finished. On 12 September 1827 the company therefore announced the start of a 9-mile (14.4 km) stretch from the forks of Chippawa Creek to Broad Creek to be finished by 1 October 1828 (the "Western Branch"). The contract went to Monson, Simpson and Company. Merritt, of course, envisaged connecting his ditch to the Grand River in a navigation system much greater than the board imagined. The feeder was never used because, as we saw in chapter 4, the crisis at the Deep Cut compelled a rethinking of the plans. When that part of the main line caved in, the board was compelled to decide whether to carry on and excavate the Deep Cut to 7 feet (2.1 m), a level that would enable them to use Chippawa Creek as a feeder, or to find another source of water supply. Time was of the essence: the canal must be open and functioning soon to prove its viability and to encourage investors and politicians to support it in the future. But what lay beneath the unexcavated parts of the Deep Cut? More "quicksand"? A safe, inexpensive, and quickly executed solution must be found.

As we know, the Grand River had figured in earlier plans: it was reckoned that a dam at its mouth would produce a depth of water of 5 feet (1.5 m) above the level of Lake Erie, giving a depth of 8 feet (2.4 m) in the Deep Cut as excavated. The dam was to be built farther upriver, but what was to become the Feeder Canal was placed under contract on 31 January 1829 and, even though late winter frosts slowed progress, the channel was built relatively quickly. The company advertised "uncommonly healthy" working conditions[16] but the malaria endemic at the time caused delays in construction. The channel would be 26 miles (41.8 km) long, 40 feet (12.2 m) wide, and 5 feet (1.5 m) deep. Laid out in half-mile sections, the contract was given to the dam builders (Monson, Simpson and Co.), who advertised for a thousand hands, most of whom came from the scaled-down works on the Deep Cut. The directors' financial position and the need for haste was exemplified by the fact that the contractors were given partial payments in amounts proportional to the funds in the directors' hands at any given time. The remainder would be paid to them when the project was finished, assuming more money would be forthcoming from the government, which would presumably be impressed by the accomplishment. Work not finished by 15 August would be re-let to other contractors, and when any one section was completed, labourers would be moved to the closest section. The workers were paid similarly, in the hope of encouraging them to apply themselves efficiently so that they would receive their wages.

Construction started in May, with 15 August as the projected completion date. But only on 3 October 1829 was the Feeder finished and, the Dunnville dam having been recently completed, water admitted. Although parts of the channel were very shallow and narrow, Merritt and two officers from the naval station at the mouth of the Grand River passed down the Feeder from Broad Creek to Marshville on 7

October. When the dam began to sink, this adjunct waterway could not be fully operational until repairs were made. Only on 5 November was the Feeder functional and the First Welland ready for navigation throughout.

WATER FROM LAKE ERIE?

All the Welland Canals operate(d) by the gravitational force of dammed up water – not by coal, electricity, oil, or petroleum. Hence the reliability and source of the water supply was paramount. Almost from its inception, the Feeder Canal was only an immediate solution to a crucial problem, a stop-gap measure, with Lake Erie regarded as the ideal source of supply. As farming and industry changed the Grand's watershed, it became increasingly inadequate as a source of water. By 1837 Merritt himself had begun to doubt the wisdom of using the Grand.[17] From the mid-1840s, authorities began seriously to consider lowering the summit level so as to draw water from Lake Erie. When engineer Samuel Power presented estimates for the cost of building the new aqueduct in 1843, he prepared two: one was based on the Grand River remaining as the source of water; the other, on using the Lake Erie level.[18] In 1848 the engineers were still debating whether the Second Canal aqueduct would be finished to suit the Grand River or the Lake Erie level. (As it turned out, the walls were raised to suit the higher Grand River level.) In the 1860s the question again received much attention, and some contracts were awarded. However, in the spring of 1867, the political leaders of the Canadas were absorbed in the pre-Confederation conferences. As a result, the local superintendant was informed that, while the Commissioner of Public Works appreciated the importance of the work, he "did not think it desirable to enter upon any large contracts until the formation of the Confederate Govt."[19] The work was postponed. After several unsuccessful attempts, the question still remained: how to tap Lake Erie without an expensive deepening of the canal's main line or the Feeder – or both?

In 1872 the Department of Public Works entertained briefly the idea of lifting water from Lake Erie by steam-powered pumps. Having been asked by his superiors to examine this scheme, Page responded that he did not approve but recommended instead the deepening of the Feeder. His report was supported by a similar response from Casimir Gzowski and Samuel Keefer. Accordingly, further improvement of the Feeder began that year. Nevertheless, this work was still regarded as only another extension of a temporary expedient. Finally,

6.2 Building the Third Canal intake at Port Colborne, c. 1880. This structure still operates as part of the Ship Canal's water regulation system. (Koudys Collection)

in the summer of 1881, after numerous attempts, Lake Erie was successfully tapped as the main source of water for the canal, after which the Feeder was used less frequently (fig. 2.4).

Nevertheless, the Feeder was always intended to be an integral part of the Welland system. We see this view reflected in Randal's reference to "The Feeder or Boat Canal."[20] When rafts of timber were floated along its length, the Feeder thrived. For example, the firm of Camp, Camp, and Kennedy brought down rafts of staves from the Grand River, and Norton and Bliss sent lumber along it to Buffalo and Lockport. Because the Feeder had become essential to the Welland's functioning, it was frequently improved. In October 1841 the company asked for tenders to widen and deepen it and in 1842 it was converted into the main line of the waterway, while the line to Port Colborne was being deepened (1845–50). At this time, the Port Maitland link to Lake Erie was built with a stone lock at Broad Creek (chapter 5). Even in the 1870s, as the second "enlargement" – the Third Canal – was underway, a turning basin at the Feeder's Dunnville end was built. In fact, even after water supply was obtained from Lake Erie in 1881, the Feeder continued to serve commerce. The last sailing vessel passed through in 1892, but as late as 1908 a shipment of railroad ties was floated through, the last record of the channel's commercial use.

CROSSING CHIPPAWA CREEK

Once the decision had been made to build a Feeder Canal across Wainfleet Marsh to connect the Grand River with the main line of the Welland, the next question was how to get this man-made stream across Chippawa Creek. For early nineteenth-century engineers the answer was obvious: an aqueduct – a bridge carrying a channel of water. The engineers decided to connect the Feeder to the main line at what became Port Robinson.

An Excellent Piece of Workmanship

In January 1829 the contract was given to the firm of Phelps (Oliver again), Theodore Brundage, and Marshall Lewis. The aqueduct allowed passage of vessels with a draft of 4 feet (1.2 m). It crossed the creek at a height of 10 feet (3 m), was 365 feet (109.5 m) long and 24 feet (7.2 m) wide (fig. 6.3). These dimensions, as reported in 1835, are different from those cited in 1832, which describe the aqueduct as being 600 feet long.[21] This discrepancy may be explained insofar as the aqueduct is also described as a "waste weir" for the regulation of the water supply. Given what we know about the dimensions of the Second Canal aqueduct, an extension of one of its approach walls incorporating a weir seems quite likely. Another puzzle is the construction material used for the aqueduct – it was probably white pine, although we can find no evidence for this. Contemporary descriptions also refer to its having "balance beams,"[22] which presumably were for guard gates, which may again have been associated with a weir. There does not seem to have been a lock closely associated with it, as was the case with the two later aqueducts.

In 1836 James Stinson of Port Colborne was hired to improve the aqueduct using masonry to strengthen the approach walls.[23] The structure tended to leak and had to be repeatedly repaired (as in 1840 and 1844). It received a new superstructure in 1846. A swing bridge (which seems to have been renewed in 1841) stood just to the south.

Although we have no precise contemporary description – in words or image – of its appearance, the aqueduct served its purpose well. In 1831 Commissioner Randal called it "an excellent piece of workmanship and a monument of the superior skill and abilities of Mr. Marshall Lewis, the builder and contractor."[24] However by 1851, when the Second Canal aqueduct (made of cut stone) was finished, the wooden one had become obsolete. Over time what applied to the Welland's channel and locks applied also to the aqueduct: it became too small

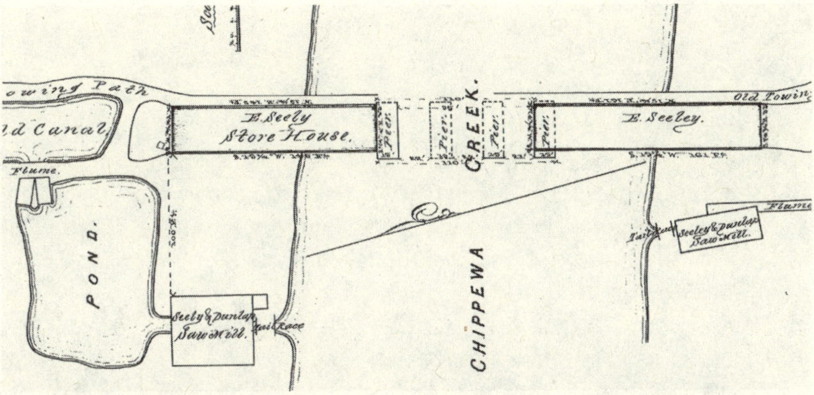

6.3 Welland 1854: remains of the First Canal aqueduct over Chippewa/ Chippawa Creek. No contemporary drawings are extant, but this plan documents the extensive industrial exploitation – in this case by Ebenezer Seeley – of the Second Canal's water. (James A. Gibson Library, Brock University, Special Collections: Welland Canal Register B, 24 August 1854, 436)

for the growing size of ships, whose captains faced the prospect of their vessels getting stuck in its narrow passage. As the canal was rebuilt in the 1840s the aqueduct had to be replaced. Many had considered it only "temporary" anyway, among them Samuel Keefer, as expressed in a letter of 1846.[25] In 1851 earthen dams were built across its two ends and the section spanning the river was demolished. The miller Ebenezer Seeley converted the approaches into storehouses.

Although navigation on the canal was of primary concern to the Welland's builders, they also had to consider the trade on Chippawa Creek (which served communities such as Wellandport). Building the aqueduct seems to have presented no technical difficulties to the engineers, but local people complained about its obstructing river traffic. Geddes advised the company that there should be space under the aqueduct for rafts and boats to pass on the creek.[26] But schooners with high masts and steamships with funnels could not pass beneath it.[27] "It is very much complained of," said Gilbert McMicking, MPP, when questioned by Mackenzie in 1836, "and I think a very great injury to the navigation of the Chippawa."[28] When similar objections were raised in 1851, Killaly (referring to the Second Canal aqueduct) defended himself to the Commissioner of Customs: When the "navigation on the Chippewa was of necessity wholly stopped, for several months, to enable the embankment at the ends of the new Aqueduct

6.4 The Second Canal aqueduct, c. 1880. Construction of the Third Canal aqueduct has begun. The Welland County courthouse (still in use today) is in the distance. This aqueduct is extant, although all but one wall have been buried. Its successor was demolished during the Ship Canal's construction in the twentieth century. A lock linked the creek with the canal. (George Monro Grant, ed., *Picturesque Canada*, 391)

to be constructed," he had given "the parties lumbering up the Chippewa" adequate notice.[29] Whether those in the timber trade agreed is not recorded.

The Most Important, Difficult, and Expensive Structure on the Line[30]

The aqueduct for the Second Canal was an imposing stone structure that had dimensions of 316 feet (96.3 m) by 45 feet (13.7 m) by 10.7 feet (3.3 m), with four arches each 45 feet (13.5 m) wide at the base (fig. 6.4). Stone aqueducts were not unusual in North America and Britain at the time; engineers and contractors in Canada West would have known, for example, about the Rochester and other aqueducts on the Erie Canal. Nevertheless, this structure was a new and major undertaking in Niagara. In his capacity as engineer, Power had submitted plans for a new aqueduct to the Board of Works in February 1841. The following May the board directed him to advertise the project and prepare tenders. The plans included a lock to be built upstream from the aqueduct on the north side of the creek so as to make a new connection from the canal to the river. In addition, a waste weir would be constructed on the south end of the east approach wall for disposal of surplus canal water into the creek (as may have been provided in the First Canal's aqueduct). The board added its customary warning that construction of the new aqueduct must not interfere with navigation on the river – although, not surprisingly, given the historical record, it did (see below). The stone came from the nearby Queenston quarries.

In July 1843 the contract was awarded to Hitchings and Company, but the firm declined to it. It was not until February 1844 that Zimmermann and McCullough (who had built the first suspension bridge over the Niagara River) got the contract. Coffer dams[31] were installed, and by February 1846 Power was able to report that the foundation had been laid and the supporting piers built, and that many of the centre columns were framed and ready.

Unfortunately, in July of 1846 Zimmerman announced that his firm could not finish the job at the tendered price and had to suspend work.[32] The four arches of the aqueduct were not yet closed, leaving the project at a delicate stage. Samuel Keefer (who had taken over as the Welland's chief engineer) reported to the Department of Public Works: "It is utterly impossible for him [Zimmerman] to complete that work at the present contract price, because that price is altogether inadequate, and all his own resources are now absorbed in the work."[33] He recommended drawing up a new contract, which was awarded to Zimmerman in October. Construction resumed, and by 17 October Keefer could report that the work was going satisfactorily. "The last arch has just been closed, and the centres will soon be struck. The masonry of the abutments has been carried up level with the crowns of the arches. Large quantities of cut stone have been provided for the parapets ... The walls have been adapted, by the plan, only to Lake Erie level, and therefore if slides should occur in the banks of the Deep Cut, upon lowering the water in it to that level, it will then be necessary to raise the parapet walls 8 or 9 feet to the higher level, but this measure must be looked upon only as a "dernier resort" [Keefer's emphasis].[34]

As Keefer would soon know, the Lake Erie level would not be achieved and the walls would later have to be raised. Financial difficulties now plagued the Board of Works as well, and political changes kept the attention of the government of the United Canadas fixed on constitutional and economic matters. On 27 October 1846 the commissioners ordered all public works temporarily halted – a decree which, of course, stalled work on the aqueduct.

Keefer was very uneasy about this suspension of work on such a vital part of the waterway. Typically, the man in charge – "on the ground" – had little sympathy with the policies of bureaucrats and politicians. "It is impossible to say how long the old one [the First Canal aqueduct] will last," he wrote nervously, "and therefore to delay the completion of the new one, would be to jeopardize the navigation. I would consider the suspension of the work in the present state of the Canal most hazardous and injudicious."

By the end of May 1847 construction had been resumed, but Keefer was still enjoining speed upon the commissioners, because, as he pleaded, "every day, experience admonishes us, that the wooden [aqueduct], now in use ... is not, by any means, so secure as it ought to be ... Several leaks in one of the abutments, some of them of a serious nature had to be repaired during the last year. It is well to be provided against the worst that can happen."[35]

By January 1848 the aqueduct's cement floor was laid and its walls finished up to the coping.[36] Nevertheless, in October the conscientious Keefer was again expressing his dismay that Zimmerman and McCullough had "not shewn any anxiety to complete this structure when it is so nearly finished."[37] The aqueduct was finally finished in 1851, after its walls had been raised in accordance with the deepening of the locks in time for the waterway's spring opening. Navigation on the Chippawa had been stopped for several months on account of the construction, which itself had been slowed by an outbreak of fever (presumably malaria) among the labourers. On 6 March 1851 Superintendent Samuel Woodruff informed Killaly that the water had been let in to the new line: "Between the Aqueduct and Junction, the level has been filled, and the water allowed to stand a few days, to test the embankments, and structures of masonry, all of which stand well, notwithstanding at the time, the Aqueduct was sustaining a pressure of 17 feet water inside."[38] The water in Chippawa Creek had been at flood level but the aqueduct withstood its battering well.

Whereas the Second Canal had been officially opened in May 1845 through the enlarged Feeder, the old wooden aqueduct was still in use and functioned until 1851. The Second Canal aqueduct also had a longer life than might have been predicted. Although a new and larger aqueduct was begun for the Third Canal in 1878, the old one was deepened by 15 inches (38.1 cm), providing a depth of 12 feet (3.6 m). Part of the floor was taken up and a small portion of the arches was lifted up. It remained in use for ships of shallow draught, although there were reports of vessels getting stuck in it. During the twentieth-century construction of the Welland Ship Canal, its northern end was filled in and one of its walls supported a construction railway. Although this aqueduct is half buried today and its beautiful arches are invisible, the upper layers of stone can still be seen in a canal-side park in Welland, the chamber having served as a community swimming pool 1946–84.

Absurd Folly[39]

The authorities considered retaining the Second Canal aqueduct for the completed Third Canal – as a money-saving measure. But fear that the structure might act as a dam that would cause floods on Chippawa Creek scuttled this plan and a larger structure was decided upon. The six-arched Third Canal aqueduct was 460 feet (140.2 m) long and 85 feet (25.9 m) wide (figs. 6.5, 6.6), and each of its limestone arches spanned 40 feet (12 m). It was built just to the west of the Second Canal structure, of limestone from quarries in Beamsville and Queenston, while lumber used in its construction came from as far away as Michigan. Hunter, Murray and Cleveland received the contract in September 1877, with 1 June 1881 as the date for completion. Until it was finished, the new aqueduct was the canal's bottleneck because only ships with a draft of eleven feet four inches – at the most twelve feet – could sail the waterway over the old aqueduct – and its construction took a whole decade!

The builders of the aqueduct were plagued with problems, not the least of which was the contractor Cleveland's encounter with two thugs who slashed his head, broke his thumb, and robbed him on a May evening in 1879 in Port Colborne! On the construction site, too, things went wrong from the start. In both January and March 1878 the cofferdam installed to control Chippawa Creek collapsed. In October of that year it gave way again, costing contractors over $5,000.[40] Resident engineer for the southern section, W.G. Thompson, had already rejected the Pelee Island stone they wanted to use, insisting that they purchase material from Niagara quarries. In November 1878 the stonecutters preparing the limestone for the aqueduct went on strike, as did the stonemasons in 1883.

By January 1880 Thompson informed Page that the work on the aqueduct was unsatisfactory. Hunter, Murray and Cleveland defended the state of their project, disclaiming any professional responsibility for delays and pointing to the aforementioned accidents.[41] We cannot know to what degree the contracting firm's work was fundamentally inadequate or to what extent natural disasters plagued their progress. Certainly a spate of bad luck continued to attend construction. In February 1880 a freshet caused the cofferdam to overflow once more, an

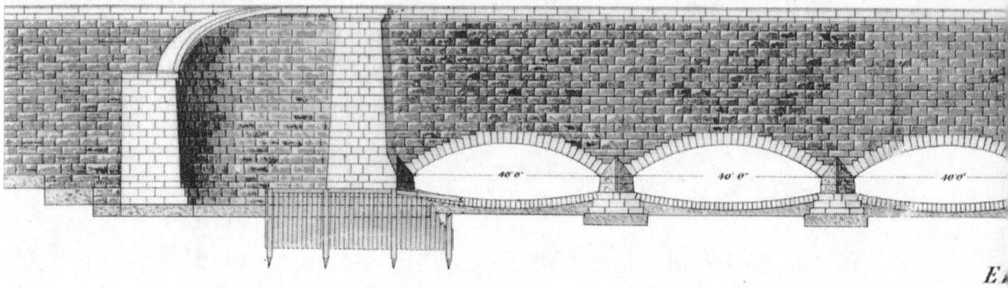

6.5 The Third Canal aqueduct (side elevation). Growing Canal traffic and the increasing size of ships necessitated its construction, only three decades after its predecessor was built, but the latter (situated to the east) remained in service for many years alongside this new version. (LAC: NMC-21825)

6.6 Building the Third Canal aqueduct, with the Second Canal aqueduct lock in background, and stone-lifting equipment. In the 1880s Canal structures were becoming monumental in size, dwarfing workers, contractors and engineers, whose employment became ever more painstaking and dangerous. (See also fig. 9.3.) (SCM: N-4618)

event that recurred at the end of March. Page, furious, telegraphed from Welland to the Department of Railways and Canals: "Dams at aqueduct have given out, water in at both sides of them, same height, nobody here, nor nothing doing, only 4 or 5 men breaking small stones, prospects bad as they can be, this state of matters cannot possibly be allowed any longer. See my general report on the subject."[42]

Hunter and company sounded a note of desperation in April, as they asked the Engineering Department to furnish them with suitable plans for cofferdams. Rejecting their plea, Page demanded that they resume the work immediately. It is possible that the contractors were overextended, for in 1877 they had also received the contract for the Grand Trunk Railway bridge piers at Section 35 in Port Colborne. Their work on that site impressed the Thorold *Post*, which was "very much struck with the solidity of the masonry work ... [It] reflects great credit on the contractors Hunter, Murray and Cleveland."[43] Despite this praise from laymen, the situation at the harbour was not promising and influenced work on the aqueduct. In late April 1880 Page again telegraphed the Department: "Hunter & Murray's work sec. 35 & McNamee's 34 prevent water from being let into Canal. Bridge works on both these contracts in backward state notwithstanding their representations & unwarranted boasting to the contrary."[44]

In fact trains were already crossing the new bridge, but with adjacent work on the piers still unfinished, water still could not be let into the canal. Page wanted the waterway opened on April 15 but Hunter, Murray and Cleveland suggested May 1. The aqueduct, of course, remained unfinished.

With their attention divided between the Port Colborne and Welland sites, Hunter, Murray and Cleveland began to rebuild the cofferdam at the aqueduct. Correspondence with Page made it clear that the chief engineer expected them to continue and to complete their work as soon as possible, but the cofferdam seemed beyond their capacity. Page was deaf to their pleas for an adjustment to the contract:

no deviation would be permitted. Seven months had elapsed since the dam collapsed, wrote Page, and the contractors should find "a more efficient way of shewing their intention ... than by writing indefinite letters."[45] In October 1880 Hunter, Murray and Cleveland finally told the Department that they wanted to give up the contract entirely.

At the beginning of March 1881, Page went again to Welland to examine the state of the aqueduct. The "old" (Second) Canal opened on May 1 with the new aqueduct still incomplete and the new waterway itself not yet finished. Notwithstanding, Page optimistically announced that the new canal would open in July, but only to ships drawing twelve feet of water.

At the end of October 1881 Beemer and Sullivan were awarded the contract to finish the aqueduct. Again (as with the granting of other Third Canal contracts) controversy swirled around the method of advertising the job and granting the work. The Ottawa *Free Press* accused the Department of "contracting in secret" insofar as they did not comply with the Public Works Act by opening competition for contracts over $10,000 to the public at large, but instead had sent private circulars to half a dozen contractors. Some of those contractors, said the *Free Press*, were connected to certain well-known "political jobbers" in Lower Canada. A few days later the *Free Press* grumbled: "It is a fair subject of enquiry whether his [Beemer's] connections with certain Quebec politicians may not have had something to do with the selection of his tender from among the secret and select few who were invited to bid for the work."[46]

From the point of view of Page and the Minister of Railways and Canals, the project was so far behind schedule that the need for speed in advertising and granting the contract was probably what drove them to cut procedural corners. Thousands of dollars had already been lost on Hunter, Murray and Cleveland's work, and shippers were clamouring for the use of the new larger canal and all its facilities to a depth of fourteen feet throughout.

Beemer put a dredge to work in December, but construction of the aqueduct would not recommence until the following spring. In May 1882 the old cofferdam was removed as Beemer pushed ahead with the work, employing 115 men on the job by the fall. The contractors soldiered on efficiently, although by November work was slowed down again by a bout of Niagara's severe fall weather.

Then in January 1884 Beemer, like Hunter, Murray and Cleveland, in turn asked the Department for financial relief; again it was refused. Haggling over prices continued throughout the spring but, when Page visited the site again in late 1884, he was pleased with the work's progress. In August 1885 the Welland *Telegraph* gave a graphic description of the work: "Concrete for the foundation of the fourth pier was laid during the week now passing, and stone work will be commenced early next week. The excavations for the fifth pier and abutments is [sic] rapidly nearing completion, and the work of placing concrete and stone will follow at once. The sheet piling at the end of the structure is nearly all placed, while the removal of stone from the old locks goes along nicely. Derricks are already in position to commence the building of the north side abutments and wing walls. The leakage is so completely under control that it does not in any way seem to interfere with the work."[47]

Construction now proceeded without incident and Beemer and Sullivan survived the aqueduct experience better than Hunter, Murray and Cleveland. After the cofferdam was unwatered in April 1886, they launched a new dredge (the CITY OF TORONTO) "in the presence of a large number of spectators, being christened by Mamie, Mr. Sullivan's little daughter," said the *Post*, much impressed by the fact that it was the first dredge built in Ontario and, what is more, by Beatty and Son of Thorold.[48]

When navigation resumed in the spring of 1886, the Third Canal aqueduct could not yet take ships; accordingly, the authorities at Port Colborne used an ingenious method to pass vessels through the southernmost stretch of the canal. They would close the lock gates at Lake Erie and at Allanburg, and open the gates connecting to the Feeder Canal, thus raising the water for several hours to permit the biggest vessels to pass. By the end of 1887, when the new aqueduct was finally completed, this complex system could be abandoned.[49]

Despite its decade-long problem-wracked construction, the completed Third Canal aqueduct impressed many observers. "One of the finest and most extensive pieces of mason work in America," said Ernest Cruikshank upon its opening in 1887.[50] It served well until 1930 when, since it lay in the path of the Ship Canal, it had to be totally demolished.

Culverts

Slicing through the landscape as it did, the Feeder Canal opened the surrounding area to settlement and farming – but it also changed natural drainage patterns. Culverts, drains, and back ditches had to be built to redirect the flow of ground water. As with much of the Welland's construction, the result was that the affected communities both gained and lost (chapters 7 and 8). The main canals as well as the

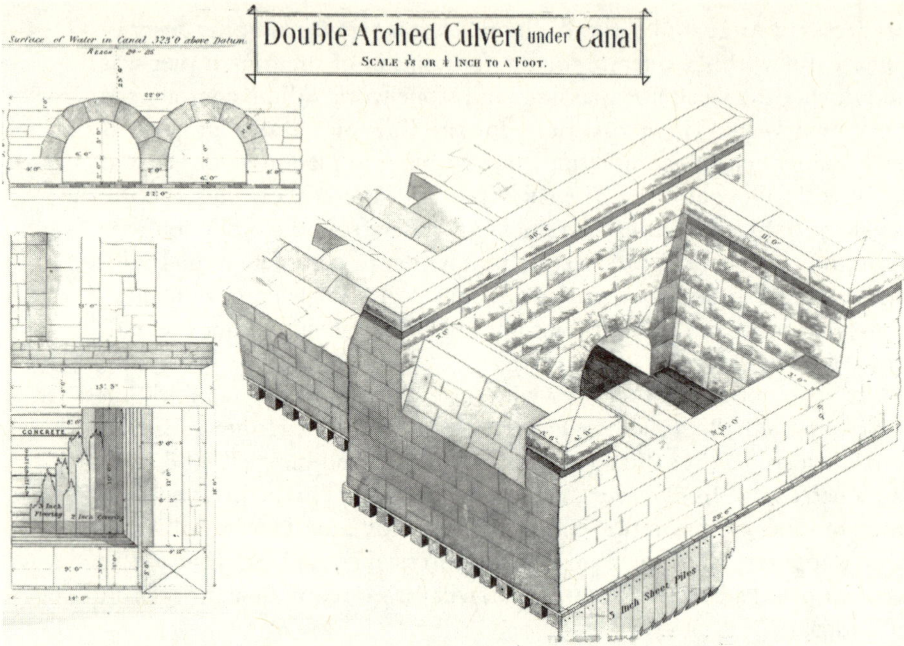

6.7 Third Canal "double-arched" culvert. This type of structure, rarely visible to the passerby, was essential for channeling ground water, especially streams, under the canal. Despite their unobtrusiveness, such features have a classic architectural beauty. (LAC: NMC-21828)

Feeder intersected a number of small streams, necessitating culverts to carry the natural running waters under the waterway. Culverts might seem to be unimportant aspects of construction, easily and cheaply built, but for the Welland they were essential. Four wooden culverts directed watercourses under the First Canal. Lyons Creek (which runs from west to east south of Welland) cut across the route of every version of the Welland. For the Third Canal, this stream was channeled under the waterway through an inverted syphon culvert with a channel 8 feet (2.4 m) wide and 3.5 feet (about 1 m) high. With its foundation 40 feet (12 m) below the surface of the towpath, the Lyons Creek culvert was a major structure of its kind (fig. 6.7).

Culverts offered solutions but they – or at least their builders – could also cause problems. Where the structure was as large and important as that at Lyons Creek, the work had to be executed precisely. Thomas Merritt Jr (a cousin of William Hamilton Merritt) was constantly at loggerheads with the board over his actions, as we have seen (chapter

3). In late 1840 he received the contract for the culvert carrying Cranberry Creek under the Feeder Canal. Assistant Engineer James Lyons reported to Principal Engineer J.S. Macaulay in 1841 that when Merritt had been reprimanded for "heaping promiscuously" both rock and earth on the bank, he informed Lyons: "his contract does not oblige him to stack them." Moreover Merritt had used blasting powder to remove stone which was "well suited for filling in frames piers etc. but to facilitate its removal, he breaks it all to small fragments with a sledge hammer, so that it can be shovelled with ease into small canal Barrows." In another letter (to Macaulay) Lyons stated that Merritt's workers found his treatment of them harsh.[51]

PROTECTING THE HARBOURS

"The contractors' operations have been considerably retarded," reported Superintendent Woodruff in 1861, "in consequence of the continuance of rough weather, which produced such frequent seas upon lake Erie, as to prevent the scows from being towed out in the lake, for the purpose of wasting the excavation."[52] Such reports remind us that the Great Lakes of Erie and Ontario, which supported the burgeoning trade served by the Welland Canal, and which were obviously essential to the waterway's functioning, were also a menace. Lake Erie was especially prone to vicious storms and to the accumulation of ice floes. We have already mentioned the special care that was taken with the locks at the canals' harbours where the basins needed sheltering from the waters of the lakes. The most important protective feature of the harbours were piers or breakwaters that stretched from the land out into the lake, breaking the force of waves in turbulent weather. They allowed ships to enter the harbour safely and controlled the movement of silt and lake currents to avoid the clogging of the gateways to the canal.

"Brush Piers"

Gravelly Bay was chosen as the waterway's southern terminus over other bays on Lake Erie because it most resembled a natural harbour: two reefs lay within 620 yards (567 m) of each other, leaving a depth of from 8 to 22 feet (2.4 to 6.7 m) of water between them. Toward the shore the water was deep enough for anchorage and the bottom was of clay – also good for anchoring. As for Port Dalhousie (the northern terminus) the mouth of Twelve Mile Creek was already a natural harbour, although a shifting sand bar intermittently blocked access to

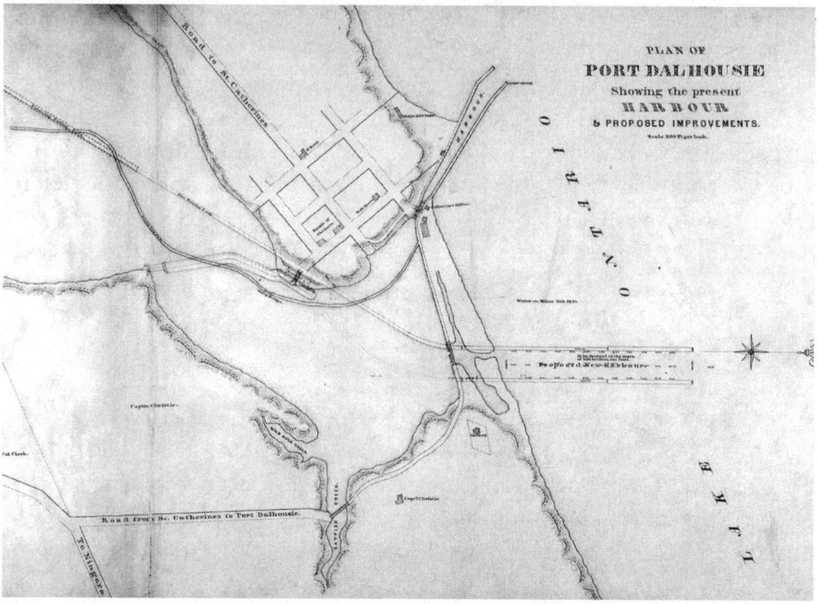

6.8 "Plan of Port Dalhousie showing the present harbour & proposed improvements." The map shows the breakwaters of the First and Second Canals at Port Dalhousie in 1845. The towpath of the First Canal can be seen. The Third Canal breakwaters were built on the site of those of the Second Canal and are now a favoured destination for both tourists and locals. (See also fig. 6.11.) (James A. Gibson Library, Brock University)

the lake. At both harbours protective breakwaters or piers would be necessary (figs. 6.8, 6.9).

While Francis Hall's report of March 1825 had recommended stone piers at Port Dalhousie, economy ruled, and the piers of the First Canal at both ports Dalhousie and Colborne consisted of sunken wooden frames or cribs filled with brush and stones – hence the name "brush piers." The two breakwaters at Port Dalhousie jutted out into the lake toward the northwest at an oblique angle. At Port Colborne one pier (on the harbour's west side) stretched out into the lake at a right angle to the shore, thus sheltering the canal entrance from Erie's waves. Another, east of the harbour, curved almost to enclose Gravelly Bay.

In 1831 the company decided to erect a pier at the mouth of the Grand River at what later became Port Maitland. Although the Feeder Canal did not yet connect directly with Lake Erie this spot had promise as a harbour because it was ice-free earlier than Gravelly Bay. Here a protective breakwater was built on the west side of the river mouth

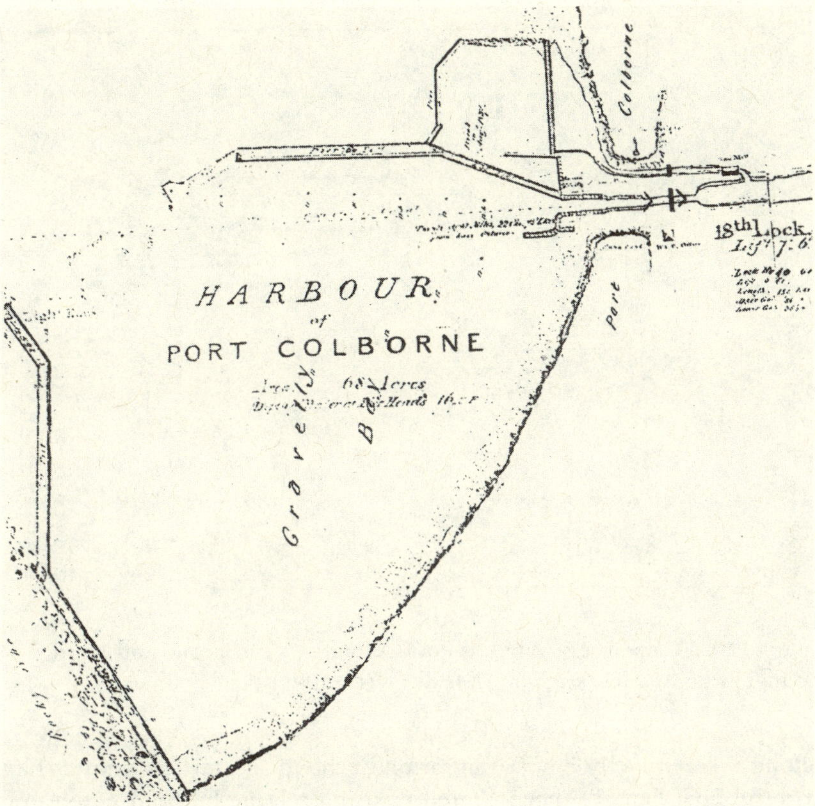

6.9 First Canal breakwaters at Port Colborne, as drawn by Nicol Hugh Baird and H.H. Killaly, c. 1837. Such protection was necessitated by Lake Erie's often ferocious storms. In the First Canal era, the water flowed south from the Junction into Lake Erie. (LAC: NMC-11848)

offering defence against the prevailing southwest wind. This structure was also made of wood and stones and supported a lighthouse.

Stone Improvements

For the Second Canal, new piers of stone were built at Port Dalhousie to extend farther into the lake, perpendicular to the shoreline. They reached through the sandbar where the weir had lain (fig. 6.8). A lighthouse at the extreme end of the longer (east) pier guided ships into the harbour. A new feature of the inner harbour was a floating towpath extending a distance from the west wall of Lock 1 into Martindale

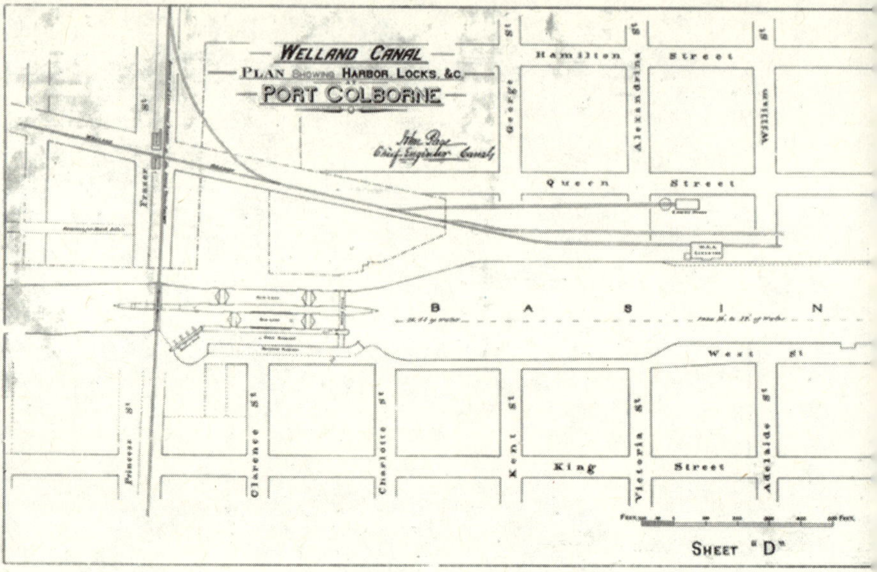

6.10 Third Canal breakwaters at Port Colborne, with Second and Third Canal locks, and intake channel. (LAC: NMC-21819)

Pond.[53] At Gravelly Bay the situation of the lock – farther inland than on the First Canal – necessitated creating a large harbour extending into the lake. Two new piers were built extending 1,500 feet (457 m) into the lake with about 180 feet (54 m) between them (fig. 6.10). The west pier, the longer of the two, had a lighthouse at its extremity and a "leading light" about two thirds of the way out. At Port Maitland improvements consisted of two new piers with a lighthouse.

In 1845 James Cotton and George Rowe were given the contracts to dredge Port Maitland harbour, to remove the old lock and approaches at Port Colborne, and to dredge Port Dalhousie. This firm was the cause of particular headaches to the supervising engineers. James Russell (their sub-contractor for the piers at the canal harbour) tried to bribe John Page (the then thirty-year-old assistant engineer). Page honourably but diplomatically rebuffed him with a chilly note: "I enclose the parcel which you I presume by mistake addressed to me for I cannot suppose for a moment that you could mean to present that to me which could only be intended to influence me improperly in the discharge of my duties" (chapter 3).[54]

The St Catharines office became increasingly irate as the work on the piers again and again failed to proceed according to the engineer's

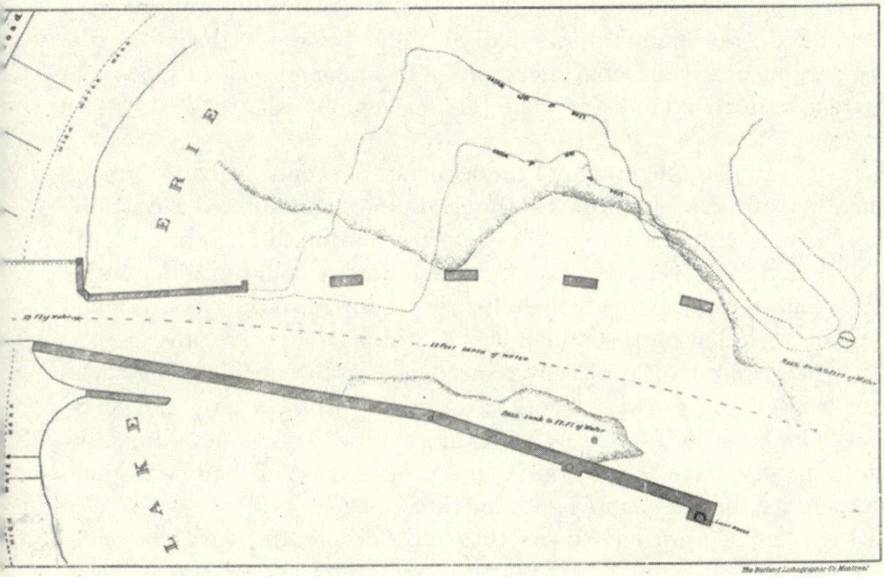

schedules. In July 1846 Samuel Keefer wrote to James Cotton: "It is absolutely essential that more vigorous measures should at once be adopted for ensuring the delivery of a sufficient quantity of stone (700 cords) during the month of August at Port Maitland in order to complete the works at that Harbor in good time this season." Keefer went on to threaten to take charge of the work himself and to "relet it to some other person or persons who will really set about it."[55] Later on, Cotton and Rowe were accused of not paying their debts and proved even more troublesome to Keefer. In July 1848 he had no recourse but to accuse them of stealing a dredge:

> You have not considered it expedient to bring back the Steam Dredge to Port Dalhousie upon my order of the 20th inst., which order, by your letter of the 24th inst. you acknowledge to have received, I am bound to consider the course you have taken in first conveying the Dredge without my leave or knowledge to a distant Port and then attempting to make terms for bringing it back, as evincing an intention and a settled plan on your part ... You were not ignorant of the fact that the Department holds a bill of sale on your dredge, and that they have advanced you £700 upon it. You must therefore have known it to be an unwarrantable proceeding for you to take it away secretly, without

> permission, and even without notifying me or any officer on the Canal of your intention ... I shall be obliged to report the circumstances to the Department and to recommend that the Contract be declared null and void. [Keefer's emphasis]

Keefer then reminded them of the sequence of events: he had stopped the work of the contractors' two horse dredges and ordered the steam dredge to continue working "on the bar or hard bottom at the ends of and outside the Piers, because the horse dredge could produce little or no impression upon it." Then, he later reported to the Department: "All of a sudden on the 19th July the Steam Dredge was missing ... They have since most positively assured me that they would bring back the Dredge and do what I required and I am now hourly and anxiously looking out for it. I will refrain for a few days from taking any steps against them in the hope that a proper sense of their condition will induce them to comply with my directions."[56]

In the end Cotton and Rowe returned the dredge and work resumed. We have no indication of what misunderstanding produced this crisis but these contractors were inclined to haggle over the contractual arrangements and in 1849 their men at Port Colborne went on strike for non-payment of wages.

Further Enlargements

The 1871 Royal Commission report advised that the northern and southern termini of the canal should be improved: both harbours should be deepened to 15 feet (4.6 m), and new breakwaters built. Accordingly, in preparation for what became the Third Canal, enlargement of the piers took place (figs. 6.10, 6.11). The new breakwaters at Port Dalhousie incorporated the older ones but were larger and extended farther into the lake. Lighthouses stood on the east pier, where they still stand today. Port Colborne harbour was deepened and its two piers were extended further into Lake Erie. Similar improvements were made at Port Maitland. In 1908 the Port Colborne harbour was deepened still further, eliminating a bottleneck for big wheat carriers, and, also to accommodate the shipping trade, a larger grain elevator was built.

Moreover, at Port Dalhousie a new floating towpath was constructed from the west wall of Lock 1 to that of Lock 2 (fig. 6.12). It consisted of a masonry dam resting on piles sunk into the soft mud of the pond bottom. A caisson in the middle of the dam released or admitted water.

6.11 Port Dalhousie, 1934. Underwater traces of the First Canal breakwaters (centre) could still be seen in 1995 aerial photographs. The Third Canal's piers have survived into the twenty-first century. Locks 1 of the Second and Third Canals are visible here to the right of the outer harbour, while Lock 2 of the Third Canal is farther to the left beyond the floating towpath. (See also fig. 6.8.) (Ottawa: Department of Energy, Mines and Resources, A4700-34)

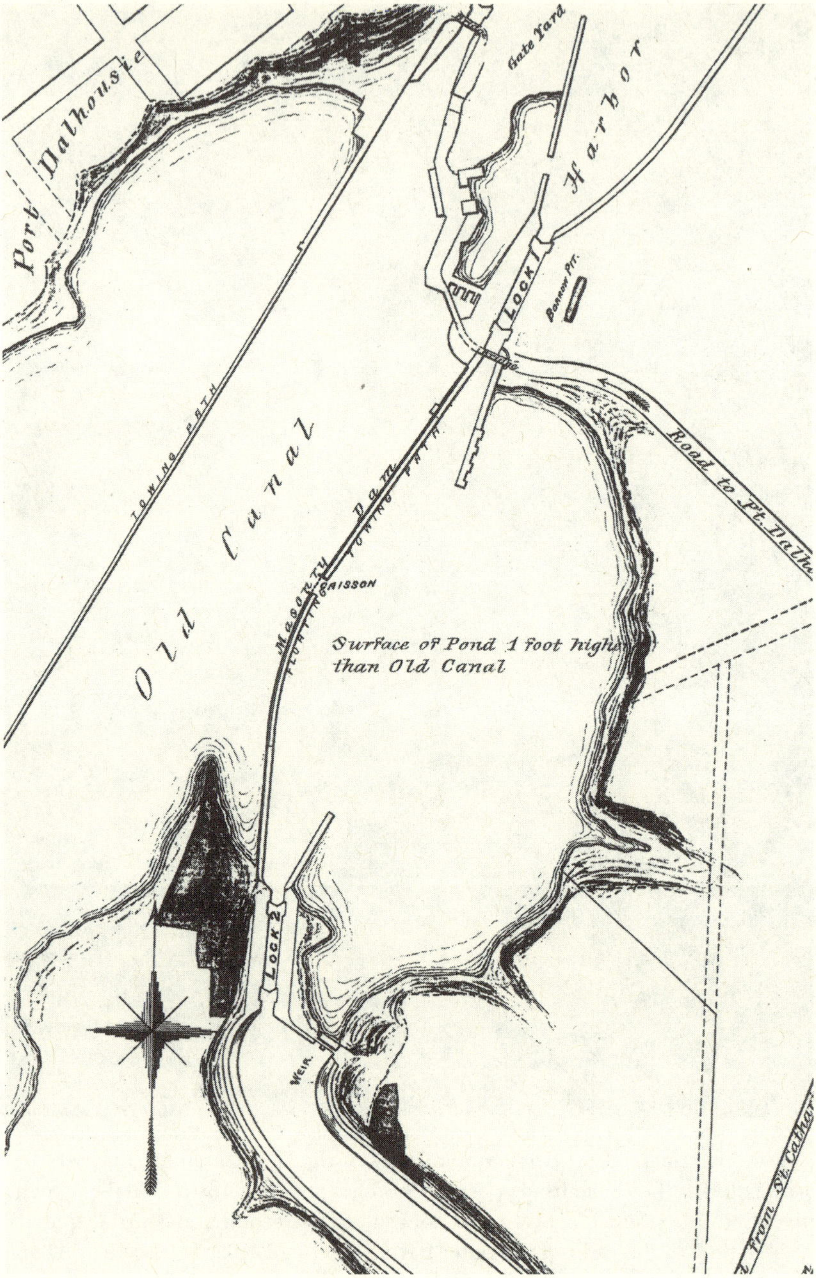

6.12 The "floating" towpaths at Port Dalhousie, with Locks 1 and 2 of the Third Canal. Lock 2 of the Second ("old") Canal is partly visible at the top. All three locks are extant. (LAC: RG 43, vol. 1747, file 8496)

6.13 A Second Canal control weir on Merritt Street in Merritton, near Lock 19, part of the extensive hydraulic system that included the channel of the First Canal. From this fixture, water was channeled into the raceway that fed the mills of Merritton and St. Catharines. (Photo: R.R.T.)

Remains of this structure could be seen well into the first years of the twenty-first century.

All in all, management of water – whether too much or too little, whether in or outside the canal – has been (and remains) of crucial importance to the waterway's operation. In the process the engineers, contractors, and those who actually operated the canal faced many a challenge. Ironically, the artificial channel they created for facilitating trade and providing water for local communities presented difficulties for those same communities insofar as it divided properties and obstructed land traffic. And so the canal builders had also to meet the challenge of providing crossings over their waterway, as we shall see in the next chapter.

CHAPTER SEVEN

Building Bridges

In the early nineteenth century water routes were the preferred avenues for transport of goods and personal travel throughout Europe and North America. As elsewhere in developing Canadian communities, roads in the Niagara peninsula were few and far between. Hence William Hamilton Merritt and the Welland Canal Company directors were not overly concerned with obstructing east-west land traffic. Nevertheless, from the outset land crossings of the canal had to be allowed for. In fact the 1824 Act of Incorporation of the Welland Canal Company required that a "secure, sufficient, and commodious bridge, for the passing of carriages" would have to be built within one month of any highway being cut.[1] But while construction of bridges would satisfy local residents who had been inconvenienced by the canal's cutting off the roads, they would cause annoyance to shippers and vessel captains since, when they were "closed" (that is, in position over the canal to receive road traffic), they would interfere with the passage of ships. On the other hand, when a bridge was "open" (that is, swung to one side or, if pivoting on a central pier, swung parallel to the canal) it could block surface traffic! Over time, population growth, urban sprawl, and the increase in both highway and ship traffic necessitated more crossings in Niagara – and made the question of number and location a much-discussed one.

THE ANNOYANCE AND INCONVENIENCE OF BRIDGES

Early in 1826 arbitration hearings were held with local residents primarily to determine the appropriate compensation to those whose land had been expropriated. Among the questions was one that referred explicitly to bridges: "If your land is divided by the Canal what do you suppose it would cost you to erect and keep in order a bridge over it or otherwise by means of a boat or scow to connect the farm?" George Marlatt said that he "would rather have had the Canal off his

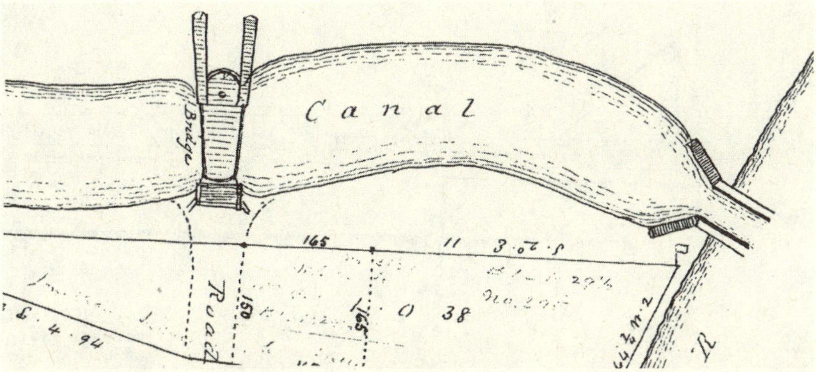

7.1 A First Canal swing bridge near the aqueduct in Welland. Such bridges were operated by bridgetenders pushing balance beams similar to those on the lock gates. (James A. Gibson Library, Brock University, Special Collections, *Survey of Lands* "1826" [1834], 127)

premises," indeed "would rather have no Canal." He was not mollifed by the promise of a public bridge to be built, because he would "have to travel a quarter of a mile or so to cross it." Several property owners noted that a public road and/or bridge would be sufficient; several others estimated the cost of a bridge at between £25 and $2,000 (£400). In the event, the arbitrators made no specific awards for bridges, but named several individuals who would not be precluded from further claims for compensation – if the company did not provide "convenient means of passage ... by bridges or scows [ferry service]." The arbitrators also affirmed that others not so named could also apply for redress if their lands were later separated by the canal.[2]

Later claims did indeed ensue. Jacob Upper (who was was numbered among the 1826 claimants) and others living in the Allanburg area in 1830 asked the company to build a bridge to take Holland Road over the waterway. The claimants were told that the directors had no objection to a bridge on that site, but that Upper and his friends would have to build it themselves.[3] This was the company's usual attitude: if given permission to construct a bridge the locals would have to pay for it and maintain it themselves, but the company had the right to approve its size and structure. However, the board did not accede to all requests. When Oliver Phelps in 1834 requested financial aid to build a bridge to connect his land in Grantham Township, which had been divided by the canal, the board turned him down.[4]

For the First Canal the directors originally planned twelve bridges, to which end they applied to the local Quarter Sessions (or Board of

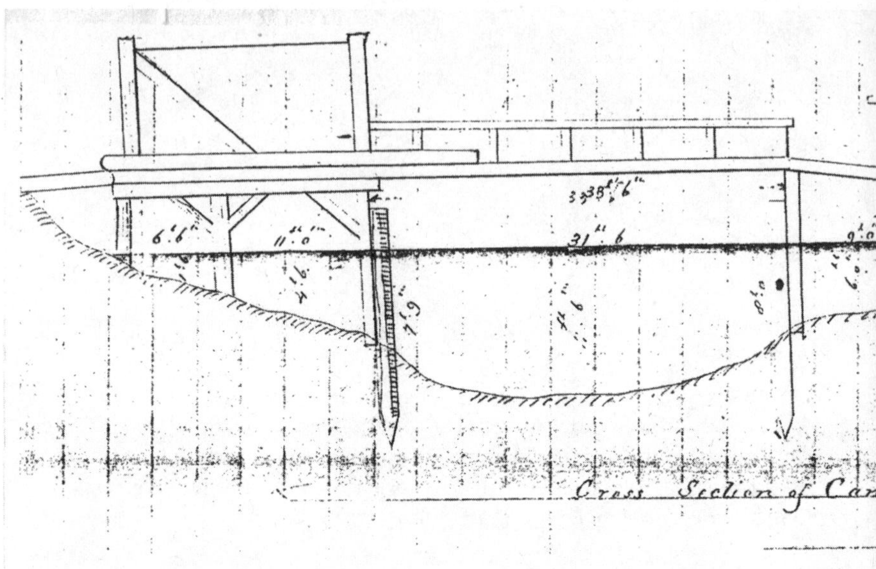

Magistrates) for an appropriation of £50 a year for each bridge for two years, to be taken from the funds of the Niagara District.[5] Any other crossings would have be paid for by those individuals interested. By 1835, partly as a result of local initiatives and partly thanks to company efforts, Francis Hall reported that there were eighteen bridges on the main canal with three on the Feeder.[6] These were of wood with iron hardware, and usually of the "swing" or "horizontal" kind, opened by human effort – that is, using balance beams, as on the lock gates (figs. 7.1, 7.2). They were painted with "McAdams' Mineral Composition," developed for coating timber work subjected to alternate wetting and drying. By the time of the Second Canal, bridges were usually provided with lights (presumably fuelled by oil) to warn ships as they approached.

Certain parts of the route required more bridges than others. Only in St Catharines was there a major pre-canal crossing, where the main trans-peninsula road was taken over Twelve Mile Creek. Between St Catharines and the Escarpment, along the summit to Port Robinson, and eventually south to Port Colborne, existing highways were cut. Problems inevitably ensued. As farmers found that they had to make great detours to get to mills or stores or even to visit parts of their property, vociferous objections arose. Pedestrians could cross at every lock, on the lock gates – although they did so at their peril, because there were no hand rails. One crossing (at Humberstone) was referred

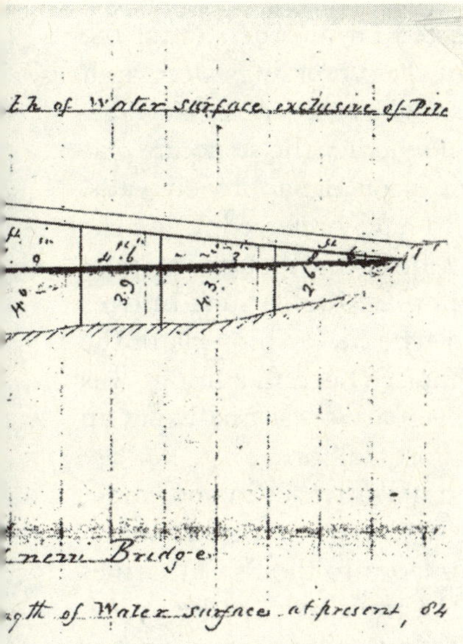

7.2 Cross section of a First Canal bridge, by H.H. Killaly, 1839. (SCM: *Letterbook "O"*)

to as the "stone" bridge (hence the later alternative name of that community, "Stonebridge"). This bridge could not have been built entirely of stone, for such a structure would have been impassable to boats. Presumably it was the supports, or piers, that were of stone, and the swinging ramp was of wood. Most communities enjoyed the privilege of only one crossing, although Port Dalhousie had two.[7]

The company and its engineers wanted to be sure that the new steamboats could enter the waterway. Bridge spans had to be long enough (that is, with the widest possible distance between the supporting piers on each bank) to accommodate ships with side-wheels. In February 1828 the directors agreed that Marshall Lewis should design and build all the bridges. At the same time they resolved that "bridges on the Mountain summit be made 40 feet wide, for the purpose of admitting Steam Boats to the large Reservoir above Lock No. 1."[8] They soon came to the conclusion, however, that Lewis's planned bridges were not long enough and in May of that year authorized Alfred Barrett to improve them.[9]

The precise location of bridges on the First Canal is open to conjecture but we know of the important crossings: at Lock 3 in St Catharines; "Vanderburg's" near Lock 21 (in the later Merritton); "Keefer's" between Locks 31 and 32 at St David's Road; Beaverdams Road; "Hellem's" at the junction of the Feeder and the main line; at Port Colborne; and at Dunnville near (or on) the dam. Obviously some bridges were named after the owner of an implicated farm; others, after the men who tended the bridges. A number of these crossings were built across the reaches of the canal but, in cases where the bridge was associated with a lock, we cannot always tell whether the structure was built over the middle of the lock chamber or on the approach walls. For financial reasons the company seems to have preferred to use the walls of the lock as the support piers for a bridge, although the public's preference was for bridges on lock approach walls; such bridges could be opened and closed regardless of whether a ship was in the associated lock. For example, at Port Dalhousie (Lock 1), a bridge was built across the chamber of the lock, but the board occasionally put up a bridge on the wing walls of a lock, as at Port Colborne.

If local residents and shippers shared negative opinions about bridges (although for different reasons), we have on record one favourable view of such crossings. In 1842 a letter to the St Catharines *Journal* conveyed the following remark: "In travelling on this canal, you are not obliged to be constantly nodding and dodging for fear of being made a head shorter by the bridges – one or more persons generally volunteering to throw open the swing bridges that span the canal, when the craft can pass on without meeting any obstacle whatever."[10] The writer may have been comparing the Welland and the Erie (barge) canal with its low-slung bridges, where passengers had to be frequently warned by the familiar cry, "Low Bridge! Low Bridge!"

Bridges on the Second Canal were similar in design to those on the First: built of wood with iron reinforcement, painted white and swinging on a pivot (fig. 7.3). In 1846 Samuel Keefer reported plans for twenty-two bridges on the Second Canal, of which sixteen were already finished and the rest under contract.[11] Unfortunately he did not include any description in his report. The increased number was a reflection of the economic and urban development in Niagara. The new bridges were usually built at lock sites, on the approach walls, but exceptions existed: Lock 7, near Merritton, had a crossing built over the middle of the chamber.

The attitude of the Department of Works to bridge-building paralleled the thinking of the Welland Canal Company: the fewer the better. As was traditional, bridges other than those planned by the Department would have to be paid for and maintained by local municipalities and had to conform to the Departmental engineer's specifications: when in 1853 the Department allowed construction of a new bridge at Lock 4 in St Catharines, the town came up with the costs. Nor were all requests agreed to: Thorold residents applied for a bridge at Wilson's tannery in 1850 but the petition was denied. At this time

7.3 Bridge over Lock 27, Second Canal, at Port Colborne, c. 1860; in the background, the Grand Trunk Railway grain elevator – one of the earliest known photographs of the Welland. (PCHMM)

the financial stringencies of the Second Canal prohibited spending any more of ratepayers' taxes on unnecessary structures – including bridges.

The exact crossing sites remained controversial. The bridges over Locks 5 and 15 (near the present-day Westchester Avenue and Glendale Avenue in St Catharines) spanned the middle of the lock chambers. By this time the positioning of bridges over locks was becoming an increased inconvenience to Niagara residents, and more and more requests came forward for them to be placed on the approach walls where they could remain open to land traffic even when a vessel was in the lock chamber. In 1846 Samuel Power felt obliged to attend a meeting of the District Council to represent the Department's viewpoint and explain why, despite local complaints, the bridge at the Allanburg lock should span the chamber of the lock.[12]

Nevertheless, residents did not in every case want bridges on the wing walls of locks. In June 1847 Humberstone and Port Colborne residents petitioned for a new bridge over the canal on the site of the old one and over the chamber of the lock itself. The Department responded somewhat disingenuously: "Present plans for the enlargement of the Welland Canal will not admit of the Bridge being built as petitioned for [over the chamber] – but with the view of inconveniencing as little as possible the inhabitants of the adjoining neighbourhood, the Bridge will not be placed over the Lock itself, as that might create delay when vessels were in the Lock, but on the wing walls, which the Commrs [sic] hope will give satisfaction to the inhabitants of the surrounding country."[13]

In a letter of 1847, Louth resident James W. Clark made an impassioned plea to Merritt about the bridge at Lock 2, near St Catharines: "I herewith enclose a Petition to the Parliament praying for the removal of the Bridge crossing the locks to some other place on the Welland Canal. It has a good number of signatures ... so great is the annoyance and inconvenience from being detained at those Bridges [Clark's emphasis] that if it had been requisite, and had there been time, the name of almost every individual in the District might have been appended thereto ... The Petition is general but the great matter of complaint in this part of the Country is at Lock number two at Rannie's Mill."[14]

Certainly this bridge (at present-day Welland Vale) stirred up more discussion than most other crossings. The town's growth as an agricultural service centre had increased the vehicular traffic on this highway in and out of the community. Ultimately the bridge was moved to a more accommodating site.

Whatever the site of bridges (over or adjacent to locks), more and more complaints were voiced by pedestrians and travellers. As older bridges went into disrepair and needed replacement, the needs of merchants, housewives, and even school children had to be considered along with those of farmers. At Port Dalhousie in 1850 locals found that the bridge was "swung" (closed to land traffic) for long periods at a time "and consequently travellers detained there to their very great inconvenience." Hence the Grantham Township Council wanted the bridge moved to the channel itself in the hope that "wayfarers and others will not suffer the interruption to which they are now subjected."[15]

Canal authorities always gave the interests of "the navigation" precedence over the needs of local residents. When Oswego merchants, for instance, protested the changing of a bridge location in Thorold in 1846, the Board of Works bowed to the interests of the shippers and denied the citizens' request.[16]

The interests of the community were not completely ignored, of course. When bridges were dismantled during reconstruction, temporary measures such as wooden floating bridges or ferry services were introduced. In late 1847 a "float bridge" was in use at Allanburg, later to be replaced by a permanent crossing. Ferry service in lieu of bridges had been foreseen from the outset, as we have already noted, and a ferry was operating at Sugar Loaf Street in Port Colborne in 1861. Such expedients became more common during construction of the Third Canal, which required larger bridges. In 1880 a temporary floating bridge was installed at Main Street in Welland, and during the deepening, ferries operated at Humberstone in 1878, and at Port Robinson in 1885. In 1881 a scow large enough to carry teams of horses and school children across the Canal in Humberstone was requested.

By the third quarter of the nineteenth century, several Niagara canal communities had grown from pioneer villages into relatively complex and sophisticated towns. The Welland Canal reconstruction of the 1870s consequently proved very disruptive to local street and highway traffic. As soon as construction of the Third Canal got under way, local authorities began making their case for bridges. In 1874 W.A. Thompson, MP for Humberstone, sent that community's "memorial" for a bridge over the canal between the fourth and fifth concessions. In the same year Grantham Township asked for a bridge where the new canal cut across existing roads.[17] When Minister of Railways and Canals Charles Tupper and Deputy Minister of Public Works Toussaint Trudeau visited Thorold to inspect the works in 1879, they were accompanied by MPs John C. Rykert and Christopher W. Bunting, as well as Henry Carlisle, mayor of St Catharines. A group of citizens lobbied the dignitaries for more bridge building[18] and local politicians no doubt seconded the motion. Port Robinson residents (alert to the vagaries of canal construction after fifty years of experience) informed the Department by telegram that they would resist the removal of the present bridge in their community until a new one was built and in operation.[19]

The most contentious of the bridge-related issues that erupted during the Third Canal era was in Welland.[20] Main Street had always crossed the waterway on a swing bridge, but the 1871 commission recommended that the bridge be demolished and a new one built to the south at Division Street – although still within the village. The Welland community approved the construction of bridges in Welland South (the former Junction) and Quaker Road (to the north), but found the suggestion of a Division Street crossing – and the whole widening itself – alarming. Consequently, at a public meeting in July 1877 the residents rejected the Department's plan. The village council met soon afterward and passed a protest resolution. The Reeve and a councillor even went to Ottawa to carry their grievance to Alexander Mackenzie (both prime minister and minister of Public Works) but their plea to retain the Main Street Bridge had no effect. Chief Engineer John Page believed that a bridge so close to the new aqueduct would impede "the Trade." As usual, ease of navigation was the government's main concern.

The Division Street bridge (of white oak with stone abutments), was duly constructed. This long (196 feet or 58.8 m) structure turned on a central pier and, when open, rested on two other piers which, in effect, created two channels for ships, one on each side of the central pier. Yet the old Main Street Bridge remained in use pending the completion of the Division Street crossing. As that date loomed, the locals revived their campaign. A delegation was again sent to Ottawa (in 1887) – again to no avail. A temporary floating bridge for pedestrians was, however, installed at Main Street in the ensuing winter months.

Only in 1904 was Welland finally able to reconnect East and West Main Streets. After the turn of the century, new bridges were built across many stretches of the Third Canal: at Port Robinson, Welland South, Humberstone, and Welland. The lobbying of W.H. German (still an MP and a Liberal supporter of Wilfrid Laurier's government), may have had an effect, but J.L. Weller (superintendent of the canal) also believed – unlike Page, the late chief engineer – that a bridge at Main Street was viable. And so the Alexandra Bridge, a steel truss swing crossing, was built.[21]

But, to return to our story of Third Canal bridges in general: tenders for nineteen road bridges were not called for until August 1879, and the contract was awarded on 21 July 1880 (figs. 7.4–7.7). Unfortunately, we have no details about the materials used in their construction, although they were likely built of wood and wrought iron. We do know that in February 1881 a contract was awarded to Toronto Bridge for two steel bridges for the Welland Railway.[22] Some bridges seem to have been of timber with a central tower from which iron suspension cables ran to support the span when they were swung open or shut. The Canada Southern Railway bridge, built in 1883–85 across the canal south of Welland, had a wrought-iron deck, but most decks were probably of wooden planks. As traffic increased in frequency and weight, all these bridges were replaced by steel truss structures in the final decade of the century. Most pivotted on stone piers standing in mid-channel.

A major change in Third Canal bridges was that, instead of being pushed by balance beams as on the first two canals, they were swung open and closed with the use of a lever from inside the turning mechanism inserted in the gearing through the floor. (Electric motors were installed around 1907.)

7.4 Third Canal bridge abutments removed from Quaker Street, north of Welland, now on Merritt Island. Increasingly, such relics are regarded as important witnesses to Niagara's past and hence worthy of preservation. (Photo: R.R.T.)

Construction was as usual slow but by the spring of 1885 most bridges were completed. The northern length of the new waterway (from Allanburg to Port Dalhousie) would have twelve road and two railway bridges, with tunnels for the Great Western Railway and St David's Road. The southern stretch was crossed by six road and three rail bridges.

As we know, the authorities traditionally preferred to install bridges on or near locks so that their operation caused a minimum of delay to shipping and to land traffic. But long-established roads (such as Niagara Street leading northwest out of St Catharines and crossing the Third Canal nowhere near a lock) were allowed to bridge the channel itself.

During the reconstruction of the Welland in the 1870s the Second Canal continued in service from Port Dalhousie to the Escarpment, and some of its crossings remained problematic. The bridge that carried St Paul Street over the canalized Twelve Mile Creek in St Catharines proving too narrow, the Department was repeatedly petitioned between 1865 and 1874 for a larger bridge that could comfortably accommodate both horse teams and pedestrians. This was built in 1878,

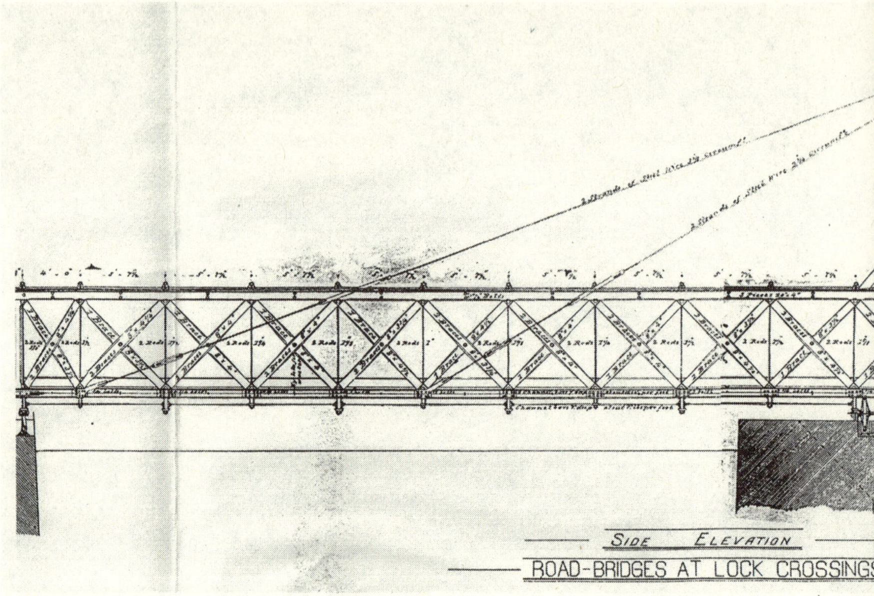

7.5 (*above*) Side elevation of a Third Canal bridge. (Report of the Chief Engineer of Canals to the Minister of Railways and Canals. 16 February 1880. Ottawa: Department of Railways and Canals, 1880, after p. 350)

only to become obsolete in its turn, so that by 1904 complaints were again heard. Finally, in 1915, the still-extant high-level Burgoyne Bridge was built as a replacement.

In 1888 St Catharines received permission to build an additional high-level bridge over the Second Canal to take Ontario Street in the direction of Merritton. When completed in 1915, this crossing (the Glen Ridge Bridge) proved to be one of the most beautiful structures in Niagara: a high-arched structure resembling the most striking of Greco-Roman architectural forms. The other "Old" (Second) Canal swing bridges with manually-operated balance beams (later winches) were also gradually phased out, but only in 1888 was the process complete. Several Third Canal bridges, when removed in the early twentieth century, were sold to local communities, to be "recycled" for further use. Wainfleet on the Feeder Canal, for example, purchased two in January 1907.

Distinctive features of the Third Canal were two tunnels built under the waterway for St David's Road and for the Great Western Railway. (On the latter, see below.) Finished in 1878 by contractor Paul Ross, the road tunnel connected the town of Thorold with the village of St

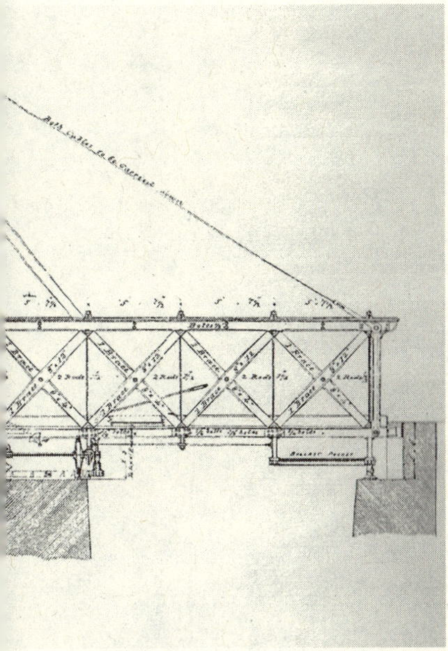

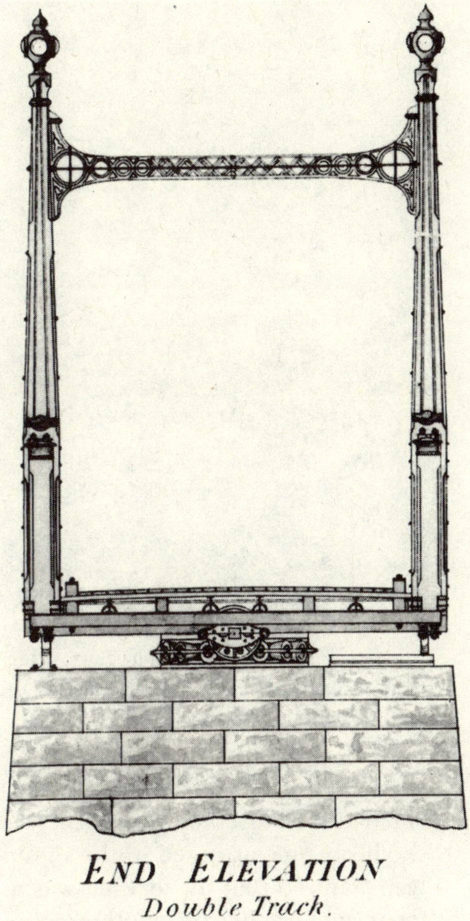

7.6 (*right*) End elevation of a Third Canal Bridge. The apparent delicacy of such structures belied their strength, for they were designed to carry heavy steam locomotives and their trains. (LAC: NMC-21823)

David's and, beyond it, Queenston on the Niagara River (figs. 7.8, 7.9). This tunnel, built of stone over a period of five years, lay under the canal reach between Locks 16 and 17,[23] where the "loop line" curved to ascend the Escarpment. With its dimensions of 14 feet (4.26 m) both high and wide, and 291 feet (88.6 m) long, engineers reasoned that this alternative to a bridge was practicable because the maximum depth under a canal was usually less than the height that a bridge over the water must achieve. A tunnel would cost more than a bridge, but it would require less maintenance. Of course (and this was most important), a tunnel would never obstruct the path of ships. Nevertheless, despite its uniqueness and the structural beauty of its approaches, the road tunnel soon began to leak badly, as the Thorold *Post* reported,

7.7 A typical Third Canal swing bridge at Port Colborne, c. 1880. This view, to the south toward Lake Erie, shows Second and Third Canal locktenders' shanties. (LAC: C-294057.8)

"much to the discomfort of those who have to travel through it." When the problem was noted in the summer and fall of 1881, local residents were assured that the leaking was not serious. Its cause seems to have been the fact that the vault was finished three years before water was let into the canal and parts of it had been exposed to the elements. Exasperated, Thorold residents petitioned for its repair in 1885.[24] It is not known what happened in the interim, but some time after 1922 the road tunnel was sealed at both ends.

Waterway versus Railway

Canal builders in the 1870s confronted a problem that had not existed when the First Canal was built: railway tracks. Of course, engineers and contractors of both the First and Second Canals had to provide bridges for roads severed by the waterway. But from the 1850s onward, when railways began threading their way through the Niagara peninsula, they, too, required bridges to cross the canal. East-west trains kept schedules that could not be interrupted without serious consequences

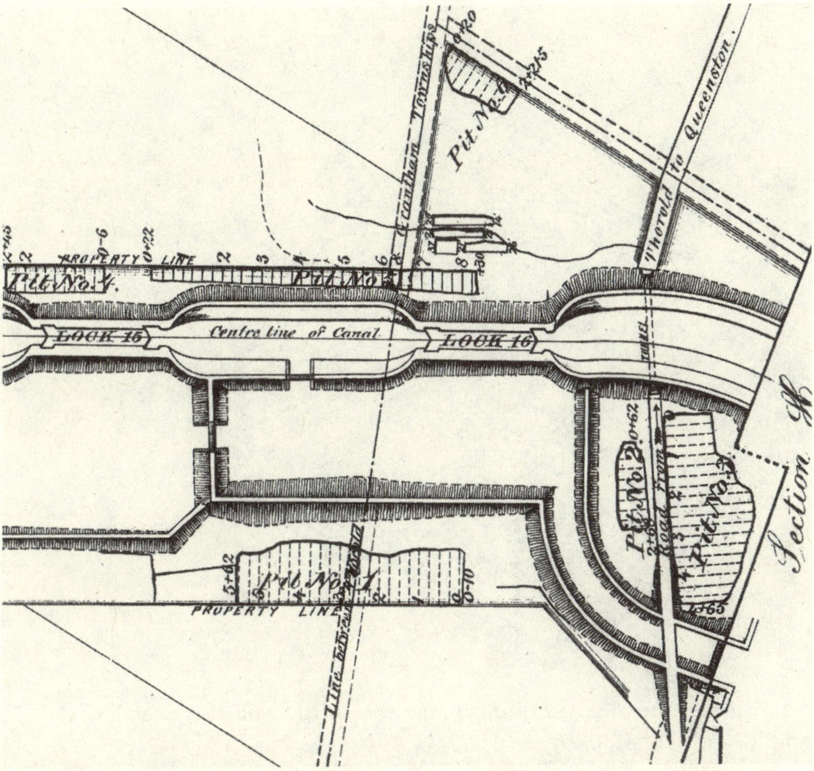

7.8 Tunnel for horse-drawn vehicles and pedestrians under the Third Canal at Lock 16, showing weirponds. Shorter than the nearby railway tunnel, it still exists. (LAC: C-20629)

for local, provincial, national and – increasingly – international economies (fig. 7.10). Not surprisingly, the Department of Public Works objected at first. In 1851, when the predecessor of the Welland Railway (the St Catharines and Merrittville Railway) asked for permission to build a bridge for its projected line over the canal, it was refused on the now familiar grounds that it would "obstruct navigation."[25]

As negotiations for the Great Western Railway bridge at Lock 12 (near the later Merritton) reveal, however, the inevitable soon had to be accepted. But where should the crossing be placed? Predictably, the railway engineers laying the tracks from Hamilton to Niagara Falls in 1852 disagreed with Samuel Keefer as to its placement. Having given careful thought to this new problem in canal engineering Keefer wrote: "To place the bridge midway betweeen Locks Ten and Eleven ... would not only prove an injury to the navigation, but a serious

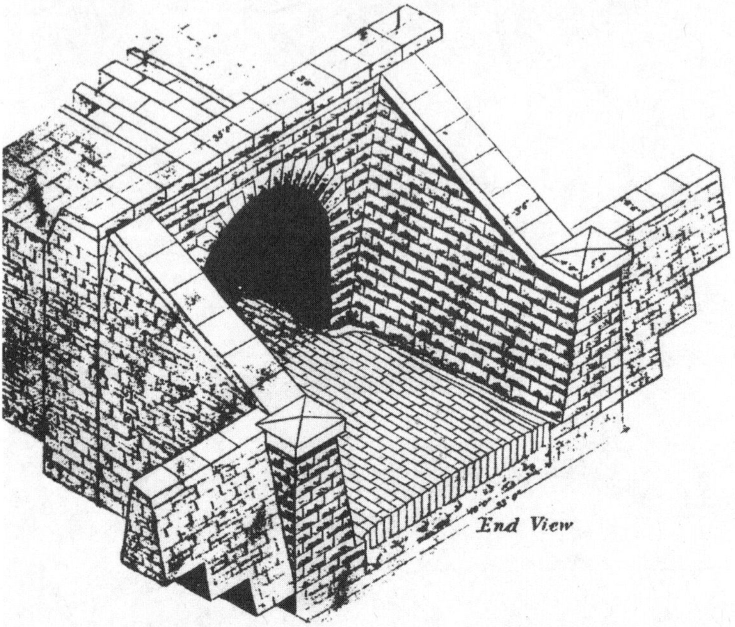

7.9 Entrance to the road tunnel under the Third Canal, between locks 16 and 17. (SCM: 977.189.107)

inconvenience to the [rail] Road; as regards the Canal, it would divide a most convenient basin into two inconvenient ones, too small to afford the necessary accommodation for passing vessels in both directions at the same time; and as regards the Railroad, it would break up a long straight line sixteen and two third miles in extent, and oblige the introduction of three or four extra curves, increasing the expense and hazard of running the Road."

The nearby community, Keefer continued, was likely to develop into a manufacturing town with many mills and related buildings that would create problems: "When this ground is built upon, the approach to a bridge by a curve, will have the view obstructed by the buildings, the engine driver will not be able to see if the bridge is open or shut, and the greatest inconvenience and danger will result from such an arrangement of the crossing. The preservation of the straight line is therefore as important to the Canal as it is essential to the safety of the life and property embarked upon the rail."[26] Canal authorities ultimately prevailed and the crossing was built just north of Lock 12 with no diversion of the railway tracks – today the Canadian National line.[27]

7.10 A Canada Southern Railway train accident at a Third Canal Bridge near Welland in 1876. As locomotives and rolling stock grew in weight and size, bridges over the "New Canal" soon became obsolete. (*Canadian Illustrated News*, 6 May 1876, 301)

Because railway companies usually built the crossings themselves, canal authorities often felt hostage to unsympathetic private interests. For example, in March 1853 the secretary of the Board of Works warned the managing director of the Great Western Railway in Hamilton that the work on the bridge at Lock 12 was going too slowly. It would not be above water level by the time the water was admitted into the channel, "unless very much increased exertions are made." Furthermore, "the consequences of [such] backwardness may be very embarrassing to the Railway Company."[28] This sort of warning became traditional over the next fifty years.

By the 1870s the heyday of the steam locomotive had arrived, and the "iron horse" would have to cross the new canal at various locations. Several railways now served the Niagara Peninsula: the Welland Railway ran north-south along the east bank of the canal; the Great Western ran east-west through Merritton; and the Grand Trunk crossed at Port Colborne. Some of these lines (or their predecessors) had crossed the canal for nearly twenty years. Of course, they were at first relatively short pioneering railways. Now, however, they had increased in mileage and economic importance. The canal builders therefore faced the prospect of new criticism from a community much broader than the eastern Niagara Peninsula. The railway companies were naturally anxious that their service (often with connections to the United States) not be disrupted for long periods by canal reconstruction. Almost as soon as rebuilding was announced, companies such as the Air Line and the Toronto, Hamilton & Buffalo Railway requested permission to cross the new canal at the Junction. The Buffalo and Lake Huron Railway (later the Grand Trunk) asked to build a bridge at Port Colborne.

For its part, the Department of Public Works remained vigilant. Engineers and bureaucrats carefully scrutinized the plans of the Buffalo and Brantford Railway for bridges over the Feeder and the main line of the canal. True to form, construction and maintenance must be carried out "without injury to the navigation." Because the line the railway company first proposed was thought to "injure the canal interests," much correspondence and exchange of maps marked in red ensued.[29] As for the pre-existing Welland Railway, it had to be crossed twice, and communications about its re-location abounded. The new canal's "loop line" would sever the railway's line running north of St Catharines to Port Dalhousie. Here the railway would span the Third Canal in Section 4 in St Catharines (near the present-day John Page Park on Scott Street), on a long bridge supported by extended embankments on either side of the waterway.

In 1872 an official of the Welland Railway objected to the Department that contractors had "completely destroyed" their track at Port Colborne. The following year the line's owners, now having learned that the new canal would require their tracks at the Escarpment to be moved, wrote to the Department stressing the "damages" this move would inflict on the railway. The complaint was referred to Casimir Gzowski and Samuel Keefer, two of the authors of the 1871 Commission's report, and adjustments were made to accommodate the rail line.[30]

For the Great Western Railway, whose tracks stretched across the peninsula on an east-west axis, a new line had to be found, and negotiations began in 1874. The deviation suggested by the government proved unacceptable to the railway authorities. They in turn submitted their own plans (including a new bridge), to which the government agreed. Before work had begun, the authorities decided (early in 1875) that the railway would be taken under the canal by a tunnel. Although the contract for the bridge and tunnel was awarded to the Great Western in April of that year,[31] construction did not begin until 1880. It began as a trench (as if for a channel of water) 650 feet (195 m) long

7.11 Grand Trunk Railway tunnel under construction, between Locks 18 and 19, c. 1885. Built "in the dry," it was then covered with earth, after which the Canal's prism was channeled over it. (Koudys Collection)

and 16 feet (4.8 m) wide, with a vault of 18 feet (5.4 m) in the centre over the level of the track. A stone vault was built over the trench, after which it was covered with soil and the canal reach laid out over it (figs. 7.11–7.13).

Controversy developed over its height, with the ever-watchful Thorold *Post* reporting that the roof of the tunnel was only four feet above the height of railway cars – which was in contravention of federal law concerning headway, which stipulated seven feet. Ultimately the tunnel was exempted from the ruling[32] and the first Great Western train passed through in March 1881 with several railroad dignitaries on board. The *Post* reported on the excellence of the road bed and relayed the general opinion that the tunnel itself was "one of the finest pieces of masonry on the new canal ... much admired."[33] As railway cars and locomotives grew larger, the tunnel soon became obsolete and by around 1902 it was replaced by a steel truss bridge. Well into the twenty-first century intrepid hikers could still walk through its derelict vault.

As large bridges had to be built across the canal in greater numbers, new opportunities – as well as complications and daunting challen-

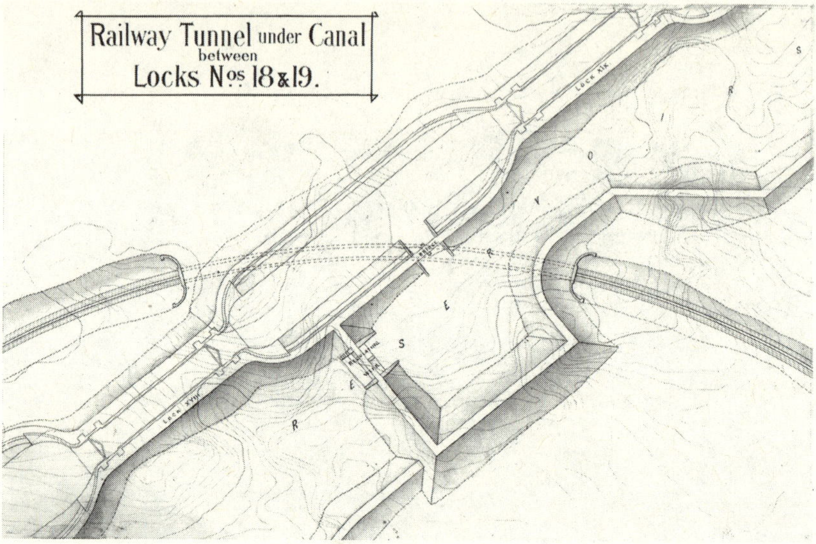

7.12 Grand Trunk Railway tunnel, showing regulating weir and "reservoirs." (LAC: NMC-21827)

ges – presented themselves to contractors. We have seen how Hunter, Murray and Cleveland's work on the Third Canal aqueduct faltered, possibly because they had over-extended themselves by working simultaneously on the Grand Trunk Railway bridge at Port Colborne (chapter 6). At the latter site in 1880, their difficulties delayed the opening of the canal until the end of April of that year. The issue reached the House of Commons, where it was discussed in March 1880. In response to questioning by Alexander Mackenzie (Leader of the Opposition), Sir Charles Tupper (Minister of Railways and Canals) described the matter of the Grand Trunk Railway bridge, confirming that the erection of its superstructure could not start until 13 April. Hunter, Murray and Cleveland's contract allowed them to work "in the dry" (that is, with the canal drained) until 26 April.[34] Nothing, therefore, could be done.

Shippers were concerned whenever new bridges were planned. Yes, the new canal would be larger and more commodious for their vessels, but the expanding railway network meant that more bridges – larger and more obstructive ones – would potentially block the waterway. These ongoing worries were intensified when bridges were replaced. When the Grand Trunk Railway started building a new bridge at Port Colborne in March 1900, for instance, J.A. Cuttle of the Montreal

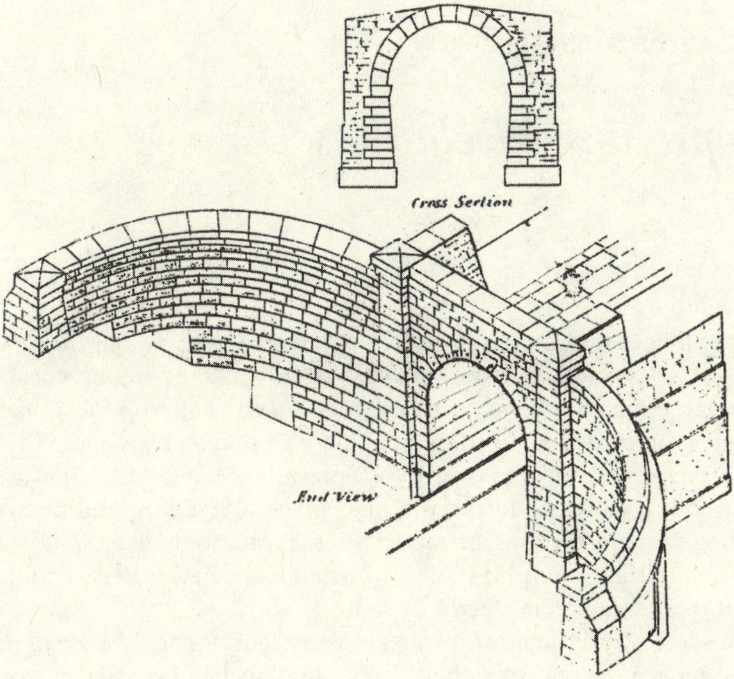

7.13 End view and cross section of the Grand Trunk Railway tunnel. Such magnificent masonry delights both industrial archaeologists and curiosity seekers, and could inspire architects. It needs to be protected and preserved as a tribute to nineteenth-century Canadian engineers and stonemasons. (SCM: Third Welland Canal file, envelope 8)

Transportation Company, wrote to his MP of his fears that its construction would postpone the opening of the canal.[35]

As we have seen, the canal divided established farms and interrupted east-west roads and, later, railways, necessitating a proliferation of bridges. While industry was attracted to the canal's banks to take advantage of the cheap and abundant water for their mills, the mills themselves were sometimes an impediment to navigation. Given these (and other) issues, canal engineers soon discovered that, if they wished to manage construction efficiently, they had to become skilled in "public relations" and, in the building of figurative as well as physical bridges. The actual bridges were obvious, but the less tangible links between the canal authorities and individuals (and the communities in which they lived) were equally important. The next chapter will deal with these invisible bridges.

CHAPTER EIGHT

Community Relations

Public dissatisfaction with the Welland Canal among local residents and enterprises was often deeply felt and highly vocal. To manage community relations, engineers and their superiors had to employ diplomatic skills for which they had had no training. Not only were there controversies over the inconvenience of bridges and waterways, but established farms and businesses suffered in tangible ways. Although industry was attracted to the canal's banks, millowners could find that their plans were thwarted if the new waterway did not meet their commercial needs.

In some ways, the most intractable obstacles to face the canal planners and engineers were their fellow human beings. Partly because of the pioneer conditions that still prevailed in Upper Canada, few people in what was still a colony could envisage a future in which British North Americans would enjoy one of the highest living standards in the world, supported by the most modern technologies and transportation systems. Imagination and enterprise were handicapped by attitude: a colonial lack of self-confidence or a sense of inferiority vis-à-vis both the great "mother country" and the bustling, aggressive neighbour to the south limited most Upper Canadians' vision of the future. William Hamilton Merritt was an exception, and his audacious sense of possibility met with pessimism, scepticism, criticism, and outright hostility from many sources as he tried to make a canal across Niagara a reality.

CUPIDITY, ENVY, JEALOUSY, AND DISTRUST

Throughout the First Canal's construction period, wrote Catharine Merritt, her husband faced "a great deal of opposition."[1] In fairness to his "enemies," we should remind ourselves that many Upper Canadians must have been aware that the Welland Canal project was initially inspired by Merritt's own need for a water supply for his mills and that the canal was designed at least in part to advance his personal interests. On the other hand, in Merritt's defence, public pessimism may have been a genuine deterrent to the canal's success. Merritt was conscious of – even offended by – this attitude. In a lengthy speech at the sod-turning in November 1824 he reminded the small gathering: "We have had difficulties and prejudices to contend with" and referred in particular to "the apathy and indifference that has hitherto prevailed among us on this subject [the canal]." Recalling that occasion, he later reinforced his point: "As a proof of how little this subject had attracted public enterprise at the time, not half a dozen gentlemen of capital or influence in the District attended this ceremony."[2]

Angered by such indifference, Merritt is reported to have declared to a group of sceptical Niagara (Newark) businessmen, "Gentlemen, I shall live to see the grass grow upon your streets."[3] Opposition to the project was certainly vociferous in that town, where many opposed the Twelve Mile Creek route (chapter 3). The directors noted that the year 1825 had "brought into action all those feelings of cupidity, envy, jealousy, and distrust, which unhappily characterize our nature."[4] Even James Gordon, the company treasurer (and married to Merritt's elder sister) wrote to Merritt in April 1826, highly critical about what he saw as Merritt's "inclination to serve yourself ... Pray may we not as well toss our money to you at once, and say, here good crafty agent, make the most of it." A later critic called Merritt a "wolf in sheep's clothing."[5] The testimony of Dr John Lefferty, MPP (1777–1842) to a Select Committee in January 1827 cast doubt on the potential profitability of the entire enterprise: "[He] does not regard it [the Welland Canal] as an undertaking which will be profitable to the country if money should be invested in it, and thinks that if the Province were to take stock it would not yield the interest of the money invested – does not think it will pay interest for many years – perhaps not for 50 years."[6]

The farming population was no more enthusiastic. Seymour Phelps, a son of the contractor Oliver Phelps (and therefore not an unbiased observer!), wrote later of Merritt: "The farmers, for the most part, as well as many other persons ... hooted at his crazy crotchet, as they then believed it to be and would not aid at all in this Canal conception ... In fact Mr. Merritt was considered by some then, as a sort of monomaniac, and was thereby spurned."[7] For a variety of motives, therefore (of which jealousy may well have been one), Merritt was frequently assailed by critics.

British opinion – with perhaps a touch of "mother country" condescension to colonials – occasionally encouraged such attitudes. John

MacTaggart, for example, denounced many aspects of the First Welland Canal.[8] In 1827 he noted that the east pier at Port Dalhousie was wrongly constructed, and that the dam that was to control the flow of Twelve Mile Creek into the lake was also inadequate, as was the towpath. In a similar vein, Colonel By warned that improvements to the St Lawrence and Welland Canals should never be entrusted to Canadians, because "the Civil Engineers in this country are either very ignorant, or have designedly Estimated these Works at less than they can be executed for."[9] Speaking as a trained military engineer, By could not be faulted, but he obviously did not appreciate the fact that at this time the colonies were obliged to rely mainly on British engineers (see chapter 3).

Merritt and his colleagues prevailed despite criticism, and the Welland, with all its faults, was opened for business at the end of November 1829. Supportive responses were heard at first. At the end of the canal's first full navigation season in 1830, the *Farmers' Journal* exulted over "the complete success of this magnificent undertaking" and reminded its readers of "the bitter and relentless opposition they [the canal's supporters] met with from almost every quarter, and the honest incredulity and prejudices of nine-tenths of the people residing upon its very banks."[10] Alas for the directors, malicious gossip continued, as indicated in their Annual Report for 1831: "A rumour, encouraged and circulated, if not invented, by some persons inimical to this useful work, that a slide of earth, or, as it was emphatically called, 'an avalanche,' had occurred in the early part of the season, at the deep cutting, and filled up the Welland Canal, had obtained general currency." The directors believed that this "unfounded report" had retarded the start of the annual construction season.[11]

In some ways, the critics may have been more realistic than the over-optimistic directors. The company's early dependence on foreign-trained engineers (chapter 3), although unavoidable, itself aroused criticism. Richard Bonnycastle, captain in the Royal Engineers and commander of the Royal Engineers in Canada 1837–39, was either ignorant of true conditions – or chose to ignore them – when he wrote in his 1841 memoirs: "there is a strong belief in the country, that men of [engineering] talent cannot be had without sending to the neighbouring states for them; and the consequence is, that people who know nothing of the profession, but perfectly understand the art of making wooden nutmegs, get the work and do it accordingly." He continued, "this disheartens persons from the old country and prevents young men of the province from studying the profession."[12]

A Shock to the Community

In the 1820s, some local residents would have believed they were living in a state of crisis. In the summer of 1825, for example, the Welland Canal Company's process of letting contracts jolted the sleepy village of St Catharines. Merritt's wife wrote to her mother on 5 July that would-be contractors "began to flock here on the thursday, and there was judged to be near 200 friday and saturday, the greatest part from the other side [the United States], there was about 60 different proposals given in & the contract for the harbor & deep cut have been let low the contractors are gone to get there sureties and will soon commence work, private families had to open there doors for the acomidation of strangers as this place is not very well provided with inns."[13]

The strangers of course brought with them their knowledge of the wider world and introduced experiences new to the inhabitants of Niagara's small, scattered communities. St Catharines would become the metropolis of the peninsula, and other places – with unpromising names like Stumptown (later Thorold) – would also thrive. Indeed, entirely new communities arose as a result of the First Welland Canal's construction.[14] In these towns interest in the canal project, at first slow to develop, soon gathered steam. We have seen that the state of the waterway and its later reconstruction projects were a frequent topic in local newspapers and, we assume, in hostelries and over fences. In chapter 2 we saw how the prospect of a branch line connecting the Welland to Newark (later Niagara, now Niagara-on-the-Lake) exercised hopes and ambitions in that town for many years. At the same time, the building and rebuilding of the canal on the chosen route often seemed to be a mixed blessing, as people found their land divided, requisitioned, or flooded, or discovered newly created pools of stagnant, disease-causing water.

"Depredations" of the Canal Builders

In the pre-industrial economy of Niagara, farming and related trades predominated. Although farmers might ultimately benefit from the presence of the Welland Canal, in the early years their interests were noticeably damaged by the waterway's construction. Indeed to some local people the immediate consequences of the First Canal must have seemed disastrous.

Few villages or rural areas prospered as did St Catharines or the canal-created towns of Thorold or Port Colborne. In the Legislative

Assembly in 1827 Lefferty, as well as expressing his misgivings about the viability of the scheme, urged the government to "sympathise with those unfortunate persons whose farms were laid waste by the canal."[15] As a consequence of the Welland's dams or weirs, some properties were flooded, even expropriated. Some communities not on the canal route were to lose businessmen to more profitable locations along the new waterway. After it became obvious that the canal would not extend to Newark, that community stagnated. But worse occurred to St John's on Twelve Mile Creek in the Short Hills. It had been an early centre of water-powered industry in Upper Canada, but when it was bypassed by the First Canal – with its more abundant and reliable power – the village nearly vanished.

Drowned Land

Flooding, which wrecked pasture land and could create ponds, was a major threat to local people's financial security and health. By the 1820s the connection between stagnant water and disease was appreciated, if not completely understood in a scientific sense. Moreover, damage to crops and buildings occurred on a large scale. Some of the early maps drawn in conjunction with the First Canal's construction show notations such as "about 3 acres actually drowned" (in this case on John Martindale's land, south of Port Dalhousie). Peter May's land in the same area is also shown to have been partly flooded (fig. Int.6),[16] because the outlet of a stream (Twelve Mile Creek) was dammed at its mouth on Lake Ontario. Flooding also occurred occasionally where weirs were constructed in association with locks.

When arbitration hearings were held in 1826 to evaluate initial damages resulting from canal construction, one of the questions was: "Does the Canal by raising the waters upon low or marshy lands in the vicinity of your premises improve the health of the situation and thereby prove beneficial to you?" Four local residents replied that raising the water was tantamount to flooding and would be injurious to public health because formerly dry land would become more marshy, especially in rainy weather. Nevertheless twenty respondents did not answer this question or thought it inapplicable, and four said "no."[17]

This relative public apathy on the question of flooding soon disappeared when residents of Wainfleet Township and Haldimand County living near the Feeder Canal and upstream from the Grand River dam found their livelihood endangered. When the dam was completed in 1829, water quickly rose behind it and flooded thousands of acres of flat land between Dunnville and Cayuga. Among them were the cornfields of the Six Nations, who had been granted strips of land 6 miles (9.7 km) wide on both sides of the river. Needless to say, they had never been asked if they approved of the canal plans. Eventually, the Welland Canal Company would face hefty claims for compensation by landowners, as we saw in chapter 7. "The people have all been waiting with much patience," the board admitted in July 1830, "and require an immediate decision." The directors, however, turned an unsympathetic ear to the plaintiffs. George Keefer responded in January 1831 that landowners had only themselves to blame for their losses. By the time the dam was closed, he said, "all the corn was perfectly ripe and could have been removed if the owners had been disposed, as I gave them notice ... Apple trees not all drowned may be transplanted, rails all on the premises may be removed at trifling expense."[18]

William Lyon Mackenzie later gave a more sympathetic description of the Grand River claimants' position and listed the situation among the Canal Company's alleged iniquities.[19] The problem persisted for the better part of fifty years: claims for flooding caused by the Dunnville dam were being made regularly as late as 1876.

For five decades the Feeder Canal carried the water essential for the operation of the main canal, but its banks and towpaths acted as dams, blocking natural watercourses. Furthermore, the eight culverts built under its channel proved inadequate to prevent overflowing. In 1847 Samuel Keefer reported: "[Given] the state of the back ditches, the capacity of the culverts, and the nature of the drainage generally along the Feeder ... it appears that the capacity of the culverts is inadequate to discharge the great body of water on such occasions, that the water sometimes rises nearly to a level with the waters in the feeder, overflowing large traces to land, and from the contraction at the culverts taking from three to four weeks to subside to its ordinary level. In the fall to[o] the lands are frequently overflown from the same cause."[20] The Department "tinkered" with the problem but with no noticeable improvement. When the Warden of Welland County requested in 1878 that the culverts under the Feeder be enlarged to improve the drainage of Cranberry Creek, he was assured that a new culvert under Lyons Creek would be sufficient to that purpose and told that the culverts under the Feeder could not be altered.[21]

If, on account of the Feeder's dam-like nature, some areas experienced flooding, others met with the opposite. Where the Lyons Creek culvert passed under the Canal south of Welland, debris tended to pile up on the western side of the channel, reducing the flow of water through the culvert and to the east. Moses Cook's mills had flourished there, but his business was eventually forced to close down because of lack of water, while lands adjacent to the Feeder continued to be frequently inundated. Even until the mid-twentieth century regular flooding of basements in Wainfleet Township continued, provoking the Department of Transport finally to commission a study of the matter by an engineer (W.G. McGeorge). Among the recommendations of his 1947 Drainage Report was that the channel be partially filled in.[22]

Other structures vital to the operation of the canal were also seen as potentially disruptive. With less justification than the flooded property owners of Wainfleet, some local opinion objected to the Second Canal aqueduct. In 1848 David Thorburn (1789–1862, warden of the Niagara District) sent a petition to the Legislature to the effect that the proposed new aqueduct would block the flow of Chippawa Creek and therefore create stagnant backwaters. The present situation was already bad enough, he said: "For the past few years the majority of the inhabitants living along its banks in some of the most populous Townships, have been confined to their beds during the most part of the summer and fall ... Such were the consequences last year that in the Townships of Wainfleet and Gainsboro there was scarcely a house in which there were not two or three laid on sick beds during the whole summer, and some of these heads of large families."[23] Despite such foreboding complaints, we have found no indication that the aqueduct exacerbated the problem.

The rapid growth of Niagara's urban centres meant that the municipal councils of towns and cities frequently petitioned the federal government to ensure proper drainage and the expansion of water mains. In 1878 (echoing earlier concerns of the warden of Niagara) St Catharines city council asked for permission to pass a water pipe under the new canal. The following year the council reported that a natural drainage ditch had been severed by canal construction. The municipality wanted to reconstitute it because the localities to be drained were "now in a very unfortunate condition." Furthermore, "many are perhaps needlessly anxious for the prompt execution of the work"[24] in case an epidemic such as cholera should break out.

By the time the Third Canal was under construction people living along the waterway were alert to the potential dangers of flooding. In 1878 Allanburg residents worried that the new channel would be higher than the level of one of their streets and asked therefore that the drainage system be improved. By 1878, "B. Tucker & Co." of Allanburg had already experienced the worst: the building of the east bank of the new canal had "obstructed the natural water channel causing the water to flow thro' his property & damaging two of his orchards."[25]

Property Laid to Waste

While part of the route of "Mr. Merritt's Ditch" traversed unclaimed land, the line inevitably ran through private property valued for its homes, farms, businesses, or profitable woodland. In many cases log cabins, barns, and outhouses had been carefully erected in clearings laboriously carved out of a wilderness by the owners or their fathers. To build the canal, the company obviously needed to acquire some of this land, and landowners were encouraged to sell parts of their property to the directors. Although certain individuals could see advantages to having a commercial waterway built past their homes and businesses, others were not at all delighted to see the surveyors and labourers appear on the scene.

The contractor Oliver Phelps foresaw no difficulty in acquiring land from local farmers, as he declared to a Select Committee in 1825: "I am confident that along the Welland Canal the proprietors could sell their lands through which it is desired that it should pass for one third more than they could before have done, and that they would in general be much disappointed if the route were not altered so as to come through their lands; some who have signed petitions against it have told me so."

His sanguine outlook was not totally reflected in public opinion. For example, in that same year Samuel Wood and others sent a petition to the Legislative Assembly alleging company "depredations." Although the co-signers approved of the canal project, they objected to the fact that Merritt's agents could "enter upon [their] lands without any previous arrangement, laying ... farms to commons and waste without compensation, to the great injury of individuals." Moreover they feared that the directors' commitment to build bridges would not be sufficiently honoured.[26]

When Jacob Upper and other local residents heard about plans to control the flow of the eastern branch of Twelve Mile Creek, they objected to the Legislative Assembly that the project would "overflow some hundreds of acres of the best meadow lands in the township of Thorold with a mass of stagnated water, much to the injury of your Petitioners and his Majesty's subjects in general, both in health and property."[27]

The Act of 19 January 1824, which incorporated the company, permitted the directors to make agreements with the owners of land through which the canal would pass, purchasing land outright or contracting to pay for damages caused by construction. Many claims for damages were immediately filed, prompting another Act of the Legislature (30 January 1826),[28] which established a procedure for arbitration between aggrieved locals and the company. Proceedings began in St Catharines in August 1826. In addition to the question about flooding referred to above, the complainants were asked the following:

> 1. What is the number of your Lot and of the Concession?
> 2. What quantity thereof is required for the Canal ...?
> 12. Has the Canal been of any disadvantage to your lands – if so, in what respect, and to what extent?
> 13. Do you apprehend any disadvantage from the Canal not yet experienced – and if so, explain in what respect and to what extent.

The many complaints voiced reflected the ambivalent attitudes of the populace. Robert Dettrick's testimony was typical of the naysayers: the canal "takes away woodland, overflows bottoms and meadows – destroys a sugar bush – takes away a good Mill seat on Dick's creek upon which he intended to buld a mill – a seat for a Saw Mill. Is shut up, has no means of getting out." Adam Gould was of the same mind: he would lose his pastures, "and apprehends about two acres of meadow more will be overflowed. Has this year been deprived of a field on the side hill – about two acres ... estimates his damages by loss of side hill field at $40 – cattle run in the woods and are not in as good condition as they would have been had he not been deprived of his pasture."

Some individuals also felt aggrieved that the company's purchasing policy undervalued their land. Fairly or unfairly, the company ultimately did compensate people whose land or homes were damaged: individual payments ranged from £300 to nearly £2,000, but the compensation often did not satisfy.[29]

By the time the Second Canal was being built, the lives of Niagara residents were less disrupted. Nevertheless (as in the 1820s) some people were inconvenienced and others must have felt their lives ruined. An April 1851 estimate of "land damages" reads in part as follows:

> Anthony Knox Boomer. Land taken opp. Merritt's Mill, St. Catharines.
>
> Land taken part of 1 town Lot No. 22, part of lot 18 in 7th Con. of Grantham £10.
>
> Sarah Dunlap. Removing house from line of Hydraulic road from opp. Lock 15 to Thorold Bridge £8.15.

G. Rother, Damages to Cellar & Garden at Stone Bridge ...
£6.5.[30]

Well-established and prosperous businesses were not immune to damage. For example in 1845 Lewis Shickluna complained that his ship repair work at St Catharines was disrupted. Engineer Power reported to the Department: "As Mr. Shickluna's business has been much deranged by his having been compelled to remove his buildings Marine railway etc. for the accommodation of the Board I would respectfully suggest the propriety of renting the Dry dock to him at a moderate sum during the ensuing season."[31]

Building the Third Canal required even larger land acquisitions – and now in a more developed and heavily populated Niagara. This gave rise to a new problem: "squatters," or people who had built homes on canal-designated land without any legal deed to the property and were reluctant to move. They were offered no compensation at all. In 1878 the Roman Catholic Reverend Dean Mulligan urged MP John C. Rykert to use his influence to prevent eviction of such people, some of whose names – such as Dooley, O'Brian, O'Meara – recalled the Irish origins of many canal labourers. However, Canal Superintendent William Ellis retorted tersely in 1880: "On no account can the request be granted" because their "continued presence on every account [was] wholly unjustifiable and very mischievous."[32]

Naturally the homes of more law-abiding citizens also occasionally stood in the path of construction and had to be vacated or moved. For these men and women the loss of or damage to land was tantamount to reduced livelihood in an age with no "social safety net." For them the Welland Canal was not an inspired commercial venture of national importance, but a threat to an existence that had been dearly achieved and was sometimes fragile. Compensation was offered, but it rarely seemed sufficient. When in 1872 N. Higgins of Port Colborne claimed $400 for the cost of moving his house and related buildings, the Department offered him only $300.[33]

Although we have no accounts of physical violence occurring when the canal authorities tried to begin work on expropriated property, we find hints of dramatic encounters with landowners. In a telegram sent by James George Currie (1827–1901), MP for Welland County, to the Department of Public Works in June 1874, concerning a problem faced by Patrick Shannon, the contractor on Section 6, north of St Catharines, we read: "Shannon's men were yesterday prevented by Potter from commencing work on his property, Potter says he has not yet been paid although it is some months since his agreement was signed." Another telegram followed up the story: "Since tel. you I have seen

Potter who has consented to allow Shannon to take possession of his land."[34] One wonders how the dispute was resolved.

Occasionally women were the injured parties in such disagreements. In 1879 Mrs Janet McCarthy of Port Colborne complained to the Department that the canal enlargement had blocked the entrance to a barn that she had rented out at $6.00 a month. Unjustly deprived "of that small income," she demanded compensation. Canal Superintendent Ebenezer Bodwell believed that she was indeed entitled to some consideration, but two years later she felt compelled to remind the chief engineer of her claim: "I am a very poor widoe [sic]," she wrote, "and the Canal enlargement at Port Colborne has done my property very serious damage." Her claim was referred to arbitrators but the outcome is unclear.[35] Some women were tenacious in their pursuit of justice. In April 1875 Mrs Mary Boyle claimed $200 compensation for the canal's flooding of her orchard along Twelve Mile Creek. When Public Works offered her $150, she refused it. Frederick Braun (the Departmental secretary) was ordered to confer with the lady – but meanwhile further damage was done to her property. Finally (in March 1876) Mrs Boyle was offered, and accepted, $300.[36]

THE WELLAND, KING OF ALL CANALS

On a civic holiday in August 1885 Thorold citizens enjoyed a parade of floats. The Welland Canal (third incarnation) was represented "by a boat with sails hoisted, and profusely embellished." On one side was printed: "The Welland, king of all canals," and on the other the couplet: "Our sailors are bold and soldiers brave; / They can hold their own on field or wave."[37]

Obviously, at this time many residents of Thorold – indeed, of all Niagara – were fascinated by the waterway and took great pride in it (fig. 8.1). This had not always been the case. As noted above, the sod-turning ceremony in 1824 had attracted little interest. And in 1841, Richard Bonnycastle had opined that: "As constructed, the Welland was a waste of money and effort, an abortive attempt to connect the two great lakes with the far west ... a mere ditch, lined with wooden locks, and its principal powers ... wasted in securing profitable mill sites."[38] Not long before, a contrasting viewpoint had been expressed by the St Catharines *Journal*: given the growth in trade and the advantages of the Welland over the Erie, "every consideration of sound policy, as well as individual and public prosperity, demands, in the strongest terms, the speedy enlargement, and permanent construction, of this perfect work."[39] The following year a ship's captain told

8.1 Curious locals at Lock 12 of the Third Canal, c. 1876. The new Welland was a source of pride for Niagara residents even as they worried about the behaviour of construction labourers and cursed the delays involved in crossing the canal's path. (*Canadian Illustrated News*, 15 January 1876, 44)

a visitor that the Welland Canal was "far better worth [wasting] time on than the Falls of Niagara."[40] In 1873 (when the Third Canal was in process) a correspondent to the Montreal *Gazette* found that there was "much stir" throughout Niagara because "every farmer in that range can show conclusively that the Canal should go right through his farm."[41]

Locals gradually became aware that the economy of their towns (and increasingly that of the whole country) depended to a large degree on the waterway. "Without the Welland Canal," wrote the editor of the St Catharines *Daily Times* in 1871, "the Dominion would be little better than 'a home for cats and badgers.'"[42] By the 1870s some town residents were scheming to have the canal as close to their community as possible, to boost the local economy. As one correspondent wrote to the Thorold *Post* in 1871: "The new Canal enlargement has created considerable interest among the inhabitants [of Allanburg], who are scheming to capture a few of those 'Almighty dollars' ... Many new dwellings have been erected for the purposes of accommodating those 'living curiosities' who have sought employment here."

As we have noted, journalists in canal-side towns made a special point of reporting on any and all canal developments. The Thorold *Post* was exemplary: in July 1876 it announced that, because construction was "interesting to our readers and the public generally," the editors were sending a representative to inspect the building site. If we are to believe the published article, the journalist walked the whole length of the canal on "a hot day's tramp."[43] The *Post* offered this kind of coverage regularly, providing readers both at the time and nearly a century and a half later with vivid accounts of progress. In fact the *Post* was an unabashed "booster" of the Third Canal because, as the editors noted in 1886, "besides being very much needed by the shipping interests of the country, the enlargement will bring comfort to many homes who have not perhaps seen it for a long time; and it is to be earnestly hoped that by the time it is completed the painful depression will have passed away, and peace and plenty once more abound."[44]

Of course the *Post* also had Thorold's specific interests at heart, fretting that the Third Canal would not run through the town and that the headquarters would remain in St Catharines. The engineer's office had been in Thorold during construction because the whole line was easily accessed from that town. Why, the townspeople asked, should the canal offices remain in a city so far removed from the main channel of the new waterway? The disgruntled editors summed up their sense of rejection in the following image: "And now that the New Canal is in operation, the almost defunct villagers can have the same privilege accorded them that the rejected young man had given to him to sit on the fence and see her go by. So we can gaze with as much admiration as our spirits will allow at the tall masts and black smoke stacks as they pass <u>us</u> by" [emphasis in the original].[45]

Specific features of the new waterway occasioned concern in some towns as locals realized how dependent their economy was becoming on canal-related business. For example, in the 1870s people in Thorold worried about the effect that the relatively small number of crossings of the Third Canal would have on their community. Several attempts by the mayor to reach the Minister of Public Works proved fruitless. However, townspeople's concerns rose considerably when John Page visited the town in 1875. But Page, said the *Post*, "was inflexible in his determination to adhere to his original plan."[46] The engineer's watchword remained, "the fewer [bridges], the better."

Community rivalries were another feature of the time. Thorold newspapermen felt a proprietary interest in the canal and were proud of their waterway expertise, sneering at the Hamilton *Spectator*'s apparent ignorance of matters relating to the mighty ditch. In the fall of 1884 the latter newspaper questioned the process of deepening the Welland, revealing (said the Thorold editor) that they were "not well posted" (was the pun intended?) and demonstrating "a lack of knowledge, if not entire ignorance on the question which is almost unpardonable on the part of the of the leading daily papers in Ontario." For a whole month thereafter the *Post* lambasted the *Spectator* for being ill-informed about water supply for the Welland. "If you want to be posted [sic!] on Welland Canal affairs," they continued, "we are just the boys that can do it. Only don't waste our time by giving us such simple questions that any school boy along the banks of the Welland Canal can answer." Finally the exasperated *Post* declared that the *Spectator* was: "still in wilful and perverse ignorance [the *Post*'s emphasis] of the fact that the banks of the new canal are only going to be raised between Lock Two and Twenty-Four. It writes a lot of nonsense about causing water to flow up hill. Well, we would as soon expect water to flow up a hill as the *Spectator* to write common sense about raising of a portion of the banks of the new canal."[47]

In fact, the rebuilding of the Welland Canal in the 1870s owed much to the pressure that journalists were able to exert on behalf of their local communities. In the early 1870s the St Catharines *Daily Times* campaigned vigorously for an enlargement and reported diligently on the efforts of local people to have the canal rebuilt. The *Times* (a Grit organ) detected Tory under-handedness and favouritism in all canal-related matters. For example, it accused the members of the 1871 Royal Commission of being "under the pay and inspiration of a 'talented member'" (presumably Conservative MP Rykert of St Catharines), a man who, said the *Times*, wanted to be appointed canal superintendent and who opposed enlargement. The *Times* blamed John A. Macdonald and his Conservative government for the snail's pace of rebuilding the canal and for any other problems associated with the waterway's functioning. On 16 September 1871 the *Times* reported on a "Preliminary Indignation Meeting" held in the city, at which nearly forty manufacturers and shipowners elected a committee to draft resolutions for a planned, larger public meeting. On 5 October the meeting was held and acted on the resolution to condemn the government for its inaction. Continuing its campaign to have the canal rebuilt, the *Times* on 2 November snorted – under the headline "WHAT ARE YOU GOING TO DO ABOUT IT NOW?": "Well, Mr. Page has been up the Welland Canal, and Mr. Woodruff [canal superintendent] has been down to Ottawa. He has interviewed Mr. Langevin [Minister of Public Works], has come home whitewashed, and now in his old buggy is pursuing the even tenor of his way along the canal, the ruined and decayed ditch into which ... he has reduced the great public work entrusted to his keeping."[48]

Something to Be Proud of for All Future Time

Although the tone of such articles did little to enhance the quality of journalism in the Niagara Peninsula, the underlying message was loud and clear: both the *Post* and the *Times* – and their readers – were deeply interested in the Welland Canal. In 1881 an "observer" sang its praises in the Thorold journal, "The canal is now a thing of beauty. Noting first its splendid masonry, we turn with admiration to the ingenious mechanical contrivances about its locks and bridges, and, last but not least, we gaze with pleasure on the clear, green tinted water rolling past our feet. Surely its engineers have done well, and Canada has something to be proud of for all future time."[49]

From the canal's early years, communities had been active lobbyists for the construction or improvement of certain fixtures such as locks, bridges, drains, and culverts. Local politicians, too, often advocated for the grassroots interests. In 1848 D. MacFarland (MPP for Port Robinson), for instance, asked that the new (Second Canal) lock in this town be enlarged to the size of the St Catharines lock. When this request was refused, he petitioned on behalf of his constituency to have one of the First Canal locks in Port Robinson used as a drydock, an appeal which was granted. In 1886 St Catharines wanted a turning basin and wharf at the Niagara Street crossing of the new Third Canal: a deputation prepared a memorandum that they took to Ottawa to deliver directly to Page. The chief engineer refused to consider building such a fixture, citing its expense.[50]

This type of public engagement was especially evident when the second enlargement (the Third Canal) was anticipated: local individuals were not slow to volunteer their suggestions for improvement. In chapter 2 we saw that John Grenville of Thorold recommended a particular line for the new waterway. John Silverthorne, who lived near the Canal north of Welland, wrote to Ottawa suggesting that the Department of Railways and Canals should use his invention of a new kind of syphon culvert.[51]

For some local residents, "the King of all Canals" could be wilful and despotic. But as the century progressed, the attitude of Niagara people to the waterway became generally one of commitment and support – albeit seasoned with a healthy dose of self-interest.[52]

8.2 Pollution of the Second Canal near Lock 24 at Thorold, 1935, with Jacob Keefer's Welland (flour) Mills (established 1846) in the background. Here sawdust and woodchips from lumber mills have been repeatedly released into the waterway. (SLSMC, Niagara Region)

INDUSTRY, TRADE, AND THE NAVIGATION

When the First Canal was put under contract, the Welland Canal Company advertised free water power in perpetuity. George Keefer of Thorold was one entrepreneur who accepted the offer, and the imposing "Welland Mills" (still standing in Thorold) bear witness to the success of his family's business endeavours.[53] But establishments such as saw mills were a liability on the canal: they sucked valuable water away from the channel and blocked it with sawdust. Canal authorities early became aware of the danger to "the navigation" posed by mills dumping material into the waterway. In 1832 the company directors ordered that "no saw mill ... be permitted to run on the line of the Canal until proper racks or floors are constructed to prevent the sawdust from getting into the canal"[54] (fig. 8.2).

The large wheels of these mills might also cause a current that could drag ships off course. In 1843 Robert Baldwin (attorney general of Canada West) was told that the Board of Works wanted to close all mills along the line of the canal, pointing out that they were obstructing the enlargement and did not provide enough revenue.[55] Despite this determination to curtail their operations, the water-driven factories along the Second Canal remained in business even after the Third Canal was completed.

In the early 1870s (before the precise depth of the new canal was known) shipping interests weighed in with their concerns. For most of them fourteen feet was the ideal depth to be achieved. From 1874 to at least 1877 the Department was assailed by letters and memoranda from the Toledo and Chicago Boards of Trade, as well as from shipowners in Hamilton, Toronto, Kingston, Port Burwell, Port Rowan, and Sarnia. Sylvester Neelon, a St Catharines shipowner, and shipbuilders (such as Alexander Muir of Port Dalhousie) begged for a depth of fourteen feet. This sort of entrepreneurial interest would have come as no surprise to Page and his fellow engineers in the Department, for since the days of the Welland Canal Company, businesses had leaned heavily on the operators of "Mr. Merritt's Ditch."

In the 1880s enterprising local entrepreneurs looked forward to opening mills on the new canal, especially on the long, straight stretch between Thorold and Port Dalhousie. Adding to the anticipation of "unlimited" water power from the locks, weirs, and ponds of the new channel, the Thorold *Post* was particularly impressed with the "immense hydraulic power" available on the new line at the Escarpment.[56] The *Post*'s enthusiasm was typical of the talk and petitioning for water rights on the new canal. But it soon became obvious that there was to be provision neither for ships stopping or turning on the route, nor for industrial sites. In 1881 St Catharines MP Rykert asked in the House of Commons why no provision had been made for a turning basin on the new canal – "a serious defect," he thought. Tupper, the Minister of Railways and Canals, explained: "the principal business on this canal, for a number of years at least, must be through trade; therefore there will be no mills, or factories or other places where vessels will be at all likely to unload or receive cargo on the new line."[57]

This decision brought considerable disappointment to the business community – and real economic loss. The communities of St Catharines, Merritton, and Thorold (writes John N. Jackson) "lost the considerable advantages of through passenger and commodity flows, as well as the service trades that had previously been enjoyed from the canal" as a result of the new northern route. Developing this point, Hannah Stanwick maintains that, although St Catharines obviously did not disappear (as did St John's when the First Canal drew business away from it), Merritt's home town "missed the boat."[58] A century ago some local people were already of that opinion. In 1897 a Thorold historian wrote: "Since the completion of the canal, the towns along its banks, with the exception of Merritton, have all shown a decrease in population and in business energy. The water power on the new canal has never yet been rented, although many applications have been made for it."[59]

Welland residents, at the hub of the Niagara Peninsula, feared that the widening of the canal would ruin the town's economy, since it would involve the destruction of a much-used raceway that served some local mills, as well as the removal of commercial wharves on the west side of the Second Canal. Public meetings, town council resolutions, and a delegation to Ottawa were of no avail. Fortunately for them, "the worst" did not happen and, after some adjustments and with the end of the long depression in the early 1890s, the community prospered.

IRRITATIONS

While "drowning" of land and blocking of roadways were the most frequent consequences of canal construction for the people of Niagara, less catastrophic, but nevertheless irritating situations also arose. Protests were heard when roads – including the most modern "Macadamized" routes – were damaged. In 1874 the St Catharines and Niagara Falls & Macadamized Road Company claimed compensation for damage to one of their roads, and in 1879 the Port Robinson and Thorold Macadamized Road Company informed the contractors on Section 17 (south of Thorold) that their towing teams had wrecked the road with heavy loads. These are just two among several such complaints.

Even if their lands were not bisected by the canal, communication routes cut off, or roads ruined, farmers suffered; as construction advanced, so too did their grumbling. As early as May 1827 the company noted that "Mr. John Gould presented an application for damage sustained in consequence of timber deposited on his land, destroying his fences, etc." The following July the board entered several claims: "A petition was presented by Luke Carrell, praying for aid towards digging a well, in consequence of his spring being destroyed by the Canal ... Adam and Benjamin Gould presented an application for payment of damage and expense in removing fences, etc. ... John Gould claimed £10 for damage in wheatfield" [emphases in the original]. (It would be interesting to know what Gould thought about the canal project.) Some complainants received compensation – others were turned down. In August 1827 the board minutes noted simply: "Elizabeth Ball presented a claim of £9 for injury sustained by covering

6 acres of land with timber. Rejected." When we read that George May in 1877 stated that he had built a fence "to protect his land from contractors"[60] we can sense some of the resentment felt by local residents *vis-à-vis* canal builders.

When the canal was widened and deepened through towns, urban businesses had to be relocated. A typical story appeared in a report in the Welland *Telegraph* in 1877: "The new canal cuts through from the wharves, taking all houses between there and Coultson, inclusive. The line takes half of Swayze's photography gallery, [the] south east corner of [the] dwelling at [the] rear, Cooper's barn and half his sheds, and misses the grist mills and Haun's factory."[61] David Cooper of Welland had to abandon his "Aqueduct Mill" when the Second Canal was enlarged in 1877. In lieu of financial compensation he asked for another site on the new canal when it opened.[62] Simple claims such as that for damage to a field of potatoes caused by the 1870s enlargement reflect the real concern of residents whose livelihood was undercut by canal construction.

The First and Second canals were built across a relatively undeveloped Niagara Peninsula, and the challenges were mostly quite predictable. Later canal builders were sometimes taken by surprise. If the living were incommoded, so were the dead! In 1874 sixteen bodies of soldiers killed in the Battle of Beaverdams during the War of 1812 were unearthed south of the Niagara Central Railway Bridge near Thorold. In 1879 sub-contractors' damage to the St Catharines cemetery was estimated at $500.00.[63] East of Thorold there was a major graveyard near St Peter's Anglican Church, consecrated in 1838. Parishioners were greatly inconvenienced when the line of the Third Canal separated the church and its cemetery from the rest of the parish. The church was demolished in the 1890s and, when Lakeview Cemetery was opened in 1886, St Peter's graveyard was abandoned.

Those working "on the ground," building and reconstructing the canals, gave little thought to the historical or "heritage" value of the structures that their work was superseding. The stonework of the Second and Third canals occasioned the admiration of contemporaries and, where it still stands today, still commands respect. But if it survives, it does so by chance. Much of it was demolished over time, regarded as merely utilitarian and disposable. Handsome old bridge masonry at Humberstone was removed in 1903, for example, when a new bridge was put in. Also long forgotten is the destruction to the natural heritage of Niagara by canal construction. When a part of Ten Mile Creek was diverted into a culvert for the Third Canal, the creek's waterfall in a gorge on the Escarpment was wiped out. Yet in fairness we cannot fault nineteenth-century engineers for not having twenty-first century sensibilities. As we saw in chapter 4, trees were, in fact, planted along the Third Canal. Granted, these plantings were done to secure the banks and berms – and most do not seem to have survived for long – but they also restored some of the natural beauty of the area.[64]

When incidents of vandalism and destruction of canal property occurred, contractors and engineers must have been hard pressed to keep a favourable attitude toward residents of the communities where damage took place. Community and personal resentment for damage done locally, as well as reaction to changes to traditional routines, occasionally provoked criminal acts. Samuel Power reported one such occurence in 1845 when the sluices on one of the gates for Lock 15 were stolen. In 1875 vandals damaged cut stone being readied for the canal. The bank of the Feeder Canal at Dunnville was cut several times in 1876 and it was also in that year that the wilful damage was inflicted on Townsend's lock gates (chapter 5). During the process of erecting light poles for electricity in 1905, farmer Kniesley stole over forty of them before they had been put up. Sometimes people's meddling with canal equipment had tragic consequences. In 1876, on a Sunday (when work had ceased and equipment lay idle), some boys were playing around with a derrick on Section 12. They tried to make the machine raise a large stone, but it crashed to the ground, killing one of them.[65]

Local residents also experienced theft and vandalism as a consequence of canal building. In the 1820s the navvies indulged in endemic thievery. In mid-century Abraham Neff of Stonebridge had timber stolen from his land by Second Canal labourers. His 1848 request for compensation was refused on the grounds that he should seek redress from "the parties doing the injury."[66] Neff must have wondered how, in the absence of a professional police force, and given the character of some canal workers, he would ever accomplish this.

On the other hand, in the process of canal building significant contributions were made to local communities, some in now-forgotten ways. For example, canal authorities donated timber and stone for building churches in local towns (chapter 10), and in 1874 Welland residents were invited to use abandoned stone for road improvement.[67]

In all settlements, rural and urban, many of Niagara's people had to make great personal and communal adjustments when the canal sliced through their towns, their property, and their lives. Perhaps the greatest challenge to their communities was the arrival of thousands of strangers, often poverty-stricken and in turmoil, seeking work. They are the subject of our next chapter.

CHAPTER NINE

Working on the Welland

A tour of the construction sites of the first three canals would have shown great mounds of earth, heaps of stone, clouds of dust, fields of mud, teams of oxen or horses, assorted equipment ranging from simple wagons to complex steam-powered shovels – and scores, often hundreds, of human beings. When describing the excavation of the trench or the building of the locks, we have occasionally referred to the labourers, but who were these unskilled navvies wielding picks and axes? Who were the more skilled men who later manoeuvred the giant shovels? Who were the men who would emerge from twelve- or fourteen-hour days covered in mud, perhaps drenched from head to foot, exhausted and occasionally resentful? (fig. 9.1)[1]

Unfortunately, the evidence regarding nineteenth-century navvies' working and living conditions is all too sketchy, and conclusions about specific individuals are difficult (if not impossible) to reach. The dearth of records for the First Canal is due largely to the nature of the Canal Company's mandate, which was to construct an operating waterway in the interests of investors and "The Trade" – not to provide social services or to preserve law and order. When the Second Canal was built, this time by the government, political and economic conditions brought questions of poverty and unrest to the fore and the records begin to provide more information. The records for the Third Canal are more complete, yet also frustrating to use.

Some aspects of navvies' lives are obvious. While employer-employee relations and the attitudes of bureaucrats, engineers, and contractors to labourers changed over the years, working conditions were always wretched, at least by our standards. Living conditions improved over the century, but the incidence of poverty and disease – though not unusual in the nineteenth century as a whole – seems to have been high in the canal communities. Ethnic and religious strife among the navvies was endemic, exacerbated by the aforementioned conditions. But we should not assume that all employers (whether government officials or contractors) were Dickensian monsters. They made attempts

9.1 Statues of canal workers in Merritt Park, Welland, designed by Bas Degroot, erected 2001. The sculptor has well depicted the drudgery and exhaustion involved in such labour. (Photo: R.R.T.)

as they could – some enlightened, some misguided – to alleviate living and working conditions. Nor did the labourers themselves remain supine: assisted in part by government legislation, they gradually organized and tried to improve their lot (chapter 10).

FROM APPRENTICE TO PROLETARIAN

Although in the 1820s an industrial capitalist economy was emerging in northwestern Europe and New England, in much of the Western world craft traditions of employment still prevailed. Employers were encouraged to take a paternal interest in their workers and to regard themselves as masters, and their employees as apprentices or journeymen, as had been the practice since the middle ages. Given this attitude, even large companies would provide food and shelter for their labourers. On canal construction in Britain and the United States, the navvy and the contractor knew each other at least by sight. The former was expected to feel a certain loyalty to his "master," and the latter to acknowledge certain responsibilities to his "apprentice." This reciprocal relationship was also active during the construction of the First Welland Canal; at least some of the contractors considered themselves "master builders" who, seeking crews of reliable labourers, hired men by the month, provided room and board, and even some medical care. This system was not necessarily superior to modern arrangements but, when it worked (as it seems to have still done in Niagara in the 1820s), it could function relatively well. When it was discarded or was subjected to stress, with nothing comparable to put in its place, its failure was catastrophic.

A Capitalist Labour Market Emerges

By the 1840s the employer's traditionally paternalistic attitude of the 1820s had shifted toward a modern capitalist view in which labour was more regarded as a commodity to be purchased. This change was in part responsible for living and working conditions on canal sites in both Canada West and Canada East becoming so bad that unemployed and starving workers resorted to violence to call attention to their misery. In addition to rock-bottom wages, alcoholism, disease, ignorance and prejudice on the part of the authorities, and feuding among the predominantly Irish navvies themselves, all contributed to the inevitable rioting. During construction of the First Canal, the Irish labourers were largely Protestant Ulstermen, some of whom had become farmers. But after about 1835 Roman Catholics from southern Ireland predominated, most of whom sought wage employment and thus in effect provided labour for Niagara's emerging capitalist economy.[2]

The social situation was in itself fraught with potential problems, but the navvies' circumstances were exacerbated by a feud between men from Connaught and men from Cork. What made matters even worse was the influx of poverty-stricken immigrants and unemployed labourers from the cessation of work on the Erie Canal, which added even more workers to the pool of the Niagara destitute, now receiving little assistance from employers or government.

Throughout North America in the 1840s (wrote Peter Way) "transient immigrant workers [were] palpably exploited by largely unknown contractors, while ... boards of works were distant and technically divorced form the labour force."[3] The fact that conditions during the Second Welland's construction confirm this observation should not brand contractors, engineers, and bureaucrats as corrupt "bourgeois" exploiters. Large-scale changes were occurring in Canada West as elsewhere, processes that no individual or institution could yet understand or control. Furthermore, the transition to the Second Welland, being a far larger project than the building of the First, created more complex problems for its builders; much more money and many more labourers were involved. Meanwhile the new Board of Works, like other public institutions, was developing a hierarchical bureaucracy, often remote from construction sites with a corps of engineers concerned mainly with technical details and finance. Concurrently, many contractors, as independent businessmen in an emerging capitalist economy, were trying to get the actual excavation accomplished "on the ground" and make a decent profit. In this stressful, evolving situation, relations between boss and worker inevitably grew more detached and more impersonal.

Navvies, seen more and more simply as "hands," grew quite divorced from any identification with the project on which they were employed. To be sure, many labourers on the First Canal had probably felt similarly unidentified, but the virtual loss of the paternalistic relationship between employer and employed (the "proletarianization" of the worker) was now made worse by the depression of the late 1830s. Faced with a shortage of capital, contractors – who were beginning to feel less responsibility to provide support for their workers anyway – believed themselves justified in lowering wages. Correspondingly, the men in the excavation trenches and the lock pits began to regard the contractor, the engineer, and the office clerk as their enemies. Complicating the situation was the fact that individual contractors – not the government – set wage rates, which could vary from section to section.

For its part, as we have already mentioned, the Board of Works refused to intervene betweeen contractor and labourer. In 1842 the board made an important pronouncement: on 19 August they informed a contractor complaining that a sub-contractor had refused to pay him: "The Board in no wise recognizes sub-contractors, therefore cannot interfere." The following year one Thomas Whitton, a stonecutter, was told: "The Board cannot in any case interfere between the Contractor and the hands employed. The prices which after careful inquiry they learn are paid on the Welland Canal are quite equal to those now being paid on any other work in the Province."[4]

Exacerbating this situation was the developing view that the interests of businessmen were increasingly allied with those of government. In other words, the canal bureaucrat regarded the success of a contracting firm as a basic building block of a sound economy and society. Contractors, for their part, not only performed the actual organization and execution of the channel digging and the lock construction, but also now carried greater responsibility for the success and failure of the venture. No wonder they tended to treat their navvies more as economic units than as co-workers! They could not afford the luxury of personal acquaintance with their many employees, much less take on the provision of shelter and sustenance. No wonder, too, that they reacted with fury when labourers refused to work or (worse) engaged in riot and pillage!

A Living Wage?

The relative absence of labour disputes on the First Canal construction site – in comparison to the Second Canal experience – was probably due to the scarcity of workers. In the summer of 1826 a shortage of available workmen actually retarded construction. Frequent newspaper advertisements for labour attest to the need for labourers. The *Farmers' Journal* in July 1826 appealed for "several hundred able bodied, sober men" to be paid wages of $10 to $13 a month.[5] In January 1827 the contractor Oliver Phelps announced: "As a further encouragement to the hands employed in completing the Deep Cut, the following advantages are afforded as a premium, to those who wish to make money themselves and see this great work speedily completed: ... Shovellers' regular wages will be $12 per month; but should they average *eleven* yards per day, (after the earth is well ploughed up,) their wages will be increased to $13; and an additional dollar per month will be paid for every extra yard of earth they may average per day" [emphasis in original].[6]

Workers were hired by the month and paid a daily rate. Piece work was rare and, according to the season, rates of pay could vary. Another advertisement by Phelps (May 1827) is representative: "$12 per month will be paid to common *shovellers*, with a privilege which will render it not difficult to obtain $15. Good, active, smart men, as teamsters and men to hold the plough, can have from $15 to $16, with a chance of earning and receiving more; smart, active men, who are capable of keeping the time and overseeing 25 men, can have $22 per month, with a chance of extending their wages to $25. Any person that will bring on to the work two good yokes of oxen and a good stout cart, shall receive $25 per month, and himself and team found; and can have employ until the Deep Cut is completed."[7]

The "want of hands" continued in 1830 and 1831, affecting progress on the cut to Lake Erie. In the latter year only 116 to 130 labourers were employed on the line to Gravelly Bay, said engineer Alfred Barrett, at the same time suggesting that the contractors had "failed to apply a sufficient force to finish their jobs according to their contracts."[8]

Whatever the promised wage rate, one problem bedevilled navvies' lives for the rest of the century: the unscrupulous contractor who did not pay his men enough or not at all. Employment on the Welland's construction was not secure, especially when contractors themselves had inadequate resources to pay their workers. They could be late in paying wages or entirely abandon their contracts – and their traditional commitment to their employees. In 1830, MPP John J. Lefferty sympathized with the workers: cheating or inefficient sub-contractors, he wrote, "often wrong their workmen ... the Company are not the losers; their contracts have been done low, but the poor labouring men have suffered greatly." In the enquiry of 1836, James Trotter, who was employed on the Deep Cut, where the shovelling of earth was let out by the yard, testified against Phelps for his treatment of his men: "[He] would pay seven cents per yard for shovelling it into the carts ... I let the work out as I thought the men could make good wages at seven cents per yard for filling in. The men worked very hard for one month and got their estimates, and had only from three to six dollars a month, after paying their board; the men turned out and would not work anymore ... I always considered that the men never got a fair statement of the quantum of the work from Mr. Phelps, as they did it by the yard."[9]

What Trotter refers to may have been an early strike and his words suggest that at least some sub-contractors in the early years were sympathetic to the labourers' plight.

When construction began on the Second Canal, little had changed. Few canal "hands" could earn enough to support a wife and two children at the subsistence level, even in the unlikely case that the wife also had a job. Because too many men were seeking work, wages were driven down and unemployment levels spiked.[10] Sometimes, when contractors found themselves in financial trouble, they cut their employees' pay, or paid them late or not at all. For example, in March 1843 several bankrupt sub-contractors failed to pay their labourers. Such a situation was just one cause of the fearful violence that often broke out on Second Canal sites. The board was aware of the consequences of the problem, and the records occasionally contain instructions to the superintending engineer to make sure that the workers were promptly paid. As early as March 1843 the Board of Works was receiving reports about the effects of certain contractors' failure to pay their men: "The laborers will be kept out of several hundred pounds, and which of course will create much excitement. The Board are very desirous that you [Power] take every possible pains to protect and see the laborers paid, at the same time carefully avoiding any official interference between the parties."[11]

Worsening the situation was the fact that, in lieu of cash, some men were paid in coupons to be redeemed at stores owned by contractors – the notorious "truck system." Contractors rationalized that, because construction sites were remote from settled commercial centres (as was Broad Creek, for example), they were providing an essential service. However, not only were prices higher at these stores than in urban shops, but some contractors used the system to make up for money lost by underestimating their job costs. Even when the contractor did not operate this system, he often owned the only nearby store, where labourers had to purchase clothing, firewood, or lumber.

Although the violence that occurred in the 1840s (chapter 10) had several causes, the desperation of poverty-stricken unemployed men with family responsibilities was the most fundamental. In a lengthy report of 1844, Magistrate David Thorburn accurately assessed the situation: "The first moving cause [of the violence] is the want of work, if not employed they are devising schemes to procure it, such as driving away the party who are fewest in number who are not of their County ... Another cause is when the wages do not suit, they combine and stop from working indeed the well disposed are compelled to go with the majority for in such cases a patrolling band with bludgeons drive off the workers."[12]

Evidence of Thorburn's second point is the reduction, by November 1843, of a navvy's average daily wage by approximately one third of what it had been a year earlier. Historians have difficulty calculating even approximately how much a labourer needed to support himself and his family. Bleasdale has estimated that food alone for one day would cost a navvy 1s/3d. We know that wages of as much as 3s/6d. a day were paid during peak construction season, which suggests that many workers could probably afford the basic necessities – at least at times.[13] How they fared between "peak" seasons is another question.

The issue of wages was not simply that they were low. In fact, in comparison to other unskilled labourers in the Province of Canada at the time, Welland Canal labourers received wages that were average or slightly above average. Moreover, wages on the Welland were slightly higher than those paid to farm labourers working in the fields nearby.[14] (On the other hand they amounted to about half the income of skilled tradesmen or mechanics.) The problem was that workers could not rely on being paid regularly for work they had done.

Responsibility for both low wages and non-payment of wages rested with the bureaucrats as much as with the contractors themselves. For example, in January 1844 Power referred to his embarrassment at not having enough money on hand to pay men who had already been discharged. Although on this occasion his request for funds was met, three months later labourers at Broad Creek petitioned him to remunerate contractors so that the latter could pay them for work done.

In August of that year Merritt himself wrote to Killaly about the contractor Van Norman, who had not been paid by the board and therefore could not pay his workers on the Feeder. Several other contractors petitioned the board in that month regarding their underpayment, an appeal that Merritt also supported.[15]

The Board of Works accordingly began to consider the wisdom of making advances to contractors to obviate the problem in the future. At a special meeting of the board in August 1845 the commissioners drew up a report to the governor general urging the speedy release of funds to pay contractors who had not paid their workers for the past two months. Power put the case succinctly: "If the payment of the laborers [sic] wages be delayed beyond the usual time, most serious disturbances may be apprehended among persons so predisposed to tumult even without cause and the safety of the vessels navigating the Canal, the peace of the surrounding Country and the security of the work itself will be greatly endangered."[16]

Despite Power's reference to the interests of the shippers — the vital and oft-mentioned "Trade" — little seems to have been accomplished. Almost as soon as construction intensified in the spring of 1846, he was again writing to the board asking for money to pay labourers for work done in 1845! Money was finally forthcoming in May, but the practice of regular payment of wages was undermined in August when the contractor Parsons (who was building the bridge at Chippawa) "absconded without paying his hands."[17] That the government's chronic shortage of funds remained the basic problem was obvious in 1848 when it was Samuel Keefer's turn to complain to his superiors that workers had not been paid for three months. Cotton and Rowe (contractors at the Port Colborne works) took up the refrain in June 1849, declaring that, because of "our inability to pay them,"[18] the navvies would not work. Other labourers struck in July for the same reason.

By the time the Third Canal was being built, strikes were common. Some were over the rights of newly unionized workers but most were about wages. Hard-pressed by the poor economic climate, contractors found it difficult to meet workers' demands for a living wage. Yet, paradoxically, despite local economic conditions and the world-wide depression of the 1870s and 1880s, the navvies' situation actually improved in these decades. Union organization helped some workers, but another factor seems to have been that labour became scarcer in the early 1880s, with the result that pay levels rose. In the mid-seventies the average daily wage for unskilled labourers was $1.25 but by 1882 it had risen to $1.50. Stonecutters were making about $3.00 a day throughout the period of construction, although this figure fluctuated.

The incompetence of certain contractors remained a problem for their labourers. For example, in July 1883 the contractors on Section 34 (Vincent Browne and Griffiths) were unable to pay their workers, leaving fifty to sixty of them "very poorly off."[19] Although the Department agreed to pay the workmen, the money did not come through until March 1884!

Another cause of wage discontent was the traditional system of subcontracting: a contract would be taken by one man or a company, then be re-let to another party or parties, after which these might again re-let to another party. The result was that the work had to be done at the lowest possible rate to allow all the members of the chain any kind of profit. This practice was one cause of the stonecutters' strike in 1878.[20]

In February of that year, "A Lover of Justice" took up the labourers' cause in a lengthy letter to the Thorold *Post*: "In the first place sub contractors are a nuisance, and should not be allowed, but when it comes to sub under sub, then it is time to stop it by some feasible means ... Is their any of these little petty foggers can say that they have any other object in view than that of feathering their own nest, and at whose expense: most certainly that of the working man – the man of labor, he, who should have the most protection."[21]

The stonecutters had originally gone out over a different issue – and, once again, the *Post* provides the details: "Messrs. Frazer, Battle & Ussher, contractors for the new bridge at Welland, being unable to make satisfactory arrangements with the union stone cutters to cut the stone at the Co.'s works at Thorold; imported a number of non-union men from Buffalo. Mr. Ussher, by the use of some strategy got the men to the works without interference, but on Wednesday the union men proceeded thither in force, and succeeded by threats and inducements in getting the non-unionists to leave their work. Revolvers were drawn and at one time bloodshed appeared imminent."

Fortunately, Police Magistrate Hill of Clifton took matters in hand. After explaining the law to the rioters, he fined two men, and by evening "matters bore a more quiet look."[22]

WORKING IN THE DITCH

Gains made by workers in the late nineteenth and twentieth centuries make it almost impossible for us now to imagine working conditions on the canal construction site in the 1820s, where no safety regulations or controls on hours and conditions applied. Men worked mainly by hand with small tools (axes, picks, shovels), assisted by animals such as oxen for the heavy hauling of earth and rock, and pulling of ploughs and scrapers.[23] Individuals who could drive teams were usually found among the local settlers and such "drivers" or carters – the aristocracy of canal labour – were paid a premium. While the average labourer provided his own small tools (such as shovels), wheelbarrows were usually supplied by the contractors. Those who had no access to wheelbarrows carried sacks of "spoil" on their backs, scrambling their way up the rugged or slippery sides of the deepening channel. These treacherous banks caused many accidents, including maiming injuries and deaths. (Protective head- or footgear was not compulsory on construction sites until 1962.)

Dangerous situations could develop quickly. Engineer Francis Hall recalled that, when a well was dug to make soil tests on the First Welland's Deep Cut, he saw the "pit nearly filled with water – the workmen informed me when the water commenced to rise, they were obliged to retreat as fast as possible."[24] Rock excavation was especially arduous and dangerous: using a sledgehammer and chisel, workmen made holes, filled them with gunpowder, and fired them by lighting fuses, preferably from a distance. John MacTaggart noted that men working on the Rideau Canal did not always heed the warnings of overseers: "I once saw a poor man blow a red stick, and hold it deliberately to the *priming* of a large shot he had just charged. I cried out, but it was of no use. He seemed to turn round his face, as if to avoid the smoke: off went the blast ... he was killed in a moment."[25] No record exists of similar disasters on the First Welland, an indication perhaps of contractors' inefficient record-keeping or perhaps of simple good luck.

Although many of the First Canal navvies were immigrant and itinerant Irish labourers who had experience of canal construction on the Erie, those straight from Ireland were often destitute farmers or impoverished artisans. Unprepared for Niagara's climate or for work in the bush, Irish navvies often arrived wearing unsuitable clothing. MacTaggart described how many Irish immigrants came to Canada wearing "breeches that bind at the knee and stockings."[26] In the colonies such "old-fashioned" and impractical wear had long since given way to trousers. Their other clothing was thin and offered no protection from Canadian winters (fig. 9.2).

While most of the Irish labourers were untrained in any craft, in 1824 Alfred Hovey (contractor for the tunnel) advertised for fifty to one hundred workers, especially "Sappers and Miners who have been accustomed to tunneling in Europe."[27] (Presumably he had encountered such labourers on the Erie.) Since he advertised for over a month

9.2 J.P. Cockburn's drawing of an Irish labourer in Upper Canada, 1830. His culottes were unsuitable for labour in the wilderness, which is still in evidence all around him. (Royal Ontario Museum, 942.48.11)

for such talent, he may not have been successful. On the other hand, local men with a knack for working with wood or creating simple iron products such as horseshoes were easy to find among the Loyalist farmers in pioneer Niagara. Generally speaking, however, although experienced carpenters and blacksmiths were needed to build the wooden locks, skilled labour was not in much demand during the construction of the First Canal.

Not surprisingly – with no experience of quasi-industrial working conditions – the unskilled navvies fell under wheels or ploughs, severed their own or others' limbs with mishandled picks, or slipped on mud or ice and broke bones. When attention wandered, repetitive and boring jobs carried their own dangers. The carelessness or importunity of contractors could also cause mishaps. Company records rarely documented accidents to labourers, but in 1825 Catharine Merritt wrote to her mother: "There was a man killed last week by the earth caving on him at the deep cut and one in the same way at the harbor last fall."[28]

Government records during Second Canal construction are just as-reticent about on-site accidents to labourers. From the point of view of the Board of Works (or the later Department of Public Works), on-site problems involved contractors and workers alone, and were therefore not the government's responsibility. Canal construction, however, was every bit as hazardous to workers as it had been in the 1820s – perhaps even more so, given the more sophisticated equipment involved, and the use of stone for the locks, and by the 1840s local journalists were beginning to report mishaps. In 1845 the St Catharines *Journal* described how, during excavation "at the stone mill" (probably at Lock 4), a bank collapsed and crushed one Peter McIntyre, who was found "fearfully mangled and quite dead." In 1844 a labourer was assisting a group of men to remove a crane (presumably for lifting stones into place at a lock) and, as he was taking up the slack on a capstan which was being worked by a horse, "the animal [gave] a sudden swing, broke the pole, which, flying back, struck the young man in the head."[29]

When "the Enlargement" of the 1870s was underway, one journalist waxed almost lyrical about the scene he had beheld: "Standing the other day on a plateau of white sun-baked clay, and surrounded by hills of the same material reaching lengthwise as far as the eye could see, we imagined that we were on the West Lake sand banks, in Prince Edward county ... Away some distance on the other side of the canal were black objects toiling like a colony of ants up and down the steep hill. On getting nearer it could be perceived that they were men and horses taking away the side of the hill."[30]

Despite the hint of difficult working conditions camouflaged in this description, labourers flocked to the new canal construction site to find employment. The Great Depression of the 1870s (which had thrown many men out of work elsewhere) drove hundreds onto the roads of Ontario. By July 1875 as canal work got underway on a large scale, about three hundred stonemasons and cutters and nearly three thousand labourers were employed on the excavation. In Thorold, remarked the *Post* in April 1877, "our police office has had many demands made on it for accommodation of tramps. On Monday night, no less than twenty were accommodated and more than that were turned away." These wanderers were not necessarily the indigent dregs of society. For example, the same journal noted in May 1886: "A family named Carroll consisting of a man and his wife and six children, arrived in Thorold on foot from Stratford, from which place they had walked to seek work on the canal. The oldest child was ten.[31]

Every labourer still faced daily the danger of maiming or death on the worksite (fig. 9.3). "There has not been a single accident" on

9.3 Workers on the site of the Third Canal aqueduct, c. 1880. A dreary, dangerous chasm in the earth, it was a workplace much larger than that of the 1820s or 1840s with more potential for accidents. (SCM: N-3967)

Section 23, crowed a local newspaper in 1878. But three years later the same journal wearily acknowledged: "There's never a day but one or more men are injured and every now and again some accident happens which results in some poor fellow being ushered out of the world in a very unceremonious manner."

Despite the "labour-saving" machinery now in use (fig. 9.4), work on the new canal was perhaps even more perilous than in the past, given the larger, more complex equipment employed, the greater size of the locks and the prism, and the use of larger stones. Steam-powered derricks were especially likely to injure labourers, as two accidents in the summer of 1875 attest. In July (at Section 2 near Port Dalhousie) the boom on a derrick broke, dropping a stone weighing several tons into a group of workers. They escaped injury, but the following month (at Section 5) a derrick under construction collapsed onto three men and "two of them had their legs broken and the other was badly cut about the head." In 1878 another derrick at the guard lock (a "wonderful labor saving machine") collapsed, lacerating the hand of its operator. The *Post* philosophically concluded that "the building of canals must

9.4 On the Third Canal, c. 1875. Workers show off their modern steam-powered shovel, a more complex implement than the shovels and picks used fifty years before, requiring skill and experience on the operators' part. Evidently their families shared in their pride, being sure to show up well dressed for the photographer. (Koudys Collection)

have their share of episodes."[32] No protective clothing was yet worn by these labourers, and safety regulations were virtually unknown.

The new steam-powered machinery, still imperfectly constructed or clumsily operated, was an additional hazard. One man was killed and six others injured when a steam boiler operating a drill exploded at Humberstone in 1881: "Herbert Harkison, aged 18 ... was sitting under the shanty covering the boiler, drying one of his socks, when all of a sudden without any warning, the boiler burst, scattering the boiler and its contents all around. The boiler was thrown about 80 yards away, so great was the force of the explosion. On some of the men proceeding to the spot it was found that Harkison was thrown about 100 feet up against the bank and on going to where he was life was found to be extinct. His boot which it is supposed he was in the act of putting on when the explosion took place was found by his side." Men nearby were "dreadfully scalded about the face and body."

On other occasions the accidents were of the more traditional sort. For example, the treacherous embankments could collapse, smothering workers, as occurred in 1876 on Section 16 where Alfred Clark was crushed to death, leaving his wife and six children destitute.[33]

The risks involved in blasting solid rock with gunpowder have been described above. Use of that dangerous aid-to-excavation gradually gave way to a new method, with the invention of dynamite by Alfred Nobel in 1866. The *Post* described its use in excavation at Port Colborne in 1876:

> After the rock has been bored to the required depth, a long tube is inserted in the hole, and this tube is charged with nitro glycerine, which is exploded by means of a galvanic battery. It is surprising to find how few accidents occur in handling this dangerous explosive. One day lately, however, the charge of exploded rock, struck the boiler of the boat on which the drill is placed and caused considerable damage thereto.
>
> We understand that in the house for storing the nitroglycerine which is situated about a quarter of a mile from the shore there is to be 10,000 lbs of it stored within a few days. We advise all nervous people to keep away from Port Colborne.[34]

A little over two months later a tragic accident occurred on the site of rock blasting in Port Colborne harbour. On 30 October one Colbert King, an employee of the contractor C.F. Dunbar, was carrying an unknown quantity of "nitro-glycerine" in a small boat to the drilling site when "a report of the most violent nature took place ... and when the shock was over a distinct rumbling could be heard, as the sound travelled to the northward and westward."[35] A Welland *Telegraph* reporter, in his office when the explosion occurred, was "surprised by the windows suddenly and violently rattling, at the same time the brick building perceptibly trembling." The explosion was reportedly heard as far away as Port Dalhousie and Fonthill, and on Lake Erie near the mouth of the Grand River. Virtually nothing was found of King, or of the boat, and no cause of the explosion could be determined. The *Telegraph* estimated that "the loss sustained by the injurie from breaking glass, tearing down plaster, &c., will ... amount to about $1000."

Obviously, because it was sensitive to rapid warming and shock, nitroglycerine could be treacherous – HANDLE WITH CARE was the watchword.

Lake Fever and the Cholera

Excavating a trench for a canal or heaving large timbers or stones into place in a lock pit was bone-crushing labour. At the same time, the workplace had even more insidious dangers. Whatever their occupations in the old world, the immigrant Irishmen who built the First and Second canals had no experience of the harsh extremes of the Upper Canadian climate and the ruggedness of a pioneer environment. Especially in the hot and humid summer months, the working day could extend to sixteen hours. Some work was carried on in the winter in snow and ice. Not surprisingly, working outdoors in such conditions was conducive to infections of many kinds – particularly among men labouring to the point of exhaustion and living in squalor. Where stagnant water lay about, mosquitoes bred and malaria thrived. Although the authorities kept no records of heatstroke and frostbite, these afflictions must have been common. However, the Welland Canal Company's documents do record when workers fell victim to "swamp fever" and "the cholera."

Our Very Bones Ache

In August 1827 Oliver Phelps (contractor on the Deep Cut) felt compelled to deny rumours that "we were dying off by scores, both men and cattle," claiming: "It was never more healthy in any place, at this season of the year" (fig. 9.5).[36] Nevertheless, in October 1828 the company secretary, writing to a contact in New York acknowledged, "much interruption ... from sickness and death."[37] Evidently the healthy conditions described by Phelps in 1827 did not last long. Worse was to come the following year (1829) when the company records are a litany of "fever and agues" among the labourers, especially on the feeder project. "Our very bones ache," said one.[38]

Scholars are in agreement that, in most cases, malaria, called "lake" or "swamp" fever, was the illness in question.[39] MacTaggart has given us a graphic description of its progress:

> [It] generally come[s] on with an attack of bilious fever, dreadful vomiting, pains in the back and loins, general debility, loss of appetite ... After being in this state for eight or ten days, the yellow jaundice is likely to ensue, and then fits of trembling—these come on some time in the afternoon ... For two or three hours before they arrive, we feel so cold that nothing will warm us ... the skin gets dry, and then the shaking begins. Our very bones ache, teeth chatter, and the ribs are sore, continuing thus in great agony for about an hour and a half; we then commonly have a vomit, the trembling ends, and a profuse sweat ensues, which

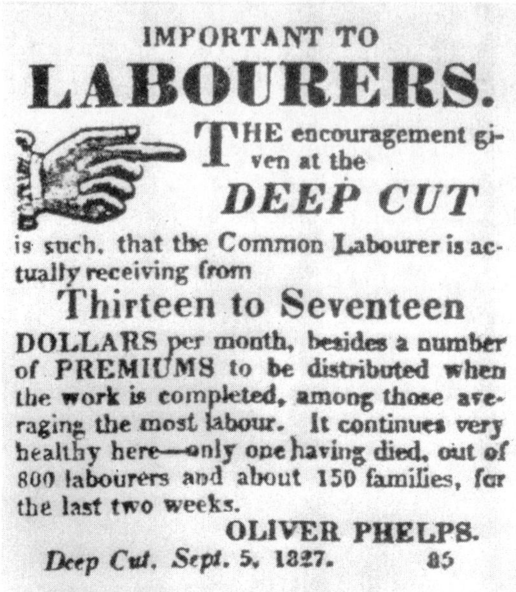

9.5 An appeal for labourers on the Deep Cut, in the *Farmers' Journal & Welland Canal Intelligencer*, 1827. (St John's Outdoor Study Centre)

> lasts for two hours longer. This over, we find the malady has run one of its rounds, and start out of the bed in a feeble state, sometimes unable to stand.[40]

Malaria was spread by the anopheles mosquito, which thrived in swampy areas, especially along the Feeder Canal and at Broad Creek in the summer. Before the 1860s North Americans had little understanding of the spread of infectious diseases, believing that exhalations from the soil were causal factors. This "miasmatic theory" maintained that "bad air" (that is, "mal-aria") arose from the decomposition of fish and animal matter. For example, in 1828 James Geddes blamed miasma for illness on the Grand River dam construction site: "For seventeen miles up, the Grand River may be called an estuary, operated upon by the motions of the Lake. Much of this level piece of water is bordered by a sedgy shore, where rotting vegetables are acted upon by the fluctuations of the Lake, and the beams of a hot sun; and from this decaying mass rises a vapour that makes the lower part of the Grand River valley unhealthy."[41] Unfortunately quinine, widely understood to be effective in the treatment of malaria, was in short supply throughout Upper Canada.

"The Devastation Made by the Cholera"

Malaria was not the worst disease on the First Canal sites. In 1832 the Welland Canal Company directors reported laconically: "The greatest activity prevailed on the line [to Gravelly Bay] this year, until interrupted by the Cholera."[42] The disease arrived in Niagara with poverty-stricken immigrants from Ireland. Hoping to find a better life in a more promising part of the Empire, these desperate migrants arrived in filthy, crowded ships to port facilities equally sordid. The first cholera deaths on the Welland occurred on 6 August 1832. They were not unanticipated, for an epidemic had been raging in Lower Canada for some months. In fact, on 25 June Niagara magistrates had decreed that all ships should wait fifty yards off shore and wait for medical inspection before entering the canal.

A letter from Merritt to his wife gives us a direct insight into local responses to the epidemic among the workers excavating the cut to Lake Erie:

> Heard the cholera had commenced its ravages that day at Gravelly Bay 3 deaths. Went on to the Bay that evening & found Coonrod, a contractor ... a man by name of Henry on lock, & one Ross a laborer at the same place, was dead, & taken only that morning — 3 or 4 others were considered dangerous — one only has since died, the others recovered.
>
> On Tuesday, went through the line, with Mr. Lewis, & as no new cases occured that day the men generally resumed their work.
>
> Slept at Holmes, Deep Cut, that night Lewis was taken — in morning Wednesday sent for Doct. Cross to St. Catharines. Cross, & Converse who was up at Gravelly Bay. He was very much alarmed, & I could not leave him until Cross arrived about 2 o'clock. Old Mr. Fuller bled him & I gave him two pills of opium — he got better immediately & is now well. Returned to Gr. B. that night to quiet the minds of the men respecting Mr. Lewis, & we found all who got medical aid & was bled in time recovered — as it was chiefly among the intemperate. Had hopes of continuing the work, but on reaching Gravelly Bay, found Doct Ellis had taken it & Mrs. Boles — remained there until 12 o'clock Thursday & left for Dam, with a determination to let every one take their own course — stopping the sale of liquor & providing doctors etc. on the spot.

The "cholera" was a particularly dreadful experience, whose consequences were social and economic as well as medical. "As soon as the cholera made its appearance," said the directors, "the affrighted workmen fled from the scene of death." Contractors were also afflicted, as Merritt noted, and at least seventy workers on the cut to Gravelly Bay died.[43] "The devastation committed by the Cholera," said the directors, made it impossible to finish the work on the extension by the end of 1832.[44] The "rock job" at the Onondaga Escarpment would have to be abandoned until the following spring.

Because the affected area was relatively remote from the larger settlements, "no competent medical aid could be procured at any price," particularly after one doctor died tending the sick and another took ill and had to return to St Catharines.[45] The newly established Board of Health at Gravelly Bay could not afford the fee of a doctor coming from York.[46] Moreover, the Act establishing Boards of Health did nothing to help the badly housed, poorly clothed and fed, and probably filthy, workers building the Welland.[47] Given the labourers' working and living conditions and the state of medical science in the early nineteenth century, the available treatment was largely useless against the most prevalent diseases. Palliative care was relatively primitive even in urban centres and on isolated canal construction sites was virtually non-existent. In the 1830s few institutions existed in Upper Canada to treat illness. The town of York had the only major facility (established in 1833) that could be considered a hospital.

The paternalism of some early canal contractors may have mitigated these medical problems to a degree. The "Rules and Regulations for the Deep Cut" set out by Phelps in 1827 provided for a "large and suitable house ... for the receipt of the sick, where medical aid, and other necessary attendance, will be administered gratis to the labourers, and at the expense of their employers."[48] Phelps referred to his "hospital" in an article in the *Farmers' Journal* in 1827, claiming that, although eight hundred men had been working on the Cut that summer, no labourer had been brought to the institution.[49] Unfortunately, we have no record of where this "hospital" stood or what sort of care it offered. Nor do we know if Phelps or other contractors were still providing such amenities during the cholera crisis of 1832. In any case, no effective remedy for cholera existed at this time. Bleeding, the traditional treatment, was more likely to hasten death than to prevent it.

Public attitudes aggravated the situation. We have already read Merritt's mention of "intemperance" in his letter to his wife. It was a common belief that "debauchery," "intemperance," or "immoderate behaviour" made one susceptible to disease. Simply put, if you ate or drank too much or were carried away by emotion, you would get sick. An attack of cholera could even be interpreted as the result of immoral behaviour.[50] In the eyes of many more affluent – and cleaner – Niagarans, "debauched" people such as Irish navvies got what they deserved!

During Second Canal construction, labourers and their families remained exceptionally vulnerable to disease, and "lake fever" continued its ravages. For example, in August 1843 it raged at Broad Creek, felling eight hundred people and killing as many as four daily, again delaying construction. "Such is the panic among the men," wrote the engineer Power, "that no inducements held out by the contractors can procure a sufficient force."[51]

In another instance of lingering paternalism, the board agreed to provide medicine for sick labourers if the contractors would pay half the cost. It is difficult to determine how well this agreement worked. We do not know whether Dr John Jarrow, a "surgeon" who sent a memorandum to the board in October 1842 about the epidemic of "marsh fever," was in the partial employ of the board. Also debatable was the work of a "Dr Campbell," who in December 1844 complained of "a considerable loss" as a result of his services. The difficulty was that, while the labourers believed that he was paid by the board and that his ministrations were therefore free, the local canal establishment would not pay him fully because they thought the contractors were paying half his salary, and the board the other half. Apparently his remuneration was cut by the contractors in November 1843 and, whatever his pay, he found it insufficient.[52] To add to the confusion, the authorities were not above using medical blackmail. In 1842 Superintendent W.B. Robinson reported that he had withdrawn medical aid from the navvies in order to find out more about the murder of one of their number.[53]

By the 1870s, a greater appreciation of the origins of disease, a certain improvement in public hygiene, and the draining of many swamps meant that malaria and cholera were much less problematic when the Third Canal was being built. Ontario's standard of living had risen appreciably, too. Medical care was becoming more scientific and no cholera outbreaks occurred.

SLABTOWNS

Poverty, disease, ignorance, and illiteracy were the lot of most unskilled labourers on the First and Second canals. Because they had no capital, they were unable to settle immediately on the land, and had the lowest standard of living in Niagara. Fortunately, as we have seen, some employers maintained a sense of patriarchal responsibility for their labourers. In 1827 Phelps, who had established the aforementioned "hospital," claimed to have built "a genteel boarding house" for labourers and promised that more "convenient boarding houses" would be established,[54] presumably only for single men. Most labourers had to make do with hovels made of discarded timber and slabs of wood rejected by local sawmills. Shantytowns proliferated in the 1840s. Here the families of married men lived on the edge of respectable communities and on the verge of starvation.

The most notorious of these settlements seems to have been known simply as "Slabtown." It consisted of approximately seventy shanties that had been cobbled together along the canal between St Catharines and the Escarpment.[55] At Broad Creek 163 shanties housed workers and their families in 1842.[56] As in the 1820s, some single men may have found shelter in barracks or boarding houses, such as Mrs McKeever's establishment on the Feeder Canal. In the early months of construction, several foremen took responsibility for their men's room and board. Evidence exists of at least one contractor who rented out shanties on the Feeder construction site in 1848, supplying furniture and provisions, and deducting rent from the labourers' pay.[57]

In the early and mid-nineteenth century, the connection between illness and poverty, dirt, and polluted drinking water was not yet clear, and a sense of public responsibility was slow to develop in Upper Canada. Local governments in Niagara regarded water supply as a matter of private business. Moreover, apart from church-sponsored charity, what we now consider the essential "social safety net" was virtually unknown until well into the twentieth century. Churches and many individuals did supply "charity," but there was not even a colonial variation of the English Poor Law to offer some organized relief to the poverty-stricken.[58] As we have seen, no Boards of Health existed in Upper Canada until the 1830s, and they were mainly concerned with fending off contagious disease.

It is difficult to discover much about living conditions of Third Canal construction labourers, but some data emerge indirectly from accounts of violence and drunkenness among their number. For example, the inquest into a savage Italian/Irish brawl of 1876 learned that eleven Italian men and two women lived in one "shanty" near Section 12. When the Irish attacked the building, they succeeded in tearing off part of the roof.[59] Clearly this was an overcrowded house of flimsy construction, larger than but probably little different from the huts built of "slabs" thirty years earlier.

On the other hand, Third Canal contractors occasionally built houses or barracks for their single employees – especially when the latter arrived in Niagara from elsewhere. For example, in 1872 Robert

Mitchell (a contractor on the Deep Cut) planned to buy an old sawmill at Allanburg and use the materials in it to erect "shanties" for his Québécois workers. The Department allowed him to "erect shanties on canal property adjoining the 'Deep Cut,' but so as not to obstruct navigation."[60]

WORKING UNDERWATER

So far, we have concentrated on the men who worked "on the ground." However, over the years there were a few men whose labours were performed underwater: as Samuel Keefer (then superintendent) noted in 1843, "there is always a diver employed."[61]

Underwater work had become safer since a hand-operated air compressor was developed in the 1770s. Rees's *Cyclopædia* shows "Klingert's Diving Machine" from the 1790s, consisting of a copper helmet and a closed costume (fig. 9.6). By 1835 a more flexible costume with a helmet and compressed air reservoir fitted around the diver's waist was introduced. We have no description of the "costume" worn by the Welland's divers at this time, but the archives do contain finely honed instructions for the use of a diving dress in 1845. They read, in part:

> Suspend the upper part or Jacket so high that a man could stand on the deck
>
> [I]n it – the man should draw up his shirt sleeves to be out of the way of the elastic wrist bands; – then get under the Jacket, raise his hands as close together as he can & as he pushes up into the dress opening his arms – the attendent should raise the sleeves to assist him, the cap should be taken off the coupling in the side of the Helmet to give him air & to speak thro' before he goes down; – the pantaloons which he will put on before he does the Jacket, is then brought over the ring in the lower part of the jacket & fastened with the ring having a screw thro' the flange ends. If the wristbands do not fit snugly put on the elastic bands to tighten them; the weights from 125 to 175 pound (four 32 lb weights are sufficient for an ordinary man) are then to be hung on the hooks, the signal line lies around the right wrist & taken in the hand of the man then being ready puts on the cap of the coupling, hoist enough to clear the deck and lower gradually over the side; – when the cap is put on immediately commence pumping.[62]

After further details, instructions are given on how to patch a hole with the accompanying can of paste!

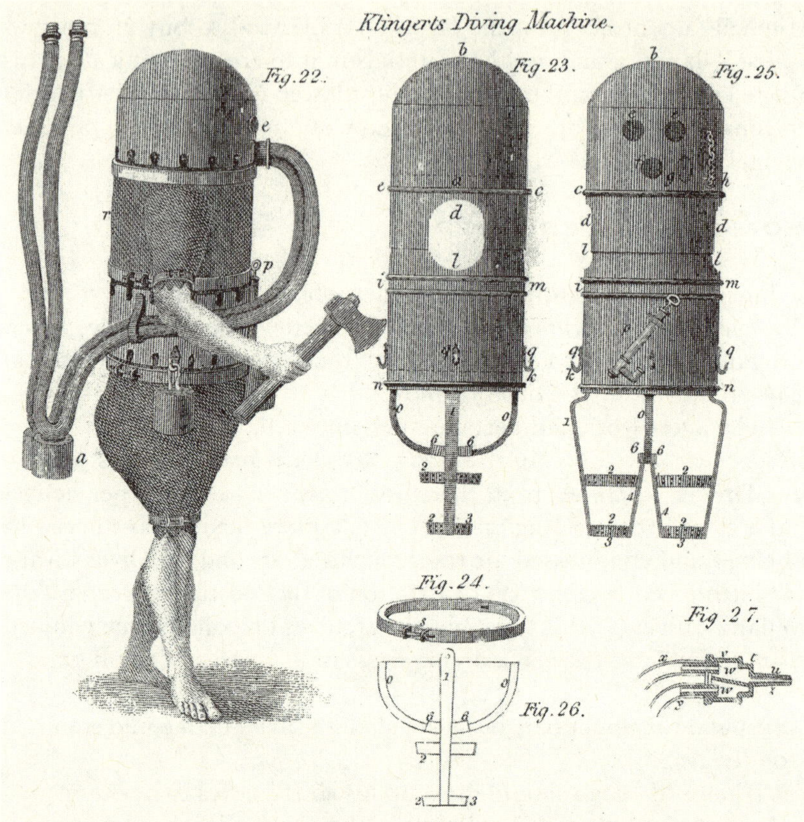

9.6 Diving equipment similar to that probably used by divers during the construction and maintenance of the First Welland Canal. (Abraham Rees, *The Cyclopædia*, Plates, vol. 3, Plate II)

Records give us little information on the divers themselves – often only their names. Nor can we be sure that they were involved in the construction process. They were certainly required at times for repairs to damaged lock gates, and we can assume that they may have played a role in hanging those gates in the first place. The first we know of, Patrick McCoy, served as locktender on Lock 14 in 1833 and 1834, and in 1846 was described as "diver and regulator of water on Old Works Staff," and also as a foreman, at a salary of £10 per month. The following year he was told that his services were no longer required. But apparently he did occasionally work as a diver after that; when he submitted an account in 1858, he was told that the charge made for diving "should be admitted only for the one day that he was actually so engaged. For the other days the same rate should be paid him that he is allowed on the canal ... with allowance for his traveling and board expenses." We have no further record of him until his death in 1876.[63]

Other First Canal locktenders may also have served as divers: Richard Fluellan (locks 18–24, from August 1831 through 1843); Jacob Switzer (assistant to William Hanin at locks 32–35, April–November 1841, and assistant to James Boothe at locks 23–31 the following year); and James Boyle (assistant to Boothe in 1841 and to Hanin in 1842).[64] It was usual for one or more of the locktenders to do occasional diving as required.

When Robert Don[n]elly of Kingston applied for a post as "diver and wrecker" in 1881, his sponsor was told that he could not be appointed, "such service being provided for." He persisted in his application; considerable correspondence follows concerning his experience, and his customary charges for the use of a pump (which he wanted to bring in duty-free from the United States). Finally, in April 1882 he was told to report for duty the following Monday or Tuesday as carpenter and diver, at $2.50/day as a carpenter, and $5 when diving.[65]

It would appear from another lengthy correspondence that the reason he was not hired on his first application was an ongoing dispute with John Armstrong, who was the tender of Lock 18 in 1855–70. In March 1881 Armstrong claimed pay for extra work – he said he had done all the diving required at that lock for fifteen years. On being told that he could not be paid for any diving, he continued to press his claim. In June of that year his MP sent in a claim for compensation for injury to his health. In April 1883 a recommendation came down that he be paid a $100 "gratuity" for his services as diver. The records are then silent until 1893, when he renewed his claim for compensation on grounds of ill-health, and the last entry we found was in 1897, when he again requested an "allowance" for deafness suffered while on the job.[66] Aside from the $100 gratuity, all his pleas were refused.

The only other reference we have found to injury sustained by a diver is a claim made for "some provision" to be made to Jacob Dell, "incapacitated from hernia and heart trouble." He had been employed since 1876, had begun diving in May 1889, and had been off work frequently in recent years. The superintendent was now recommending that he be retired on grounds of ill health.[67] By this time divers' equipment had become less cumbersome, and could be worn with pride and confidence by those who worked underwater.

Obviously, the navvies, whether working "on the ground," or in the water, underwent many difficulties in the nineteenth century. Their response to these vicissitudes was often irrational at first, as was the reaction of the authorities. Over time, however, labourers began to tackle their challenges in an organized, constructive way. So too, government and canal bureaucrats found more positive methods of dealing with poverty and its potentially criminal consequences. Our next chapter will examine some of the main issues that arose between labour and authority throughout the nineteenth century on the Welland Canal project.

CHAPTER TEN

Conflict and Survival On the Ground

Working on the Welland Canal was difficult, even occasionally life-threatening, as we have seen. The navvies, however, had other struggles, some of their own making, others beyond their control. The abuse of alcohol, endemic in the society at large, made their lives even more unstable. The Irish labourers – and later the Italians – brought their own issues with them to Niagara. Their internecine feuds, which often led to violent encounters, were not mitigated by the prejudices of the local population. Canal and governmental authorities were both flummoxed as to how to deal with canal-side poverty, disease, and criminality, for much of the nineteenth century. They found that charity and the old methods of dealing with the poor and the vagrant, combined with punishment, no longer were effective. Gradually, however, as Canadian society became more sophisticated and as the navvies themselves learned new methods of self-help, including the acquisition of literacy, their standard of living and working conditions began to improve. Nevertheless, the beginnings were not auspicious.

We have previously discussed the lack of skilled engineers and contractors in the early canal years. Equally rare were artisans – bricklayers, stonemasons, even carpenters. In a community where many settlers built their own homes, demand for such men was low. Even unskilled labour was initially hard to find as well – a wage-earning proletariat scarcely existed yet. Consequently, advertisements for navvies appeared frequently in local newspapers. With settlements still scattered and linked by unreliable roads, information, people, and goods travelled much more slowly than they would a mere thirty years later when the railways came on the scene.

Such impediments did not prevent the construction of the First Welland Canal, however, and, while the nay-sayers and critics of the canal project were many, even John MacTaggart was moved to assure the colonial government in 1829: "A canal ... will certainly be made of it by and by, in spite of *private interest*, obstinate *management*, and *perversion* of the laws of nature: but when, I will not take upon myself to say."[1]

When authorities decided to proceed with building the Second Welland Canal in the early 1840s, "times had changed." The political climate was more stable, and trade and commerce were growing. Labour was now abundant, thanks to an influx of Irish navvies and experienced Scottish stonemasons who were attracted to North American construction projects. While the increase in skilled labour was welcomed, the vast numbers of unskilled navvies were more difficult to deal with.

By the 1870s increasing literacy, the organization of workers into unions, changing attitudes on the part of officialdom, and the role of the new Dominion Government were contributing to further changes on the labour front.

LIQUID DAMNATION

The difficult working and living conditions described in the previous chapter were problematic for both labourers and their employers. Long hours of back-breaking labour for low pay drove men to alcohol for relief, exacerbated ethnic tensions, and led to violence, all of which could occasion repressive measures by government authorities. To protect themselves and their families, navvies (even though illiterate) took what measures they could, including mutual aid and, eventually, unionization. Oliver Phelps's 1827 "Rules and Regulations" for workers on the Deep Cut urged upright behaviour but made no reference to the abuse of alcohol.[2] However, one striking aspect of working conditions on the First Canal is the fact that the company tolerated the daily serving of whisky to construction labourers.

Over-consumption of alcohol was a perennial problem on the First Canal. Reminiscing about his youth, Seymour Phelps recalled the much-appreciated role of the "Grog boss" during his father's tenure:

> When the Welland Canal was being built in 1827, we being only but a boy of 11 years old, was what was then called "Grog boss," and used to carry up and down the line of the canal a large pail of whiskey, with sometimes a handful of tansey, from Hartzell's garden in it, and deal it out in a small tin cup, called *tots*, six times a day to each laborer, of whom in our beat there were 250 or 300 in all. We then tho't we were not only doing the laborers a benefit, but assisting in completing the work, as well as doing good. Our approach was hailed by the men with smiles and delight; often would some of the hardest drinkers plead earnestly for an extra *tot* which we seldom refused them.[3]

The fact that the company was still spending money on whisky for labourers in 1834 greatly irritated William Lyon Mackenzie, the great critic of the canal project.[4] He noted that for one part of the line "nine barrels or 300 gallons" of whisky were consumed in ten days. Is this a printer's mistake, he asked? He went on to point out that "such unlimited supplies of whisky [about thirty gallons a day] must have incapacitated the workmen for the performance of their labour, and surely it afforded a pernicious example."[5]

While it is hard to judge the quality or potency of the whisky served, we should not assume that scores of labourers were to be found reeling drunk about the excavation sites. Later Victorians were justified in bemoaning the consequences of excessive alcohol consumption (that "liquid damnation"[6]), but the use of whisky in difficult working situations was not confined to the Welland's construction – and some good reasons existed for drinking it on the job. At Upper Canadian logging bees "whisky boys" regularly made the rounds.[7] "Spirits" slaked thirst, were a good substitute for unreliable local water, and may have improved mood.

Perhaps in response to criticism such as Mackenzie's, canal authorities began efforts to control the sale and consumption of liquor on or near the Welland's construction sites. For example, in April 1834 the directors resolved: "No liquor will be allowed to persons employed on the Canal."[8]

Second Canal labourers, mired in hopeless poverty, often sought comfort in alcohol. But in this period, the distribution of whisky *gratis* was a thing of the past. Aware that alcohol oiled the wheels of anger and violence, the authorities sought even more vigorously to curb its sale and consumption. In late 1842 certain contractors petitioned the board to control the sale of liquor, and in 1843 the board condemned the operation of "grog shops" near construction sites, urging district magistrates to limit the number of taverns in the vicinity of public works. The problem does not seem to have been solved, for in April 1845 the board asked the superintendent of the Canal Police for a list of grog shop proprietors because, they said, whether licensed or not, such businesses were "injurious and likely to excite disturbance and outrage." The complete list included 124 *un*-licensed premises near the canal![9]

High Old Times

By the 1870s many conditions had improved, but some elements of the labourers' lives had not changed. Despite the federal law of 1869 prohibiting the sale of liquor in the vicinity of public works, the Thorold *Post* in 1877 counted no less than six shanties selling liquor to canal labourers on Section 13 alone. Paydays and periods of layoff were occasions for drunken sprees. In 1878 the Port Colborne *Free Press* commented that fifteen hundred men would be hired to work on canal construction there in the coming winter: "Look out for high old times on pay days."[10]

On these occasions canal towns could indeed be rowdy and violent. Reflecting on the previous week's payday in 1879, the *Post*'s editor marvelled that it was "the quietest fifteenth that has been seen in Thorold for some time past. Not a single arrest was made."[11] A long-time Welland resident later said: "I remember some terrific struggles between our local constables and the powerfully built chaps on the works. We had four stalwart men on the force in those days ... and they fought many a battle."[12] One of these "battles" may have been the set-to in October 1886 when canal workers tussled and broke Burgar's Drugstore window. The cause, said a journalist, was payday and drunkenness.[13] Demanding the services of a "Night Policeman," the *Post* complained that same year that, "Quite frequently the streets are made hideous late in the night by drunken brawls, and one man cannot possibly be on duty both day and night."[14] Such disturbances remained the rule in all canal communities until the project was finished.

However, on-site evidence of consumption of alcohol was now grounds for dismissal. As the *Post* wrote in 1877: "The contractors on Section 11 complain bitterly of the illegal sale of intoxicating liquor which is carried on there, demoralizing their men to a considerable extent about pay days."[15] Some contractors took action: on the site of new aqueduct, H.J. Beemer gave notice that he would create "a good example" by firing any worker found drunk.[16] Nevertheless, nearly a decade later no improvement was noticed. In 1887 the *Post* editor described the behaviour of canal labourers on payday: "A large number of them pointed direct from the 'contractor's' office door to the nearest hotel where a large share of their hard-earned money was left for liquor."[17]

Ethnic Strife

No amount of medical assistance, control of alcohol sales, traditional charity, or moral indignation could prevent outbreaks of violence among the workers. Peter Way has calculated forty-seven riots and twenty-six strikes on Canadian canals in the 1840s, in comparison to only six riots and three strikes in the 1820s. Of these, many on the

Second Welland Canal construction sites were among the Irish. On Third Canal sites conflicts were more likely between Irish and Italian immigrants.[18]

The Irish War

Between 1842 and 1849 virulent incidents occurred almost continually. The first outbreaks happened in August 1842 and were briefly described by H.H. Killaly: "Several riots have taken place within the last day or two. These gentlemen report that the unemployed men have intimidated, and maltreated those at work, have assembled tumultuously, and broken open and plundered the stores, and that their conduct has been so outrageous as to make it necessary that two companies of the Rifles should be forthwith quartered in the neighbourhood of that work."[19]

In St Catharines, unemployed and hungry labourers had plundered contractor Barnett's storehouse for food, as well as the "Red" Mill and Henry Mittleberger's mill. They also took eighteen barrels of pork from the schooner MARINER. Such disturbances continued well into the fall. Then in 1843 an attempt by some contractors to lower wages led to a work stoppage. Disgruntled navvies well knew the importance of "the Trade" to the Welland's managers and in July 1844 some of them had manifested a "disposition ... to interfere with boats" passing through the canal.[20] Now faction fights among labourers were also becoming a problem.

The causes of these outbreaks – unemployment, poverty, hunger – have been noted above. Another factor, often-overlooked, was the predominance of young, single men in the canal workforce. More energetic and excitable than older labourers (and perhaps with less to lose), they were traditionally more prone to violence. But the flares of violence also had origins that were peculiarly Irish, described in the *Journal* as the "Irish War."[21]

As hundreds of Irish drifted down to Niagara from the St Lawrence canals, from the ports of Quebec or westward from the Erie Canal where they had found temporary work, an element entered the picture which had little to do directly with poverty or unemployment: a feud between men with roots in County Cork in the southwest province of Munster (Corkorians) and Connaughtmen (also know as Far-downers) from the province of Connaught on the west coast of Ireland. Most of the Welland Canal workers came from one of these areas, as did some of the contractors – who naturally liked to employ men of their own background. Irish traditions of county rivalries, local allegiances, and violent social conflict were a powerful factor in an age before mass communication and homogenized popular culture. Differences of dialect, dress, and custom loomed large and engendered a strong sense of identity and clanship. However, this feud (which was not primarily sectarian) may have been a new phenomenon developed on canal construction sites in England or in North America, including those on the St Lawrence River. Whatever its origins, competition between Corkorians and Connaughtmen for jobs aggravated pre-existing economic and social tensions in Niagara.

For many labourers, writes Way, "faction fights were rational labour strategies."[22] Contractors, however, promoted the dividing of workers into cliques, a process that could work to the advantage of the contractors themselves. If the occasion required it, the pre-existing feud could be exploited to avoid paying their navvies – divide and conquer.

In Niagara, Connaughtmen settled at Slabtown, and Corkorians lived below Port Robinson, but both groups roved the length of the canal seeking work, inevitably and abrasively encountering each other. The Connaughtmen seem to have outnumbered the Corkorians – which only seemed to inspire the latter to greater belligerence. David Thorburn (warden of the Niagara District, responsible for preserving the peace along the canal) gave a biased but vivid account of these "frays":

> They are armed with all and every kind of weapon, consisting of guns, pistols, swords, pikes or poles, pitch forks, scythes, &c, &c. They are determined to do evil when they think that by doing so will answer some end consonant with their views which hath no bounds their affrays or riots are against each other or against their contractors as yet in every instance their plans have been promptly met and put down with the destruction of some shanties, cooking utensils &c &c and often broken heads which generally takes place at the commencement of their rows, when uneasiness takes place on any of the works the firing of guns and blowing of horns throughout the night on such works is the sure presage of trouble.

Thorburn continued with a description of events in a shanty town at Stonebridge on Christmas Day 1843, which was caused, he said, "by the fighting of two drunken men in one of the shantys."

> Like wild fire the evil spirit ran throughout every work on the whole line when the Cork and Connaught party immediately

> were roused in the worst character every part of the works were stopped ... The Cork men began it, in several instances bodies of four, five and six hundred of them (every one of the men in arms) were met and dispersed, their women & children flew from their shanties for safety, and took refuge where ever they found a door whether it was a stable, barn, dwelling house or even a church, and many of them fled to the woods. As they battled, their women and children flew from their Shanties for safety and took refuge where ever they found a door.[23]

Canal police, contractors, foremen, and local citizens quelled this riot, which left the Connaughtmen feeling defeated by the Corkorians. In January 1844 the former sought revenge by seizing blacksmith shops, making weapons, and attacking the Corkorians. Only with the help of troops was this fray brought to an end.

Needless to say, local journalists delighted in recounting these exciting events – no doubt adding to the locals' fear of the Irish. For example, in June 1842 the St Catharines *Journal* described the Corkorians' efforts to drive Connaughtmen from the worksites. The latter rallied, driving their rivals "flying in all directions through houses, yards, and over fences." The militia was called in to suppress "these strange and mad belligerent factions – brothers and countrymen – thirsting like savages for each others blood – horrible infatuation."[24]

On some construction sites, another source of tension emerged: "the long cherished feelings of hostility," in Power's words, "existing between the Irish laborers, and the lower class of Orangemen." Corkorians and Connaughtmen were largely Roman Catholic and, however much they may have hated each other, they hated Protestants even more. Not only were townsmen and farmers in Niagara largely Protestant (and hence "Orange") at this time but Superintendent William B. Robinson (according to Power) favoured appointing Orangemen as constables, part of whose job it was to control disturbances along the canal. The perceptive Power wrote to Merritt: "I cordially detest ultra politics of every description, and hope that the laborers may not be unnecessarily exasperated by placing them beneath the surveillance of those whom they view as their old tyrants."[25]

The sectarian aspect of these disturbances occasionally had a bizarre aspect. For instance, on 12 July 1844 the steamer ADMIRAL, carrying several hundred "conservatives" from Toronto, and the steamer ECLIPSE from Hamilton, with a smaller number aboard, arrived at Queenston, where the passengers disembarked and proceeded by rail and other vehicles to Niagara Falls. The authorities had learned in advance that canal labourers were going to leave their work and attack the "conservatives" with picks and shovels, because: "Some mischievous people had told them [the workers] that they were Orangemen and antipapist."[26] A detachment of the Royal Canadian Rifles was called in to protect the passengers.

The most notorious example of sectarian conflict was the "Battle of Slabtown" (July 1849) in what later became Merritton. While some of those involved were not construction labourers (two were locktenders), nevertheless the incident – with its overtones of a shootout in a Western film – exemplifies the hostilities that still ran rampant along the waterway. At Duffin's Tavern a group of twenty Orangemen were set upon by a Catholic crowd and the ensuing melee left two dead and several wounded.[27]

Other immigrants were caught up in the atmosphere of violence: in 1844 Scottish stonecutters were "threatened and beaten" by fellow Scots.[28] Even foreigners traversing the canal were not safe. In 1846 a group of navvies assaulted American sailors for allegedly insulting a priest. On another occasion (also in 1846) – in an incident that smacked of Luddism – Irish workers attacked and burned a steam dredge at Port Dalhousie. The set-tos were occasionally internecine and took place off-site; in November 1843 Corkmen at the Thorold quarries fought among themselves. After they had hurled stones and shot at each other, two were dead and several injured. Tensions between groups of labourers seemed to go even beyond ethnic or religious differences. In 1846 Samuel Keefer referred cryptically to "hostile feeling" between "the pier men and the Lockmen," but gave no details.[29]

Italian Blood Runs Hot in Italian Veins

In the 1870s, as a large and impoverished group of immigrant labourers found work rebuilding the Welland Canal, history repeated itself. Now Italian labourers faced the same situation – and often fought the same battles – as had the Irish on the Second Canal. Between 1861 and 1900 about seven million Italians emigrated for reasons similar to those that brought about the Irish diaspora. Especially in the 1880s a large-scale exodus began from northern Italy, as the agrarian way of life was being transformed into an industrial, capitalist economy. As with the earlier Irish, some came to Canada from the United States while others came here directly, making Toronto or Montreal their base.[30] Willing to accept seasonal work on Central Canada's canals and railways, they became the largest non–Anglo-Celtic group in the labour force of the Third Canal. Again, as with the Irish earlier, many citizens of Niagara believed that Italians were a "violent" group, prone to riot and crime. And – again – there was a grain of truth in the overstatement.

The unfortunate political and social conditions of their homeland had conditioned many Italians to use physical violence as a way of handling conflict with both peers and employers. Moreover, generations of oppression had made these people – again like the Irish – hostile to their superiors. Common sense dictated the need for communal solidarity and even the carrying of weapons. Arriving on the construction sites of the Third Canal, many Italian workers found no need to abandon their traditions.[31]

Ironically, the first sign of trouble with Italians involved workers of Irish descent. Describing events on 18 June 1876, the Thorold *Post* wrote: "the usual stillness of our Sabbath evening was broken by the shrill calls of the bugle" as the local military was called out to suppress a battle between Irish and Italian labourers on Section 12 near the Escarpment. By the time the soldiers arrived, the trouble had subsided but one Italian had been killed, from either a kick in the head or a blow from a stone. According to witnesses, a drunken Irishman had accosted an Italian who was returning from grocery shopping in the town. As some of their respective countryman intervened, a riot had ensued. The Irish mob proceeded to plunder two "shanties" near the Canal where many Italians lived. The latter defended themselves with revolvers against the Irish sticks, pickhandles, and axes. Witnesses claimed that anywhere from sixty to two hundred Irishmen had attacked about thirty Italians.[32] Whether the "Irish" were actually recent immigrants or the adult children of the traumatized Irish of the Second Canal era we cannot know. In any case, the Italians referred to the Irish as "Englishmen"!

This was only the first of several incidents involving Italian immigrant workers. In August 1878 stabbings were reported among the Italian community in Port Colborne and in 1886 an "Italian scare" occurred in Thorold. In early July twenty-four Italians arrived from Syracuse, New York, hired by Raynor and Co. on their contract for deepening the loop on the Escarpment. The non-Italian navvies already employed there decided to drive them away and staged a general strike in protest.[33] The Italians sensibly agreed to leave – provided their expenses were paid. Once the contractor had agreed to raise a subscription to do this, they "solemnly marched down to the station" and stated through an interpreter that, if their numbers had been larger, they would have fought before leaving. The *Post* grimly observed:

"When the troubles of old canal times with the same class of people are remembered, it is easy to believe they would. The Italian blood runs hot in the Italian veins, and perhaps serious trouble has been averted by the fact that their numbers were small."[34] Local attitudes to "foreigners" had not changed since the 1840s, and public opinion was slow to adopt a more tolerant attitude to any action labourers might take to better their conditions.

Several days later a representative of Raynor and Co. quite credibly told the *Post* that his firm "found the Italians good workers, minding their own business, and always on hand sober in the morning" – an interesting comment on the habits of Canadian-born labour. On the other hand, the Thorold town council concluded their discussion of the crisis by remarking: "Every Italian recently in the town was armed, carrying both revolvers and knives. They were a dangerous class."[35]

Anti-Italian hysteria in the community surfaced again a month later when Carroll and Shields (contractors on the eastern section of the St Catharines and Niagara Central Railway from Thorold to Niagara Falls) hired Italian labourers. Learning of their presence, Dr Lucius Oille, president of the firm, saw to it that they were fired. The St Catharines *Journal* commented ambivalently that the Italians were a "quiet, orderly lot, and would no doubt have proved good servants, but were sent away by the firm. It is said they were all armed."[36]

RESPONSES OF THE AUTHORITIES

If, from a twenty-first century perspective, the attitudes of some of these employers seem at times arbitrary and unfeeling, we should remember that individuals such as Merritt or members of the Family Compact did not question the fairness of a rigid social hierarchy. Nor did they doubt that poverty was inevitable. Local prejudice against the Irish (and especially against the Catholic Irish) was also rife, so much so that "Irish," "Catholic," and "destitute" became almost synonymous terms. At the same time, in the early nineteenth century, "right-thinking" people assumed that the lower orders were more inclined to immorality than were "their betters." The paternalism of employers had, therefore, a righteous dimension – which scarcely served public or medical purposes.

Maintaining the Moral Tone

Contractors occasionally felt obliged to try to raise the "moral tone" on construction sites. In a notice to his workers, Phelps affirmed that "a comfortable house will soon be erected for the worship of God,"[37] presumably in the vicinity of the Deep Cut. The same notice declared that "As *profane language* [emphasis in the original] is highly offensive to God, and dishonorable to rational men it will be wholly discountenanced; and those who cannot bring themselves to dispense with it cannot be longer employed on this work."[38]

Phelps's efforts to control the behaviour of what must have seemed unruly, if not actually criminal, labourers went beyond surveillance of language and were possibly intended to improve their hygiene: "It is the particular request of your employer," his "Rules" continued, "that every person as soon as he quits work at night, will put on suitable clothes to preserve health, and at an early hour retire to rest. No gambling will be countenanced."[39] Some hints of the canal labourers' way of life emerge from this notice: scruffy clothing, gambling, coarse language. At the same time, we have a sense of the ignorance and insensitivity of the employers: did the navvies actually possess a change of clothes? Whether these imprecations had any effect in the 1820s is hard to know. Efforts to make the same recommendations in the 1840s seem to have changed nothing, but of course the social and economic problems of the canal labourers were much worse in that decade.

In the Last Stages of Starvation

When reading about the Second Canal era, some of today's readers may be shocked that the weight of government, soldiers, and clergy was aligned with the interests of private businessmen. Nevertheless, their bumbling and ultimately ineffective efforts were typical of prevailing attitudes to social order and public behaviour. To take only one example of a canal community, St Catharines had known a long period of civil and international peace since the end of the War of 1812. Pauperism certainly existed, but the poor "knew their place" and traditional charity was often adequate to alleviate the worst suffering. However, by the 1840s many citizens of Niagara felt under seige. Beggars with foreign (Irish!) accents appeared on their doorsteps regularly, taxing the resources of personal charity. Moreover the locals had little sympathy with rioters and looters. As for the immigrant labourers, they found that their accent, faith, dress, and social background differentiated them radically from the United Empire Loyalist settlers of Niagara, who resembled the people the Irish workers had regarded as oppressors back home.

A long letter to the St Catharines *Journal* in June 1842 reveals the unsympathetic consternation of the solid burghers of that village when faced with the sudden influx of unemployed, poverty-stricken, mainly Irish labourers, seeking work on the Welland's reconstruction. Headlined "To Strangers," the letter gave threefold advice to immigrant workers. First: "Keep far away from the taverns. These places are intended for travellers to eat in, and sleep in, and have their horses fed." Second, honour the Sabbath by avoiding the "reading [of] newspapers, or talking of politics." Third, go to church.[40] Other responses to the newcomers were less benign. By 1844 an element of hysteria had entered the psyche of "respectable" people. For example, the Niagara *Chronicle* asserted: "The offences taking place on the Welland Canal demand the severest and most exemplary punishment for they are calculated to destroy the whole fabric of civilized Society."[41] Yet many of the labourers were by no means amoral anarchists, as is evident in the banner which some of them had carried through St Catharines in August 1842. On one side it read "Bread or Work," and on the other "Peace and Union – God Save the Queen."[42] In fairness we should note that business men and merchants in St Catharines took up a subscription to aid the workers in 1842.

Typically, it was believed that the Irish had brought their misery on themselves by "intemperance," which meant not only by their excessive drinking but by their intense response to life in general. Public officials and canal engineers also tended to denounce any efforts made by the navvies to better their working or living conditions. In 1843 Power described a group of unemployed, sick, and starving as merely "a party of idlers."[43] Of disturbances in that year Thorburn wrote that the labourers had "shown a disposition to be troublesome" so that "like wild fire the evil spirit ran throughout every work on the whole line." Not that Thorburn or others were especially vicious in their attitudes to their fellow human beings, but the phenomenon of great crowds of workers massed in one place – an industrial labour force paid by wages – was new. In Britain, where the industrial revolution had begun some sixty years previously, the nation's best minds were still working out how to deal with the birth of a new form of human society.

The paternalistic attitudes prevailing along the First Canal construction site had ameliorated labourers' living and working conditions to some degree. As we know, however, public attitudes had changed measurably by the 1840s. The navvy building the Second Canal was often expected to work as long as fourteen hours a day – two hours longer than work days on the First Canal. He was now employed by the day, not by the month, as had been the case earlier. His pay was less than that of his counterpart on "Mr. Merritt's Ditch" and was usually reduced in the winter. Benefits such as barracks for living quarters were rarely provided and, if such accommodation was made available by contractors, it was overpriced. During construction of the First Canal, the labour market had been relatively favourable to navvies, but by the 1840s the situation was reversed. Desperate for work, many came to Niagara even before construction began, so that from the start there were more labourers available than jobs. (Full-scale building did not start until 1843.) In August 1842 the St Catharines *Journal* described the scene: "For several weeks past, hordes of Irish laborers from the state of New-York – where all public works have been suspended – have been pouring into this village and its vicinity, together with a large number of newly-arrived emigrants, in search of employment upon the contemplated improvements of the Welland Canal."[44]

In the same month Killaly (chairman of the Board of Works) wrote to R.W. Rawson (civil secretary to Governor General Bagot): "I regret to have to acquaint His Excellency that the employment ... afforded is by no means adequate to the demand which exists for it this season, in consequence of the large immigration."[45] This statement greatly underplayed what was a major social catastrophe: some observers estimated that only one in ten men could find work. For example, nine hundred men and four hundred women had settled at Broad Creek in October 1842, but the number employed there never rose above three hundred and forty.[46] Matters were slow to improve. In July 1843 three thousand men on the Welland were without work and near starvation[47] and the total grew to five thousand by the winter (with almost as many women and child dependents).[48] Some found part-time work, but in November 1843 wages were cut back while the cost of food rose. By January 1844 about ten thousand men women and children lived in the shantytowns – but only about three thousand labourers were employed.[49] The following month, the St Catharines *Journal* published its estimate that well over three thousand men, women and children were involved with canal labour along the length of the construction site from Port Dalhousie to Allanburg alone, hundreds of whom were "in the last stages of starvation."[50]

In 1842 some of these men had appealed to a St Catharines parish priest, Father Constantine Lee, begging him to find work for them. Lee turned to Merritt, who then wrote to Killaly about the crisis. Merritt also allied with the local Presbyterian minister, John William Baynes, in sending a petition to the Governor General. But neither priest, pastor, businessman, nor engineer-bureaucrat could prevent seven years of disturbances.

Unemployed, hungry, and faced with the suffering of their starving wives and children, labourers took to pilfering. From neighbouring farms, they stole wood (for building shanties or for heating), textiles, and fruit – sometimes cows. Even before violence flared, the Irish navvy had a criminal reputation – not surprising, given that living and working conditions were almost calculated to distort any labourer's sense of proportion.[51]

Preventing Bloodshed

The company directors seem to have practised a fair degree of religious tolerance. A "Notice to Labourers" in 1827 enjoined contractors: "It has been represented to the Directors, that many labourers professing the Roman Catholic religion, are deterred from working on the Canal through fear of ill usage from persons of other persuasions, this is therefore to give PUBLIC NOTICE, that the Contractors are required to use every lawful means in their power to prevent such conduct; and not only to dismiss those who may be guilty of violating the peace, but institute legal proceedings against the offending party without delay."[52]

This notice implies that not every Niagara citizen was as broadminded as the directors, although the latter were probably motivated as much by practical considerations as by a sense of social justice. On the other hand, Roman Catholics had been granted full civil rights under the Quebec Act of 1774 and in Britain the Catholic Emancipation Act was passed by parliament in the year the First Canal opened. So, conceivably the board was not far out of step with enlightened contemporary thinking.

The engineers and bureaucrats who supervised the building of the Second Canal continued to exhibit some more "modern" attitudes, resembling those of their predecessors on the First. "I do not know to this day," wrote Samuel Keefer in 1848, "and have never concerned myself to know who are Roman Catholics and who are orangemen on this canal." He was responding to charges that Catholics had been denied permanent jobs on the new waterway.[53] Unfortunately, as the strife among the navvies shows, Keefer was probably a minority in society at large.

For the Protection of the Labourer[54]

Certain engineers and bureaucrats were insightful in another way, too. In August 1842, as social conditions along the canal deteriorated, Killaly recommended providing regular employment, specifically urging the usefulness of proceeding immediately with the works of the Welland Canal on a more extensive scale: "There is no time when they can be so economically carried on as at the present, and the proceeding with several works will prevent that crowding on one point which must lead to disturbance and bloodshed."[55]

Although he requested that troops be stationed along the waterway, he also suggested speed in allocating contracts. At the same time, Superintendent W.B. Robinson recommended that work such as laying out the new canal embankments should be started, to provide employment as soon as possible. Keefer (at this time assistant engineer of the Board of Works) expanded the work underway with a view to meeting employment needs. The results were not clear; a year later, Power was urging Carmichael and Co. to start work at the Deep Cut without waiting for the board's orders. He wrote to the commissioners: "I shall not I trust be considered to have acted precipitately in thus urging forward the work." He continued to ask the board to expedite the awarding of contracts not – be it noted – for charitable reasons, but "to obviate disturbances & bloodshed."[56]

For his efforts to expedite construction for employment purposes, the board censured Power. Furthermore, when he tried to force subcontractors to pay their labourers on a daily basis (thus ensuring that the men were paid promptly), the commissioners criticized his actions, saying that a government bureaucrat had no power to intervene between employer and worker.[57] On the other hand, the board tried to control the truck system and did not object when Power in 1842 included a clause in contracts giving commissioners the right to regulate prices at contractors' stores. Killaly, too, seems to have realized that the "truck system" or "store pay" was an evil. Father Patrick William McDonagh (1808–1863), hired by the board to act as a "moral agent," expressed some concern to him over this practice in 1843. In 1846 Power remained critical of it, informing McDonagh that he was investigating the contractors Clark and Woods – in particular their "treatment of their laborers." He was "fully resolved to prohibit their system of 'truck pay.'"[58] Unfortunately, we have no record of its successful abolition in this period.

As we have seen, in the 1820s Oliver Phelps's concern for the dress and language of his workers revealed traces of the declining paternalism of an earlier era. In the 1840s, we find a similar effort (although seasoned with more practicality) in an appeal to the moral sense of labourers. In October 1842 the board had hired Father McDonagh to help control the violent impulses of the navvies. In a letter to McDonagh, Killaly mandated him to help secure "peace and order along the line of the works of the Welland Canal." The priest's work would benefit, wrote Killaly, from "the influence, which I know you to possess over the laborers, from your profession, from being from the same country with much the greater number of them, and from your being enabled [to] address them in their native language." Killaly urged McDonagh not to "lose a moment in going through the works generally and exert[ing] all your authority, religious and moral, in repressing insubordination, & all tendency to outrage."[59] Obviously McDonagh was not intended to act as a consoling padre.

In fact, the priest intervened in the strike on the Feeder Canal in January 1843, urging the men to return to work. In December of that year he helped to separate the Connaughtmen from the Corkorians at Stonebridge.[60] The extent of his influence may be questioned, since he was himself from Connaught and hence likely to be suspect among the Corkorians. Nevertheless, in 1843 (in a more diplomatic move) McDonagh invited James Buchanan, the Irish-born British Consul at New York, to speak to the labourers. At the arranged meeting Buchanan did so, as did McDonagh and Thorburn (fig. 10.1). But the workers (mainly Connaughtmen) interjected: "Give us work to earn a living, we cannot starve, the Corkmen now have all the work, give us a share of it."[61]

Another of McDonagh's duties seems to have been to operate as a one-man "fifth column." Killaly wrote to Begly, "I consider no one so likely to obtain early and due information of any ... scheme or plot as Mr. McDonagh not only from the advantages which his calling gives him but also from his knowing all the men their characters &c."[62]

Records contain no firm evidence that by December 1849 (when he was dismissed) McDonagh's work had reduced the navvies' discontent or that he ever fully understood the social and economic dynamics of the labourers' discontent. Nor can we tell whether a more bureaucratic approach to the worker's moral sense succeeded. In early 1844 McDonagh, Thorburn, and Power distributed "affidavits" to the navvies, which they were required to sign before being considered employable on the canal. The St Catharines *Journal* described these documents as "a solemn affirmation ... in which they declare, in substance, that they have not in possession any gun or other firearms or offensive weapon of any description; and that they will henceforward keep the peace towards all persons; and use all their endeavors to prevent its disturbance by others."[63] As might be expected, this program had limited success, in part because the stonecutters refused to take the oath and many contractors refused to co-operate. Then in March 1845 the Legislature passed an act requiring that all firearms belonging to labourers on or near Public Works projects be registered. This, too, seems to have been non-productive.

FALLS OF NIAGARA,
12th January, 1844.

TO THE SONS OF ERIN,

Engaged on the Welland Canal, who are known as Cork men and Connaught men.

MY BELOVED COUNTRYMEN:

After having filled the office of Her Majesty's Consulate at New York for about 26 years, and having in my old days been permitted by Her Majesty to retire from that honourable Office, and come to reside in Canada, to which I have sent thousands of my countrymen, believing it superior to any other country for a sober, industrious poor man to provide for his family, I deem it prudent, in order to layclaim to your confidence so as to effect the object in view by this Address, to state; that during the Rebellion in Ireland I became a Magistrate, and commanded the Barons' Court Corps of Yeomanry in Tyrone, yet such was the course of my conduct, that I was honoured with a vote of thanks and a piece of Plate by the Catholic Board of Ireland, a testimony which I value very highly.

In addition thereto, I have also to mention, that upon my leaving the City of New York, among numerous testimonials, I was honored with an Address, signed exclusively by my countrymen of the Roman Catholic faith, headed by the Very Rev. Dr. Power, a gentleman, a native of Cork, and an honour to our country, who takes a deep interest in the welfare of his countrymen, and to whom I promised I would endeavour to reconcile and heal the divisions of my countrymen in Canada, so as to promote their true interests, and the happiness of their families.

In order to consult about the best means to effect the object I have in view, as a first step, I request that five married men and their wives, and five single men, of the Cork party, and the same number of the Connaught men, may be chosen as Delegates to meet me, to whom I wish to submit for their approval my purposed measures. I therefore propose to meet the Delegates of the Cork men at Port Robinson, on the 18th day of January inst., at 10 o'clock in the morning, at Coleman's Hotel; and those of the Connaught men at Thorold, on the same day, at 2 o'clock P. M., at Henderson's Tavern. Punctual attendance is requested.

I further request that the persons so to meet me, may be furnished with the approval of the Rev. Mr. McDonnagh or of Wm. Bonallie, Esq. Superintendent on the Canal, whose co-operation I rely on in this good work, without which no Delegate will be admitted to the Conference.

I remain,

Your affectionate countryman,

JAMES BUCHANAN.

10.1 Notice to Irish labourers from James Buchanan, 1844: one of several efforts to reduce violence on the Second Canal construction site. (LAC: RG 11, 68-5)

Concern for the moral welfare of the navvies occasionally had a literally constructive aspect. Phelps, himself a Presbyterian deacon, contributed lumber to the construction of a church of that denomination in St Catharines, which was completed in 1834. At the instigation of Father McDonagh, the Board of Works donated stones from its Thorold quarry for building the Roman Catholic Church St Catherine of Alexandria (later Cathedral) in St Catharines. Many Irish canal workers contributed labour to this edifice, the cornerstone of which was laid in 1843. Similarly, in 1874 a Lutheran congregation in Humberstone was allowed to take stone (presumably left over) from the canal banks to build a church.

A Disposition to Be Troublesome

By the 1840s the authorities were aware that canal workers were becoming militant, having identifiable leaders and experimenting with work stoppages. Even such peaceful activities terrified both the local population and the engineers. In an effort to ensure law and order, the Board of Works tried to discover who among the labourers might be inciting them to organize or to plan possible violent action. To this end, a blacklist was created of "ringleaders" never to be employed on the canal. In February 1843 Power was asked to "transmit a minute description of them" to the board.[64] Later that year the board sent him a list of men who seemed to have inspired recent riots on the Lachine Canal, in case they showed up on the Welland seeking work. Soon specific individuals were being targeted for dismissal. John and Richard Allen were fired in January 1845 for allegedly causing disturbances, while in September of that year Power was told never to hire one Patrick Mitchell, "age about thirty-five, hair and whiskers dark – height about 5 feet 10 inches and rather stout ... employed as a foreman on the Lachine and Beauharnois Canals, where he has been considered a troublesome character – creating insubordination amongst the labourers, etc."[65]

What bothered the authorities more than individuals' inciting labourers to strike or to riot was the movement to organize. The attitude of the Public Works Commissioners to such a phenomenon must be understood as both rational and rooted in contemporary attitudes (which always seem reasonable to those who maintain them). Throughout the Western world, the notion of a group of men "ganging up" on one individual had always seemed "unfair." Thus in the early years of the Industrial Revolution, the prospect of fifty or a hundred machine operatives "combining" to "extort" concessions from the one or two men who operated a mill was condemned as "conspiracy." Of course, the phenomenon of one individual employing hundreds of others was relatively new, and the economic dynamics of the situation were not understood. On the Welland Canal, defending the right of the isolated contractor against a mob of workers seemed only natural. Especially in 1846, fear of "the existence of a conspiracy among the unpaid laborers" was expressed by Samuel Power and would have resonated in Toronto and Montreal – indeed virtually anywhere in North America.[66]

At the same time, because the bureaucrats did not regard themselves as employers, their attitude toward canal construction workers was an "arm's length" one. As we have seen, in 1843 Power had already been urged to avoid interference between contractors and sub-contractors. The commissioners' attitude was clearly stated in 1846: "They consider that when the men are unpaid by a contractor, the Department is not in any way called upon to interfere, relative to the payment of the men, further than to the extent of funds remaining in hand, due to the contractor."[67]

For the Preservation of the Peace[68]

Many engineers and contractors – as well as Merritt – believed that the presence of armed force along the waterway had become essential and so, to subdue the starving workers, physical coercion was used. In Canada the use of troops to suppress labour unrest had begun on the Rideau in 1827, and became common over the next century. Nor was it unknown in the United States, where federal soldiers had been called out in 1834 to stop rioting by workers on the Chesapeake and Ohio Canal. Circumstances in 1842 seemed to warrant the deployment of force but, before the troops were summoned, moral support was sought from David Thompson, a magistrate in Indiana on the Grand River who, it was believed, carried more weight than local magistrates. Moreover, in the fall, Parliament approved the appointment as magistrate of Baron de Rottenberg – who had some success suppressing disturbances until December 1842.[69]

In the summer of that year canal authorities called on Her Majesty's Royal Canadian Rifles at Drummondville to control the labourers. Ultimately, mounted soldiers were stationed along the line of the canal to intimidate the navvies and crush any illegal activities. Sixty men were stationed at St Catharines, sixty at Thorold, and thirty at Port Maitland. Occasional help came from the Royal Canadian Rifles at Chippawa. Finally a special group of black soldiers, the "Colored Corps," was called on. These men (originally attached to the 1st Incorporated Militia of Hamilton) were commanded by Captain Alexander MacDonald, whose headquarters was at Port Robinson. "This spirited company turned out ... in a handsome manner," said the St Catharines *Journal* approvingly.[70] The arrival of the Colored Corps, however, may have only exacerbated discontent. The Irish labourers (who hated everything British) were enraged that their traditional enemy would use black soldiers – for whom they had contempt – to quell their efforts to improve their conditions.

The stated aim of these "police forces" was to protect the navvies who wished to carry on working during a strike, but the authorities were not entirely happy with this arrangement. On the one hand, they may have been aware that the soldiers were mainly Orangemen, a fact that could only irritate the largely Roman Catholic labourers. As well, the Board of Works fretted about "the great expense" of maintaining a military force on the Welland Canal while at the same time fearing what would happen if the soldiers were removed. A tortuously worded letter from Begly to Power in December 1845 reveals the bureaucrats' discomfiture. The board, he stated, wanted to reduce or eliminate the cost "involved in the maintenance of the Police and military forces, which would only be justified on the ground that if this force were not kept up, the Canal would be obstructed, and not available to the Trade. With this view and having in mind that the great mass of men are by your own shewing employed upon works which however desirable it may be to have completed, yet if interrupted will not tend to interfere with the navigation of the Canal next season, the Board requests that you will reconsider the subject, and furnish a further report with the least possible delay."[71]

Killaly also professed to be unhappy about the use of troops on public works, justifying his calling for them in 1843 by "the peculiar circumstances alone which had preceded the (as I conceive) necessity for their assistance."[72] Possibly the chief engineer sensed that the use of black troops – or indeed of any troops in the hire of the British Empire – deepened Irish resentment.

That the soldiers were successful in limiting violent outbreaks on the canal is possible but difficult to determine. For their part, the black soldiers may have themselves only added to the level of lawlessness – at least in Port Robinson. In 1845 local worthies complained of "frequent depredation committed in the village of Port Robinson and its environs" by "the Colored Core" [sic], who had "become a Public Nuisance" and were believed responsible for "pilfering" and more serious robberies in the area.[73] At a remove of nearly two centuries we find it hard to know how much racial bigotry was behind these accusations

– the blacks being regarded by many locals as a species lower than even the Irish Catholic navvies! In the end, the canal's military forces were disbanded by 1850.

Suitable and Proper Lock Houses

Despite the obvious callousness of some of their responses to serious social problems, the canal builders found at least one positive solution to those difficulties. Realizing that poverty made for dissatisfied and unreliable employees, the authorities endeavoured to assure themselves of a contented workforce by building lock-side buildings for the on-duty comfort of locktenders and even by providing domestic housing near the locks for locktenders and their families.

Such a program had actually begun in 1831 when the Welland Canal Company directors authorized the construction of locktenders' "houses" at Locks 2 and 3, each to be "one story 14 foot posts, consisting of two rooms and one chimney." A map of Port Colborne in 1870 shows an "old Lock House" on the west side of the harbour, almost at the pier, at the site of the lock of the First Canal.[74] Unfortunately, we know little about such structures on this version of the waterway. They seem to have been what were later called "shanties," or offices and shelters from the weather for the men in charge of operating the locks. No trace of these structures remains today, and the preceding references to them are all that exist in the records.[75]

When the Second Canal was under construction, the program was revived. In December 1842 the board purchased the necessary land, and by the summer of 1845 several dwellings were under construction. Power described one such house as "a single lockhouse 24 x 6 chains 1½ stories high windows of upper story in the gable 4 rooms plastered and well finished in every respect."[76] These dwellings seem to have been of wooden frame construction (in contrast to those built several years later). In his annual report of October 1846, Samuel Keefer made a constructive recommendation: "The trade being continually on the increase, demands every year a greater portion of [the locktenders'] time, and it therefore becomes necessary to look forward to the period when vessels will have to pass through the Canal both night and day, and the Locktenders must then be always near at hand. [Therefore we need] erection of suitable and proper Lock houses, and I have accordingly estimated for 15 Lock Houses."

Keefer went on to specify that "along the Mountain range," there should be one house for every three locks, each built of rubble masonry "in a substantial manner with cut quoins sills and lintels."[77] Because his

10.2 A double locktender's house near the Second Canal in Merritton, built of stone c. 1850 (now demolished). The provision of comfortable homes for staff was an effort to attract committed canal operators and thus to ensure efficient operation of the waterway. (Photo: R.R.T.)

suggestion seems to have made no impression on the Board of Works, he revived the idea in March 1849. He now included bridgetenders among the permanent canal staff to be provided with homes, urging: "That authority should be given to erect accommodation at each Lock for the Lock tender [and] That each Locktender should be required to live in his respective Lock house."[78] On this occasion, Keefer was more successful, for in the spring of 1849 it was announced that tenders would be called for the construction of lock houses.

In fact, no evidence exists of such homes being built at this time. Certainly the labour turmoil on the canal would have given Keefer and Killaly's superiors second thoughts about such amenities. The cholera outbreak of 1849 and the contemporary financial exigencies were doubtless also retarding factors. What is known is that almost as soon as those tenders were called for the Department of Public Works suspended the program.

When the financial situation stabilized, the social climate had calmed, and the canal itself appeared near completion, the Department revived its plan to build locktenders' homes. By May 1851 the contractor John Bradley was building such houses at Locks 13 and 23.

10.3 A locktender's shanty at Lock 4 of the Third Canal. Consisting of an office for record-keeping and temporary sleeping accommodation, such canal-side structures were provided on the Second Canal as well, but we have no evidence of similar amenities built on the First. (AO: Murphy Collection [5])

More houses of frame construction were built in 1852, 1855, and 1860. These buildings were sometimes combined with toll collectors' offices and dwellings – as at Lock 1 in Port Dalhousie. Many were double houses (fig. 10.2), but one brick structure (near Lock 23 in Thorold) was a triple family house. Only two of these buildings (both double-stone structures) survive and may be seen on Bradley Street in St Catharines.

Some small "shanties" to serve as offices and to protect locktenders from the elements were also built beside the Second Canal locks, but none of these still stand. Although little reference to them is found in the written documents, they appear on Department of Public Works maps of the 1850s. For example, at Lock 4 both a locktender's house and a lock-side shanty are shown.[79] Unfortunately the surviving data on these structures is spotty. Moreover the authorities often referred to these as "lockhouses" – which can be confused with the afore-mentioned homes built for locktenders and their families.

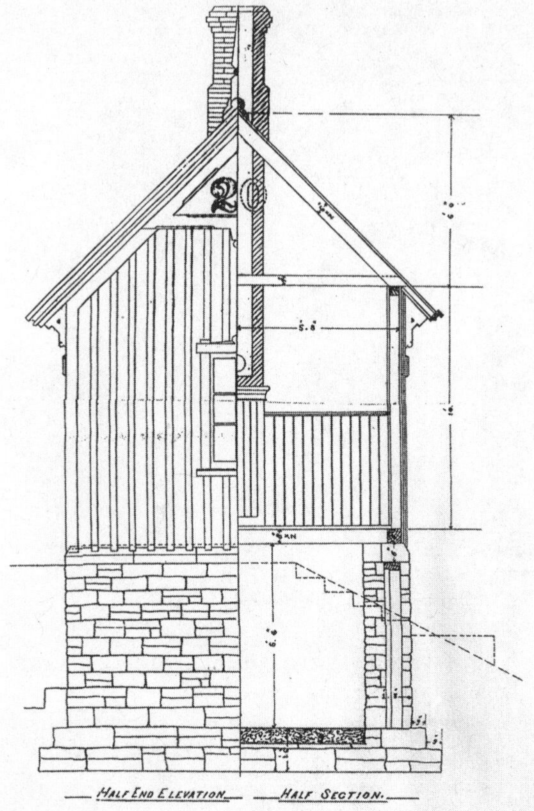

10.4 Side elevation of a Third Canal locktender's shanty, 1882: a stable structure, built to last. (Only one of these, at Port Dalhousie, has survived.) (SCM: Canal Gallery)

On the Third Canal, no new domiciles for lock- or bridgetenders were built, although these employees were given a house rent allowance as part of their wages. On the other hand, substantial shelters for locktenders (confusingly also called "shanties") were again built at every lock. Most had two rooms and a stove (figs. 10.3, 10.4). Only one of these remains today, at Lock 1 in Port Dalhousie. Some of the shanties standing beside Second Canal locks were moved to the Third Canal; in other cases new ones were built, most being completed in 1884. Eventually privies were also installed – across each lock from the shanty.

Fitful Progress of the Navvies

Despite difficult working conditions, labourers on the First Canal site were relatively passive. On the other hand, faced with an even more challenging workplace, Second Canal construction workers found ways to defend themselves and began to organize and, if necessary, to refuse to work. By the 1870s, trade unions were legal and working class literacy had improved. Working conditions had not appreciably improved, but the navvies had learned how to advance their interests without violence.

An Organized System Exists Among the Labourers

What inspired the earliest strikes was more than simply a sense of injustice or an empty stomach; it was also a tradition of self-help. Like the oppressed everywhere and at all times, the canal workers practised mutual aid. In fact they had brought with them from Ireland a tradition of solidarity vis-à-vis authority. Having cultivated a deep hatred of British political and military institutions, they tended to take action directly against their enemies in ways that could involve personal assault or property damage.[80] Moreover, Thorburn was correct to note in 1844 that "an organized system exists amongst the labourers."[81] Traditional secret societies (the Hibernian and the "Shamerick") seem to have been as powerful a cohesive as sectarianism or Cork/Connaught county origins. While Second Canal labourers still lacked the stabilizing influence of a trade union, their *ad hoc* banding together seems to have had some effect in forcing contractors to pay relatively high wages compared to those in effect on the St Lawrence canals.

When the First Welland was under construction, unions were unknown, but by 1833 the Organization of Carpenters and Joiners had been formed in York. Other labourers in the building trades (such as bricklayers and stonemasons) would follow suit. By the 1840s a modern labour movement was developing in Canada West. For example, the York Typographical Society, an association of apprentice typesetters, had been established in 1832 and was revived in 1844.

The problem for students of the union movement on the Welland Canals in this era is that we have little primary documentation on the degree of organization among the navvies and skilled workers. Nonetheless, the building of the Second Welland probably reflected a growing sophistication on the part of the skilled labourers, notably the stonemasons, largely Scottish. In their homeland, many of the Scots had benefitted from a superior educational system. Furthermore, as talented craftsmen, they derived self-respect from the skill with which they dressed, shaped, and placed the stones in the lock walls or weirs. Associated stonecutters in nearby quarries seemed to share their sense of dignity.

Moreover, certain other occupations were developing which required training and experience and which inspired a greater degree of self-respect. Many of the skilled labourers on the Second Canal were now literate and could write cogent letters outlining their position and requests. One example occurred in 1843, when Charles Whitton represented his stonemason colleagues in complaining to the board about the wages paid them by contractors.[82] No doubt some of this progress was inspired by the Mechanics Institutes, such as the one in St Catharines, which by the 1850s were encouraging literacy and education among the working class.

When confronted by intractability on the part of contractors or the board, labourers (both skilled and unskilled) began to organized and use the weapon of the strike. Just as employers were beginning to assume that labour was a commodity to be bought and sold, stonemasons had become equally "modern" – seeking to control the price of what they had to sell. The year 1841 saw the first manifestation of skilled workers' organized activism. Supported by stonecutters in the local quarries, stonemasons petitioned for a wage increase. Their petition was read at a Board of Works meeting and was (not surprisingly) rejected. Rumblings of stonemason discontent were heard again in 1844. In fact, between 1842 and 1845 the canal labourers (skilled and unskilled) struck ten times.[83] When unskilled labourers first struck for higher wages in March 1842, some contractors wanted to suspend construction of certain locks, presumably to intimidate the workers into withdrawing requests for pay increases. Typically, the authorities supported the contractors' position. Power, for instance, was told in May 1842: "The Board are not by any means desirous to force the Contractors to submit to the extortion of the laborers and workmen."[84] Therefore Power temporarily suspended the masonry work.

Nothing is heard of unrest again until February 1845 when the stonecutters announced their intention to strike if the contractors would not increase their pay. The authorities were alarmed by this threat, fearing "so great a calamity as the work not being ready for the Trade."[85] On 4 March the men carried out their threat and struck, causing another suspension of the works. The board responded vigorously and Power was informed that he could use force to suppress these "turbulent and & evil desposed [sic]" men.[86]

Strikes sometimes worked their desired effect. When in July 1843 labourers working on the canal between St Catharines and Thorold downed tools for higher wages, they soon returned to work, "the contractors having considered it advisable," said Power, "to comply with their demand in consideration of the high price of provisions."[87] Whatever their success rate, strikes were frequent until the completion of the new canal.

The response of the authorities may seem excessive, but we should remember that construction was already behind schedule, with shippers inquiring regularly about the readiness of the new locks and the precise opening date. Moreover, frightening outbreaks of violence by the unskilled workers had already occurred. As well, canal authorities had local opinion on their side. In 1845, noting that the works had been suspended, the St Catharines *Journal* opined that a large pay raise "would not be beneficial for the majority of the labourers, it would furnish larger means for vicious indulgences," and would also turn public opinion against the workers.[88]

Growing Sophistication of Labour

In the two decades after the Second Canal was completed, the social independence and maturity of the navvies had developed. Signs of this had been apparent during the first reconstruction but now, with growing literacy, self-confidence, and legislative support, certain groups (such as the stonecutters) were even more organized and militant. We now know the names of more of the labourers. In fact, even some unskilled workers were sufficiently literate to at least sign their own names on paysheets, rather than simply marking an "X".[89] A symptom of the new new standards of literacy and self-confidence among labourers was the occasional request for compensation for on-the-job injury. In January 1882 one Thomas Cunningham wrote to the Department of Railways and Canals seeking recompense for an accident he had suffered while working as a mason on the canal enlargement. Although the Ontario Act to Secure Compensation for Workmen was not passed until 1886, Cunningham ultimately received $75.[90]

As we have seen, since the 1840s, a capitalist labour market had emerged in Canada's nascent industries and on constructions sites. Mr Cunningham's efforts were given more likelihood of success by the authorities' growing awareness of this development. The earlier image of the militant worker no longer applied. The formation and activity of unions had been particularly aided by federal legislation such as the Trade Unions Act of 1872, which decreed that unions were not illegal conspiracies against owners. (In 1889 the Royal Commission on the Relations of Labour and Capital also defended unions as legitimate forms of organization.)

The Canadian Labour Union was founded in 1873, followed by the Trades and Labour Congress of Canada in 1883. Many industrial communities saw the formation of local labour councils. The American-based Knights of Labor entered Ontario around 1880. As well, the Civil Service Act of 1868 introduced superannuation pensions in certain cases, and various Public Health acts in Ontario improved living conditions.

Although, again, specific documentation is often lacking, we find that these changes were reflected in the activities of workers on Third Canal construction sites. Local stonecutters and masons (members of the Dominion Co-operative Stonecutters' Association) had the contract for the masonry on Sections 33 and 34 at Humberstone, for which they leased a quarry near Beaverdams. In 1878 the Thorold *Post* noted that "the 'boys' seem to be getting on well with their contract."[91] In 1880 the Ontario Co-operative Stone Cutters Association felt confident enough to file a lawsuit against the contractors Clarke and Co.

The social and intellectual life of stonecutters began to be considered as well. In 1879 the Stonecutters' Association purchased a well-known Thorold building (the Crobar House) and converted it into a Lodge Reading Room. The *Post* announced in December 1886 that the stonecutters' "Beaver Assembly" would hold a "grand ball and supper" at Cloy's rink, "one of the events of the season [which] will be attended by brethren from St. Catharines, Merritton, Welland, Niagara Falls and elsewhere."[92] The following August the Knights of Labor (of which the stonecutters were a part) were represented in a civic holiday parade.

The peaceful, constructive solidarity exhibited by these activities helps to explain the vigorous strikes launched by stonecutters during the Third Canal's construction. The year 1875 saw their first major strike action, on Sections 8 and 9, where the contractors acceded to their demands for a wage raise. Aggrieved by the anti-union actions of a foreman, stonecutters taking stone from quarries on Pelee Island for Lobb (the contractor on Section 12) struck in 1877. Unionized stonecutters in Welland and at a Beamsville quarry (working on stone for the aqueduct) struck for higher wages in November 1878. Similarly in 1879 Hunter, Murray and Co. provoked a strike at the Queenston Quarry in 1879 over their hiring of scabs and over one foreman contradicting what another said about wages. In 1883 stonemasons struck when hours were reduced from ten a day to nine, and daily wages cut.

In Niagara, fear of organized workmen still prevailed. In 1878 the Welland *Tribune* described an incident during which unionized workers on the bridge contract of Frazer, Battle and Ussher used "threats and inducements" to drive non-union men off the job. The report does not describe violence or bloodshed, but typically refers to the unionists as "rioters." In that year, the stonecutters' strike inspired local authorities to bring in special constables and call out the militia, actions that reveal the unchanging state of official opinion since the 1840s. But something *had* changed: when the striking labourers were of British background, some local public opinion disapproved of contractors depending on the threat of force.[93] The Thorold *Post* thought such a step was unnecessary, referring to the "imaginary riot," a phrase that suggested arbitration rather than reliance on soldiers. Its editors criticized the custom of sub-contracting and supported the efforts of workers to organize unions. "It is strange that the contractors have such a hatred to the Stonecutters' Union," wrote the editors in 1879: "They look on the Union as a body of men combined together for the sake of destroying them."[94]

However, public opinion had not changed in one respect: the sight of idle men on the streets of Niagara's villages and towns occasioned fear in the minds of many locals. Memories of violence thirty years before nurtured such apprehension, as did the fact that seasonal unemployment (as well as the general downturn in the economy) meant that the sight of "a large number of men ... laying around the streets"[95] was common in the late seventies and early eighties. For example, in January 1880 the village of Stonebridge was alarmed at the rumour that "unless the unemployed labourers were immediately given work, they would plunder the village."[96] Fortunately the anticipated pillage did not occur and most men found work.

Of course, the problems of the Welland Canal labourers reflect the difficulties of the working classes everywhere in the Western world before the social legislation passed in the late nineteenth and twentieth centuries. Because of the seasonal nature of their employment, and the itinerant nature of their lives, their suffering was probably greater than that of the urban proletariat. Their response, too, was more violent, at least at first. As we have seen, residents of canal-side communities as well as local authorities were profoundly shocked by both the behaviour and living conditions of the navvies. Nevertheless, the Irish, Italian, and other migrant workers survived. Although they were at first a disruptive presence, most of them (with their families) settled down in the Niagara Peninsula, where they and their descendants often became model – even influential – citizens in their respective communities.

Conclusion

Into the Future

In this book, we have chronicled the experiences of the men who built and rebuilt a great canal "on the ground" – the challenges, frustrations, and triumphs of engineers, contractors, artisans, and navvies. As the visionary instigator of the project, William Hamilton Merritt has been granted a prime role in this saga, but we have also shown that politicians, soldiers, businessmen, and local worthies all saw this waterway connecting lakes Ontario and Erie as contributing to the increase in prosperity of British North America – and, not coincidentally, to their own fortunes. In particular, entrepreneurs, both local and from farther afield, profited from contractors' need for machinery and supplies. Businessmen and politicians, of course, were not the men who had to struggle with ice, rain and heat, with hardpan, rock and mud, with remote bureaucracy, local sensitivities, and each other's personal quirks. The engineers and contractors planned and argued, overspent and sometimes cheated. In the muck and among the stones, the labourers toiled long hours and occasionally fell ill, or were injured – even killed – on the job.

All these issues considered, building the Welland was in fact another example of that quintessentially Canadian saga of "people against nature." As for the inhabitants of local communities, they had a "love-hate" relationship with the canal, appreciating its role in providing employment through its construction (and later operation), but also expressing anger at construction-related flooding and disruption to east-west road traffic. At the same time they, like visitors from beyond Niagara, were fascinated by the spectacle of the construction process.

The locks, weirs, and channels built by the contractors and navvies, now neglected, overgrown, or buried, remain as monuments to the builders' imagination, planning, skill, and grit. Although often abandoned, crumbling and half-hidden, these structures are historical documents that reflect the foundations of a modern country. As such, they await the attention of future archaeologists and historians. Indeed, they have almost untouched – yet great – potential as tourist, educational, and recreational sites. Twenty-first century Canadians might do well to consider establishing a national park in the Niagara Peninsula to commemorate their forefathers' achievement in linking the Great Lakes of Erie and Ontario.

At the beginning of the nineteenth century, the success of the Welland Canals could not have been foreseen. Canada was a relatively poor agricultural, British colony with limited trading links. By 1900, however, it was a domestically autonomous, prosperous, and expanding Dominion. In both the Niagara area and the evolving federation, the three successive Welland canals played an important role in this development. Economic, social, political, and technological conditions changed dramatically during the century, and "Mr. Merritt's Ditch," constantly being expanded, reflected those changes and occasionally played a role in causing them.

Construction methods, building materials, bureaucratic systems, and labour organizations had become more sophisticated, while traffic on the waterway had expanded tremendously. The economy and society of Niagara was transformed. In fact, some have argued that, for Central and Atlantic Canada, the Welland played a role comparable to that of the Canadian Pacific Railway in opening up the prairies and establishing Canada beyond the Rocky Mountains and on the West Coast. This theme, of course, could be the subject of another book!

By the 1890s, with the Third Canal in operation, Niagara communities, indeed the whole of Canada (and the wider world), were about to undergo dramatic and fundamental changes. The great transformation would begin in the years of Sir Wilfrid Laurier's government (1893–1911), when the country enjoyed an economic boom and the inadequacies of the Third Canal were in turn becoming increasingly apparent. Even before the First World War began in 1914, many features of twentieth-century Canada, such as urbanization and the use of motor cars, were already in evidence.

It is against this background that in 1910 the Laurier government made the decision that the Welland Canal must once again be enlarged. The story of that expansion, that of the Welland Ship (Fourth) Canal, will be told in the second part of this study, *Building the Welland Ship Canal: The Twentieth-Century Welland Canal.* As the builders of the previous century discovered, twentieth-century engineers, contractors, and labourers found that building such a huge waterway was not accomplished without difficulties and disasters, in a saga that had political, social, economic, and ecological ramifications in Niagara and beyond. Nevertheless, by the 1960s the new Welland had become an integral part of the extensive St Lawrence Seaway system. As we

11.1 Near Port Robinson, c. 1972. Reconstruction of the Welland Canal continued in the twentieth century, as engineers responded to the growing size of boats. Here a typical laker passes under a lift bridge, both characteristic of the era of the Fourth Canal, built 1913–30. In the background, work is underway on the Welland By-Pass, built 1965–73. (SLSMC: Niagara Region)

are now well into the twenty-first century, this forthcoming companion volume, complementing the nineteenth-century chronicle of the Welland's construction and reconstruction, will also offer a "look into the future" for the Welland and the Seaway, to bring up to date a unique study of a great Canadian technological and human epic (fig. 11.1).

ABBREVIATIONS

AO	Archives of Ontario
Biog.	Jedediah P. Merritt, *Biography of the Hon. W.M. Merritt, M.P.* St Catharines: Leavenworth, 1875
Cowan	P.J. Cowan, *The Welland Ship Canal between Lake Erie and Lake Ontario 1913–1932*. London: Offices of Engineering, 1935
DOT	Department of Transport
DPW	Department of Public Works
DRC	Department of Railways and Canals
Koudys	William Koudys Collection
LAC	National Archives of Canada (now Library and Archives Canada)
MP	Member of Parliament (Canada)
MPP	Member of the Provincial Parliament (Upper Canada; United Province of Canada; Ontario)
NMC	National Map Collection
Page's *Atlas*	H.R. Page, *Historical Atlas of the Counties of Lincoln and Welland, Ont.* Toronto: Craig, 1876
PANS	Public Archives of Nova Scotia
PCHMM	Port Colborne Historical and Marine Museum
RMS	Roberta M. Styran
RRT	Robert R. Taylor
SCL	St Catharines Centennial Library
SCM	St Catharines Museum
SLSMC	St Lawrence Seaway Management Corporation
SP	*Sessional Papers of the Dominion of Canada*
Third Report	Ontario. Parliament. House of Assembly. *Appendix* to the *Journal of the House of Assembly of Upper Canada* 1836–37. Toronto: William Lyon Mackenzie, 1836, vol. 2
WCR	Welland Canal Records (St Catharines Centennial Library)

NOTES

INTRODUCTION

1 William Kingsford, *The Canadian Canals*, 59.

2 Foreword to Roberta Styran and Robert R. Taylor, with John N. Jackson, *The Welland Canals: The Growth of Mr. Merritt's Ditch*, vii.

3 Styran and Taylor, *Mr. Merritt's Ditch: A Welland Canals Album*, 1992; *The Great Swivel Link: Canada's Welland Canal*, 2001; *The Welland Canals Corridor, Then and Now*, 2004. See Bibliography for the works of Jackson and other local authors.

4 So wrote Seymour Phelps, a St Catharines journalist, author of a series of columns, "A Walk Around Town," for the St Catharines *Journal* in the 1850s, under the pseudonym "Junius." The remark quoted here appeared on 16 October 1856, in "A Walk Around Town W." (*St. Catharines A to Z*, 60).

5 Tonnage of ships is not given in metric figures because vessels were not yet required to be registered in metric.

6 Montreal *Gazette,* 23 September 1818.

7 On this subject, see Robert R. Taylor, "Merritton, Ontario: The Rise and Decline of an Industrial Corridor, ca. 1845–1939," *Scientia Canadensis*, vol. 14, nos. 1–2, 1990, 90–130; and John N. Jackson, *The Welland Canals and Their Communities: Engineering, Industrial, and Urban Transformation*.

8 See Donald Creighton, *The Commercial Empire of the St. Lawrence 1760–1850*, 252.

9 Upper Canada. House of Assembly. *Third Report of the Select Committee Appointed to Examine and Enquire into the Management of the Welland Canal*, 218; henceforth cited as *Third Report*.

10 The entrance lock at Port Dalhousie was 185 by 40 by 10 feet (56.4 by 12.2 by 5.05 m).

11 This was the case in St Catharines and Welland, and at the Little Deep Cut.

12 William Notman and Jennings Taylor, *Portraits of British Americans*, Montreal: Lovell, 1865, vol. 2, 296.

13 "General Report of the Commissioners of Public Works for the Year 1856," *Sessional Papers for the Province of Canada*, 20 Victoria, Appendix No. 29, A. 1857, in Appendix 5, vol. 15.

14 John Page, Annual Report of the Chief Engineer of Public Works, 29 April 1872, *SP for 1873*, vol. 6, pt. 6, 1873, 2.

15 They planned to enlarge the waterway either by twinning the remaining locks, or by constructing four huge "super locks." As a result of changing economic conditions, neither plan could be implemented, although the southern section was deepened and straightened with the "Welland By-Pass" (1965–73). A new, larger siphon culvert carries Chippawa Creek under the By-Pass.

16 Some of the maps, plans and engineers' drawings surviving from the nineteenth century have been published, but many have not, or at least not in sources readily accessible to the general public.

17 "Diagram of J. Martindales Land in Grantham," *Survey of Lands* (1826–?) [after 1831] (Niagara Collection, James A. Gibson Library, Brock University), 21.

18 "Port Robinson," *Survey of Lands* (1826) [1834], 101.

19 "Map of the District of Niagara in Upper Canada shewing the Course and a Section of the Welland Canal. Compiled from Actual Survey by order of the Directors," in Ogden Creighton, *A General View of the Welland Canal in the Province of Upper Canada; together with a Brief Examination of its Advantages*, 1830. These locks had a slight lift, but were essentially two sets of guard gates.

20 Nicol Hugh Baird and H.H. Killaly, *Report*; NMC 11848.

21 Ibid.

22 See, for example, William Hamilton Merritt's "Account of the Welland Canal, Upper Canada," *American Journal of Science and Arts*, wherein he writes, complicating the matter further(!), "From the termination of the deep cut, to that part where the mountain descends (or lock No. 1, as it is called, although it is properly No. 2,), the distance is four miles and twenty three chains" (vol. 14, July 1828, 161).

23 The introduction of electronic mail in the late twentieth century will render the research of scholars in the future even more difficult!

24 At the beginning of the twenty-first century, Kingsford's 1865 observation that the Welland's history had "to be traced out from official documents, and the records of legislative proceedings" still held true (Kingsford, *The Canadian Canal*, 59).

25 Directors to J.B. Robinson, 5 June 1833 (LAC, RG 43, vol. 2099, 239).

CHAPTER ONE

1 H.H. Killaly to Merritt, 3 January 1842 (LAC, RG 11, vol. 116, #414 or #416).

2 Some might claim this to be an apocryphal tale, for our source is Jedediah P. Merritt, *Biography of the Hon. W.M. Merritt, M.P.*, 16 (henceforth cited as *Biography*), which we have found to be occasionally erroneous. However, Jedediah presumably heard it from his father, and we sense that it has the ring of truth. Certainly the younger Merritt later includes a quotation from the senior Merritt's journal: "As I passed Bridgewater on my ride from Black Rock, thinking of Pell's Canal, brought up the idea again" (Saturday, 22 February 1823, LAC, MG 24, E1, Merritt Papers, vol. 33, 50).

3 For example, in 1799 a bill had been placed before the House of Assembly of Upper Canada asking for authority both to improve the road from Queenston to Lake Erie, and to build a canal to facilitate the passage of boats (*Preamble*

to a Bill to Improve and Amend the Communication between the Lakes Erie and Ontario, 15 June 1799. Printed by S. & G. Tiffany, Printers to the Province, 1799; reproduced by Brock University, 1968).

4 Robert Fleming Gourlay (1778–1863), who immigrated to Upper Canada in 1817 and wrote a guide for other immigrants (published as *Statistical Account of Upper Canada,* 2 vols.), was considered a radical and was refused a grant for land on which he had planned to settle newcomers.

5 Gourlay, *Statistical Account*, 274. William Kingsford wrote in 1865 that "the friends of the late Mr. Merritt assert that he communicated the idea [of a Niagara canal] to Gourlay" (Kingsford, *Canals of Canada*, 61).

6 Robert Legget, *Canals of Canada*, 166.

7 From fewer than 1,500 to over 3,000; Charles Hadfield, *The Canal Age*, 208, 78.

8 Ibid., 192.

9 Response of Grantham Township, 29 November 1817, Gourlay, *Statistical Account*, 424.

10 *Biography*, 81.

11 The Erie Canal was a government-funded undertaking from its inception. An American historian of the Erie has written, however, that New Yorkers "built their own canal," implying direct citizen involvement in the project. We assume he means that voters supported political candidates who would approve canal bills. The Welland, on the other hand, was truly a local "grassroots" initiative (Richard H. Wright, "Clinton's Ditch: Comment and Chronology," in Lionel Wyld, ed., *40′ x 28′ x 4′: The Erie Canal – 150 Years*, Rome, New York: Oneida County Erie Canal Commemorative Commission, 1967, 13).

12 Mackenzie, a journalist and politician, at first supported the Welland. Several times elected to the Legislative Assembly and first mayor of Toronto, he was appointed a director of the Welland Canal Company by the Legislature in 1834. From this experience came his charges against the directors. Defeated in the 1836 election, he was the principal leader of the Rebellion of 1837.

13 William Lyon Mackenzie, *The Welland Canal: A Weekly Journal*, 16 December 1835, 3.

14 William Notman and Jennings Taylor, *Portraits of British Americans*, vol. 2, 295.

15 See J.B. Yates and J. Warren, "Report," 1 June 1831 (LAC, RG 43, vol. 2099, *Minute Book of the Welland Canal Company, 7 December 1825–3 April 1837*, 144–5; hereafter *Minutes 1825–37*; also in *Third Report*, 473–4). Robert Randal, a contemporary, also praised Merritt's "indefatigable exertions" (Randal's "Report," 31 May 1830, ibid., 450).

16 "G.W.B's" Letter to the Editor of the St Catharines *Journal*, 2 June 1842, 3). Nevertheless, Merritt lacked the American's personal wealth and political position.

17 A translation from *Praesto et persto*, the family's Latin motto. Historian Donald Creighton referred to Merritt as the "eager, pushing, incurably romantic promoter ... of the First Welland Canal project" (*The Commercial Empire of the St. Lawrence 1760–1850,* Toronto: Ryerson, 1937, 256).

18 James K. Johnson, *Becoming Prominent*, 118.

19 Notman and Taylor, *Portraits*, 285.

20 Ibid.
21 *Journal*, 23 March 1823; LAC, MG 24, E1, *Merritt Papers*, vol. 33.
22 Merritt to Prendergast, 13 February 1825 (AO, F662, MS74, *Merritt Papers*, Package 12).
23 LAC, MG 24, K2, *Coventry Papers*, vol. 15, 263–4. For a diagram of the flume and weir at Merritt's sawmill at Lock 3, see "Diagram of William Hamilton Merritt's Land," *Survey of Lands 1826,* n.p.
24 Hugh Aitken, "A New Way to Pay Old Debts: A Canadian Experience," in W. Miller, ed., *Men in Business,* 71–90.
25 Keefer, a Thorold millowner, was the first president of the Welland Canal Company and the biggest shareholder in that enterprise. His sons Samuel and Thomas Coltrin were engineers active on the Welland.
26 13 February 1825, AO, F662, MS 74, *Merritt Papers*, Package 12.
27 Ibid.
28 23 September 1818, Montreal *Gazette;* 11 March 1824, LAC, MG 24, K2, *Coventry Papers,* vol. 15, 288–9.
29 Copied into his journal, LAC, MG 24, E1, vol. 33.
30 Ibid. For example, when the surveyor Hiram Tibbett suggested that a "railway" or inclined plane be used to overcome the Niagara Escarpment, a reader of the Niagara *Gleaner* on 25 November 1823 wrote: "To haul loaded boats over a Railway would be a bad plan, besides it would put a stop to all rafts of timber coming down, which might be a great branch of trade" (quoted in E.A. Cruikshank, "Inception," 71).
31 The Act of 1824 authorized the issue of 3,200 shares, each valued at £12.10, for a total of £40,000. According to Aitken, "almost the whole of this amount was subscribed by the end of 1824" (Aitken, *The Welland Canal Company*, 77).
32 S.J.R. Noel, *Patrons, Clients, Brokers*, 121. The First Welland was "a magnificent feat, not of engineering technology, which was ordinary, but above all of original and creative brokerage" (ibid., 123).
33 Ibid., 294.
34 Copied into his journal (LAC, MG 24, E1, vol. 33).
35 Merritt to Catharine Merritt, 10 April 1825 (AO, F662, MS 74, *Merritt Papers*, Package 12).
36 Catharine Merritt to Mrs Prendergast, 27 January 1826 (AO, F662, MS 74, *Merritt Papers, Package 12).* Catharine's spelling was only slightly more erratic than that of many of her contemporaries.
37 *Journal,* 16 March 1823 (LAC, MG 24, E1, *Merritt Papers*, vol. 33).
38 Catharine Merritt to Mrs Prendergast, 11 March 1828 (AO, F662, MS 74, *Merritt Papers*, Package 12).
39 Merritt to Simon McGillivray, Montreal, and to James Irvine, Quebec City, 5 November 1825 (LAC, RG 43, vol. 2101).
40 Merritt, "Account of the Welland Canal, Upper Canada," 167.
41 Merritt to Prendergast, 11 January 1824 (AO, F662, MS 74, *Merritt Papers*, Package 12); 13 February 1825. The Twelve Mile Creek route, of course, ran past his mills.
42 John MacTaggart, *Three Years in Canada*, vol. 2, 156.

43 Merritt to the Board of Directors, Welland Canal Company, 10 November 1831, quoted in Mackenzie, *The Welland Canal*, 3.
44 A point made long ago by Margaret Hamilton Alden in her preface to Thomas C. Keefer, *The Old Welland Canal and the Man Who Made It*, 9.
45 17 February 1836, *Third Report*, 14.
46 As early as 1823 he lamented in his journal (23 March 1823, LAC, MG 24, E1, *Merritt Papers*, vol. 33) that he had "spent money & gave myself much trouble to no benefit."
47 6 September, 1824 (LAC, RG 43, vol. 2098, *Minutes 1824–1825*, 8).
48 18 October 1824 (AO, F662, MS 74, *Merritt Papers,* Package 12).
49 Noel, *Patrons, Clients, Brokers,* 123.
50 Mackenzie, *The Welland Canal*, 2.
51 M.J. Patton, "Shipping and Canals," in Adam Shortt and Arthur Doughty, eds, *Canada and Its Provinces*, vol. 10, 524.
52 Merritt to Hillier, 12 December 1823 (LAC, RG 43, vol. 2101).
53 *Biography,* 65.
54 Quoted in Keefer, *The Old Welland Canal and the Man Who Made It*, 11.
55 A Scottish soldier and administrator, Lord Dalhousie was a supporter of Merritt and the Welland Canal Company: Port Dalhousie is named after him.
56 *Biography,* 96.
57 LAC, MG 24, E1, *Merritt Papers*, vol. 33.
58 "Memorandum for the Board April," undated but probably 11 April 1827 (LAC, MG 24, E1, *Merritt Papers*, vol. 33).
59 Black to Seaman, New York, 15 October 1828 (LAC, RG 43, vol. 2102; and see *Biography,* 110).
60 Merritt to Prendergast, 13 February 1825 (AO, F662, MS 74, *Merritt Papers,* Package 12).
61 "St. Catharines, November 1832" (*Third Report*, 504–12).
62 "Memorandum Concerning the Enlargement of the Welland Canal," 21 March 1837 (LAC, MG 24, E1, *Merritt Papers*, vol. 34).
63 Merritt to George Arthur, 16 February 1839 (LAC, RG 5, A-1, *Upper Canada Sundries*, vol. 216).
64 St Catharines, *Journal*, 9 May 1850, quoted in *Biography,* 373.
65 LAC, RG 11, vol. 65.5, 83, 105.
66 *Journal*, 24 July 1844 (LAC, MG 24, E1, *Merritt Papers*, vol. 34). Merritt's journal contains several lengthy memoranda relating to the next two months, but on 22 October he resigned (ibid., 83–4).
67 Merritt to Power, 26 May 1845, ibid.
68 Killaly to Merritt, 3 January, 1842 (LAC, RG 11, vol. 116, #416).
69 J.E. Hodgetts, *Pioneer Public Service*, 68.
70 Notman and Taylor, *Portraits*, 293.
71 Ibid., 294.
72 MacTaggart, *Three Years*, 147.
73 Bibliothèque Nationale (Paris), AN Colonies, C11A 31, 173–4. We are grateful to our colleague in the History Department at Brock University, Dr Jane McCleod, for obtaining photocopies of these documents for us.

74 Report of the Select Committee on Internal Resources, 31 March 1821, "Journal of the Legislative Assembly of Upper Canada," in Ontario Bureau of Archives, *Tenth Report of the Bureau of Archives for the Province of Ontario*, Toronto: Cameron, 1913, 433.

75 Nehemiah Merritt to Merritt, 18 July 1823, quoted in Mackenzie, *The Welland Canal*, 16 December 1835, 3. In its 1821 report to the colonial government, the Committee on Internal Resources had also stressed the colony's poverty ("Report of the Select Committee on Internal Resources," 31 March 1821, Ontario. Bureau of Archives, "Journal of the Legislative Assembly of Upper Canada, 1821," *10th Report, 1913*, 433–4).

76 Ibid.

77 Report of the Joint Committee Appointed to Confer upon the Improvement of the Internal Navigation of the Province of Upper Canada, 6 April 1825 (Quoted in Cruikshank, "Inception," 84).

78 "Annual Report" for 1830, 6 (*Third Report*, 444).

79 This policy was "diplomatic" and "astute," wrote Patrick Brode (*Sir John Beverley Robinson*, 109).

80 Ibid.

81 Francis Bond Head, *A Narrative*, 215.

82 AO, F662, MS 74, *Merritt Papers*, Package 12; and *Third Report*, 235.

83 Brode, *Sir John Beverley Robinson*, 120.

84 John Heisler, *Canals of Canada*, 88.

85 Randal, "Report" of 21 May 1830 (*Third Report,* 449).

86 The committee inspected the books of the company and came to the conclusion that, while anomalies existed, no "intentional fraud" had been committed (*Third Report*, 4). Mackenzie maintained that important documents "were withheld" from the inspectors (Mackenzie, *The Welland Canal*, 16 December 1835, 1).

87 *Third Report, 2.*

88 Mackenzie, *The Welland Canal,* 2. Patrick Grant Beaton, the company bookkeeper, was "of intemperate habits ... absent, and it is believed drunk, a state not unusual to him" (ibid.). We have found no evidence to support this description.

89 Ibid., 4.

90 *Third Report,* 4–5.

91 Ibid., 9.

92 *Biography*, 159.

93 Douglas McCalla, *Planting the Province*, 393.

94 William Kingsford, *The Canadian Canals*, 68.

95 Nicol Hugh Baird (1796–1849), a Scot, had worked with his father, an engineer on the Forth and Clyde Canal. In Canada he was employed as Clerk of Works on the Rideau in 1828 and later by the Board of Works in the Newcastle District. Hamilton Hartley Killaly (1800–1874) had served under his father, an Irish engineer, and emigrated to Upper Canada in 1835. He was Company Engineer on the Welland, 1838–40. In 1841 he was appointed chairman of the new Board of Works. From 1848 to 1851 he was "Engineer" on the Welland; from 1851 to 1859, Assistant Commissioner of Public Works.

96 Report of the Directors of the Welland Canal Company to Sir Francis Bond Head, 12 February 1838 (LAC, RG 43, vol. 2100, 59–60).
97 3 March 1838, Upper Canada. House of Assembly. *Journal*, 1837–38, 428.
98 Macaulay to Justice Jones, 5 March 1838 (AO, F662, MS 74, *Merritt Papers*, Package 13).
99 Following the Act of Union of Upper and Lower Canada, an Act of 18 September 1841 granted £1,659,682 to the newly created Board of Works.
100 John George Lambton, 1st Earl of Durham, was named Governor General and High Commissioner to British North America in 1838 with a mandate to report on the recent rebellion.
101 "Lt. Col. Phillpotts' letters of 12 February 1840 and 5th May 1841 relative to his first and second Reports on the Inland Navigation of the Canadas ..." (R. Louis Gentilcore and C. Grant Head, eds, *Ontario's History in Maps*, 185.) See also George Phillpotts, "Report," *Papers on Subjects Connected with the Duties of the Corps of Royal Engineers*, vol. 5, no. 6, 1842. Phillpotts's map is more detailed and suggestive than the text of his report.
102 Merritt to H. Bliss, 18 August 1840 (LAC, MG 24, E1, *Merritt Papers*).
103 *Letters from Lord Sydenham*, 113–14.
104 Hodgetts, *Pioneer Public Service,* 192.
105 Ibid., 191.
106 These events did not materially affect Killaly's career. He served on the Welland until 1851, when he was appointed Assistant Commissioner of Public Works. Relieved of this position in 1859, after having disagreed with the then chief commissioner, he continued to serve the Department in various capacities for many years.
107 Throughout North America in the 1840s, canal building involved "direct state participation" (Peter Way, *Common Labour*, 266).
108 In 1841 Samuel Keefer was appointed as the first Chief Engineer of the Board of Public Works of the United Canadas.
109 27 October, 1846 (LAC, RG 11, vol. 113, #296).
110 Keefer to Thomas Begly (Secretary of the Board of Works), 6 November 1846 (LAC, RG 43, vol. 2249, 114; and ibid.).
111 Most contractors accepted this change as necessary, but there was enough opposition that cash payments were resumed in 1850 (LAC, RG 11, vol. 123, *Letterbook January 1850–July 1851,* #7288, 25 May 1850).
112 Killaly to Begly, 25 November 1848 (LAC, RG 43, vol. 2250, 273–7).
113 LAC, RG 11, vol. 122, #4812 (30 December 1848); RG 43, vol. 1250, 355 (23 January 1849).
114 Begly to Killaly, 4 January 1849 (LAC, RG 11, vol. 122, 357, #4832).
115 Killaly to Begly, 23 January 1849 (LAC, RG 43, vol. 2250, 353).
116 Kingsford, *Canadian Canals,* 5 and 16.
117 Board to Woodruff, 3 May 1867 (LAC, RG 11, vol. 616, *Register 1860–1867*, #62405).
118 St Catharines *Daily Times*, 7 January 1870, 2.
119 St Catharines *Daily Times*, 5 March 1870, 2. Noting that a francophone, Hector-Louis Langevin, was Minister of Public Works, the *Times* earlier objected that so much money seemed to be spent "to please and pamper French Canadians"

(26 February 1870, 2). In anglophone Canada, certain grievances seem to be traditional.

120 St Catharines *Daily Times*, 11 March 1870, 2.

121 Ibid., 25 August 1871, 2.

122 *SP (No. 54) for 1871*, vol. 4, pt. 6, 56. The commissioners, who reported in February 1871, were Sir Hugh Allan (1810–1882), D.D. Calvin (1784–1884), Pierre Garneau (1823–1905), Alex Jardine, and S.L. Shannon (b. 1816). Sir Casimir Gzowski (1813–1898) chaired the commission and Samuel Keefer (1811–1890) replaced the original secretary on 6 December 1870.

123 John Page was referred to as "an officer of sterling integrity" (Thorold *Post,* 4 July 1890). He was an assistant engineer on the Second Welland Canal, then Chief Engineer of the Department of Public Works of the United Canadas and later Chief Engineer of the Department of Railways and Canals. Thomas Monro was the widely experienced resident engineer in charge of construction of the Northern Division of the Third Welland Canal.

124 27 July 1875, "Annual Report for 1874–75," *SP (No. 6) for 1876*, 46.

125 Legget, *Canals of Canada*, 173.

126 DPW to Bodwell, 12 September 1874 (LAC, RG 11, vol. 668, #26899).

127 Quoted in the Thorold *Post*, 23 July 1875, 2.

128 Ibid., 2 April 1880, 1.

129 St Catharines *Daily Times*, 20 August 1875, 2.

130 Ibid., 29 September 1875, 2.

131 Deepening to 14 ft (4.3 m) was accomplished in 1886–87.

132 "The facilities for this canal through Canada are much better than through the U.S." (Quoted in Thorold *Post*, 14 December 1883, 1).

133 Keefer, *Canadian Waterways from the Great Lakes to the Atlantic*, 17.

134 We plan to tell that story in another volume, *Building the Welland Ship Canal.*

135 By to General Mann, 13 July 1826 (LAC, RG 8, "C" Series, *British Military and Naval Records*, vol. 42, 58–60). He recommended a scale of up to 130 feet (39 m) in length and up to 50 feet (15 m) wide.

136 He maintained that any British government loan to the company should be conditional on the locks being no less than 20 ft (6 m) wide, to accommodate gunboats (LAC, RG 8, "C" Series, *British Military and Naval Records,* vol. 208, 50–1).

137 The various creeks running into Lake Ontario were named by their distance from the Niagara River. In 1819 the Royal Engineers' Lieutenant J.R. Portlock had rejected the idea of any Niagara canal, finding no route practicable (LAC, RG 8, *British Military and Naval Records*, vol. 39).

138 AO, F662, MS 74, *Merritt Papers*, Package 12.

139 Baird and Killaly, *Report.*

140 Phillpotts, "Report," 152.

141 "Memoranda Respecting various Public Works heretofore in progress, or projected in the Province of Canada ... prepared and submitted for the consideration of His Excellency the Governor General" (12 August 1841, Upper Canada House of Assembly, *Journal*, 1841, Appendix [C.C.]).

142 Such a route would follow "the course of the Grand River from Lake Erie, as far as Caledonia Bridge or Brantford, and from thence to be carried in the

most favorable direction into Burlington Bay with a view to its communication with Lake Ontario" (LAC, MG 12, Adm. 7, *Admiralty Secretary, Misc., 1845–46*, vol. 625, case 165, in Captain Warden's *Report on Canada*, dated 27 January 1846).

143 Samuel Keefer, "Annual Report," 17 October 1846 (LAC, RG 43, vol. 2249, Letterbook *1846–1847*, 90).

144 An Order-in-Council of 1861 (#56543) approved construction of "Block houses on the Canal" (LAC, RG 11, vol. 616, 137; see also LAC, RG 11, vol. 616, 139, #39685).

145 23 November 1883, Thorold *Post*, 2. The *Post* urged Ottawa to supply a small gunboat, because "it might be lonesome on Lake Erie."

146 Nevertheless, in 1823 Merritt's U.E.L. uncle Nehemiah of Saint John, New Brunswick, told him that to invest in a Niagara canal would be a "wild speculation ... I recommend to you to have nothing more to do with the canal, and not to build any more castles in the air" (Nehemiah Merritt to Merritt, 18 July 1823, quoted in Mackenzie, *The Welland Canal*, 3).

147 "Ontario," *Canadian Encyclopedia*, vol. 3, 1576.

148 Way, *Common Labour,* passim.

149 Killaly to the Receiver General, 20 February 1843 (LAC, RG 11, vol. 117, #1978; Killaly to Power, 27 August 1844 (LAC, RG 11, vol. 118, #4924).

150 Begly to Power, 22 October 1845 (LAC, RG 43, vol. 2129, #6905); Power to Begly, 4 November 1845 (LAC, RG 43, vol. 2248, 198).

151 Power to Begly, 14 February 1846 (LAC, RG 43, vol. 2248, 279, #9733).

152 Upper Canada's population was about 100,000 in 1821; about 210,000 in 1830; and about 407,000 in 1839 (Wesley Turner, *Life in Upper Canada*, 32).

153 Notman and Taylor, *Portraits*, Vol. 1, 296.

154 Edwin Guillet, *Pioneer Travel in Upper Canada*, 81, 87, 95.

155 Ibid., 136.

156 William Cosgrave to Henry Goulburn, 18 January 1819, quoted in Cruikshank, "Inception," 65. By 1839, ten years after the First Welland Canal opened, over one-third of the oak timber and one-fifth of the staves passing across Lake Ontario came from southwestern Ontario or the north shore of Lake Erie (McCalla, *Planting the Province*, 50).

157 "Preamble to a Bill to Improve and Amend the Communication between the Lakes Erie and Ontario," 1799.

158 "Petition of Sundry Inhabitants of the District of Niagara to the Legislative Assembly, 4 November 1818"; Ontario. Bureau of Archives, "Journal of the Legislative Assembly of Upper Canada, 1818," *10th Report, 1913,* 50.

159 James Strachan, *A Visit to the Province of Upper Canada*, 106. On the other hand, a Black Rock resident feared possible Canadian projects, because "it is so easy ... to improve the navigation of the St. Lawrence, that all our efforts to divert the trade will prove in vain" (ibid., 107, 110–11).

160 "Report of the Select Committee of the Legislature of New York, on the petition of the Inhabitants of the County of Oswego." In Assembly, 14th April 1834, 189–90, in Phillpotts, "Report," 52.

161 Wright had been superintendent of the Erie Canal. Originally a judge, he and his assistant, James Geddes, taught themselves canal engineering – run-

ning practice levels, designing locks, weirs, dams, etc., how to use hydraulic cement, and how to build machines to move earth and rock, and to cut roots and pull stumps (Elting Morison, *From Know-How to Nowhere*, 40).

162 C.J. Burckle (an Oswego merchant) to Phillpotts, 2 June 1839, Appendix D of Phillpotts, "Report," 184.

163 "An Observer" to the Editor, Niagara *Gleaner*, 8 November 1823, n.p.

164 J.M.S. Careless, *Union of the Canadas*, 58.

165 Christopher Andreae, *Lines of Country*, 126.

166 Keefer to Bronson, 27 March 1847 (LAC, RG 43, vol. 2249, 249); Keefer to Begly, 9 April 1847 (ibid., 266–7).

167 Hodgetts, *Pioneer Public Service*, 185.

168 Heisler, *Canals of Canada,* 97. The precise amount was $7,638,239.83.

169 For example, the First Welland "was not even remotely successful in commercial terms" (McCalla, *Planting the Province*, 124).

170 Thomas F. McIlwraith, "Freight Capacity and Utilization of the Erie and Great Lakes Canals before 1850," *Journal of Economic History*, vol. 36, 1976.

171 McCalla, *Planting the Province*, 124.

172 St Catharines *Evening Journal*, 23 August 1871.

173 Arthur Hickman of Buffalo in a speech to the New York State Assembly, Albany, 23 March 1882, quoted in Hill, *An Historical Review*, 194.

174 Heisler, *Canals of Canada*, 115.

175 Ibid., 116.

176 Hodgetts, *Pioneer Public Service*, 178.

177 18 March 1877, *Debates of the House of Commons*, 40 Victoria 1877, vol. 3, 1877, 1049.

178 Quoted in Thorold *Post*, 4 April 1879, 1.

179 Ibid., 18 August 1882, 1.

180 Ibid., 14 December 1881, 1.

181 New York *Herald,* quoted in Thorold *Post*, 21 May 1880, 3.

182 Merritt's journal, 21 July 1824 (*Biography*, 57).

183 Welland Canal Company Annual Report for 1825, in *Third Report*, 242.

CHAPTER TWO

1 Thorold *Post*, 4 June 1875, 2.

2 The so-called North Summit, just south of Thorold, did not present as much of a challenge. These two "summits" can be seen on a cross-section of canal on *No. 1 Rough Sketch of The Welland Canal from The Welland River to Lake Erie by Capt. J.E. Alexander* ... (Royal Geographical Society Map Room: Canada S/S. 76). These rises are still clearly visible on geological cross-sections prepared for the twentieth-century construction (P.J. Cowan, *The Welland Ship Canal between Lake Erie and Lake Ontario 1913–1932*, London: Offices of *Engineering*, 1935, 7).

3 George Phillpotts, "Report," 149.

4 In modern times, part of this break has been used for Highway 406. The present Welland Canal passes through another break to the east, the course of Ten Mile Creek.

5 Board of Works meeting, 11 August 1843 (LAC, RG 11, vol. 112, #78, 107–9).
6 This location, at the north end of the "Little Deep Cut," near the power station of the Third Canal, was known as "Kelly's Crossing."
7 Samuel Keefer to Begly, 3 August 1846 (LAC, RG 43, vol. 2249, 18); Killaly to Begly, 25 November 1848 (LAC, RG 43, vol. 2250, 273).
8 On 16 January a reporter for the Thorold *Post* commented on conditions on Section 26.
9 "Diagram of Widow E. Ball's land," *Survey of Lands 1826 (1834),* n.p.; *Survey of Lands 1826 (1831),* 157; No. 2: Rough Sketch of The Welland Canal from The Welland River to Lake Erie ...
10 Hiram Tibbett's Report of 10 May 1823 (*Third Report,* 213).
11 *Third Report*, 463–5.
12 10 November 1830, *Farmers' Journal and Welland Canal Intelligencer*, n.p.
13 SCM, 979.56.2.
14 John MacTaggart, *Three Years in Canada,* vol. 2, 153.
15 *Survey of Lands 1826* shows a reservoir and weir for outflow of Beaverdams Creek on George Marlatt's property ("Diagram of George Marlatt's Land," 87).
16 J. Bainbrigge, Royal Engineer, *Sketch of the Principal Roads in the Niagara District* ... 1840 (London: Public Record Office, MPHH 688, PFH/616).
17 Merritt to Hillier, 12 December 1823 (LAC, RG 43, vol. 2101, *Letterbook 1823–1825).*
18 Board Meeting, 20 September 1825 (LAC, RG 43, vol. 2098, *Minutes 1824–25*, 39–40). See also Merritt's article "Account of the Welland Canal, Upper Canada," 164: "Lake Erie will serve as a feeder."
19 "Memorandum Concerning the Enlargement of the Welland Canal," 21 March 1837 (LAC, MG 24, E1, *Merritt Papers*, vol. 34).
20 Phillpotts, "Report," 156.
21 Minutes of the Board of Works, 11 August 1843 (LAC, RG 11, vol. 112, 107–8); on 24 June 1843, engineer Samuel Power submitted comparative estimates for deepening to the level of either the Grand River or Lake Erie (LAC, RG 43, vol. 2097); Contract #439 with C.H. French, 4 November 1846 (LAC, RG 43, vol. 2359). Subsequently, a number of contracts were awarded to Thorold contractor, John Brown.
22 Robert Gourlay, *Statistical Account*, 274.
23 *Biography*, 42; LAC, MG 24, K2, Coventry Papers, vol. 15, 264.
24 Charles Hadfield, *Canal Age*, 208.
25 Robert Legget, *Canals of Canada,* passim.
26 Thomas Keefer, *Canals of Canada*, 16.
27 23 March 1823 (LAC, MG 24, E1, *Merritt Papers*, vol. 33).
28 Gourlay, *Statistical Account*, 426.
29 The names reflect the approximate distance from the Niagara River.
30 Robert and Abraham Nelles to Edward McMahon, 10 January 1817 (LAC, RG 5, A-1, *Upper Canada Sundries,* vol. 31).
31 James Chewett (1793–1862). In 1824 Commodore Robert Barrie of the Royal Navy recommended such a route to Sir Peregrine Maitland (15 June, LAC RG 5, A-1, *Upper Canada Sundries,* vol. 67).

32 On this tunnel, see R. Louis Gentilcore and C. Grant Head, *Ontario History in Maps*, 181.

33 11 December 1845 (LAC, Adm.7/625, "Admiralty – Secretary, Misc. 1845–46 – Captain Warden's Report on Canada").

34 "Preamble to a Bill" (1799).

35 "An Act to render effectual certain securities to be given by the Welland Canal Company, for a loan advanced by his Majesty's government ... and also for authorizing the making of a lateral cut from the Welland canal, through the town of Niagara, to the mouth of the river Niagara, by a company incorporated for that purpose" (10 Geo. IV, Ch. IX, 20 March 1829).

36 *Third Report*, 517–28.

37 Board Meeting, 20 November 1835 (LAC, RG 43, vol. 2099, 369–72).

38 An Act to provide for the permanent completion of the Welland Canal, and for other purposes herein mentioned, 7 William IV, 1st Session, Ch. XCII.

39 Bonnycastle, *The Canadas in 1841*. The "Frontier Route" was again urged in early 1873 during discussions on the route for the Third Canal.

40 Welland County Historical Society, *Papers and Records*, vol. 5 (1938), 232.

41 *Third Report*, 212–13; 214 ("Address to the Inhabitants of Upper Canada and Lower Canada," 27 June 1823); 222–3; 217–18; 221–2. Nathan Roberts (1776–1852) was described by the pre-eminent American engineer Benjamin Wright as "a prudent, careful man, and free from any visionary plans of internal improvement" (Wright to William Hamilton Merritt, 1 October 1824, ibid., 253).

42 Ibid., 222–3.

43 Ibid., 245–6.

44 Don Thompson, *Men and Meridians: The History of Surveying and Mapping in Canada*, vol. 1, 243. See below, chapter 10, on the "grog bosses" during the First Welland's construction.

45 *Third Report,* 244–5.

46 Ibid., 250.

47 8 June 1825, ibid., 286. John DeCew (1766–1855).

48 William Lyon Mackenzie on the First Welland Canal's route (*Third Report*, 137).

49 Ibid.

50 Meeting of 1 January 1829, following consideration of reports from engineers Alfred Barrett and James Geddes (LAC, RG 43, vol. 2099, 104). Originally Merritt had suggested only a small auxiliary cut from Chippawa Creek to the Grand River – that is, the "Western Branch."

51 J.E. Alexander, *No. 1 Rough Sketch*, Map Room, Canada S/SS. 76; Welland Canal Company *Survey of Lands*, c. 1826 (Brock University, Niagara Collection); map accompanying "Report" by Baird and Killaly to the Welland Canal Company, 23 February 1838 (Upper Canada House of Assembly, Appendix to *Journal*, 339).

52 23 February 1838, "Engineers' Report to the President and Directors of the Welland Canal Company" (Appendix to the *Journal* of the House of Assembly, 340). The First Canal on the Escarpment would become "exclusively the channel for the discharge of the surplus water" (341). In the text of their

report, Killaly and Baird also considered "a line direct from Port Dalhousie to near Thorold" (such as was followed for the Third Canal), but rejected it on the grounds of expense (340).

53 DPW to the Welland's Superintendent, 18 September 1854 (LAC, RG 11, vol. 126, #16098).

54 T.C. Clarke suggested three possibilities: opening a canal from the St Lawrence to Lake Champlain and enlarging the Welland; a ship canal from Georgian Bay to Lake Simcoe and thence to Lake Ontario (the "Hurontario" line); Lake Huron via the French River to Lake Nipissing and down the Ottawa River to Montreal (the Georgian Bay route) (Canada. *Sessional Papers for 1857*, "Annual Report of the Department of Public Works," Appendix to Appendix No. 29, Section A). Construction of either of the latter might have reduced the Welland to secondary importance.

55 23 January 1872 (*SP [No. 6] for 1874*, Appendix 7, 47–59).

56 Merritt to Lieutenant-Governor Maitland, Welland County Historical Society, *Papers and Records*, vol. 5 (1938), 232.

57 *Third Report*, 219–20.

58 Ibid., 221.

59 LAC, RG 43, vol. 2098, 39–40.

60 *Third Report*, 273.

61 Ibid., 367–8.

62 *Biography*, 87.

63 R.H. Bonnycastle, *Royal Engineers ... Shewing situation of new Fortress*. Brock University Map Library 141-C (NMC, Ottawa).

64 Merritt, *Account*, 159–68. Although the Grand was eventually connected to Chippawa Creek through the Feeder Canal, the link was not built as Merritt envisaged it (chapter 6).

65 Ibid., following 208.

66 LAC, RG 43, vol. 2103, *Estimate Book 1824–29*, 55, 74. There is still a ditch, running parallel to the Feeder but separated from it by a road, which could well be that trench. We are grateful to Mr William Lewis, a local historian from Welland, who discovered this ditch while out driving, and brought it to our attention. It follows almost exactly the route shown in the Keefer map, dated 5 June 1828.

67 28 December 1828, *Third Report*, 383.

68 LAC, RG 43, vol. 2099, 104–5.

69 Memorandum re Grand River Dam, late 1828/early 1829, LAC, RG 43, vol. 2097, *Letters and Memorandums Respecting the Welland Canal, 28 October 1828–3 November 1829*, n.d., n.p.

70 This idea came up again during discussions for the Fourth Canal.

71 *Third Report*, 221.

72 Theodore Dwight, *The Northern Traveller*, 79 and 99.

73 At a meeting on 26 October 1830, the company's board resolved: "To connect the Lakes by the shortest possible route, it is necessary to make a lateral Cut to the most direct & best point on Lake Erie which will cost $100,000" (LAC, RG 43, vol. 2099, 132).

74 By Samuel Keefer in late 1830 and early 1831 (*Third Report*, 454–8).

75 During this debate, John Strachan (later Bishop) wrote to another member of the Family Compact, John Macaulay: "Whatever he [Boulton] touches he poisons and while he remains agent [of the Bank of Upper Canada] any increase of capital is doubtful, or any additional assistance to the Welland Canal ... It is reported that several members will vote against the measure [to lend the Welland Canal further aid] because they say it is enriching the Attorney General" (AO, F32, MS 71, *Macaulay Papers*, 28 February 1831).

76 23 May 1831, *Third Report*, 473.

77 Robert Randal, *First General Report from Robert Randal, Esquire*, York, Baxter, 1831, 10.

78 Report of J.B. Yates and John Warren on possible Lake Erie harbours, 1 June 1831 (*Third Report*, 474).

79 23 February 1838, "Engineers' Report to the President and Directors of the Welland Canal Company," *Upper Canada, Journal of the House of Assembly for 1838*, Appendix, 341.

80 Phillpotts, "Report," 155.

81 9 October 1840 (LAC, RG 43, vol. 2100, 143).

82 LAC, RG 11, vol. 688, #28189.

83 Report of 23 April 1872 (*SP [No. 6] for 1873*, Appendix 7, 45).

84 "Petition of the Mariners and Vessel Owners on the Inland Waters and Great Lakes of North America, 16 April 1874 (LAC, RG 11, vol. 162).

85 On 25 July 1827, Bonnycastle, then Commander at Kingston, wrote to Merritt: "I have suggested to the Home Govt the practicability of a canal from yours to the Short Hills, either by Ball's Valley to Beckitt's Mills, or, above the Deep Cut" (quoted in *Biography*, 86).

86 Niagara *Gleaner*, 11 December 1824, 2.

87 Ibid., 5 February 1825, 3. The Twelve Mile Creek route had "disadvantages"; to build a harbour at Port Dalhousie would be "impractical" (ibid., 2 April 1825, 3). See also Francis Hall's reports: on the Twelve Mile Creek route, *Third Report*, 219–20; on the "Chippawa Canal" (from Chippawa to the Niagara River below the Escarpment), ibid., 236–7 and 242; and on Port Dalhousie harbour, ibid., 245.

88 Niagara *Gleaner*, 2 April 1825, 3.

89 Ibid., 22 January 1825, 2; 22 January 1825, 3; 5 February 1825; 2 April 1825, 3; 28 May 1825, 3.

90 *Farmers' Journal and Welland Canal Intelligencer*, quoted in the Niagara *Gleaner*, 29 April 1826, 3.

91 Niagara *Gleaner*, 2 April 1825, 3.

92 23 August 1824, *Third Report*, 221.

93 Merritt to his wife, 5 March 1825 (AO, F662, *Merritt Papers*, MS 74, Package 12).

94 2 December 1825, *Third Report*, 262 and 352.

95 Niagara *Gleaner*, 2 April 1825, 3.

96 MacTaggart, *Three Years*, 148 and 156. Nevertheless MacTaggart approved of the route chosen!

97 *Third Report*, 16.

98 Ibid., 4.
99 Baird and Killaly, "Report," 23 January 1838, 339.
100 *Third Report*, 8–9.
101 Bonnycastle remained a critic of the Welland project, doubting that there would ever be "a fortunate termination of this interminable job" (*The Canadas*, 196).
102 20 December 1844 (LAC, RG 43, vol. 2248, 44–5).
103 *Debates of the Legislative Assembly of United Canada, 1841–1867*, vol. IX, Part 1, 1018–24. Shanly's letter was dated 11 October 1854 (Province of Canada, *Journal of the House of Assembly*, Appendix No. 29, 1857).
104 24 March 1855 (LAC, RG 11, vol. 127, #17174).
105 E. Parent to Department of Public Works, 1 May 1872 (LAC, RG 11, vol. 643, #22655).
106 Toronto *Mail*, 10 January 1873.
107 Ibid., 3, 6, 7, and 8 February 1873.
108 L.S. Lundy et al. to DPW, 20 January 1873 (LAC, RG 11, vol. 668, #28011, #28190, and #28207).
109 29 April 1872 (*SP [No. 6] for 1873*, Appendix 7, 38–9).
110 24 August 1895, Royal Commission on Transportation to Department of Railways and Canals (LAC, RG 43, vol. 469, #140520).
111 22 November 1825, *Third Report*, 137.
112 St Catharines *News*, 20 February 1873, 2.
113 Toronto *Mail*, 4 February 1873, 3 (LAC, RG 11, vol. 159, 3222).
114 *Journal*, quoted in Thorold *Post*, 27 August 1886, 3.
115 Gourlay, *Statistical Account*, 436–7.
116 The Americans had opened the Weitzel lock (515 by 80 by 17 feet, 156 by 24.3 by 5.1 m) and the Poe lock in 1897 (800 by 100 by 21 feet, 243 by 304.6.4 m) at Sault Ste Marie, and the Canadian lock at the "Soo" had opened in 1895 (900 by 600 by 18.25 feet, 274.3 by 18.3 by 5.56 m).

CHAPTER THREE

1 Because this chapter presents a detailed discussion of the role of the engineers and contractors involved with the canal, and in particular of the assignment of the contracting sections, readers who are more interested in the day-to-day construction of the Welland may wish to go directly to chapter 4, "Digging the Ditch." They may, however, want to refer back to chapter 3 later, to check specific details.
2 *Biography*, 42.
3 27 November 1846 (LAC, RG 43, vol. 2249, 140).
4 Thomas Begly to the firm of E. & G.W. Blunt of New York, 8 June 1853 (LAC, RG 11, vol. 125, #13499).
5 Ronald Shaw, *Canals for a Nation*, 161–2.
6 Daniel H. Calhoun, *The American Civil Engineer: Origins and Conflict*, 22, quoted in Shaw, *Canals for a Nation*, 161.
7 Shaw, ibid., 163.

8 Roberts, who was a mathematics teacher, speculator, and engineer with experience on the Erie Canal construction, offered invaluable advice to the First Welland Canal builders. "A prudent, careful man" (*Report of a Hearing Before a Select Committee of the Upper Canada Assembly*, 7 December 1825).

9 Much of our biographical information on the engineers' careers was compiled from a variety of sources for our volume "*The 'Great Swivel Link*,'" published by The Champlain Society, and has been paraphrased from the footnotes contained therein. References to payments for work on the Erie Canal are to be found in the Comptroller's Reports of the State of New York Canal Commission. Payments to engineers on the Welland Canal are in LAC, RG 43, vol. 2107.

10 LAC, RG 5, A1, vol. 60, *Civil Secretary's Correspondence.*

11 Robert Passfield, *Building the Rideau Canal*, 84.

12 While there, he spent time with his uncle, Charles Poulett Thomson, who became first Baron Sydenham following his appointment as the first governor general of the United Canadas.

13 Nicholas Flood Davin, *The Irishman in Canada*, 435–6.

14 J.E. Hodgetts, *Pioneer Public Service,* passim.

15 Samuel Power to Thomas Begly, Secretary of Department of Public Works, 25 June 1846, LAC, RG 43, vol. 2248, 412.

16 Power, 17 February 1845, LAC, RG 43, vol. 2248, 78.

17 Robert Legget, "John Page," 50.

18 LAC, RG 11, vol. 681, 668, 689.

19 LAC, RG 43, vol. 433, #85620, #151597.

20 LAC, RG 43, vol. 432, #137839, #137936.

21 LAC, RG 43, vol. 442, #160702, vol. 2115, #161373.

22 LAC, RG 43, vol. 445, #180200, vol. 465, #128050.

23 William Hamilton Merritt, *Account*, 159–68, map and drawing following p. 208.

24 *Survey of Lands 1826*, passim.

25 J. Rodney Millard, *The Master Spirit of the Age*, 6.

26 23 February 1842 (LAC, RG 11, vol. 116, #536). Similar letters were sent to several other engineers in Michigan and New York State.

27 LAC, RG 43, vol. 2107, 68, 79.

28 A survey of the records of the Engineering Institute of Canada in Library and Archives Canada in 1995 included a number of Keefers: Charles Henry, Edward Coltrin, George Alexander, and Joseph Alexander of Victoria, BC, Samuel and Thomas Coltrin Jr of Ottawa (LAC, MG 28, I.277, vol. 9).

29 Known as the "Dean of Canadian Engineers" and an expert on water control and supply, Thomas C. Keefer worked on the building of the Second Welland Canal and advised on the Third.

30 George A. Rawlyk, "Thomas Coltrin Keefer," 190.

31 Abraham Rees, *The Cyclopædia*, 41 volumes, 1810–1824.

32 David Stevenson, *Sketch of the Civil Engineering of North America*, 169–70.

33 Thomas C. Keefer, *The Canals of Canada*, 10.

34 Annual Report of the Board of Directors for 1827 (*Third Report*, 364).

35 E.V. Bodwell to DPW, 13 September 1878 (LAC, RG 11, vol. 693, #76190).
36 Thorold *Post*, 20 September 1878, 4.
37 10 December 1829, *Third Report*, 403.
38 John Donaldson, 5 April 1835 (AO, F662, MS 74, *Merritt Papers*, Package 13).
39 8 April, 1836 (AO, F662, MS 74, *Merritt Papers*, Package 13).
40 Thorold *Post*, 23 March 1877, 1.
41 Killaly to Collier, 18 January 1849 (LAC, RG 43, vol. 2250, 344–5).
42 Neilson and Co. to F. Braun, 15 January 1872 (LAC, RG 11, vol. 643, #20496).
43 "Report of the Select Committee of the Legislature of New York, on the petition of the Inhabitants of the county of Oswego," 14 April 1834, in Appendix H of George Phillpotts, "Report," 189.
44 The letter is dated "York, November 23, 1825" (*Third Report,* 287–8).
45 For example, Colonel John By, in charge of construction of the Rideau, wrote to General Gother Mann in England on 13 July 1825, urging locks of 110–130 feet by 40–50 feet width (LAC, RG 8, "C" Series, *British Military and Naval Records*, vol. 42, 60), and to Lieut.-Gov. Maitland's Secretary on 1 March 1827, advocating locks of 150 by 50 feet (LAC, RG 5, *Upper Canada Sundries*, vol. 83).
46 John L. McWhirter to Frederic Braun, Secretary, DPW, 27 June 1872 (LAC, RG 11, vol. 158, #24159).
47 Samuel Keefer to Begly, 25 August 1847 (LAC, RG 43, vol. 2249, 374–5).
48 DPW to Killaly, 30 December 1848 (LAC, RG 11, vol. 122, 351, #4812).
49 Henry Robert Emmerson (1853–1914), 8 July 1904, *Debates of the House of Commons*, 1904, vol. 4, 6351.
50 30 November 1880 (LAC, RG 43, vol. 398, #89892).
51 Ellis to Railways and Canals, 4 March 1882 (LAC, RG 43, vol. 795, file 48).
52 In fact, electricity was not used in either the construction or the operation of Canada's canals until the early 1890s. Thomas Monro had a small hydroelectric plant built near Lock 4 of the Beauharnois Canal in 1891. Two years later Monro began to prepare plans to operate the Soulanges completely with electricity (Passfield, *Technology*, 95).
53 DPW to Monro, 9 April and 20 May 1886 (LAC, RG 43, vol. 413, #68500; 20 May #111584).
54 Ibid., 4 June 1875, 2.
55 Prescott to Begly, 18 February 1844 (LAC, RG 11, vol. 118, #4044).
56 Begly to Power, 22 March 1844 (ibid., #4165).
57 Killaly to Begly, 14 March 1849 (LAC, RG 43, vol. 2250, 445).
58 Report by Baird and Killaly to the Welland Canal Company, 23 February 1838 (Upper Canada. House of Assembly. *Journal*, Appendix, 339; re-printed in St Catharines by Hiram Leavenworth, 1838).
59 20 September 1842, "Articles of Agreement entered into between George Barnet of St. Catharines ... and the Board of Works of Canada for all the masonry work timberwork puddling and earth work" for the Mountain Locks of the Welland Canal (LAC, RG 43, vol. 2247, file "Legal Documents 1842–1843").
60 Contract #5439 for Section 27, 26 September 1877 (LAC, RG 43, vol. 2492).
61 Ellis to Department of Railways and Canals, 28 April 1880 (LAC, RG 43, vol. 398, #87693).

62 In his *Journal*, 21 July 1824 (LAC, MG 24, E1, *Merritt Papers*, vol. 33).
63 Ronald Shaw, *Canals for a Nation*, 38.
64 LAC, MG24, E1, *Merritt Papers*, vol. 33.
65 Ibid.; LAC, RG 43, vol. 2101.
66 LAC, RG 43, vol. 2098, 11.
67 24 November, AO, F662, MS 74, *Merritt Papers*, Package 12.
68 LAC, RG 43, vol. 2098, 26–8.
69 Ibid., 50–1.
70 Oliver Phelps, a miller, philanthropist, and controversial contractor on the First Welland Canal, was "a hard working, active, stirring and wide-awake driving person" ("Junius," "A Walk Around Town," n.p.).
71 *Third Report*, passim.
72 Ibid., passim.
73 LAC, RG 43, vol. 2247.
74 They were daunted by some of the colonel's methods and declined to apply them in Niagara (Legget, *Rideau Waterway*, 51). Unfortunately, Legget did not identify them.
75 22 March 1836, *Third Report*, 155.
76 LAC, RG43, vol. 2099, 104.
77 Ibid., 106–7.
78 Ibid., 111.
79 This assumption has been made on the basis that only Lewis and Newlove (both of whom had come from the Erie and settled in the area) had been paid on the Erie, and the other names do appear locally.
80 2 June 1831, *Third Report*, 478–9.
81 19 September 1829, AO, F662, MS 74, *Merritt Papers*, Package 12.
82 LAC, RG 43, vol. 2100, 84, 132; LAC, RG 43, vol. 2097; SCM, *Letterbook "O"*, 8–9; LAC, RG 43, vol. 2106, 177.
83 LAC, RG 43, vol. 2100, 149; ibid., 150; there may have been two contracts to Doushon & Merritt – according to *Letterbook "O"* in the St Catharines Museum, on 2 December a contract was issued to Douthele & Merritt to excavate rock and earth from Stone Bridge to Port Colborne, which contract was cancelled 9 February 1841 and awarded to Merritt alone.
84 Macaulay to Harrison, 11 January 1841, SCM, *Letterbook "O"*, 63–4.
85 Lyons to Macaulay, 14 January, 1841, SCM, *Letterbook "O"*, 67–8; 29 January, ibid., 70; 2 March, ibid., 73; Macaulay to Lyons, ibid., 75.
86 *Journal* of the House of Assembly, 1841, Appendix (C.C.), 1.
87 27 December 1841; LAC, RG 11, vol. 116, #396; 17 February 1843, LAC, RG 11, vol. 117, #1965; 10 April 1846, LAC, RG 43, vol. 2248, 342–3. In this endnote, as in some in following chapters, several references are presented in one note.
88 LAC, RG 43, vol. 2539 – List of Contracts. From here on, unless otherwise indicated, information on the allocation of contracts has been taken from this volume.
89 Sharpe and Quinn's sureties were two innkeepers, one from St Catharines, the other from Chippawa. Information on sureties comes from LAC, RG 11, vol. 114, 64.

90 SP *(No. 6) for 1873*. All the quotations and statistics cited on pages 110 and 112 are from this *Sessional Paper*.

91 Three in St Catharines, one each from Thorold, Queenston, and Dunnville, and two from Welland; one each from Hamilton, Cookstown, Oil Spring, Walkerton, Belleville, Whitby, Prescott, Ottawa, and Montreal, two from Brantford.

92 Thorold *Post,* 30 June 1876. Brown had died on 28 June.

93 SP *(No. 58) for 1878.*

94 Correspondence in LAC, RG 11, vol. 668.

95 LAC, RG 11, vol. 689, #31388; *Daily Times* of 24 August.

96 LAC, RG 43, vol. 2491, 27 July 1875.

97 Board of Works to contractor J. & A. Wood, 19 August, LAC, RG 11, vol. 94, #1020.

98 Between MacDonald's Point near Coteau Landing and Cascades Point.

99 François Cartier, *Canal de Soulanges*, 39.

100 Passfield, *Technology,* passim.

101 James Angus, *A Respectable Ditch*, passim.

CHAPTER FOUR

1 George Keefer, quoted in *Biography*, 67.

2 Report of the Directors, 18 December 1826 (*Third Report*, 306).

3 John MacTaggart, *Three Years*, 147.

4 *Biography*, 77.

5 Annual Report of the Welland Canal Company for 1824 (*Third Report*, 227).

6 The spelling is in the original (*Third Report,* 196).

7 Eight named American directors writing to George Keefer, President of the Welland Canal Company, 22 December 1824, in *Third Report*, 235.

8 Ibid., 196, 226, 227.

9 Annual Report of the Welland Canal Company for 1824 (ibid., 227). See also Niagara *Gleaner*, 12 February 1825, 3, for Keefer Sr's letter to stockholders.

10 M.J. Patton, "Shipping and Canals," in Adam Shortt and Arthur Doughty, eds, *Canada and Its Provinces*, vol. 10, 525.

11 Merritt to Prendergast, 13 February 1825 (AO, F662, MS 74, *Merritt Papers,* Package 12).

12 *Third Report*, 44.

13 He had circulated a pamphlet to this effect in September, 1824 (William Lyon Mackenzie, *The Welland Canal*, 1).

14 Report of the Directors, 18 December 1826 (*Third Report*, 304).

15 Merritt, "Account," 160. One chain was equal to sixty-six feet.

16 AO, F662, MS 74, *Merritt Papers*, Package 12.

17 Annual Report of the Welland Canal Company for 1829, 31 December 1829 (*Third Report,* 431).

18 Postscript to Merritt's "Account," 168.

19 Annual Report of the Welland Canal Company for 1827 (*Third Report*, 364).

20 Report of the President and Directors of Welland Canal Company to Shareholders, *Third Report,* 18 December 1826, 302–3.
21 Extract from the *Farmers' Journal and Welland Canal Intelligencer*, quoted in the Niagara *Gleaner*, 29 April 1826, 3.
22 Christopher Andreae, *Lock 24*, 44.
23 *Third Report*, 75, 79, 84, and 79.
24 Lefferty's testimony, 16 January 1830 (*Third Report*, 419).
25 Ibid., 142, 574, 9, and 10.
26 7 July 1827 (ibid., 54–5).
27 LAC, RG 43, vol. 2099, 102.
28 Ward to Merritt, 30 August 1852 (AO, F662, MS 74, *Merritt Papers,* Package 16). At the time, Ward lived in Montezuma, New York. On 5 December 1859 Ward again wrote to Merritt, referring to Merritt's having presented his petition to the government "last winter," and asking him to bring his plea for assistance forward again in the coming session of the Legislature. There the matter disappears from the record.
29 Hiram Tibbett(s)'s report of 23 May 1823, *Third Report*, 213.
30 Mann to Lord Dorchester, 6 December 1788 (LAC, MG 11, Colonial Office 42, *Original Correspondence* – "Q" Series, vol. 20, #258).
31 10 May 1823 (*Third Report,* 213).
32 "A.B." [from Thorold], 25 November 1823, Niagara *Gleaner*, 29 November 1823, n.p.
33 LAC, RG 43, vol. 2248, 415. The concept was revived in 1898 but never seriously considered again for the Welland.
34 James Geddes Report, 27 December 1828 (*Third Report*, 384).
35 Mackenzie's wording in his "Twenty-Ninth Charge" (*Third Report,* 4).
36 4 February 1836 (ibid., 435).
37 In his Report of 3 October 1833 Benjamin Wright diagnosed the problem as "quick-sands" (*Third Report,* 519). The situation was not limited to the area of the Deep Cut, however. A "sandy bottom" was discovered on the feeder route as well (Capt. J.E. Alexander, *No. 1 Rough Sketch of the Welland Canal from the Welland River to Lake Erie*, 77).
38 Randal's "Report," 31 May 1830 (*Third Report*, 446).
39 Twenty-ninth charge (*Third Report*, 4).
40 *Third Report,* 236, 53, and 52–3.
41 Ibid., 53, 383, and 16.
42 23 February 1838, Baird and Killaly, *Report*, 341.
43 *Third Report,* 9. In 1836 George Keefer Jr agreed, stating that "no effectual remedy could have been adopted to avoid slips," the basic problem being quicksand well below the surface (*Third Report*, 170). For Francis Hall's testimony on the matter, see ibid., 44–5.
44 Kingsford, *Canals of Canada*, 77.
45 Minutes of the Welland Canal Company, 2 June 1831 (*Third Report*, 478).
46 James Ross, on Oliver Phelps's work at the Deep Cut, evidence given to the 1836 enquiry, 24 March 1836 (*Third Report*, 163). On the tools and equipment used on the Welland, see *Third Report,* 3, 9, 12, 27, 48, 81–4, 160, 172, and 179. As well, see Abraham Rees's *Cyclopaedia*, vol. 6 for contemporary machinery.

47 Report of Rheddy Cusack, 10 May 1824 (*Third Report*, 222).

48 On 21 July 1824 he recorded in his journal: "An advantage will be derived for beginning early, as many of the contractors being out of work wil have all their tools on hand and prepared to commence immediately" (LAC, MG 24, E1, vol. 33).

49 Merritt to Macaulay, 22 June 1825 (LAC, RG 43, vol. 2101). In 1827 the Welland Canal Company paid a total of £149.11.4 to various merchants for cordage. By September of that year one Thomas Akenhead was able to supply the company's needs (LAC, RG 43, vol. 2103, "Cash Journal").

50 Merritt to a Select Committee of the Legislature, 15 December 1825, on a petition for remission of import duties (*Third Report*, 256).

51 According to the Cash Journal, contractors were paid a total of £682.4.3 for duties on imported goods in 1826 (LAC, RG 43, vol. 2107).

52 30 November 1825 (*Third Report*, 256). When Yates was authorized to buy a steam dredge in 1834, the authorities were again persuaded not to enforce import duties on it (Mackenzie, *The Welland Canal*, 16 December 1835, 4).

53 Testifyng at the Select Committee on 3 March 1836, on his loss of shanty furniture and other property which the company had helped him to buy, Phelps listed "250 yoke of oxen and yokes, 150 large carts, 55 Waggons, 44 horses, 25 sets of harness ... Machines purchased ... scrapers and crow-bars." His evidence included several inventories of materials purchased from sub-contractors, including shovels, axes, wheelbarrows, and ploughs (*Third Report,* 81–4).

54 Prices are taken from the *Third Report*, and Minutes of the Welland Canal Company (LAC, RG 43, vol. 2098).

55 LAC, RG 43, vol. 2103, 32, 55–7, 74, 67.

56 LAC, RG 43, vol. 2098, 21; 11; and 10 September 1825 (LAC, RG 43, vol. 2098, 36); 7 December 1825 (LAC, RG 43, vol. 2099, 3).

57 *Third Report*, 75, 86, and 84.

58 Robert Passfield, *Building the Rideau Canal*, 78.

59 *Third Report,* 84.

60 Board Minutes, 9 June 1827 (*Third Report*, 375).

61 *Third Report*, 374; LAC, RG 43, vol. 2101.

62 *Third Report*, 376. Phelps, Pratt & Simpson, and probably also Donaldson, had been contractors on the Erie.

63 Merritt, "Account," 160. George Keefer Jr's description of this machine is on page 167.

64 Ibid., 167.

65 Phelps to Merritt, 16 May 1827 (*Third Report*, 85). See also E.P. Johnson, "Canal Engineering Yesterday and Today," 368.

66 On "barrow runs" see Terry Coleman, *The Railway Navvies*, 46. See also Asa Briggs, *The Nineteenth Century*, 16 for a description of such a device on the excavation of cuttings for the London to Birmingham Railway in 1837. This may be a case of a universal problem inspiring a common solution.

67 MacTaggart, *Three Years*, 103–4; Ronald Shaw, *Canals for a Nation*, 39, states that trees "were brought down using a cable attached a hundred ft up their trunks, which wound around a roller turned by an endless screw and crank" (ibid.).

68 Scows were flat-bottomed boats, usually with broad squared ends.
69 *Third Report*, 212–13.
70 Merritt to Prendergast, 29 April 1829 (AO, MS 74, *Merritt Papers*, Package 12).
71 *Third Report*, 385.
72 LAC, RG 43, vol. 2099, 271, and vol. 2102, passim. In 1840 Louis Shickluna was paid $400 (£100) for building a pile driver (LAC, RG 43, vol. 2106, 184).
73 *Third Report*, 163.
74 Ibid., 173, 171; MacTaggart, *Three Years*, 159 and *Third Report*, 424; LAC, RG 43, vol. 2103; an assumption based on specifications in a contract with Marshall Lewis et al. on the Gravelly Bay extension, 3 June 1831 (LAC, RG 43, vol. 2097).
75 MacTaggart, *Three Years*, 159.
76 Alfred Barrett (*Third Report*, 404, 442–3).
77 From 24 March 1834 through June 1835 either Clark, the company secretary, or Merritt himself was in correspondence with the firm or with the American financier Yates who, it appears, initiated the project, over what became a "useless" expenditure of the company's money (LAC, RG 43, vol. 2099; *Minutes of the Board*, passim; LAC, RG 43, vol. 2102, passim).
78 LAC, RG 43, vol. 2102.
79 3 July and 1 July 1835 (LAC, RG 43, vol. 2099, 327, 321).
80 *Third Report*, 91.
81 Directors of the Welland Canal Company to J.B. Robinson, 5 June 1833 (LAC, RG 43, vol. 2099; *Minutes 1825–1837*, 239–40).
82 An act passed 4 March 1837, ch. 92.
83 Begly to W.B. Robinson, 4 March 1842 (LAC, RG 11, vol. 116, #556).
84 DPW to Dominick Daly, Provincial Secretary, 2 November 1843 (LAC, RG 11, vol. 94, #3490).
85 LAC, RG 43, vol. 2250, 257. Proof of the need for an adequate supply of basic equipment was an order placed by the company's secretary with Bronson and Crocker of Oswego on 31 October 1836 for six dozen shovels (LAC, RG 43, vol. 2102).
86 23 June 1845 (LAC, RG 43, vol. 2248, 144).
87 15 May 1845 (LAC, RG 43, vol. 2248, 127; LAC, RG43, vol. 2250, 388; Power's report, 26 May 1846 (LAC, RG 43, vol. 2248); 12 May 1845 (LAC, RG 43, vol. 2248, 124–5).
88 LAC, RG 43, vol. 2097, 12 July; vol. 2248, 33.
89 11 August 1849 (LAC, MG 24, E1, *Merritt Papers*, vol. 31).
90 20 February 1846 (LAC, RG 43, vol. 2248, 286); Annual Report of Samuel Keefer, 10 January 1848 (LAC, RG 43, vol. 2250, 49).
91 Appendix C to *SP (No. 4) for 1861*.
92 Brown, a trained stonemason, had numerous contracts on both the Second and Third Canals.
93 Power to Begly, 25 August 1843 (LAC, RG 43, vol. 2097, #2671).
94 Killaly to Merritt, 23 February 1850 (AO, F662, MS 74, *Merritt Papers*, Package 16, #1424).
95 Kingsford, *Canals of Canada,* 61.

96 Toronto *Mail*, 16 July 1875, 2.

97 SP *(No. 54) for 1871*, 1. Among the "Commercial Aspects" studied was the trade rivalry with the United States.

98 Contract #3464, to enlarge and deepen the harbour at Port Colborne (LAC, RG 43, vol. 2539 – Contracts List).

99 St Catharines *Daily Times*, 23 July 1875, 3; 6 July 1875, 2.

100 Thorold *Post*, 25 May 1877, 1; ibid., 7 September 1877, 1; St Catharines *Journal*, 1 April 1875, 2; Thorold *Post*, 21 September 1877, 1.

101 4 March 1878, *Debates of the House of Commons*, 41 Victoria, vol. IV, 714–16.

102 28 February, 4 and 13 March, 24 April 1878, ibid., 623–62, 714–17, 1095–119, and 2151–2. The quotation is from 626. The Thorold *Post* also published part of the debate (3 May 1878, 2).

103 Toronto *Globe*, 26 March 1880, 3, quoted in Thorold *Post*, 2 April 1880, 1.

104 J.K. Hartwell to DPW, 0/31 March 1874 (LAC, RG 11, vol. 668, #39725).

105 Thorold *Post*, 11 June 1880, 3, and 16 July 1880, 4.

106 Bodwell to DPW, 13 September 1878 (LAC, RG 11, vol. 693, #76190).

107 Thorold *Post*, 20 September 1878, 4.

108 Ibid., 28 September 1881, 3.

109 The Thorold *Post* opined that "the government finds it inadvisable, in the present state of the Dominion finances, to proceed with the work this year" (19 February 1886, 2).

110 Thorold *Post*, 11 March 1887, 3.

111 A reflection of this development is Robert Thurston's *A History of the Growth of the Steam-Engine* (1878), which describes in great detail the many advances made since c. 1820.

112 Thorold *Post*, 4 June 1875, 2.

113 Ibid., 16 July 1875, 2.

114 20 September 1842 (LAC, RG 43, vol. 2247); 27 July 1875 (LAC, RG 43, vol. 2491, Contract #4728).

115 Thorold *Post*, 28 January 1876, 4. This drill may have been the same as "Ingersoll's Rock Drill" mentioned on later occasions.

116 *Canadian Illustrated News*, 15 January 1876, 35.

117 26 September 1877 (LAC, RG 43, vol. 31760, book 39).

118 Thorold *Post*, 21 July 1876, 1. Not surprisingly, costs rose with size and efficiency! An Order-in-Council of 13 December 1883 authorized spending $2,250 for a Sisley steam pump. In 1884 a smaller pump could be obtained from Ingles & Hunter for $750, and the Gate Yard at Thorold had made ten small hand pumps (LAC, RG 43, vol. 411).

119 Thorold *Post*, 3 May 1878, 1; ibid., 3 May 1878, 1.

120 12 August 1881 (LAC, RG 43, vol. 394, #56226). This was, in effect, an interest-free loan, since the contractors agreed to repurchase the equipment and have the use of it in the meantime. The total value of the plant was $13,820; the explosive, $3,500 (LAC, RG 43, vol. 793, #1179).

121 Thorold *Post*, 23 April 1886, 3.

122 Ibid., 2 September 1881, 2.

123 Page to DRC, 23 November 1882 (LAC, RG 43, vol. 800, #97102); Ellis to the DRC, 27 May 1882 (LAC, RG 43, vol. 2261, 312–13). On 29 November 1882 Order-in-Council #2276 authorized the purchase from Townsend.
124 24 September 1885, William Ellis, Annual Report to the Department (*SP [No. 1] for 1886*, 116).
125 Thorold *Post*, 27 May 1887, 3.
126 Ibid., 14 September 1877, 4.
127 Ernest Cruikshank, *History of the County of Welland*, 120.

CHAPTER FIVE

1 Locks at the entrance to a canal are not necessarily "lift" locks but serve to ensure that the water level inside and outside the canal remains the same (as at Port Colborne on Lake Erie). If the entrance is on a sea coast and affected by tides, the entrance lock is referred to as a "sea lock."
2 31 December 1835, *Third Report*, 562. Engineer Hall referred to them as "stop gates," which implies that they were "stop logs," but the context of his remark suggests swingable gates. Stop logs, installed at the upstream end of each lock, fitted into vertical grooves in the sides of locks and formed a wall to hold back the water when the lock was emptied for repairs. Little evidence exists of stop logs on the First Canal, but they were used on the Second and Third canals, and a variation is in use on the present canal.
3 The American David Thomas (1776–1859), briefly the Welland's resident engineer, seems to have been responsible for suggesting this feature. (See his report of 12 May 1826, *Third Report,* 308.) John MacTaggart was disturbed by this apparent anomaly. "The gates of the locks are not of proper construction, the upper and lower being both alike in dimensions – this they should not be. The upper gate should not have the lift of the lock added to it." (MacTaggart, *Three Years*, 157). See also Robert Passfield, *Building the Rideau Canal*, 26–8.
4 Christopher Andreae, *Lock 24*, plans after 178.
5 "Annual Report of the Directors," 18 December 1826 (*Third Report*, 305).
6 Although a lock was built near each of the aqueducts of the Second and Third canals, connecting the canal to Chippawa Creek, no such structure seems to have been built at the First Canal's aqueduct. Access to the creek was effected through the two connecting locks at Port Robinson.
7 AO, F662, MS 74, *Merritt Papers*, Package 12; see also *Third Report*, 235, for the letter from the New York stockholders.
8 Marshall Lewis was a man of many talents, variously described as a millwright and architect, and sometimes acting as a contractor. He was responsible for building the bridges for the First Canal (chapter 7).
9 LAC, RG 43, vol. 2098, 50–1.
10 LAC, MG 24, E1, *Merritt Papers*, vol. 33.
11 Annual Report of the Board of Directors for 1827 (*Third Report*, 365).
12 On the matter of lock construction materials, see MacTaggart, *Three Years*, 163.
13 J.B. Yates to James. H. Samson, Chair of the Committee of the House of Assembly on the Welland Canal Petition, 31 December 1833 (*Third Report*, 541).

14 He thought the locks would last from twelve to fifteen years (16 January 1830, *Third Report*, 421).

15 Nevertheless, the 1837 Act that authorized conversion of government loans to the company into public stock aimed to "effect the completion of the said Canal, in a substantial and permanent manner" with stone as the designated material (4 March 1837, 7 William IV, Ch. XCII).

16 Thomas Proctor to J.N. Dunn, 17 May 1825 (*Third Report*, 289).

17 J.B. Yates to James H. Samson, Chair of the Committee of the House of Assembly on the Welland Canal Petition, 21 December 1833 (*Third Report*, 543); and see also Board Meeting, 22 November 1828 (*Third Report*, 396ff.).

18 MacTaggart, *Three Years*, 153–4.

19 Randal, "Report," in *Third Report*, 31 May 1830, 448.

20 3 October 1833, *Third Report*, 518. His estimates of the relative cost also explain the choice of wood: a wooden lock cost $9,663.61; a stone lock of comparable size, $19,248.90 (*Third Report*, 522).

21 MacTaggart, *Three Years*, 154.

22 Daniel H. Calhoun, *The American Civil Engineer*, ch. 5, "Conflicts and Trends: The Progress of Benjamin Wright," 122.

23 Benjamin Wright's Report, 3 October 1833 (*Third Report*, 522, 518, and 521).

24 Quoted in William Lyon Mackenzie, *The Welland Canal*, 23 December 1835, 4.

25 Hall's testimony to Mackenzie's inquiry, 27 February 1836 (*Third Report*, 45).

26 Yates refers to "fraud on the part of the Contractors" in a letter to James H. Samson, Chair of the Committee of the House of Assembly on the Welland Canal Petition, 31 December 1833 (*Third Report*, 541).

27 *Biography*, 122.

28 An "extremely liberal" payment, said Hall (Hall to W.L. Mackenzie, 23 September 1835, *Third Report*, 51).

29 Board Meeting, 13 August 1829 (LAC, RG 43, vol. 2099, 118).

30 Randal's Report, 31 May 1830 (*Third Report*, 446).

31 Hall's testimony of 27 February 1836 (*Third Report*, 47). No lock was built here in the First Canal era, possibly because it would have been too expensive and, strictly speaking, was beyond the Welland Canal Company's mandate. It may simply have been overlooked in the characteristic haste of the First Canal's construction! (Colin Duquemin and Daniel Glenney, *A Guide to the Grand River Canal*, 48.)

32 Minutes of the Board, 4 November 1836 (LAC, RG 43, vol. 2099, 449).

33 Killaly refers to this request in a letter to the company secretary on 24 May 1839 (SCM, *Letterbook "O"*, 1).

34 Minutes of the Board, 4 October 1839 (LAC, RG 43, vol. 2102, 108). The entry for 5 October 1836 (LAC, RG 43, vol. 2099, 442) reads "reconstruct," which suggests that the Dunnville guard gates were to be supplemented with another pair, creating a genuine lock.

35 Board Meeting, 5 June 1835 (LAC, RG 43, vol 2099, 317–19).

36 Board Meeting, 21 June 1837 (LAC, RG 43, vol. 2100, 20–9).

37 Barrett's Report of 1 January 1828 (*Third Report*, 366).

38 Andreae, *Lock 24*, 59–60.

39 The gates do not close like two panels on a barn door, flush with the wall, but, when shut, are always at an oblique angle to the lock wall.

40 *Farmers' Journal and Welland Canal Intelligencer*, 17 October 1827, n.p. Unfortunately, no drawings of Lewis's gate valve have survived. Further archaeological research may reveal the existence of iron valves on First Canal lock gates. Such parts, however, may not have survived the dewatering of that waterway. The relatively high value of iron in the colonial economy could have led to their being salvaged and "recycled." The excavation of Lock 24 revealed wooden paddles.

41 Welland Canal Company Board to Robinson, 5 June 1833 (LAC, RG 43, vol. 2099, 239).

42 Hall to Merritt, 8 April, 1836 (AO, F662, MS 74, *Merritt Papers*, Package 13).

43 Thomas McIlwraith, "Freight Capacity ...," *Journal of Economic History* 36:876.

44 Report of the Government-appointed Directors of the Welland Canal Company, in *Journal of the House of Assembly for 1836*, Appendix (No. B).

45 Minutes of the Board, 15 June 1837 (LAC, RG 43, vol. 2199, 7); the letter can be found in LAC, RG 43, vol. 2102; Baird and Killaly, *Report*; the map is in the Map Collection of Library and Archives Canada (NMC, 11848).

46 "Memoranda Respecting various Public Works heretofore in progress, or projected in the Province of Canada ... prepared and submitted for the consideration of His Excellency the Governor General" (H.H. Killaly to Lord Sydenham, 12 August 1841, Upper Canada. House of Assembly, *Journal*, 1841, Appendix [C.C.]).

47 The phrase used in the Act of 4 March 1837 (7 William IV, Ch. XCII).

48 Begly to Power, 22 April 1843 (LAC, RG 11, vol. 117, #2365).

49 This lock may still be seen, near what is now Clarence Street. Whether the decision to move the lock further inland was made before the gale of 19 October 1844, we cannot be sure. We do know that the gale caused a great deal of damage to the harbour. We also know, from a letter from engineer Power to the Board of Works (20 February 1846, LAC, RG 43, vol. 2248, 288), that the location of the lock had been changed some time after a contract had been signed with Gleeson & McDonagh in early 1844. Power pointed out that he had "always intended that the lock should be situated at the end of the rock cut remote from the lake" and that the "change McDonagh complained of was of about 450 yards." Power also noted that McDonagh had been unable to work on the contract during the summer, and resumed only in December. Thus, the change of site could well have been caused by the gale. In a later letter, Power observed that McDonagh's work was in a "very backward condition" (LAC, RG 43, vol. 2248, 303), and on 11 September 1847 the work was re-assigned to the reliable firm of Brown & McDonnell, who successfully completed the lock in 1850.

50 See Power's "Annual Report," 26 February 1846 (LAC, RG 43, vol. 2248, 303) and Keefer to W.B. Robinson, Chief Commissioner of Public Works, 7 July 1846 (ibid., vol. 2249, 12).

51 St Catharines *Journal*, 13 September 1844, 3.

52 Before the First Canal was completed, the locks were numbered from the top of the Escarpment to Lake Ontario; i.e., Lock 1 had been in the area of Stumptown (later Thorold). See, for example, Francis Hall's report of 10 December 1824 (*Third Report*, 235).

53 Killaly, Memorandum for the Board of Works, 16 September 1845 (LAC, RG 43, vol. 2129, following entry for 14 November); see 18 November for Board Meeting.

54 *Biography*, 289.

55 Board of Works, 11 April 1843 (LAC, RG 11, vol. 112, #83084).

56 Killaly to Brown and McDonnell, 1 March 1849 (LAC, RG 43, vol. 2250, 423).

57 Killaly to the Board, 29 January 1849 (LAC, RG 43, vol. 2250, 358); 6 February 1849, vol. 2250, 379–80).

58 Ronald Shaw (*Canals for a Nation,* 10) describes the effort of William Weston to perfect an underwater cement: "He recorded his preparation at the Mohawk Lock of mortar, mixing four and a half bushels of terras, five and three-quarter bushels of lime, and two and a half bushels of sand as he struggled with formulating a cement that would harden under water." Despite Weston's efforts, Shaw claims (39) that: "The perfection of an underwater cement was the invaluable achievement of Canvass White of Whitesboro ... who was sent to England, where he examined the underwater cements used there. He returned to find a variety of limestone that could be made into a quicklime cement superior to any made in America ... White took out a patent on the cement."

59 Thomas C. Keefer, *Canadian Waterways*, 18.

60 20 February 1873, St Catharines *News*, 2. Keefer's letter was reprinted from the Toronto *Daily Mail,* 5 February 1873, 3.

61 Ellis, "Annual Report for Year Ending 30 June 1882," 22 September 1882 (*SP [No. 8] for 1883*, 100).

62 Thorold *Post*, 3 May 1878, 1.

63 "Notice to Contractor," *Canadian Illustrated News*, 13 September 1873, 175.

64 Brown operated quarries on the Escarpment, one of which was at the foot of York Street in Thorold (Thorold *Post,* 2 June 1876).

65 DRC to Page, 24 April 1880 (LAC, RG 43, vol. 398, #53330).

66 Thorold *Post*, 21 July 1876, 1.

67 Ellis to DRC, Telegram, 30 May 1881 (LAC, RG 43, vol. 394, #91540).

68 Thorold *Post*, 8 July 1881, 2.

69 Ellis to A.P. Bradley (Secretary, DRC), 2 September 1882 (LAC, RG 43, vol. 2261, 405).

70 Thorold *Post*, 9 July 1880, 2.

71 St Catharines *Journal*, cited in Thorold *Post*, 18 June 1880, 2.

72 Thorold *Post*, 11 February 1881, 3.

73 Page to DRC, 11 February 1881 (LAC, RG 43, vol. 398, #90604).

74 Townsend to DRC (LAC, RG 43, vol. 398, #90589). Monro hired a detective to identify the culprits (LAC, RG 43, vol. 39, #55239).

75 LAC, RG 43, vol. 798, file 59, #96027; LAC, RG 43, vol. 394, #58840, #96027, #64273.02; LAC, RG 43, vol. 798, file 60, #96147; LAC, RG 43, vol. 800, #97102.

76 L.K. Jones, Secretary of the Department of Railways and Canals, to Weller, 21 January 1907 (LAC, RG 43, vol. 2125, #440).
77 Nassau W. Gowan (1856–1924) ran a music store in St Catharines, but was a "home inventor" who persuaded government officials to try out his brainchild on the Welland Canal (*Evening Journal*, 11 June 1910, 8; 20 May 1912, 1).
78 26 September 1912, LAC, RG 43, vol. 2230, file 19653.
79 "Annual Report" of Superintending Engineer, 27 June 1914, 369; 30 June 1915, 360 (*SP [No. 20] for 1915 and 1916*). The figures for damage repair come also from the Superintendent's Reports. Publication of these reports was suspended during the rest of the First World War, and when they resumed, the heavy repair bills were for damage to bridges, not to lock gates.
80 Thorold *Post*, 14 September 1877, 4; ibid., 17 August 1877, 4.
81 Ibid., 2 June 1876, 4.
82 William Hunter to DPW, 26 June 1878 (LAC, RG 11, vol. 693, #74779; 10 July #44949).
83 Thorold *Post*, 27 April 1877, 1.

CHAPTER SIX

1 Alfred Barrett's Report to the Directors of the Welland Canal Company, 1 September 1827 (*Third Report*, 368). In July 1828, even before the catastrophic land slips, Merritt had the related idea of "throwing a dam over and constructing a lock in the Welland river [Chippawa Creek] below the entrance of the canal, and raising the locks two feet, the water may be raised throughout the canal to a depth of ten feet, with very little additional expense" ("Account," 164). Such a dam was not built, but was planned – and abandoned – again in the 1920s.
2 27 December 1828, *Third Report*, 383.
3 Barrett to the Directors, 30 June 1829 (*Third Report*, 140).
4 James Black to Bosanquet, 25 May 1829 (LAC, RG 4, vol. 2102, 127).
5 Merritt's journal, 4 October 1829, quoted in *Biography*, 122.
6 Report of the Board of Directors of the Welland Canal Company for the Year 1832, *Third Report*, 490; Barrett's report, 30 June 1829 (ibid., 140).
7 Randal's "Report," (ibid., 446).
8 William Lyon Mackenzie, *The Welland Canal*, 23 December 1835, 2–3.
9 Russell Harper, *Early History*, 35.
10 1 September 1829 (AO, F662, MS 74, *Merritt Papers*, Package 12); Board Meeting, 30 July 1830, *Minutes 1825–1837* (LAC, RG 43, vol. 2099, 128): Wilkinson was a leading advocate of the Erie Canal (LAC, RG 43, vol. 2099, *Minutes 1825–1837*), 235.
11 Letter to the Niagara *Gleaner*, 8 November 1823, quoted in Ernest Cruikshank, "Inception," 71.
12 George Phillpotts, "Report," 147.
13 The "Western Branch" (chapter 2).
14 John MacTaggart, *Three Years*, 161.
15 James Geddes's "Report" of 27 December 1828 (*Third Report*, 383–4).
16 "The Feeder Canal," *Chronicles of Wainfleet Township: 200 Years of History,* Wainfleet Historical Society, 1992, 100.

17 *Biography*, 168.
18 Power to Begly, 28 June 1843 (LAC, RG 43, vol. 2097, 74–5).
19 DPW to S.D. Woodruff, 3 May 1867 (LAC, RG 11, vol. 616, #62405.
20 Randal's "Report," in *Third Report*, 447.
21 *Third Report*, 562; ibid., 491.
22 Ibid., 402.
23 Board Meeting, 4 October 1836 (LAC, RG 4, vol. 2099, 436–41).
24 Randal's "Report," in *Third Report* , 447.
25 Keefer to Begly, 10 December 1846 (LAC, RG 43, vol. 2249, 146).
26 Geddes's "Report" to the Welland Canal Company, 27 December 1828 (*Third Report*, 383).
27 Mackenzie, *The Welland Canal,* 23 December 1835, 2.
28 *Third Report*, 156.
29 Killaly to S.M. Bouchette, 14 May 1851 (LAC, RG 11, vol. 123, #9003).
30 Samuel Power, "Annual Report," 26 February 1846 (LAC, RG 43, vol. 2248, 303).
31 Temporary enclosing dams built in the water and pumped dry to protect labourers while performing some work, such as the construction of piers.
32 Samuel Zimmerman (1815–1857) emigrated from Pennsylvania to Canada West in 1842. In the 1840s he was granted seven contracts, either alone or in partnership, on the Second Canal.
33 LAC, RG 43, vol. 2249, 10.
34 Keefer's "Annual Report," 17 October 1846 (LAC, RG 43, vol. 2249, 87).
35 Keefer to Begly, 10 December 1846 (LAC, RG 43, vol. 2249, 146); Keefer's "Annual Report," 22 May 1847 (ibid., 330).
36 Report by Keefer to Begly, 10 January 1848 (LAC, RG 43, vol. 2250, 45). He was probably referring to hydraulic cement.
37 Keefer to Killaly, 10 October, 1848 (LAC, RG 43, vol. 2250, 242).
38 Woodruff to Killaly, 6 March 1851 (LAC, RG 11, vol. 67-2, 8–9, also RG 43, vol. 2253, #2075).
39 "It does appear strange that the most difficult portion of the canal should have been the last to contract for as the other work will not only be useless, but will be injuriously affected by the delay" (Monck, *Reform Press*, quoted in Thorold *Post*, 29 October 1880, 3).
40 Thorold *Post,* 13 October 1878, 1.
41 Hunter, Murray and Cleveland to DRC, 12 February 1880 (LAC, RG 43, vol. 398, #86939).
42 Page to DRC, Telegram, 31 March 1880 (LAC, RG 43, vol. 398, #87365).
43 Thorold *Post*, 30 April 1880, 1.
44 Page to DRC, 21 April 1880 (LAC, RG 43, vol. 398, #87619).
45 Page to Hunter, Murray and Cleveland, 15 September 1880 (LAC, RG 43, vol. 398, #89100 and #54323).
46 Quoted in Thorold *Post*, 21 October 1881, 1, and 28 October 1881, 2.
47 Welland *Telegraph*, 7 August 1885, 1.
48 Thorold *Post*, 23 April 1886, 3. Matthew Beatty (1808–1901) emigrated from Ireland with his parents in 1810. In 1842 he moved from the United States to Canada and settled in St Catharines. Then, in 1860, he moved to Welland and

set up a machine shop. By 1887 he had brought his sons into a prospering business which shipped agricultural machinery all across Canada. The firm was also producing dredging machinery, some of which was used on the Welland Canal. After his retirement in 1897, his sons carried on the business.

49 The saga of the Third Canal aqueduct can be followed in Library and Archives Canada through RG 11, vols. 689 and 193, and RG 43, vols. 398 and 411; as well as RG 43, vols. 394, 417, 441, and 798. The Thorold *Post* adds gloss and depth.

50 Ernest Cruikshank, *History*, 119.

51 The correspondence between Lyons and Macaulay is in SCM, *Letterbook "O"*, 67–75.

52 S.D. Woodruff, "Annual Report," 19 December 1861, *SP (No. 3) for 1862*, Appendix B, "9."

53 Despite the growing prevalence of self-propelled ships, all three nineteenth-century waterways were provided with towpaths, sometimes on the east side; otherwise, on the west; sometimes on both sides. The location and function of the towpaths merits an independent study.

54 Page to James Russell, 17 February 1845 (LAC, RG 43, vol. 2248, 78).

55 Keefer to James Cotton, 29 July 1846 (LAC, RG 43, vol. 2249, 9).

56 Keefer to Cotton and Rowe, 27 July 1848 (LAC, RG 43, vol. 2250, 174); Keefer to Begly, 9 August 1848 (ibid., 190–1).

CHAPTER SEVEN

1. Upper Canada, 4 George IV, Ch. XVII, Section X.

2 23–31 August 1826, *Third Report*, 313; 319–20; 343.

3 8 March 1830 (ibid., 439). When local people were told to build and maintain bridges themselves, not only did this relieve the company from an onerous responsibility, but it continued the tradition of *corvée* or statute labour that would be familiar to some Niagara residents.

4 3 April 1834, *Third Report*, 557.

5 20 June 1827, *Third Report*, 381.

6 24 October 1835, Upper Canada. House of Asssembly, *Journal 1835*, Appendix 3, 4.

7 John N. Jackson, *The Welland Canals*, 17.

8 18 February 1828, *Third Report*, 392. The "40 feet" referred to the span of the bridge over the channel, not its width as a thoroughfare.

9 10 May 1828, *Third Report*, 392–3. In 1828 Merritt referred to "four twin bridges" being constructed, but his meaning is unclear (William Hamilton Merritt, "Account," 161.)

10 G.W.B., letter to the editor of the St Catharines *Journal*, June 2, 1842 (cited in Colin Duquemin and Daniel Glenney, *Grand River Canal*, 32).

11 Samuel Keefer's "Report," 17 October 1846 (LAC, RG 43, vol. 2249, 89).

12 LAC, RG 11, vol. 119, #74536.

13 10 June 1847 (LAC, RG 11, vol. 120, #1697).

14 James W. Clark to Merritt, 28 June 1847 (AO, F662, MS 74, *Merritt Papers*, Package 15).

15 LAC, RG 11, vol. 67, #15354.
16 27 January 1846 (LAC, RG 11, vol. 112, 415).
17 W.A. Thompson to DPW, 7 April 1874 (LAC, RG 11, vol. 668, #40622), and J.S. Bessy to DPW, 24 August 1874 (#43655).
18 Thorold *Post*, 19 December 1879, 1.
19 John Wilson to DRC (telegram) 23 March 1880 (LAC, RG 43, vol. 398, #87277).
20 William L. Lewis, *Aqueduct, Merrittsville and Welland*, vol. 2, chapters 15 and 16.
21 See *Building the Welland Ship Canal* (Styran and Taylor, in progress) for the fate of this bridge a scant two decades later.
22 LAC, RG 43, vol. 2539 – List of Contracts.
23 The contract was awarded on 5 August 1873 (LAC, RG 43, vol. 2539 – List of Contracts). The tunnel still exists, although both entrances are blocked.
24 Thorold *Post*, 24 June 1881, 3; Thorold *Post*, 2 Sept. 1881, 3; Minister of Inland Revenue to DRC, 29 July 1885 (LAC, RG 43, vol. 441, #108056).
25 LAC, RG 11, vol. 124, #9616.
26 Keefer to the Secretary, DPW, 22 December 1852, *Journal of the Legislative Assembly of the Province of Canada,* vol. 11, Appendix 8 (1852), 1853, 29.
27 Page dealt with these problems in his "Report of the Chief Engineer of Public Works," 29 April 1872 (*SP [No. 1] for 1873,* 11).
28 LAC, RG 11, vol. 125, #13022.
29 LAC, RG 11, vol. 124, #108641, #11173, and vol. 125, #12201.
30 T.R. Merritt, MP, to DPW, 24 April 1872 (LAC, RG 11, vol. 643, #2246); LAC, RG 11, vol. 668, #28983, #18739, #29492, #29625.
31 22 April 1875 (LAC, RG 43, vol. 2539 – List of Contracts).
32 The *Post* was referring to 44 Vict. Ch. 24 (Thorold *Post*, 16 May 1879, 1; and 3 February 1882, 3.
33 16 Thorold *Post*, 11 March 1881, 3.
34 22 March 1880, *Debates of the House of Commons*, 1880, vol. VIII, 783–4.
35 LAC, RG 11, vol. 668, #21570.

CHAPTER EIGHT

1 Catharine Merritt to her mother, 27 January 1826 (AO, F662, MS 74, *Merritt Papers*, Package 12).
2 Niagara *Gleaner*, 3 December 1824, printed in *Biography*, 66; Merritt's testimony, 29 March 1836 (*Third Report,* 212).
3 Thomas Keefer, *The Old Welland Canals*, 10.
4 "In the Year 1825" (*Third Report*, 242).
5 28 April 1826, quoted in William Lyon Mackenzie, *The Welland Canal*, 23 December 1835, 3.
6 *Third Report,* 359. Lefferty (Lafferty) served as a government-appointed director of the Welland Canal Company 1829–31.
7 "Junius," "A Walk Around Town: W." in *St. Catharines A to Z,* 60.
8 John MacTaggart, *Three Years,* passim and 150–3.
9 The home government, Colonel By said, should undertake their construction. Quoted in George Raudzens, *The British Ordnance Department*, 64. By was

especially irritated by what he believed were the miscalculations of Samuel Clowes, who had surveyed the routes of both the Rideau and the Welland.

10 *The Farmers' Journal and Welland Canal Intelligencer* concluded that "falsehood and foolery cannot now prevail" (10 November, 1830, n.p.).

11 Report of the Board for 1831 (*Third Report,* 487).

12 Richard Bonnycastle, *The Canadas in 1841*, 200. On the other hand, the presence and experience of talented Britons and Americans was an incalculable asset to Niagara's waterway and to Upper Canada's professional establishment. Although it is difficult to document specific examples of British or American engineers who functioned as agents in any "transfer of technology," further research may yield instances. Those working under them could have learned a great deal (Elting Morison, *From Know-How to Nowhere,* and Darwin H. Stapleton, "The Transfer of Early Industrial Technologies to America, With Especial Reference to the Role of the American Philosophical Society," *Proceedings of the American Philosophical Society*, vol. 135, no. 2, 1991, 286–98).

13 Catharine Merritt to Mrs Prendergast, 5 July 1825 (AO, F662, MS 74, *Merritt Papers*, Package 12).

14 See John Jackson, *The Welland Canals,* passim.

15 Quoted in the Niagara *Gleaner*, 17 March 1827, 1.

16 *Survey of Lands,* 1826 [1831], n.p., and 14.

17 *Third Report*, 313; ibid., 309–43.

18 Ibid., 30 July 1830, 440; George Keefer's report, 20 January 1831 (ibid., 461).

19 Mackenzie, *The Welland Canal,* 16 December 1835, 2.

20 Keefer to Begly, 20 September 1847 (LAC, RG 43, vol. 2249, 394).

21 Warden of Welland County to DPW, 7 June 1878 (LAC, RG 11, vol. 693, #74337).

22 W.G. McGeorge, *Report on the Welland and Feeder Canals*, 1947.

23 10 February 1848 (LAC, RG 43, vol. 2248, 453).

24 St Catharines Council to Minister of Railways and Canals, 17 May 1887 (LAC, RG 43, vol. 1350, 1791 file "St. C. Sewage Sys. 1887–88").

25 P.S. Muslin et al. to DRC, 12 August 1878 (LAC, RG 11, vol. 693, #75648) and B. Tucker and Co. to DRC, 12 November 1878 (LAC, RG 11, vol. 693, #7758).

26 Phelps's testimony, 5 November 1825 (*Third Report*, 261); ibid., 256–7.

27 1 November 1825, Petition of Sundry Inhabitants of the District of Niagara, *Third Report,* 254. Merritt disagreed on the grounds that the water "is to escape over a waste weir, and I think cannot be prejudicial to health" (*Third Report*, 255).

28 4 George IV, Ch. 17; 7 George IV, Ch. 19.

29 *Third Report*, 323; 25 August 1826 (ibid., 315); see "Proceedings of the Board of Arbitrators" (*Third Report*, 309–35) and "Award of the Arbitrators" (ibid., 335–43).

30 LAC, RG 43, vol. 1786, *Estimates of Works 1848–1854*, 221.

31 Power to Begly, 18 February 1845 (LAC, RG 43, vol. 2248, 64).

32 See LAC, RG 43, vol. 398, #87426; LAC, RG 11, vol. 693, #44221; LAC, RG 43, vol. 398, #88719 and #87785.

33 N. Higgins to DPW, 11 April 1872 (LAC, RG 11, vol. 643, #22150, #1450, #22789).

34 James M. Currie to DPW (telegrams), 12 June 1874 (LAC, RG 11, vol. 668, #41914 and #41912).
35 Janet McCarthy to DRC, 28 August 1879 (LAC, RG 11, vol. 707, #84392; see also LAC, RG 43, vol. 398, #85658, and vol. 790, #90585).
36 Files beginning 22 April 1875 (LAC, RG 11, vol. 689, #49869) and ending 22 March 1876 (#58101)
37 Thorold *Post*, 28 August 1885, 3.
38 Richard Bonnycastle, *The Canadas*, 196.
39 St Catharines *Journal*, 4 June 1840.
40 An Emigrant Farmer [Joseph Abbot], *The Emigrant to North America* ..., Edinburgh: Blackwood, 1844, 74, quoted in John N. Jackson, *St Catharines*, 239.
41 Montreal *Gazette*, 7 February 1873.
42 St Catharines *Daily Times*, 15 August 1871, 3.
43 Thorold *Post*, 28 December 1878, 1; ibid., 21 July 1876, 1.
44 Ibid., 6 January 1886, 2.
45 Ibid., 23 February 1877, 1; 19 August 1887, 2; 21 April 1882, 3.
46 Ibid., 9 July 1875, 1.
47 Ibid., 3, 10, and 31 October 1884, 2.
48 St Catharines *Daily Times*, 9 September 1871, 3; 13 September 1871, 2, 3, 5, and 6 October 1871, 2; 2 November 1871, 2.
49 Thorold *Post*, 2 September 1881, 2.
50 F. Bullivant to DRC, 0/12 March 1886 (LAC, RG 43, vol. 411, #110614); H.A. King, Mayor, to DRC, 27 February 1886 and 27 June 1886 (LAC, RG 43, vol. 411, #110615).
51 AO, MS 191, *Welland Canal Papers*, file 3571.
52 On the other hand, in 1875 a St Catharines newspaper described an old farmer who lived within four miles of the canal who said he would never go to see it, because years ago he had declared that any man who said that a canal could be built there was "a blasted fool" (St Catharines *Daily Times,* 21 October, 1875, 3).
53 General Beach of Rochester, New York, was originally Keefer's partner, but withdrew from the arrangement.
54 Board Meeting, 9 April 1832 (*Third Report*, 497–8).
55 Begly to Robert Baldwin, 24 August 1843 (LAC, RG 11, vol. 117, #3143).
56 Thorold *Post*, 4 June 1875, 2.
57 8 February 1881, *Debates. House of Commons.* 44 Victoria 1881 vol. XI, 904.
58 Jackson, *The Welland Canals*, 148; Hannah Stanwick, "Did St. Catharines Miss the Boat?"
59 Thompson, *Jubilee History of Thorold*, 113.
60 Board Meeting, 3 May 1827, *Third Report,* 373; Board Meeting, 6 July 1827, ibid., 376; Board Meeting, 9 August 1827, ibid., 377; George May to DPW; 10 September 1877 (LAC, RG 11, vol. 689, #69430).
61 Welland *Telegraph*, 27 July 1877, 1.
62 David Cooper to DPW, 23 April 1877 (LAC, RG 11, vol. 689, #66567).
63 19 April 1879 (LAC, RG 11, vol. 694, #81257).

64 Some disagreement surrounded tree-planting, but its origins are obscure. In 1887 Monro expressed concern to Page that the trees being planted might be uprooted in storms and rip open the canal banks, whereupon he was told that the minister ordered the discontinuing of planting without the approval of the chief engineer (Monro to Page, 4 November 1887, LAC, RG 43, vol. 417, #117510; DRC to Monro, telegram, 7 November 1887, ibid., #73190).

65 8 September 1845, LAC, RG 43, vol. 2248, 172; 3 September 1875, Thorold *Post*, 4; 2 May 1876, LAC, RG 11, vol. 451, #58991; 9 May 1905, LAC, RG 43, vol. 469, #200904; 7 July 1876, Thorold *Post*, 4.

66 DPW to Abraham Neff, 8 March 1848 (LAC, RG 11, vol. 121, #2973).

67 10 August, LAC, RG 11, vol. 668, #26419.

CHAPTER NINE

1 The working and living conditions of labourers on the First Canal construction site have remained something of an unknown to scholars. On the other hand, with the better records on the Second Canal, several historians have described the lives and work of these men. One of the first was J. Lawrence Runnalls, who was deeply sympathetic to the condition of the Irish on the Second Welland, but whose work is outdated and inaccurate (*The Irish on the Welland Canals*). Ruth Elizabeth Bleasdale has also written a brief account of the navvies' labour on the Second Welland, in comparison to the Cornwall and Williamsburg canals ("Irish Labourers"). Peter Way has published a monograph on labour conditions on several North American canals in the early nineteenth century (including the Second Welland), in which he describes "the moulding of a modern industrial workforce" and "the rise of industrial capitalism" on canal construction sites (Way, *Common Labour*). Construction labourers on the Third Canal have, however, been neglected.

2 Bleasdale, "Irish Labourers," 5.

3 Way, *Common Labour*, 266.

4 19 August 1842, LAC, RG 11, vol. 94, #1020; 17 February 1843, LAC, RG 11, vol. 117, #1965. Whitton was not acting alone: he wrote on behalf of the stonecutters.

5 *Farmers' Journal,* 12 July 1826, n.p.

6 *Third Report*, 12 January 1827, 381.

7 23 May 1827, *Farmers' Journal*, n.p. According to Bleasdale ("Irish Labourers," 40–2), a typical daily wage before heavy immigration began was 3s/6d, a figure that dropped to 2s/6d in the period from 1830–1850. Lt. E.C. Frome, in an Appendix to George Raudzens, *British Ordnance Department*, noted that labourers on the Rideau Canal were paid from 2s/6d to 3s/6d per day, while masons received from 5s to 6s/6d (184).

8 Barrett's Report, 4 August 1831 (*Third Report*, 482).

9 16 January 1830, *Third Report*, 419; 24 March 1836, 163.

10 Even in 1843 the board was occasionally receiving requests from men in Ireland for employment on the canal. They were told that no jobs were available and that they should not emigrate (LAC, RG 11, vol. 117, #374).

11 Begly to Power, 6 March 1843 (ibid., #2066).

12 Thorburn to Daly, 10 January 1844 (LAC, RG 11, vol. 68-5, 34–43).
13 Bleasdale, "Irish Labourers," 40–2.
14 During the winter of 1843, Power believed that Welland labourers were receiving the highest wages in North America (Bleasdale, "Irish Labourers," 23–5).
15 19 January 1845, LAC, RG 11, vol. 94, #3686; 19 April 1845, ibid., #4331; 4 August, LAC, RG 11, vol. 65-6; ibid.
16 Power to Begly, 8 August 1845 (LAC, RG 43, vol. 2248, 155–6).
17 Samuel Keefer to T.C. Street, 29 August 1846 (LAC, RG 43, vol. 2249, 31).
18 Cotton & Rowe to Killaly, 26 June 1849 (LAC, RG 11, vol. 65-5, 153).
19 C.M. Gripton to DRC, 17 August 1883 (LAC, RG 43, vol. 411, #100461).
20 See the quarry owner James Walker's defence of this practice in the Thorold *Post*, 15 March 1878, 1.
21 Thorold *Post*, 8 March 1878, 1.
22 Ibid., 8 February 1878, 3.
23 In England and on the Rideau, labour-saving tramways or "barrow runs" were constructed, consisting of planks laid up the sides of the trench for wheeling barrows up and down. Ropes attached to the barrow were connected to the belts of the men. These cables ran up the embankment and around a pulley at the summit. (Terry Coleman, *The Railway Navvies*, 46 gives a good description of the "barrow run.") No evidence exists for the use of these on the Welland.
24 Upper Canada. House of Assembly. *Journal 1836–39*, *Appendix*, vol. 2, "Welland Canal Report," 44.
25 John MacTaggart, *Three Years*, 245–6.
26 Ibid., vol. I, 290.
27 For example, Niagara *Gleaner*, 20 November 1824, 3; 11 December, 2.
28 Mrs Merritt to Mrs Prendergast, 25 December 1825 (AO, F662, MS 74, *Merritt Papers*, Package 12).
29 St Catharines *Journal*, 27 February 1845, 3; ibid., 13 September 1844, 3. Another early report of an accident reads: "On the morning of Monday last, a laborer on the canal fell into one of the locks above the village and fractured his skull so severely as to cause instant death." Typically, no name is given (ibid., 2 February, 1844, 3).
30 Thorold *Post*, 23 July 1875, 2, quoting the Toronto *Mail*.
31 Ibid., 13 April 1877, 4; ibid., 21 May 1886, 3.
32 Ibid., 3 May 1878, 1; ibid., 1 April 1881, 3; ibid., 9 July and 27 August 1875 (both page 4); ibid., 15 March 1878, 1.
33 Ibid., 18 February 1881, 3; ibid., 18 February 1876, 3.
34 Ibid., 1 September 1876, 4.
35 Welland *Telegraph*, 3 November 1876. According to this report, King was aged about 36, had had "about ten years experience with nitro-glycerine, having had charge of what was used at the Hoosac Tunnel, and left a wife and five children." Donald Anger, in *The Age of Sail*, 101–3, suggests that "Colbert" may have been a misunderstanding of "Gilbert."
36 Oliver Phelps to the editor, *Farmers' Journal,* 15 August 1827, n.p. He did admit, however, that three workers had died since May.
37 Black to Seaman, 15 October 1828 (LAC, RG 43, vol. 2102).

38 See, for example, Merritt to Mrs Merritt, 24 August 1829 (*Biography*, 120).
39 On the incidence of malaria in North America, see Andrew Spielman and Michael D'Antonio, *Mosquito*.
40 MacTaggart, *Three Years*, 17–18.
41 27 December 1828 (*Third Report*, 383).
42 Ibid., 489.
43 AO, F662, MS 74, *Merritt Papers*, Package 48; Report of Board for 1832 (*Third Report*, 490); ibid.
44 Ibid., 178 and 501.
45 Report of Board for 1832, ibid., 490.
46 In 1833 "An Act to Establish Boards of Health and to Guard Against the Introduction of Malignant, Contagious and Infectious Disease in This Province and for the Formation of Local Boards" (13 Febuary 1833, 3 William IV, Ch. XLVIII) was followed by an instruction from the Quarter Sessions that all districts should set up such boards.
47 On the Rideau Canal construction, specific provisions for medical care existed. Surgeons were hired and provided with medicines, but only for permanent employees of the military, including engineers, Royal Sappers and Miners, and some civilian functionaries. For them, deductions from pay were made in return for medical treatment. A hospital was also built (William Wylie, "Poverty, Distress and Disease," 24). As on the Welland, however, contractors were regarded as responsible for navvies, and no system of insurance existed for them. The cost of visits to a doctor and of medicine were, of course, beyond the means of most workers.
48 12 January 1827, *Third Report*, 381.
49 Oliver Phelps to the editor, 29 August 1827, *Farmers' Journal*, n.p.
50 See Charles Godfrey, *Cholera Epidemics*, 11, or Geoffrey Bilson, *A Darkened House*, 175.
51 Power to Begly, 25 August 1843 (LAC, RG 43, vol. 2097, #2671). In 1849 cholera made another appearance on the canal but was less virulent than in 1832; Power to Begly, 18 August 1843 (ibid., 93).
52 Power to Begly, 20 December 1844 (LAC, RG 43, vol. 2248, #5995).
53 W.B. Robinson to Begly, 19 October 1842 (LAC, RG 11, vol. 67-11, 73).
54 *Farmers' Journal,* 25 July 1827 and 8 August 1827, n.p.
55 St. Catharines *Journal*, 18 August 1842, 3.
56 Memorandum of John Jarrow (LAC, RG 11, vol. 67-11, 50–1).
57 Walter Shanly to Begly, 28 February 1850 (LAC, RG 11, vol. 65-5, 332–4).
58 Such a system had been rejected by the Upper Canada Legislature in 1792 (Splane, *Social Welfare*, 68–70). The District Councils Act of 1841 (amended in 1846) allowed townships to use property taxes to provide help to the poor. By 1866 the Municipal Institutions Act created a system of "houses of industry" (shelters).
59 Thorold *Post*, 23 June 1876, 1.
60 13 March 1872, LAC, RG 11, vol. 643, #13948.
61 27 April 1843 (LAC, RG 43, vol. 2097).
62 LAC, RG 43, vol. 2248, 103–4.

63 In 1835 McCoy was paid $9.46 for services (LAC, RG 43, vol. 2099, 306); 18 October 1847 (LAC, RG 43, vol. 2249, 411); 25 June 1858 (LAC, RG 11, vol. 130, #24727); 16 September 1876 (LAC, RG 11, vol. 689, #61928).

64 Dates taken from LAC, RG 43, vols. 1786, 2105, 2106.

65 1 August 1881 (LAC, RG 43, vol. 404, #92198); LAC, RG 43, vol. 394, #94009, #57380, #94377; 27 April 1882 (LAC, RG 43, vol. 2261, 285).

66 16 March 1882 (LAC, RG 43, vol. 394, #94341 and passim); 2 June (LAC, RG 43, vol. 407, #111677); 25 April 1883 (LAC, RG 43, vol. 404, #60757); 20 February 1893 (LAC, RG 43, vol. 433, #143803); 14 September 1897 (LAC, RG 43, vol. 465, #166726); 7 October 1897 (LAC, RG 43, vol. 465, #106791).

67 12 June and 26 June 1918 (LAC, RG 43, vol. 2142, "Staff 1918").

CHAPTER TEN

1 John MacTaggart, *Three Years*, 163.

2 *Third Report*, 380–1.

3 "Junius," "A Walk Around Town 'T'," St Catharines *Journal*, 25 September 1856.

4 William Lyon Mackenzie, *Welland Canal,* 30 December 1835, 4.

5 *Third Report*, 22.

6 "Junius," "A Walk Around Town 'N'," St Catharines *Journal*, 31 July 1856.

7 Thomas Conant, *Life in Canada*, 83; Rev. M.A. Garland and J.J. Talman, "Pioneer Drinking Habits," 341–64.

8 3 April 1834, *Third Report*, 557; LAC, RG 43, vol. 2099, 273–4.

9 Begly to Power, 23 April 1845 (LAC, RG 43, vol. 2129, #5879); Benson to Power, 2 May 1845 (ibid., vol. 2248, 117–19).

10 Thorold *Post*, 20 July 1877, 4; quoted in Thorold *Post,* 22 November 1878, 4.

11 Quoted in the Thorold *Post*, 19 February 1879, 4.

12 Quoted in William Lewis, *Aqueduct, Merrittsville and Welland, vol. 2,* 182.

13 Thorold *Post*, 22 October 1886, 3.

14 Thorold *Post*, 22 October 1886, 3; ibid., 17 July 1886, 2.

15 Ibid., 17 August 1877, 4.

16 Ibid., 17 August 1877, 4; ibid., 12 May 1882, 3.

17 Ibid., 17 August 1877, 41; ibid., 12 May 1882, 3; ibid., 21 January 1887, 3. Of course, labourers who headed straight home to their families or to the baker's or butcher's shops were not noticed by the editor. The exact percentage of canal workers visiting public houses on payday cannot be known. Nevertheless, alcoholism was a serious problem throughout Canadian society at the time and the difficult working and living conditions of the Welland's navvies did nothing to alleviate the situation.

18 Peter Way, *Common Labour*, 2.

19 Killaly to R.W. Rawson, Chief Secretary to Governor General Bagot, 19 August 1842 (LAC, RG 11, vol. 116, #1018).

20 Thorburn to Board, 1 July 1844 (LAC, RG 11, vol. 94, #4726).

21 St Catharines *Journal*, 1 September 1842, 2. During the Napoleonic Wars, which ended in 1815, tillage farming had prospered in Ireland and the potato

became the staple food. But after the European conflict subsided, pasturage gradually replaced tillage and many Irish peasants were thrown out of work. Nevertheless, for a time these people could survive on small plots of land where they grew potatoes. Eventually about two-thirds of a population of eight million lived on these nourishing vegetables. After 1845, however, a blight ruined the potato crops causing mass starvation. For thousands of Irish, the only solution (short of slow death) was to leave home. Emigration had been commonplace for several decades but now thousands left each year. In 1847 alone 109,680 Irish immigrants, mainly unskilled, impoverished peasants, came to the Province of Canada (Charles Godfrey, *Cholera Epidemics,* 49). However, by the time the effect of this wave of immigration was felt in the Niagara area, construction on the Welland was virtually completed and the disturbances almost at an end.

22 Way, *Common Labour*, 194, 197.

23 David Thorburn to Dominick Daly, 10 January 1844 (LAC, RG 11, vol. 68-5, 34–43).

24 St Catharines *Journal*, 11 August 1842, 49. Frightening as these outbreaks were to St Catharines' respectable citizens, they made "good copy" and probably sold newspapers.

25 Power to Merritt, 4 January, 1843 (AO, F662, MS 74, *Merritt Papers*, Package 15).

26 Niagara *Chronicle*, 17 July 1844, 2.

27 This incident is well described by Paul Hutchinson and Michael Power in *Goaded to Madness*.

28 Thorburn to Daly, 17 January 1844 (LAC, RG 11, vol. 68-5, 49–51).

29 Keefer to W.B. Robinson, 1 September 1846 (LAC, RG 43, vol. 2249, 36).

30 In 1888, 600 Italians worked on the construction of the Hereford Railway in Quebec. Between 1890 and 1898, 360 Italians came to Canada each year (Bruno Ramirez, *The Italians in Canada*, n.14, 3–6).

31 See, for example, Jean Morrison, "Ethnicity and Violence."

32 Thorold *Post*, 23 June 1876, 1. In an amusing postscript to this incident, the murder suspect (who had fled to Michigan) returned to visit family in Port Colborne: "He was arrested on Monday. While at the depot waiting to be conveyed to Welland gaol, he managed to knock down one of the two constables and left his empty overcoat in the hands of the other, making his escape again, it is thought to Uncle Sam's domain. Those constables must have felt simple when they found their man gone" (Thorold *Post*, 29 February 1884, 3).

33 Cheap Italian labour – "these south of Europe Chinese … mere birds of passage who pay none of the taxes" – brought down wages, said the *Canadian Labor Reformer* in 1886 (10 July 1886, 10).

34 Thorold *Post*, 16 July 1886, 3.

35 Ibid., and 9 July 1886, 2.

36 St Catharines *Journal*, 13 August 1886, 3.

37 *Third Report*, 381. On the other hand, the church mentioned may have been the original Presbyterian Church in St Catharines.

38 *Third Report*, 380–1. An American journalist who visited the Deep Cut in the autumn of 1827 wrote: "We received a printed copy of the regulations adopted

for the government of the laborers and workmen. Their moral tendency is excellent, and being every way judicious, we understand they proved effectual for the promoting of order, industry and good morals" (quoted in Merritt, "Account," 168).

39 *Third Report*, 380–1.

40 "Z," "To Strangers," St Catharines *Journal*, 30 June 1842, 3.

41 Niagara *Chronicle*, 10 July 1844, 2.

42 St Catharines *Journal*, 18 August 1842, 3.

43 Power to Merritt, 4 January 1843 (AO, F662, MS 74, *Merritt Papers*, Package 15).

44 Thorburn to Daly, 10 January 1844 (LAC, RG 11, vol. 68-5, 34–43); St Catharines *Journal*, 7 July, 11 August 1842, 3.

45 Killaly to R.W. Rawson, 19 August 1842 (LAC, RG 11, vol. 116, #1018).

46 Way, *Common Labour*, 237.

47 Ibid., 238.

48 Thorburn to Daly, 10 January 1844 (LAC, RG 11, vol. 68-5, 34–43).

49 Ibid..

50 The *Journal* estimated that, on the Feeder and at Broad Creek, the number of canal workers was: "working, 658; idle, 645; women, 666; children, 1209; total 3178." Of that number, only forty-two were sick. This total did not include skilled labour (St Catharines *Journal*, 16 February 1844, 2).

51 A description by two local historians of the work on the Feeder Canal in 1842 is apt: "The men were making a relatively deep cut across marshland; they were moving by hand stinking black muck, and underneath that, very likely, old and heavy blue-grey clay; the mosquitoes were aroused and malaria was acute; potable water was scarce and sanitary conditions poor, so that catching typhoid fever was a high risk. But above all else, there was a labour force ill-served by contractors, irregularly employed and shuttled from place to place, where 'home' was most likely a hastily built shanty at best. Wives and children were dragged along and they fended for themselves as best they could" (Colin Duquemin and Daniel Glenney, *A Guide to the Grand River Canal*, 22).

52 "Notice to Labourers. Welland Canal Office. St. Catharines, June 20th, 1827" (*Third Report*, 381). In the late eighteenth century British legislation allowed Catholics to have their own schools, to practice Mass and to inherit property. The political *Catholic Emancipation Act* of 1829 lay shortly in the future.

53 Keefer to Begly, 17 October 1848 (LAC, RG 43, vol. 2250, 232–5).

54 Power to Begly, 25 August 1843 (LAC, RG 43, vol. 2097, 96). Power was concerned about "the frauds of the contractors" which provoked the workers to riot, and suggested the insertion of clauses into contracts that would limit the rapacity of certain contractors. Taking such steps would, of course, not only "protect the labourer" but would also protect the canal authorities from financial loss.

55 Killaly to Rawson, 19 August 1842 (LAC, RG 11, vol. 116, 20–1).

56 Power to Begly, 17 July 1843 (LAC, RG 43, vol. 2097, 80); Power to Begly, 6 August 1843 (ibid., 90–2).

57 Begly to Power, 21 August 1943 (LAC, RG 11, vol. 117, #3101).

58 Power to McDonagh, 28 May 1846 (LAC, RG 43, vol. 2248, 387–8).

59 Killaly to McDonagh, 7 January 1843 (LAC, RG 11, vol. 117, #1679).

60 An account (possibly apocryphal) of McDonagh's forceful personality describes how, at the scene of one potential riot, he rode up to a mob on his black horse, dismounted and drew a line across the road with his riding whip, threatening to excommunicate anyone who dared to step over it. Then he remounted and rode into the workers, whipping them (Ernest Green, "Upper Canada's Black Defenders," 388).
61 Thorburn to the Board, 17 January 1844 (LAC, RG 1, vol. 94, #3668).
62 Killaly to Begly, 16 March 1849 (LAC, RG 43, vol. 2250, 451–2).
63 St Catharines *Journal*, 2 February 1844, 3. (See also Power to the Board, 19 January 1844 [LAC, RG 11, vol. 94, #3688]).
64 Begly to Power, 10 February 1843 (LAC, RG 11, vol. 117, #1915).
65 Begly to Power, 3 September 1845 (LAC, RG 43, vol. 2129).
66 See, for example, Power to Begly, 2 May 1846 (LAC, RG 43, vol. 2248, 359–60).
67 Begly to S. Keefer, 25 September 1846 (LAC, RG 11, vol. 120, #396).
68 Power to Begly, 1 August 1843 (LAC, RG 43, vol. 2097, #2482). Power praised the "exertions of Mr. Bonnalie the Chief of the Police & and the cooperation of Col. Elliott."
69 Baron George Frederick de Rottenburg (1807–1894) was probably born in England, a son of Francis (Franz) de Rottenburg, who had served with distinction in the British army in the War of 1812. The son apparently followed his father's footsteps in a military career, serving in the Militia in Canada West.
70 St Catharines *Journal*, 14 July 1842, 2.
71 Begly to Power, 27 December 1845 (LAC, RG 11, vol. 119, #7258).
72 Killaly to Governor General Metcalfe, 11 October 1843 (LAC, RG 11, vol. 117, #3334).
73 Robert Holmes and Dilly Coleman to Merritt, 11 April 1845 (AO, F662, MS 74, *Merritt Papers*, Package 15).
74 DPW, "Map of the Village of Port Colborn [sic]," *Welland Canal, Book 3,* c. 1870, 20.
75 Board Meeting, 4 August 1831 (*Third Report*, 481–3; LAC, RG 43, vol. 2099, 158.)
76 Power to Parsons, 18 September 1845 (LAC, RG 43, vol. 2248, 174).
77 Keefer, "Annual Report," 17 October 1846 (LAC, RG 43, vol. 2249, 90).
78 Keefer to Begly, 21 March 1849 (LAC, RG 11, vol. 65-6, Part 1, 189).
79 DPW, *Welland Canal, Book 1*, 13.
80 Wylie, "Poverty, Distress, and Disease," 23 and 25.
81 Thorburn to Daly, 10 January 1844 (LAC, RG 11, vol. 68-5, 34–43).
82 Charles Whitton et al. to the Board, 11 February 1843 (LAC, RG 11, vol. 94, #1125.
83 Hutchinson and Power, *Goaded to Madness*, 11.
84 Begly to Power, 14 May 1844 (LAC, RG 11, vol. 118, #4450).
85 Begly to Power, 25 February 1845 (LAC, RG 43, vol. 2129, #5590).
86 Begly to Power, 5 March 1845 (LAC, RG 43, vol. 2129, #5625).
87 Power to Begly, 17 July 1843 (LAC, RG 43, vol. 2097).
88 St Catharines *Journal*, 6 March 1845, 3.

89 For example, in 1880 the *Post* recorded the departure of "Messrs. D. Brown, D. Barrett, John Thompson, Alex Malcolm, John Sutherland and Alex Chisholm" and "Messrs. McPherson, Cowie and Force" for jobs in the United States (Thorold *Post*, 14 May 1880, 4). Moreover, long letters from stonecutters to the editors of local newspapers reveal their command of English.

90 Thomas Cunningham to DRC, 11 January 1882 (LAC, RG 43, vol. 394, #93597 and #57420). Another change concerned the replacement of "grog boys" with "water boys," most of whom were about thirteen years old. We assume this change would have occurred earlier, on Second Canal construction, but have no evidence.

91 Thorold *Post*, 3 May 1878, 1.

92 Ibid., 17 December 1886, 3.

93 Welland *Tribune*, 8 February 1878, 3; ibid., 8 February 1878, 1, and 15 February 1878, 1.

94 Thorold *Post,* 28 February 1879, 1.

95 Ibid., 16 January 1880, 4.

96 Ibid., 16 January 1880, 4; ibid., 30 January 1880, 1.

GLOSSARY

ABUTMENT: a solid pier of stone or timber designed to support bridges or other similar works.

APPROACH WALLS: walls of considerable length leading up to locks, designed to protect locks and gates by allowing vessels to pull up alongside well before the lock itself.

APRON: the platform or sill at the entrance to a lock.

BALANCE BEAM: see GATE LEVER

BASIN: the enclosed part of a dock where ships are moored to load, discharge, or be repaired.

BERM: an earthen embankment forming the side of a canal channel.

BOLLARD: a low, thick post of iron or concrete, set on the berm along a canal, to which mooring lines are secured when docking a vessel. Also used for controlling a rope or cable that is running.

BOOM (on a lock): see GATE FENDER

BORROW PIT: an area where material such as sand or gravel has been excavated for use on another site.

BREAKWATER: a structure for protecting a harbour from the force of waves.

BREASTWALL: a section of wall leading up to the gates of a lock.

CANALLER: a ship designed to fit snugly into the locks of the Second and Third Canals to maximize carrying capacity. It had a box-like hull with bow and stern rising almost vertically out of the water. Modern canallers ("lakers") are still built for a similar purpose, with a maximum length of 730 feet (222.5 m), and are easily distinguishable from the "salties."

CHAMBER: see LOCK

COFFERDAM: a temporary enclosing dam built in the water and pumped dry to protect labourers while some work, such as the construction of pier foundations, is in progress.

COPING: the top course of a lock wall, of stone or steel, sloping to shed water.

CRANE: a machine for lifting heavy weights, consisting of a vertical post bearing a horizontal projecting arm on which the hoisting tackle is fixed.

CRIB: a wooden or concrete frame upon which to build a wall or pier.

CULVERT: any artificial covered channel for the passage of water under a road, canal, or embankment.

CURTAIN WALL: that part of a wall which connects two advancing or more lofty portions.

DAM: a barrier of earth, wood, stone, or concrete for holding back or confining water.

DERRICK: a lifting device consisting of a post, at the bottom of which is attached an arm attached by a cable to the top of the post. Like a crane, it can move freely in every direction.

DRAFT/DRAUGHT: the depth of water that a ship needs for floating, or the depth to which a vessel is immersed when bearing a given load.

DRAGLINE: a lifting system which consists of a large bucket suspended from a boom and manoeuvred by ropes or chains to scoop up soil.

DRY DOCK: a basin or chamber with watertight gates for controlling the water level, used in the construction or repair of boats.

FLUME: a narrow channel or pipe to carry water from a canal, river, or raceway to drive a mill wheel.

GATES: movable barriers swinging on hinges for closing the passage into a lock.

GATE CHAMBER: the recess in the lock wall into which a gate may swing so that it is flush with the wall when fully opened.

GATE LEVER: a man-powered device employed on the First and Second canals to open and close the lock gates. Large beams acting as levers extended out from the top of each gate and were pushed or pulled to operate the gate.

GATE YARD: a canal maintenance yard for building or repairing gates or other lock mechanisms.

GLANDERS: an infectious disease afflicting horses, mules, and donkeys. Symptoms include lesions in the lungs and ulceration of the mucous membranes in the upper respiratory tract.

GRAVING DOCK: a dry dock for examining, cleaning, and repairing a ship's hull.

GUARD GATE: a safety gate pointed towards the flow of water, to prevent flooding in case of accident, or to stop the flow of water when repairs are needed. A guard gate was placed above Thorold at the beginning of the summit level on the Second, Third, and Fourth canals as a safety gate to prevent flooding in the system below it.

HARBOUR: a sheltered area for a ship, either natural or man-made.

HARDPAN: a layer of hard, unbroken clay, usually found underneath the uppermost layer of topsoil.

HEAD GATES: the upstream gates of a canal lock.

HEADRACE: see FLUME

HEELPATH: the side of a canal bank opposite the towpath.

HEEL POST: the post in a lock wall to which the gate is hinged.

HOIST: a load-lifting device that uses a drum or lift-wheel around which is wound a rope or chain.

HOLLOW QUOIN: the vertical recess in the lock wall into which the end of the gate leaf fits.

HYDRAULIC RACE: a man-made channel to carry water at a higher level than a canal. In falling to a lower level, the water can provide power for mill wheels. Such a system paralleled the first two Welland canals from Thorold to St Catharines and was dewatered and abandoned after 1929.

INTAKE: the point at which water is taken into a pipe or channel.

LAKER: a ship intended primarily to serve on the Great Lakes.

LEAF: a division or part of a pair of lock gates or bridge spans. See GATES

LEVEL: see REACH

LIFT: the distance that a ship is raised from one reach to another by means of a lock.

LIGHTERING: unloading all or part of a ship's cargo to reduce its draft.

LIGHTHOUSE: a tower containing a light for guiding navigators by night or during inclement weather, erected at the entrance to a port or at a point of danger.

LOCK: an enclosure with gates at each end used in raising or lowering ships as they pass from one water level to another.

LOCKMASTER/LOCKTENDER: canal worker responsible for locking boats into a canal, opening and closing gates, and recording ship passages.

LOWER GATES: the downstream gates of a lock.

MILLRACE: see HYDRAULIC RACE

MITRE: the angle of closed lock gates, pointing toward the upper water level.

MITRE SILL: wood or stone structure along the bottom ledge at each end of a lock, shaped in a "V," pointing upstream, upon which the lock gates close.

PADDLE: see SLUICE

PASSING BASIN: a wide point in a canal channel to enable approaching vessels to pass one another.

PIER: a structure extending from land into a canal, acting as a breakwater to provide a safe point of entry for vessels approaching the canal system. Also, any solid support for the ends of adjacent spans in a bridge.

PILINGS: heavy pointed timbers or steel beams forced into the earth to form a foundation for a wharf or building.

PINTLE: the post on which a lock gate swings.

PIVOT POST: see PINTLE

POND: a basin of water built up behind a regulating weir.

PORTAGE: the act of transporting boats and cargo overland from one navigable body of water to another..

PORTLAND CEMENT: invented in England by Joseph Aspdin in 1823, by burning ground chalk with clay in a lime kiln until carbon dioxide was driven off.

PRISM: the cross-section of a canal channel: also used to refer to the channel itself.

PUDDLE: clay combined with water and spread in layers on the bottom and sides of a canal in order to make the banks watertight.

QUAY: landing stage built alongside a basin or harbour for loading and unloading cargo.

RACEWAY: see HYDRAULIC RACE

REACH: the level expanse of water between locks.

REGULATING WEIR: a dam-like structure that maintains a correct level of water in a pond and/or reach above a lock.

SAFETY WEIR: a weir used in conjunction with a guard gate to regulate canal water in the event of an accident.

SALTY: an ocean-going vessel, as opposed to a "laker."

SCHOONER: a small ocean-going sailing vessel with two, three, or four masts carrying one or more topsails.

SCREW: a propeller-driven ship, as opposed to a sailing vessel.

SILL: see MITRE SILL

SLAB: protection on the side banks of a canal.

SLUICE (paddle): a frame of timber or metal within a lock gate for the purpose of regulating the flow of water.

SPILLWAY: a passageway in or around a dam to release the water in a reservoir.

SPOIL: excavated material.

STOP LOGS or GATES: gates placed at intervals along a waterway and usually kept open, but which can be shut when required to isolate a stretch of water containing a breach of the walls, or when repairs of any kind are necessary. Originally a stack of logs kept beside a canal to form a gate or dam.

SUMMIT LEVEL: the highest level in a canal system from which no further lifts are necessary.

TAILRACE: a channel for returning "used" water from industry to a canal.

THEODOLITE: a surveyor's instrument for measuring both horizontal and vertical angles.

TOWPATH: a path along one bank of a canal where teams of horses or mules walked while pulling ships.

TRANSIT: the action of passing through a canal.

TURNING BASIN: an area of water wide enough to allow vessels to turn around and reverse their direction.

UNWATERING: emptying a canal of water. Necessary when inspecting or repairing lock mechanisms.

VALVE: a contrivance that opens or closes an aperture. See, for example, SLUICE.

WASTE WEIR: a dam-like structure along a canal berm with openings for controlling the water level. Water not required for lock operation may be diverted to the weir and pond system which parallels the canal locks.

WINCH: cranking mechanism that opens or closes valves in lock gates in order to fill or empty locks.

WING WALLS: walls that are flared at an angle, forming the approach ends of locks.

BIBLIOGRAPHY

PRIMARY SOURCES

GOVERNMENT RECORDS

Admiralty, London
Archives of Ontario, Toronto
British Military and Naval Records
Colonial Office
Department of Public Works
Department of Railways and Canals
Library and Archives Canada, Ottawa
Upper Canada Sundries

MANUSCRIPTS

Archives of Ontario, Toronto
Baird Papers
Macaulay Papers
Mackenzie-Lindsay Collection
Merritt Family Papers (Additional)
Norris and Neelon Papers
Welland Canal Papers

British Museum, Department of Manuscripts, London
Huskisson Papers

James A. Gibson Library, Brock University, St Catharines
Welland Canal Records

Library and Archives Canada, Ottawa
Coventry Papers
Cruikshank Papers
Dalhousie Papers

Engineering Institute of Canada
Killaly Papers
Merritt Papers

St Catharines Museum
Welland Canal records

MAPS, PLANS, GRAPHICS

Archives of Ontario, Toronto
Map Collection
Murphy Collection

James A. Gibson Library, Brock University, St Catharines

William Koudys Collection

Library and Archives Canada, Ottawa
Documentary Art and Photography Division
National Map Collection

Ministry of Defence, Hydrographic Office, Taunton, Somerset, UK

New-York Historical Society, New York City

Port Colborne Historical and Marine Museum

Public Archives of Nova Scotia, Halifax
Francis Hall Papers

Public Record Office, Kew, UK

Royal Geographical Society, London, England

St Catharines Centennial Library

St Catharines Museum
Welland Canal Archives

Toronto Reference Library, Baldwin Room
John Ross Robertson Collection

Welland Historical Museum

PRINTED PRIMARY SOURCES

Government Publications

Canada. *Reports in Relation to the Huron and Ontario Ship Canal.* 3rd ed. Toronto, 1871.
– *Sessional Papers.*
– *Statutes.*
Province of Canada. *Journals of the Legislative Assembly.*
– *Papers respecting Claims of Shareholders in the Late Welland Canal Company for Arrears of Interest.* Quebec, 1853.
– *Statutes.*
Ontario. *Debates in the House of Commons.*
– *Sessional Papers.*
– *Statutes.*
Upper Canada. *Journals of the Legislative Assembly.*
– *Statutes.*

Municipal Records

St Catharines Board of Trade. Committee on Transportation. *Papers on the Subject of the Enlargement of the Welland Canal.* St Catharines, 1875.
– Board of Trade. *Minute-Book.* St Catharines, 1876–1903.
– Chamber of Commerce. *Welland Canal Centenary. St. Andrew's Night Dinner, Saturday, November 29, 1924.* St Catharines, 1924.
Thorold Township. Board of Trade. *Advantages of Thorold Township for Industrial Purposes.* Thorold, n.d.
– *Township of Thorold 1793–1967.* Thorold, 1967.

NEWSPAPERS AND JOURNALS

Anglo-American Magazine
Canadian Engineer
Canadian Illustrated News
Canadian Labour Reformer
Colonial Advocate
Dominion Illustrated
Engineering
Farmers' Journal and Welland Canal Intelligencer
Montreal *Gazette*
Niagara *Chronicle*
Niagara *Gleaner*
Ontario *Gazette*
Picturesque Canada
St Catharines *Constitutional*
St Catharines *Daily Times*
St Catharines *Evening Journal*

St Catharines *Journal*
Scribner's Magazine
Thorold *Post*
Toronto *Mail*
Welland *Telegraph*

PRINTED SECONDARY SOURCES

Aitken, Hugh G.J. "The Family Compact and the Welland Canal Company." In J.K. Johnson, ed., *Historical Essays on Upper Canada*. Toronto, 1975, 153–70.

– "A New Way to Pay Old Debts: A Canadian Experience." In William Miller, ed., *Men in Business: Essays on the History of Entrepreneurship*. Cambridge, Massachusetts, 1952, 71–90.

– *The Welland Canal Company: A Study in Canadian Enterprise*. Cambridge, Massachusetts, 1954. Reprinted by the Canadian Canal Society, 1997, with a "Note on Sources" and "Errata" by Roberta M. Styran.

– "Yates and McIntyre: Lottery Managers." *Journal of Economic History*, 13 (1963), 36–57.

Andreae, Christopher. *Lines of Country: An Atlas of Railway and Waterway History in Canada*. Erin, Ontario, 1997.

– *Lock 24, First Welland Canal*. London, Ontario, 1988.

Anger, Donald G. *The Age of Sail*. Port Colborne, Ontario, 2006.

Angus, James T. *A Respectable Ditch: A History of the Trent-Severn Waterway 1833–1920*. Kingston and Montreal, 1988.

Andrews, Mark E. *For King and Country: Lieutenant Colonel John By, R.E., Indefatigable Civil-Military Engineer*. Merrickville, Ontario, 1988.

Baird, N.H., and H.H. Killaly. *Report of the Present State and Proposed Deviations and Improvements of the Welland Canal*. St Catharines, 1838.

Bilson, Geoffrey. *A Darkened House: Cholera in Nineteenth-Century Canada*. Toronto, 1950.

Bleasdale, Ruth Elizabeth. "Class Conflict on the Canals of Upper Canada in the 1840s." Paper submitted to the Canadian Historical Association, London, Ontario, 1978.

– "Irish Labourers on the Cornwall, Welland, and Williamsburg Canals in the 1840s." MA thesis, University of Western Ontario, 1975.

Bonnycastle, Richard S. *The Canadas in 1841*, 2 vols. London, 1841.

Briggs, Asa. *The Nineteenth Century: The Contradictions of Progress*. London, 1970.

Brode, Patrick. *Sir John Beverley Robinson: Bone and Sinew of the Compact*. Toronto, 1954.

Burtniak, John, and Wesley B. Turner, eds. *The Welland Canals. Proceedings of the First Annual Niagara Peninsula History Conference*. St Catharines, 1979.

Calhoun, D.H. *The American Civil Engineer: Origins and Conflict*. Cambridge, Massachusetts, 1960.

Careless, J.M.S. *Union of the Canadas: The Growth of Canadian Institutions 1841–1857*. Toronto, 1967.

Carter, Dewitt. "Relative Sizes and Capacities of our Canals Reflected in Trend of Traffic." *Ontario Historical Society, Papers and Records,* 23 (1926), 19–27.

– *The Welland Canal: A History*. Port Colborne, 1960.

Cartier, François. *Canal de Soulanges: D'un défi à l'autre/Meeting the Challenges*. Montreal, 1999.

Coleman, Terry. *The Railway Navvies: The Men Who Made the Railways.* Harmondsworth, 1968.

Conant, Thomas. *Life in Canada*. Toronto, 1903.

Coyne, J.H. "Unveiling of Merritt Cairn at Allanburg, November 29, 1924," *Welland County Historical Society, Papers and Records*, 2 (1926), 126–34.

Craig, Gerald M. *Upper Canada: The Formative Years.* Toronto, 1968.

Creighton, Ogden. *A General View of the Welland Canal in the Province of Upper Canada*. London, 1830.

Cruikshank, Ernest A. "Centenary of the Welland Canal." *Welland County Historical Society, Papers and Records*, 1 (1924), 1–35.

– "The Fenian Raid of 1866." *Welland County Historical Society, Papers and Records*, 2 (1926), 1–49.

– *The History of the County of Welland*. Belleville, 1887–1972.

– "The Inception of the Welland Canal." *Ontario Historical Society, Papers and Records*, 22 (1925), 60–88.

– "The News of Niagara a Century Ago." *Ontario Historical Society, Papers and Records,* 23 (1926), 45–64.

Davin, Nicholas Flood. *The Irishman in Canada*. Toronto, 1877.

Duquemin, Colin K., and Daniel J. Glenney. *A Guide to the Grand River Canal.* St Catharines, Ontario, 1980.

Dwight, Theodore. *The Northern Traveller.* New York, 1826.

Garland, Rev. M.A., and J.J. Talman. "Pioneer Drinking Habits and the Rise of the Temperance Agitation in Upper Canada Prior to 1840." *Ontario History*, 27 (1931), 341–64.

Gentilcore, R. Louis, and C. Grant Head, eds. *Ontario History in Maps.* Toronto, 1984.

Gibson, Rev. Jesse. *Thomas Bone – The Sailors' Friend: The Story of His Work on the Welland Canal.* Toronto, 1908.

Gilham, E.B. *The Welland Canal Mission*. St Catharines, 1981.

Glazebrook, G.P. de T. *A History of Transportation in Canada.* 2 vols. 2nd edn. Toronto, 1964.

Godfrey, Charles M. *The Cholera Epidemics in Upper Canada 1832–1866.* Toronto, 1968.

Gourlay, Robert. *Statistical Account of Upper Canada,* 2 vols. London, 1822.

Grant, George Monro, ed. *Picturesque Canada: The Country As It Was And Is.* Toronto, 1882.

Green, Ernest. "Upper Canada's Black Defenders." *Ontario History*, 27 (1931), 365–91.

Guillet, Edwin C. *Pioneer Travel in Upper Canada*. Toronto, 1933/1963.

Hadfield, Charles. *The Canal Age*. Newton Abbott, 1981.

Harper, Russell. *The Early History of Haldimand County*. Martindale, 1950.
Head, Francis Bond. *A Narrative: With Notes by William Lyon Mackenzie*. Toronto, 1969.
Heisler, John P. *The Canals of Canada*. Ottawa, 1973.
Hill, Bruce Emerson. *The Grand River Navigation Company*. Brantford, Ontario, 1994.
Hill, Hamnet P. "The Construction of the Rideau Canal, 1825–1832." *Ontario Historical Society, Papers and Records*, 22 (1925), 117–24.
Hill, Henry Wayland. *An Historical Review of Waterways and Canal Construction in New York State*. Buffalo, 1908.
Hodgetts, J.E. *Pioneer Public Service: An Administrative History of the United Canadas, 1841–1867*. Toronto, 1955.
Hutchinson, Paul, and Michael Power. *Goaded to Madness: The Battle of Slabtown*. St Catharines, 1999.
Innis, H.A., and A.R.M. Lower, eds. *Select Documents in Canadian Economic History*. Toronto, 1933.
Jackson, John N. *St. Catharines, Ontario. Its Early Years*. Belleville, 1976.
– *The Welland Canals and Their Communities: Engineering, Industrial and Urban Transformation*. Toronto, 1997.
Jenson, Albert C. "Engineering Clinton's Ditch." *Civil Engineering* (September 1963), 48–50.
Johnson, E.P. "Canal Engineering Yesterday and Today." *Ontario Historical Society, Papers and Records*, 13 (1926), 365–9.
Johnson, J. George. "When Fort Erie was Distributing Centre for Middle West." *Welland County Historical Society*, 3 (1927), 80–5.
Johnson, J.K. *Becoming Prominent: Regional Leadership in Upper Canada, 1791–1841*. Montreal, 1989.
Keefer, Thomas Coltrin. *Canadian Water Ways from the Great Lakes to the Atlantic*. Boston, 1893.
– "The Canals of Canada." *Transactions of the Royal Society of Canada*, Sec. 3 (1893), 25–60.
– *The Canals of Canada, Their Prospects and Influence*. Toronto: Armour, 1850.
– *The Old Welland Canal and the Man Who Made It*. St Catharines, 1920.
Kingsford, William. *The Canadian Canals: Their History and Cost*. Toronto, 1865.
Kos-Rabcewicz-Zubkowski, Ludwik and William Edward Greening. *Sir Casimir Stanislaus Gzowski: A Biography*. Toronto, 1959.
Langbein, Walter B. "Our Grand Canal." *Civil Engineering* (October 1988), 75–8.
Legget, Robert F. *Canals of Canada*. Vancouver, 1976.
– "John Page: Another Great Pioneer." *Canadian Consulting Engineer* (April 1988), 50–1.
– *Ottawa River Canals*. Toronto, 1988.
– *Rideau Waterway*. Toronto, 1955.
– "Search Continues for Early Engineer's Manuscript." *Canadian Consulting Engineer* (September 1984), 42–3.

Letters to Lord John Russell from Lord Sydenham, Governor-General of Canada, 1839–1841 (ed. by Paul Knaplund). Clifton, New Jersey, 1973.

Lewis, William. *Aqueduct, Merrittsville and Welland: A History of the City of Welland,* vols. 1 and 2. Welland, 1997 and 2000.

Livermore, Daniel. "The Welland Canal Company: A Study in Motivation." BA thesis, Brock University, 1969.

MacTaggart, John. *Three Years in Canada: An Account of the Actual State of the Country in 1826–7–8.* London, 1829.

Martine, Gloria. "The Role of the Welland Canal in Industrial Location." BA thesis, University of Toronto, 1961.

Mather, Fredric C. "Water Routes from the Great North West." *Harper's New Monthly Magazine*, 63 (1881), 415–35.

McCalla, Douglas. *Planting the Provinces: The Economic History of Upper Canada, 1784–1870.* Toronto, 1993.

McDougall, John Lorne. "The Welland Canal to 1841." MA thesis, University of Toronto, 1923.

McGeorge, W.G. *Report on the Welland and Feeder Canals.* Chatham, 1947.

Meany, Carl Frank Patrick. "The Welland Canal and Canadian Development." MA thesis, McMaster University, 1980.

Merritt, Jedediah Prendergast. *Biography of the Hon. W.H. Merritt, M.P.* St Catharines, 1875.

Merritt, William Hamilton. "Account of the Welland Canal, Upper Canada." *The American Journal of Science and Arts*, vol. 14 (July 1828), 159–68.

– *Brief Review of the Origin, Progress, Present State, and Future Prospects of the Welland Canal.* St Catharines, 1852.

– *A Lecture Delivered by the Hon. W.H. Merritt before the Mechanics' Institute of St. Catharines.* St Catharines, 1857.

– A Projector [William Hamilton Merritt]. *A Concise View of the Inland Navigation of the Canadian Provinces.* St Catharines, 1832.

Michener, David M. *The Canals at Welland.* Welland, 1973.

Millard, J. Rodney. *The Master Spirit of the Age: Canadian Engineers and the Politics of Professionalism, 1887–1922.* Toronto, 1988.

Morison, Elting F. *From Know-How to Nowhere: The Development of American Technology.* New York, 1974.

Morrison, Jean. "Ethnicity and Violence: Southern Europeans in Strikes on Thunder Bay's Waterfront before World War I." In John Potestio and Antonio Pucci, eds, *The Italian Immigrant Experience.* Thunder Bay, 1988.

Noel, S.J.R. *Patrons, Clients, Brothers: Ontario Society and Politics, 1791–1896.* Toronto, 1990.

Notman, William, and Jennings Taylor. *Portraits of British Americans.* Montreal, 1865.

Owen, David. *The Manchester Ship Canal.* Manchester, 1983.

Owram, Doug. *Building for Canadians: A History of Public Works, 1840–1960.* Ottawa, 1978.

Page, H.R. *Illustrated Historical Atlas for the Counties of Lincoln and Welland.* Toronto, 1876; Stratford, Ontario, 1984.

Passfield, Robert W. *Building the Rideau Canal: A Pictorial History.* Don Mills, Ontario, 1982.

– *Technology in Transition: The "Soo" Ship Canal, 1889–1985.* Ottawa, 1989.

Patton, M.J. "Shipping and Canals." In Adam Shortt and Arthur Doughty, eds, *Canada and Its Provinces.* Toronto, 1914, vol. 10.

Pentland, Clare. *Labour and Capital in Canada 1650–1860.* Toronto, 1981.

Phelps, Seymour ("Junius"). "A Walk Around Town," St Catharines *Journal*, 1856; St Catharines and Lincoln Historical Society. *St. Catharines A to Z.* St Catharines, Ontario, 1967.

Phillpotts, Lt. Col. "Report on the Canal Navigation of the Canadas." *Papers on Subjects Connected with the Duties of the Corps of Royal Engineers*, vol. 5, Part 6. London, 1839.

Ramirez, Bruno. *The Italians in Canada.* Ottawa, 1984.

Raudzens, George. *The British Ordnance Department and Canada's Canals.* Waterloo, Ontario, 1979.

Rawlyk, George A. "Thomas Coltrin Keefer and the St. Lawrence–Great Lakes Commercial System." *Inland Seas*, vol. 19, no. 3 (fall 1963), 190–4.

Rees, Abraham. *The Cyclopaedia,* 41 volumes. Philadelphia, 1810–24.

Rehabilitate the Old Feeder Canal Association, Inc. *A Feasability Study on the Welland Feeder Canal.* Wainfleet, Ontario 1979.

[Rice, A.B.] (ed. by John Burtniak). *The History of the County of Welland.* Belleville, 1972.

Runnalls, Lawrence. *The Irish on the Welland Canals.* St Catharines, 1974.

St Catharines Historical Museum. *A Canadian Enterprise: The Welland Canals. The "Merritt Day" Lectures, 1978–82.* St Catharines, 1984.

Sayles, Fern A. *Welland Workers Make History.* Welland, 1963.

Seibel, George A. *The Niagara Portage Road.* Niagara Falls, 1990.

Shanly, Water. *Report on Mr. W. Shanly's (Civil Engineer) Survey on a Branch Canal to Connect the Welland Canal with the Mouth of the Niagara River.* Toronto, 1854.

Shaw, Ronald E. *Canals for a Nation: The Canal Era in the United States, 1790–1860.* Lexington, Kentucky, 1990.

Spielman, Andrew, and Michael D'Antonio. *Mosquito: A Natural History of Our Most Persistent and Deadly Foe.* New York, 2001.

Splane, Richard A. *Social Welfare in Ontario, 1791–1893.* Toronto, 1965.

Stanwick, Hannah. "Did St. Catharines Miss the Boat? The Political Economy of the Welland Canal in the 1800s." MA thesis, Brock University, 1994.

Stevenson, David. *Sketch of the Civil Engineering of North America.* London, 1838.

Strachan, James. *A Visit to the Province of Upper Canada in 1819.* Aberdeen, 1820.

Stretton, R.W. *Dunnville, Ontario: Centennial Year 1950.* Dunnville, 1950.

Styran, Roberta M. "From Merritt to Multinationalism." *Proceedings of the Eleventh Annual Niagara Peninsula History Conference* (1981), ed. John N. Jackson and John Burtniak. St Catharines, 1992, 71–90.

Styran, Roberta M., and Robert R. Taylor, eds. *The "Great Swivel Link": Canada's Welland Canal.* The Champlain Society. Toronto, 2001.

Styran, Roberta M., and Robert R. Taylor. "Purges, Prosperity and Doorian's Pizzeria." *Proceedings of the Third Annual Niagara Peninsula History Conference* (1981), ed. John Burtniak and Patricia G. Dirks. St Catharines 1981, 122–36.

– "The Welland Canal: Creator of a Landscape." *Ontario History*, 72 (1980), 210–29.

– *Mr. Merritt's Ditch: A Welland Canals Album.* Erin, Ontario, 1992.

– With John N. Jackson. *The Welland Canals. The Growth of Mr. Merritt's Ditch.* Erin, Ontario, 1988.

– With Thies Bogner. *The Welland Canals Corridor: Then and Now.* St Catharines, 2004.

Taylor, Robert R. "The Growth of Merritton's Industrial Corridor, c. 1845–1914." *Proceedings of the Eleventh Annual Niagara Peninsula History Conference* (1981), ed. John N. Jackson and John Burtniak. St Catharines, 1992, 1–20.

– "Merritton, Ontario. The Rise and Decline of an Industrial Corridor, c. 1845–1939." *Scientia Canadensis: Journal of the History of Canadian Science, Technology, and Medicine,* 14, no. 102 (1990), 90–130.

Taylor, Robert R., ed. *Voices from the Great Ditch: The Historic Welland Canals in Pictures, Prose, Poems, and Songs.* St Catharines, 2004.

Taylor, Robert Stanley. "The Historical Development of the Four Welland Canals, 1824–1933." MA thesis, University of Western Ontario, 1950.

Thompson, Don W. *Men and Meridians: The History of Surveying and Mapping in Canada.* Ottawa, 1966.

Thorold and Beaverdams Historical Society. *Jubilee History of Thorold*, ed. by John H. Thompson. Thorold, 1897–98.

Thurston, Robert H. *A History of the Growth of the Steam-Engine.* New York, 1978.

Turcotte, Dorothy. *Port Dalhousie: Shoes, & Ships & Sealing Wax.* Erin, Ontario, 1986.

Turner, Wesley B. *Life in Upper Canada.* Toronto, 1980.

Watson, J.W. "The Changing Industrial Pattern of the Niagara Peninsula." *Ontario History*, 37 (1945), 49–58.

Way, Peter. *Common Labour: Workers and the Digging of North American Canals, 1780–1860.* Cambridge, 1993.

Welland *Telegraph. The Hub of the Peninsula, Anno Domini 1907.* Welland. 1907.

– *Souvenir of the Town of Welland.* Welland, 1902.

Wells, George. "Welland When Young." *Welland County Historical Society,* 5 (1938), 192–8.

White, Richard. *Gentlemen Engineers: The Working Lives of Frank and Walter Shanly.* Toronto, 1999.

Whitford, Noble E. *History of the Canal System of the State of New York*, 2 vols. Albany, 1906.

Winearls, Joan. *Mapping Upper Canada, 1780–1867.* Toronto, 1991.

Wylie, William N.T. "Poverty, Distress and Disease: Labour and the Rideau Canal, 1826–1832." *Labour/Le Travailleur*, 7 (September 1983), 7–29.

Yates, George W. "The Welland Canal." *Canadian Geographical Journal*, 2 (1931), 23–37.

INDEX

An italic *f* indicates the presence of an illustration; an italic *m* indicates a map or chart; an italic *t* indicates a table. The following abbreviations are used for references to the first three Welland Canals: FWC (First Welland Canal); SWC (Second Welland Canal); TWC (Third Welland Canal)